*Aestheticism and the Canadian Modernists*

# Aestheticism and the Canadian Modernists

## Aspects of a Poetic Influence

BRIAN TREHEARNE

McGill-Queen's University Press
Kingston, Montreal, London

© McGill-Queen's University Press 1989
ISBN 0-7735-0710-8

Legal deposit 2nd quarter 1989
Bibliothèque nationale du Québec

Printed in Canada on acid-free paper

This book has been published with the help of a
grant from the Canadian Federation for the
Humanities, using funds provided by the Social
Sciences and Humanities Research Council of
Canada.

---

**Canadian Cataloguing in Publication Data**

Trehearne, Brian, 1957–
    Aestheticism and the Canadian Modernists
    Includes index.
    Bibliography: p.
    ISBN 0-7735-0710-8
    1. Canadian poetry (English) – 20th century – History
    and criticism. 2. Aestheticism (Literature). I. Title.
    PS105.M6T74 1989        C811'.5'09        C89-090097-3
    PR9190.5.T74 1989

---

Material from Robert Finch's *Poems,* from John
Glassco's *Memoirs of Montparnasse, A Point of Sky* and
*Selected Poems,* from Leo Kennedy's *The Shrouding,*
from F.R. Scott's *Selected Poems* and from A.J.M.
Smith's *Poems New and Collected* is quoted by
permission of Oxford University Press Canada.
Material from W.W.E. Ross's *Shapes and Sounds* is
quoted by permission of Harcourt Brace Jovanovich.
Material from F.R. Scott's *Collected Poems* is quoted by
permission of the Canadian Publishers, McClelland
and Stewart, Toronto.

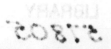

*For my father, who would have preferred
this work*

# Contents

# Acknowledgments

The works of Robert Finch have been quoted with the permission of Robert Finch, Toronto, Ontario. The works of John Glassco, F.R. Scott and A.J.M. Smith have been quoted with the permission of the three poets' mutual literary executor, Mr William Toye of Oxford University Press, Don Mills, Ontario. Quotations from Frederick Philip Grove by permission A. Leonard Grove, Toronto, Ontario. The works of Raymond Knister have been quoted with the permission of Imogen Knister Givens, Harley, Ontario. I am grateful to all of these persons for their ready encouragement and support and prompt responses to inquiries. Every effort has been made to contact the owners of copyright for material in this volume, and the author would be grateful to hear of omissions so that they may be corrected in subsequent editions.

Many people have assisted me in the preparation of this study, whether through persistent moral support or intellectual challenge and encouragement. Heartfelt thanks to Mrs H.W. Trehearne and to Mr and Mrs R.V. Cattell, for encouragements of infinite variety. Thanks are also due to David Bentley, provocative interlocutor and boon companion during the final stages of my work. To Louis Dudek, for his unfailing enthusiasm for the project and his demanding criticism of it, my whole-hearted gratitude and affection.

The thesis from which this book emerged was undertaken with the support of the Social Sciences and Humanities Research Council of Canada and the Administrative Committee of Huron College, London, Ontario. Final stages of revision were completed while the author was a Webster Fellow in the Humanities at Queen's University, Kingston. The book was published with the assistance of an Aid to Scholarly Publications Grant from the Canadian Federation from the Humanities. To all these agencies, my thanks for their generosity and understanding.

The patience and encouragement of my wife have sustained me throughout the years in which this book grew into its present form; I will not have thanked her enough for many years to come. Another debt beyond words is acknowledged in the dedication to this volume.

*Aestheticism and the Canadian Modernists*

# Influence, Aestheticism, Modernism

Critics of Canadian poetry have been little urged by the conventions of their discipline to address the legacy of European Aestheticism. Most would acknowledge the degree to which the Confederation poets were influenced by the various cross-currents of Aestheticism and Decadence,[1] but a comprehensive accounting of that literary relationship has yet to appear. The influence of Aestheticism on more modern Canadian poetry has never been proposed, much less documented. Only for the prose of John Glassco has a backdrop of Decadence been consistently asserted, and then with an insufficient grasp of the Decadent literature ostensibly reflected in his canon.[2] Critical convention notwithstanding, the influence of the various schools of Aestheticism on a number of Canadian poets whose careers were initiated in the 1920s was direct and forceful and had a significant impact on the development of Canadian Modernism. Given reasonable variations as to the source, tenure, and degree of each influence, such poets as Raymond Knister, W.W.E. Ross, Robert Finch, Leo Kennedy, F.R. Scott, John Glassco, and A.J.M. Smith received the example of Aestheticism with some approval and were willing to be influenced by it, primarily by adopting the themes, symbols, imagery, and diction of the earlier movement, occasionally by experimenting with prosody and form learned from the Decadents. The many names indicate the pervasiveness of the Aesthetic influence and suggest the degree to which a sensitivity to Aestheticism could alter the present appearance of Canadian literary history.

Proof of my contention lies in the poetry of each man, not only in the recognized canon but in the uncollected and unpublished pieces as well, in the private documents, manuscripts, correspondence, and notes that have been made available in this still obscure period of our literary history, in such critical prose as they published

or left unpublished during their lives, and in such biographical information as may be gleaned from their own memoirs or from the
publications of others in the field. In submission to the resulting
scope of the present study, I have divided the poets in this book
into groups and thence into chapters. While this structure may unfortunately reduce our sense of their having assisted one another,
it will necessarily increase the degree to which we may clarify the
problem of influence in each case and will reduce the tendency to
see these poets as cogs in the wheel of a larger Canadian Modernism.
That latter phrase too often encourages a blurring of the differences
between these radically different poets and urges us to look no
farther than Modernism for an explanation of their developments.

To avoid these tendencies, the following order will be imposed
on a group of richly inter-connected poets. In chapter 2 I discuss
the Canadian "Imagists," Raymond Knister and W.W.E. Ross, redefining the nature of their Imagist practice, relating that practice
to literary Impressionism, and discussing possible causes of their
refusal of typical Imagist poetics. Chapter 3 includes a number of
minor Canadian poets who began their careers or attained some
prominence during the 1920s: briefly, F.O. Call, Frederick Philip
Grove, Louis Mackay, and Neil Tracy; in greater detail, Robert Finch
and Leo Kennedy. Each poet manifests a strong textual affinity with,
or some plausible influence from, European Aestheticism in his poetry, thus offering an entirely new context for the criticism of our
minor moderns. In chapter 4 I examine the Aesthetic inheritance in
the early uncollected poetry of F.R. Scott that appeared pseudo-
nymously in the *McGill Fortnightly Review*, show that Scott's time at
Oxford coincided with a revival of Aestheticism at that institution,
and apply these conclusions to his recognized canon to render some
occasionally surprising readings. In chapter 5 I relate the recent
critical image of John Glassco as a Decadent memoirist to his poetry
and demonstrate therein a wide range of typically Decadent obsessions, thus challenging a surprisingly common view of Glassco
as a Canadian Wordsworth. Chapter 6 completes these studies with
an inquiry into A.J.M. Smith's early poetry, buried in back copies
of the *McGill Daily*, as well as the *McGill Daily Literary Supplement*
and the *McGill Fortnightly Review*, and relates the Aesthetic characteristics of that poetry to Smith's later, more noted publications. In
the conclusion I relate the book's evidence to a few pressing critical
issues in Canadian literary history.

The repercussions for that history suggest themselves readily. A
consensus that European Aestheticism worked a significant influence upon so many poets of the Modernist generation will not only

constitute a major shift in our attitudes to their individual histories, but will force a shift in our entire approach to Canadian Modernism as a literary phenomenon. Significant as it is that these poets welcomed the particular Aesthetic influence in their youth, it is an even more significant proposition (and this is the first study to argue) that *anything* other than Modernism had an impact upon them; it will no longer be possible to criticize these major poets with sole reference to one immediately obvious governing tradition.

This is not the place to address at length the reasons for such lacunae in our criticism; but I would suggest briefly that we have been content, in the past, to study these poets by analysing the canon largely *as they have passed it on to us*; we have paid too little attention to their journals, manuscripts, and private papers; and we have regularly failed to see in his or her critical prose an important measure of the poet's work and thought. The present argument draws on such information whenever profitable, a practice that makes for a loose method, but which provides a surer footing for the critic than an orthodox analysis, however perspicacious, of a volume of collected poems assembled by the poet.

The degree of my variance from critical orthodoxy will of course be different with regard to each poet, and in certain cases I will insist upon a slender point of distinction. By no means am I trying to prove that any of these poets was not in fact modern; I take that fact for granted and will spend no time demonstrating or parsing their modernity, the current of Canadian critical opinion having already done so. Instead I will provide an alternative focus for our approaches to the poetry, which alters and sharpens our understanding of their Modernism without undermining it. By attempting a greater precision in the way we speak of this obscure period of Canadian literature, we will see in the orthodox attitude to it occasional fundamental inaccuracies which must be corrected. The *McGill Fortnightly Review*, for example, may informally be referred to as a "Modernist" journal;[3] but, if we are describing it as a part of our task of criticism, that phrase needs vigorous qualification and (now and then) outright contradiction. Such a distinction between a casual account and a critical accounting I have sought to maintain.

I have limited the study to the generation of the 1920s for a number of reasons. First, it seems helpful to trace an influence through a group of later poets who are linked in some way, so that we approach a roughly similar chronological and intellectual situation in each case. Second, that particular generation of Canadian poets demonstrates the influence in the most central and subtle ways. Canadian poets of the 1890s, when they felt the influence of Aestheticism, revealed it in manners more imitative of the original, adapting less freely, presumably because of their closer coincidence with the influencing movement. But the inter-generational influence discussed here suggests more strongly the potency of the precursor school and more significantly alters our sense of the ways in which Canadian literature has tended to adopt international artistic models. Third, since Aestheticism does have particular theoretical affinities with Modernism, it seems natural and necessary to trace its relationship above all to the first generation of modern Canadian poets and to exclude the Modernist poets who came after them, in order to show that the primary influx of Modernism into Canada occurred concomitantly with an early Aestheticism in the poets who were to receive it. Fourth and last, as I shall argue in the conclusion, the chronology is fitting: that roughly thirty years passed between the heights of Aestheticism and the first signs of Canadian Modernism parallels a general pattern of inheritance in Canadian poetry, which has led many of our poets to adapt after roughly three decades the innovations occurring across the Atlantic. I will not qualify or insist upon this familiar generalization until later in the book, but it may prove a useful backdrop as the chapters progress.

Of the three terms crucial to this argument – influence, Aestheticism, Modernism – the most notorious at present is the belaboured concept of "influence." Since the study of influences betrays an essentially Romantic and biographical orientation, the New Critical reaction against "biographical criticism" has made it easy to dismiss the concept as yet another cancerous growth in the body of Romantic theory. More recently, the inarguably impressive influence-theory of Harold Bloom and the delineation of intertextuality by Julia Kristeva and others have cast the question of influence onto a higher level of inquiry where literary chronologies, poets' developments and archival gleanings appear as the stuff of an old-fashioned disposition towards the earth-bound and the practical.

My insistence on the older term here should not be construed, however, as a glum manifesto against recent theorizing. Intertextuality provides the critic with a dramatic, imaginative, and enriching approach to the relations between literary texts, and its rejuvenation of the study of such relations, after the arid hyper-textuality of declining New Criticism, has been necessary and gratifying. Bloom's "theory of poetry," deriving from his conception of an influence that is more psychological and irrational than literary and orderly, has had an enormous impact on a generation of critics eager to circumvent the more mundane historical connections between artists, texts, generations, and periods. Such achievements do not indicate, however, the triumph of a sufficient theory of literary relationships; they indicate a necessary step forward, another part of the difficulty resolved. They cannot account for the means by which two texts became related to one another except in the loosest terms, for example; indeed, they find it difficult to explain why textual relations are crucial but the means by which they came about of marginal concern; they betray little or no interest in the literary education of a particular artist or group of artists; they presuppose a sufficient understanding, or the irrelevance, of detailed literary chronology. Such gaps do not undermine their value as theories; they merely undermine any claim for their supremacy in the field. A rationalist will distrust theories that examine literary effects independent of their causes and will eventually insist that the paramount interest of the former need not override the necessary examination of the latter.

I for one cannot help feeling that the rejection of the conventional models of literary history, chronological and clinical as that history must sometimes appear, is a greater danger in Canada than in cultures whose literary history has been charted and re-charted for decades or for centuries. We need the information before we rule upon its relevance. Without an archival and literary-historical interest, the Aestheticism in these Canadian poets might well have gone, indeed was going, entirely unnoticed. Future critics might choose to ignore this information, but there is an enormous difference between willed ignoring and wilful ignorance.

Relating such information obviously requires an orientation and a terminology that does not render it irrelevant; hence "influence," not "intertextuality," in the pages that follow. Bloom's sense of the anxiety created in the influenced poet by the precursor is a powerful and central vision – and some will want to argue that the repression of the Aesthetic influence by the poets considered in this book reveals a promising "anxiety." But Bloom's terms are not intended to explicate the post-creative embarrassment of an influenced poet; they constitute instead a "theory of poetry," an explication of the creative process in relation to prior and influential works of art. Nor would Bloom's methods have proved the influence satisfactorily; they may become stimulating *post facto*, but they are not intended for reliable methods of literary-historical analysis. If there is a defined method to which this study will adhere, it is implicit in the pages of Goran Hermeren's *Influence in Art and Literature*, a startling and complex theoretical text that describes precisely what we assume when we use such terms as "influence" and "transmission." Hermeren is himself the first to deny that influence-study lends itself to any such precision; his effort is to make as precise as possible those terms that have been clouded by semantic misunderstanding or methodological sleight-of-hand. His parabolae and algebraic definitions of literary terms, intended primarily to demonstrate their daunting complexity as discourse, are of no use to the practical critic; his capacity for exhaustive precision is a quality to emulate.

The final complication in the influence-theory of this book is demanded by the centrality of the Aesthetic influence to most Canadian Modernist poetry of the 1920s, necessitating a look at a larger number of poets than would normally be treated within the limits of a single study. If it is true that the study of influences should involve us not only in superficial source-hunting but also in a larger and more thorough sense of one artist's reception and development of the ideas and techniques of another (as the burden of contemporary influence-theory clearly demands), surely to study several artists in that manner, each with equal attention to complications, will yield even larger and more fruitful results for our understanding of the nature of the Canadian tradition. The result will be an enriched and fortuitously complicated sense of what "influence" means when passed to a group rather than to a single artist, since any influence, if seen correctly, is not a neat absorption of this or that artistic detail, but a vast, complicated, indefinite, and necessarily sloppy process by which traditions grow and reconcile themselves to one another. Partly, then, this book is an effort, to borrow a discard of T.S. Eliot's, to "do the influence in different voices," the resulting juxtaposition and interpenetration of patterns of influence providing a very close approximation of "what actually happened" in the literary 1920s, which ought to be the end of all studies of such influences. A cacophony of individual influences can give us the most accurate sense of what the general influence of a prior work was; to perform such a study with an ear for "different voices" promotes both accuracy and relativity and precludes the error of definite and entirely unambiguous conclusions.

Such caution is particularly demanded by the present case, since theories of influence involve significant ramifications for the study of colonial and post-colonial literatures. In Canadian and in most colonial literatures, poetry began in an effort to maintain or extend the artistic, social, and moral standards of the mother country in a geographical and cultural situation that was perceived as inhospitable to received normal behaviour. "Influence," under such conditions, became something avidly sought, a life-giving transfusion of order and authority when no such order was provided by the environment, or by the present means of mastering it. Rejecting the influence of older poets is unthinkable in such a difficult case, and so the literature of the mother country dominates in technique (and usually in quality) the literature of the colony for some time.

As prosperity increases, however, and social standards are reconciled to the realities of a new situation, the colonial literature gradually arrives at a sense of its own development and seeks, inevitably, to demonstrate its viability as a national literature, independent of foreign models. Perhaps such a phase is initiated in Canadian poetry in 1864, when Edward Hartley Dewart published his *Selections from Canadian Poets* – an astonishing publication from our modern point of view, since he had so few poets from whom to choose. But the passing of time and the gradual success of civilizing influences from the mother-countries made that year seem propitious for a gathering together of Canadian poetry, and the anthologies that follow in rapid succession lead, within a mere sixty years, to the first movement in Canadian letters to demand a clean break with the colonial attitude. Influence from foreign sources becomes, within those six decades, a sign of intellectual subservience, lack of imagination, or insufficient national feeling, and the importation of foreign models is felt as an irritation of pride, an imposition upon an otherwise mature group of artists. At such a juncture poets naturally seek to throw off their influences (at least, those that had previously dominated) and to build, with or without new models, a self-justified literature braving foreign standards. Influence, at that point in colonial history, becomes a thing to be shunned, where once it had been the life-blood of a pioneering culture.

Canadian literature has rarely been clearly addressed in these terms. The coincidence of our anti-colonial period, climaxing in the 1920s, and that phase in English criticism that avidly sought since the 1930s to shatter the respectability of influence studies has perhaps produced in our attitude to our literature too great a pride in our independent national achievement, too little willingness to understand the influences that have shaped our country's artistic traditions. We have been very ready to find in new poets further and further evidence of an independent and vibrant Canadian tradition; we have needed to do so, and it has helped us to what are indeed the most significant achievements of our literary history. But it may be that we have arrived at a point of cultural security at which we will not be afraid to discover the influences that have shaped us, a point at which we can seek and take pride in the ways in which our artists have seized upon, and adapted with their own efforts, the traditions of other countries and of foreign artists.

As for Aestheticism, a moderated criticism rising above mere approval and condemnation has only recently been consolidated, and it may be a century after the trial of Oscar Wilde before we speak as accurately of this uncertain period as we wish to of most others. "Aestheticism," a term comprehending the many different versions of the phenomenon, suffers among other difficulties from the obvious dangers of any generic name: the single noun suggests inevitably a single movement, a single group of like-minded artists, rising and passing at roughly the same point in literary history. The limitations of such terms have been proven repeatedly, of course; we recurrently posit such period-titles as a means of preliminary understanding, then realize the inevitable shades of meaning attendant upon them. Further difficulty arises here, however, because "Aestheticism" connotes at once the entire movement – Pre-Raphaelitism, Aesthetic criticism, Decadence, literary Impressionism, and so on – and one particular phase of that movement: "Aesthetic" poetry, that of Dante Gabriel Rossetti, Algernon Charles Swinburne, and William Morris. As a result one is forced to use the adjectival "Aesthetic" to refer both to the period as a whole and to the earlier style of Rossetti and Morris, in order to distinguish this from poetry written by, say, Ernest Dowson and Arthur Symons, which is "Decadent." While it may be tempting as a result of this difficulty to realign the terms – to call, for instance, Rossetti's and Morris's poetry "Pre-Raphaelite" and use "Aesthetic" only in the more general sense – there is as much danger in newly imposed terminology as in old. "Pre-Raphaelite" suggests a richly visual medievalism, and the term therefore runs the risk of excluding a good deal of "Aesthetic" poetry that is, in a purer sense, concerned with abstract beauty of whatever epoch. For such reasons this study will use "Aesthetic" in the general sense as well as the specific; if I need to evoke the entire period, I shall refer to "Aesthetic literature," "Aesthetic criticism," and so on; if I wish to suggest "Aesthetic poetry" as opposed to Decadent, the context of the usage will always make that opposition clear.

Nomenclature aside, the image of the Aesthetic period, especially of the decade that supposedly incarnated its beliefs, the 1890s, has come under increasingly dubious scrutiny. Although major critical texts have usually sought to underline elements common to most Aesthetic literature, briefer skirmishing articles tend to highlight the difficulties of any unified version of the period. Certainly the diversity of reaction both for and against Aestheticism that took place from about 1880 to 1900 (Rudyard Kipling, William Ernest Henley and the Counter-Decadents, Realists and Naturalists, George Bernard Shaw, the Rhymers' Club, Impressionists, Symbolists, Decadents proper; W.B. Yeats, Thomas Hardy, Gerard Manley Hopkins, even Alfred Lord Tennyson also active through much of the "Aesthetic" period) makes it readily apparent that no single conception can adequately describe the two decades most closely associated with Aestheticism.

Nevertheless, we can perceive certain clusters within these many groups; the chronological period does break roughly into two generalized literary tendencies: approaches to and reactions against a prominent Aestheticism. For this reason, we must remember and chart the remarkable diversity of the period, but may seek when we have done so some general aesthetic propositions that run loosely through a significant number of the groups then active and modern. This will leave us with the most comprehensive possible view of a period that has proved, despite its brevity, such a challenge to the modern critical temper.

The meanings of Aestheticism derive above all from a sense of its place in literary history. Far from interrupting the flow of European literatures from the Renaissance to the modern age, Aestheticism rose naturally and of necessity from the movements that preceded it and gave rise to the movements that followed. The pattern is perhaps clearer in English literary history than in others, but casts light on French, German, and Italian Aestheticism as well. During the "high Victorian" period, English Romanticism, facing criticism as a quasi-revolutionary, hyper-individualistic, and potentially sensualist doctrine, appeared to have reached an end. The Spasmodics struggled to defend moribund Romantic dogma; the greater Victorian poets, who obviously inherited the burdens of primal Romanticism, felt called upon to struggle beyond it, to turn its renovation of the human spirit outward to a reconstitution of society, to which endeavour their greatest cultural achievements seem fundamentally linked. In doing so they eventually rejected, or repressed as incompatible with the regulation of a self-consciously moral society, such Romantic concerns as individual perceptions of beauty enriched by the imagination and the need for the individual to be fulfilled by a life of struggle or contemplation or intensity (the "Byronic," the "Wordsworthian," the "Keatsian"). As a consequence these tendencies, not exclusively Romantic but basic paradigms for humankind that the Romantics particularly explored, went underground, accepted a temporary silence, until they appeared again, perhaps inevitably, in mid-century. The first Aesthetic poets, perhaps because some were Pre-Raphaelite painters with strong visualizing capacities, found especially conducive to their artistic needs and temperaments a Romantic fascination with glimpses of earthly and spiritual beauty – for Wordsworth, "spots of time" – which had special force in their struggle against both the Royal Academy and the received poetic practice of their age. In their poetry, therefore, they would pursue a distillation of Romanticism: the increasing antinomianism of the submerged Romantic spirit encouraged them to adopt those qualities of Romantic doctrine that would most sharply distinguish them from prevailing Victorian culture. Rossetti, Morris, and Swinburne, the chief of these poets, are standardly referred to as the Aesthetic poets, since they drew from a particular facet of Romantic aesthetics a comprehensive philosophy of art.

"Aestheticism" was not confirmed as a tangible doctrine in English literature, however, until the famous pronouncements of Walter Pater in his *Studies in the History of the Renaissance* (1873), despite the obvious affinities between his thinking and elements of the earlier poetry of Swinburne, Rossetti, and Morris. Although we locate in these poets certain qualities that we rightly call "Aesthetic," and despite the campaign by Swinburne to import the concept of *l'art pour l'art* into England before Pater wrote his first essays, Aestheticism as a self-conscious and increasingly organized movement required the work of Pater to coalesce and publicize certain of the themes and techniques of the earlier poets in a form that could be transmitted to the next generation tellingly enough to produce those odd variations in the *oeuvres* and careers of the Aesthetes maturing in the 1890s. The more sensational principles of Paterian Aestheticism have been much belaboured, the obvious being the adoration of beauty, the pursuit of intensity, "not the fruit of experience, but experience itself";[4] but as a theory of the arts Paterian Aestheticism is, at root, a doctrine of the removal of art and the artist from all other human activity and of pursuit in his specialized realm of affective beauty in objects commonly recognizable as "art."[5]

Decadence begins, however, when creative personalities too active to persist in the ethereal contemplation of timeless art seek to unite that life of Paterian contemplation with the life of worldly experience – to perceive all of life as an art work yielding, potentially, moments of extreme aesthetic pleasure. The plot thickens because the world, thus re-entered, cannot realistically maintain an aspect of beauty and intensity for the inquiring soul. Pressure is thus brought to bear upon the late Aesthetic artist to create intensity and beauty, while consciously or unconsciously recognizing the incompatibility of his enterprise with reality. The contradiction implied in this spiritual state produces those extreme efforts at intensity that bring the seeker closer and closer to Arthur Rimbaud's "systematic derangement of the senses." These efforts involve him in more direct conflict with social codes than was brought to bear upon the more spiritual Paterian aesthete, and the stage is set for the pattern of despair and lassitude that seizes at last upon the pilgrim of beauty and is manifested in what we refer to as his "Decadent" poetry.[6]

Of course, the application of such extreme aesthetic principles to the "pursuit" of life has often clouded the necessary distinctions between the Decadent's writings and his moral character. I have no interest in suggesting relations between the two; his character is his business, his aesthetic beliefs only are the business of the critic. "Decadence," therefore, whenever it appears in the following pages, is an *aesthetic* term, descriptive of certain techniques, doctrines, or preoccupations of certain works of art, and has nothing whatsoever to do with the personal histories of any poet involved in the discussions.

While it is easy to mistake the Decadent version of Aestheticism for a wilfully perverse approach to aesthetics and to life, a deliberate effeminacy of spirit that seeks decay and failure where they need not be found, such a sense of decay and falling off was a manifestation of a keenly felt cultural impasse, and these young men and women, while they did perhaps over-dramatize the despair they felt at the spiritual state of Victorian England, were in part reflecting a situation first perceived clearly for the first time by their generation. Their response to their cultural situation was to take it within themselves and demonstrate its worst effects upon the human condition; had they not been quite so flamboyant in their expression of those effects, we might now think them the better poets of their day for their original and honest approach to problems with which our culture still grapples.

My claim that the Aesthetic movement is a late and rarefied development of English Romanticism will be obvious to most readers. It is important to recognize, however, that although Aestheticism is a late *version* of Romanticism, it is not the same as what we may call "late Romanticism," an attempt by slighter poets to maintain well into the twentieth century Romantic diction, sentiment, and formal properties, with a significant falling off of Romantic genius. This distinction is especially crucial to Canadian literature, where so much poetry from 1900 to 1925 was simply late Romanticism. The Canadian Modernists are set keenly apart from the poetasters of their time by virtue of their recent Aesthetic rather than late Romantic poetic derivation.

Meditation upon "late Romanticism" helps to emphasize that there is more seriousness to Decadence, and more serious cause for it, than is often admitted. Indeed, it is increasingly common to question the infamously "degenerate" nature of the Decadent poets, both biographically and theoretically. Russell Goldfarb, in his "The Dowson Legend Today," has demonstrated convincingly that much of the image of Ernest Dowson as a whoring alcoholic was created by a journalistic spirit in early biographers and critics who wanted for England her very own *poète damnée*, to counter the primacy of France in that area. John Allan Quintus, in a different vein, has argued for "The Moral Implications of Oscar Wilde's Aestheticism." William E. Buckler has found in Pater's *Marius the Epicurean: His Sensations and Ideas* not a record of "sensations" but "the focal document for a study of the transformation of the creative spirit of the nineteenth century into the creative spirit of the twentieth," "an examination of touchable possibilities for the self-renewal of a certain type of distressed modern man."[7] The list of such works will grow as scholars cast aside preconceptions of the period and realize how many of the twentieth century's aesthetic and cultural problems are foreshadowed in the tensions of Aestheticism manipulated and suffered by such artists as Pater and Wilde.

Such positive assessments must be based on attitudes to Aestheticism at least akin to those proposed above. Only if we can accept Aestheticism as a serious aesthetic theory in which the arts are removed from other forms of human commerce in an effort to preserve their beauty and integrity, and can understand Decadence as an inevitable modification of that theory to the point where the poetry demonstrates little but woe, rejection, and failure, will it be possible to learn from and to emulate the Aesthetes and Decadents, to avoid their pitfalls and to partake of their peculiar and considerable gifts. We may then approach an understanding of a variegated movement that rises above the clutches of evaluative criticism.

The ways in which the above definitions of Aestheticism and Decadence lead to the kinds of poetic activity manifested in the two schools should suggest themselves readily. The poetry of Aestheticism expresses an exhaustive appreciation of beauty,[8] in an atmosphere more or less of poignancy, and reflects a concomitant search for intensity of experience, whether in religious passion, aesthetic rapture, or a sexual intensity that uplifts the lover to a vision of his beloved as "Blessed Damozel." Such experience is realized not in fixed and sculptural visions but as a to-and-fro of more or less continuous "moments," heightened experiences that pass quickly but offer a temporary bliss; a tendency which also accounts for the delicate anguish that frequently informs Aesthetic poetry (as distinct from the more truly Decadent obsession with failure, with the passing of pleasure, with the *post coitum triste* of daily life). Such a preoccupation also helps us to place poetic Impressionism, practised by Wilde and Symons among others, at the centre of Aestheticism, since the "impression" struggles to capture with fleeting touches those visual elements that have created in the poet a particular refined mood.

To the first Aesthetic poets such concerns permitted visions of a more intense medieval world than ever existed in fact and licensed image-rich addresses to women of great beauty and soul: this world was exchanged for another that was more in keeping with the aesthetic principles of the school. Perhaps unfortunately, such an exchange is not available to all. Given a more withering self-consciousness, the Decadent typically writes a poetry obsessed with failure, since desire for unceasing intensity and beauty must inevitably leave the poet embittered; this fixation may manifest itself in poems in which love is unrequited, either from indifference or because of the beloved's death, or in poems of nature, in which Autumn, the "failure" of the year, emerges as the typical Decadent setting, or in poems of creative exhaustion, in which the poet laments his artistic failure (while struggling, by recording it, to surmount it). Since the transience of beauty, the brevity of impressions, is largely responsible for the Decadent's misery, a hatred and fear of natural processes, of inescapable decay, is also central to Decadent literature. The passing of time ages the beloved, or clouds the memory, or buries the beautiful impression under falling leaves, or (if the Decadent is also a dandy, an aesthete of his own flesh) leaves the artist himself wrinkled, withered, and hobbled, an unattractive "impression" ripe for ridicule.

Finally, in pursuit of intensity, the Decadent finds that the sensations of the past – past art, past "sins," past amours – soon become a source of boredom, since any intensity, once mastered, becomes a commonplace, causing ennui. One reaction is to record the ennui, but that soon becomes boring as well; the Decadent then goes out of his way to write about deeper and darker intensities, to find heightened moments the Romantics, for instance, had not found, in an effort to stimulate himself for one more day of life. The Decadent thus begins to record "dangerous," unnatural, or artificial intensities: to create intensities, as it were, rather than find them in nature or in the beauty occasionally offered by the company of others. This tendency in Decadence necessarily gives rise to a fascination with the lurid, the sordid, and the sinful, which probably did more than any other quality of the school to call down ignominy and public venom upon it. Sexuality in this way tends to perversion, beauty tends to evil, delicacy to corruption, each of which qualities, while rarely announced openly in Decadent literature – there are scarcely three remotely homosexual poems in all the work of Wilde and Lord Alfred Douglas[9] – bring to it an atmosphere of willed immorality.

The shift of emphasis between Aesthetic and Decadent poetry must not be insisted upon too finely, however; as the one passes into the other within three or four decades, it is rare (and needless) to find careers that fit the categories decisively. We must be equally cautious when speaking of any distinct stylistic tendencies in Aesthetic and Decadent poetry. At first glance, early Aesthetic poetry, say that of Rossetti and Morris, certainly developed characteristics of style distinct from the dignity and "manliness" of Matthew Arnold, or the stateliness of "Idylls of the King," and maintained a similar distance from typical Decadent style by virtue of a still strong attraction to the English tradition, which drew the poetry towards ballads and sonnets and regulated phonetic effect, rhythm, and diction to a degree the experimenters of Decadence would find restrictive. Thus we find in Rossetti's "The Blessed Damozel" a style evoking sexual sanctity, ideal vision, and a patent medievalism:

> Her robe, ungirt from clasp to hem,
>   No wrought flowers did adorn,
> But a white rose of Mary's gift,
>   For service meetly worn;
> Her hair that lay along her back
>   Was yellow like ripe corn.[10]

Rossetti's balladic rhythm, simple diction, and rich imagery are essential to his vision – as that has been ideal and spiritual, no complicated mannerism can be permitted to intrude between the speaker and his audience. He similarly manipulates highly traditional formal qualities in order to counterpoint and highlight the speaker's fallen condition; the form of the poem bespeaks a continuity with the past, which the poet also desires to attain, but cannot.

The Decadents, however, tend towards a delicacy of impact and refinement of style engendered to capture exactly that falling off, that failure, even degradation, which the earlier poet makes clear only in his final stanza. These stylistic qualities bring their poetry to a trembling standstill, a quiet hush as the thin lines whisper by; nowhere is this more evident than in the poems of Dowson, which have an almost palpable paperiness, suggestive of the dead leaves that drift through so many of them:

> ... Oh, the white
> Gaunt ghosts that flutter where thy feet have sped,

Across the terrace that is desolate,
And rang then with thy laughter, ghost of thee,
That holds its shroud up with most delicate,
Dead fingers, and behind the ghost of me,

Tripping fantastic with a mouth that jeers.[11]

The rhythm lulls, the diction enforces an overwhelming melancholy, the sibilants hiss like the ghosts they capture. The style itself seems to have achieved a superlative tension, so that one drop more of despair would collapse the whole thing in upon itself in utter failure. A situation roughly similar to Rossetti's, the passing of some beautiful beloved, produces an entirely different style, the only end of which is to express pain, emptiness, and bitterness. While Rossetti looks up to heaven and attains a brief, searing glimpse of his beloved transfigured, Dowson's persona is stuck harshly in the abandoned earth, lunging hideously after a mere ghost, after an echo of past laughter. He never attains, perhaps never seeks, an ideal vision of the dead woman; his chief concern is with his surroundings and how they reflect the burden upon his soul. His focus is down and in, while Rossetti's is up and out, and one can argue such a distinction as successfully from properties of style as from content.[12]

A few typical poems do not two movements make, and while certain stylistic distinctions can be generally sketched in this way, they do not hold a clean boundary between Aesthetic and Decadent poetry. Certainly Rossetti produced sonnets entwining diction and rhythms much like Dowson's, and Dowson on the other hand produced poetry that we would have a hard job to distinguish, stylistically at least, from much of Swinburne's. Swinburne in fact produced stanzas as foreign to the English mould as those of "Faustine," and rhythms as explosive as the most stunning of Hopkins's; he could capture either the whispers of Dowson, or the balladic regularity of Rossetti's "The Blessed Damozel"; and yet in chartings of the period he is generally placed with Rossetti and Morris as a craftsman of "Aesthetic" poetry. Swinburne is therefore a compelling reminder that the line between Aesthetic and Decadent form and style is an unreliable and faint one, with clearly different habits manifested by each only when a poet touches the heights of his particular gift.

The very diversity of the Aesthetic movement, however successfully it has been brought to first principles here, poses a question with some revealing answers. The period from 1880 to 1900 was a jumble of movements and counter-movements, many of which were efforts to shatter the grip of Aestheticism on impressionable young minds; yet many of the greatest writers of the period remained largely undisturbed by the Aesthetic battles in England. If, as has become increasingly clear, Aestheticism and Decadence are only two related schools among several that had far greater popularity as literature (rather than as public spectacle), why have we, Modernists and the heirs of Modernism, taken our understanding of the 1890s not from the cacophony but from the Decadents we began the century by deriding? Why does the end of the Victorian empire strike us as a Decadence, when Tennyson passed the mantle of that empire into the able hands of Kipling with such apparent grandeur? Why, on a simpler level, do we remember the Aesthetes and Decadents so well, when we have all but forgotten Henley, Francis Thompson and the name of the laureate next after Tennyson?

We do so because we find in Aestheticism and Decadence the movements of the Victorian period closest to English Modernism, and are pleased, even gratified, to find some foreshadowing of the revolutions of the early twentieth century under the darkest shrouds of the late Victorian period. This is to argue that there are elements in the literature of Aestheticism that are not only congenial to Modernist theory but central, that Aestheticism was a necessary cultural step taken before the Modernist revolution could be initiated. The fact that we rely on Dowson, Symons, Wilde, and the others for our sense of the 1890s is insufficient grounds for that conclusion, however; so we must seek other means of delineating that strange rivalry of allies that took place between Aestheticism and Modernism.

Those who speak of the theoretical and aesthetic relationship between Aestheticism and Modernism usually do so from one of three perspectives: they see Modernism as a deeper, more pervasive and more serious Decadence and, therefore, as a carry-over of the spirit of the "Nineties"; or they see Modernism as a health-giving overthrow of all that Decadence represented; or they understand Modernism to have developed in part out of an elaboration of Aesthetic and Decadent principles, while also remembering that Decadence provided the focus of attack for a generation of young poets in the early years of our own artistic epoch. Primarily the first of these positions is held by the detractors of Modernism, now fairly well routed, the second by the original apologists of Modernism, who felt keenly the need to attack a ready-made opponent, and the third by more recent critics sympathetic to Modernism but interested above all in its antecedents, in its continuity despite all claims to the contrary with various strains of nineteenth-century thought.

Each school of thought delineates some form of influence: in the first and third cases a positive influence – the acceptance of certain

principles of an earlier school – and in the second a negative influence – a process of self-definition by rejection of such principles.
Those who seek the roots of Modernism in Aestheticism have been
most thorough in their study of how the one movement passed into
the other, necessarily involving a study of individual cases of influence as well as larger speculations as to theory and tradition. These
are, of course, the critics of greatest interest here.

Morse Peckham's "Aestheticism to Modernism: Fulfilment or Revolution?" ranges through modern music, sculpture, painting, and
literature with startling ease and argues from a number of premises
that the various manifestations of nineteenth-century Aestheticism
were "logically necessary strategies for encompassing that breakthrough into the comprehension of the very principle of self-trans-
formation, which is Modernism."[13] Peckham argues that
Aestheticism occurs as a result of "the abandonment of the superficial aspect of the Romantic program" (216). That abandonment
meant that new sources of faith had to be found, faith that rose
neither from the materialistic society surrounding the artist, nor from
the outworn premises of Romantic genius, nature, intuition, imagination, and the like: "A functional substitute for faith was obviously
needed, a substitute which would be metaphysically neutral; it
would not commit the individual to any illusory goal, nor would it
leave him defenseless. The answer lay in commitment to style in its
own right" (216–17). Peckham likens the disintegration of this Romantic program to the disintegration of a personality and notes that
in both cases a stylization results in any creative product, which
makes it "more limited and less flexible in its responses and more
repetitive … The behavioural pattern is applied almost indifferently
to an increasing variety of situations without correction or adaptation" (217).

The rigid pursuit of style for its own sake brings a multitude of
pressures to bear upon the artist: to refine and to innovate perpetually, to sacrifice all the pleasures of life to such refinement, to see
art as the highest of life's goals and yet to live in the lower world,
and to survive there long enough to produce ever finer and more
rarefied styles. Such pressures are, however, all the artist has to
motivate his genius, so he uses his style, "not as the neurotic does,
to decrease the threat of disintegration, but, on the contrary, to
increase it" (221).

Such a situation can hardly be maintained past the first generation.
The pressure becomes unbearable, and the pursuit of intrinsically
limited art forms leads to creative exhaustion, since these forms are,
for the artist's purposes, chronologically dead. At the breaking point,
a new destiny for the arts must be developed: "the appearance of

Art Nouveau upon the scene was a sign that the pressure which the Stylist was seeking strategies to achieve had very nearly reached the necessary degree ... When the pressure was enough, the lid blew off, and the modern styles emerged, not in an embryonic form, or only briefly, but almost at once in maturity" (224–5). Thus the progress from "Aestheticism to Modernism" is a fulfilment, a continuity, by virtue of its explosive discontinuity, which was implicit in, in fact demanded by, the premises pursued to the death by the "Stylists." Peckham resolves in these terms the central tension underlying the history of Modernism.

J.E. Chamberlin's "From High Decadence to High Modernism" arrives at conclusions with a different emphasis from those of Peckham, but which support his central vision of artists under wilful creative pressure: "The paradoxical conjunction of beauty and despair, of joy and sorrow, is one which poetry has always employed ... But the artists of the nineteenth century that were called decadent intensified this juxtaposition to a dangerous pitch, to the point that it became unclear whether the pleasure that one felt was in the beauty evoked or in the deliberate and often suicidal despair that accompanied its evocation."[14] But the chief aesthetic link to be found between Aestheticism and Modernism, according to Chamberlin, is their mutual antagonism to the vulgarization of the arts taking place in an increasingly democratic and literate culture:

Both, in ways that are congruent, were informed by an almost puritan zeal to maintain standards appropriate to what were received as the sacred values of art, and to protect these values against compromise ... a defence against the futile institutionalizing of language and other forms of communication was to break them down into their smaller constituent elements – images, words, sounds, and so forth. Decorative and other similarly abstract forms of art were in a way a defence of this sort against the perversions of representative art; just as symbolism, with its isolation of the elements of a numinous reality, was (in Arthur Symons' view) a defence against materialism. (598)

Thus the formal breakdown we tend to associate with Modernism is inherent in the "dissolution" of form apparent in the literature of the Decadence (599), and this preoccupation was passed on to the next generation: "The disunity, the separateness, the disintegration, that seemed to define decadence both fascinated and bothered the artists who moved from decadence to modernism, and few escaped the ambivalence" (600).

Jacques Barzun's scintillating *The Use and Abuse of Art* confirms the efforts of Peckham and Chamberlin to establish a general continuity of purpose and occasionally of practice between the generation of the 1890s and that of the 1910s: "The phase of Estheticism and Abolitionism which fills the quarter century 1890–1914 ... is the formative period from which all our present ideas and attitudes are derived,"[15] and it is the application of Art as the destroyer of so-called "bourgeois values" – a meaningless term which Barzun invalidates consummately – which particularly links the Decadent and the Modernist halves of that span of years. The pursuit of beauty and intensity, launched in Barzun's opinion primarily as an attack upon conventional Victorian pieties, "earnestness," "manliness," and the like, gives the Aesthete a self-definition and defence against an aesthetically and spiritually hostile society. But the pursuit of beauty becomes repetitive, and, because the concept of beauty itself is acceptable to the philistine enemy, "Reconcilement through beauty is almost bourgeois complacency. It damns the world too indirectly. The war against the bourgeois, the infidel, the hated Turk at our gates must reach a new intensity."[16] The new intensity, Decadence, involves among other things an attack on conventional beauty itself and inaugurates the "Abolitionism" to which art in Barzun's opinion has dedicated itself, in one form or another, ever since. The resulting institutionalization of an abolitionist avant-garde brings about an emasculation of true avant-gardism, since there is no longer an establishment rear- and middle-guard against which to militate. The problems of contemporary art are, therefore, a direct result of the Decadent strategy as Barzun conceives it.

Supporting such vast cultural criticism is a wide range of articles and texts dealing with individual Modernists who have inherited some part of the Aesthetic burden. T.E. Hulme, T.S. Eliot, Ezra Pound, Virginia Woolf, and W.B. Yeats have been criticized revealingly in the light of their common Aesthetic inheritance.[17] It is an unfortunate fact, nonetheless, that no sizeable, thorough critical volume exists on a scale to combine the brilliant theorizing of Barzun with the meticulous commentaries and individual studies necessary to make such a theory respectably solid. In the absence of such a landmark text one must conclude that the notion of Aesthetic roots for Modernism is still thinly spread and needs significant further development. Although the immediate result of the studies to follow will be an illumination of the specifically Canadian Modernist tradition, they are also devoted to the larger task: to establishing the profound continuity of Modernism with the prior literary traditions it appeared at first to have routed.

## CHAPTER TWO

# Impressionism and Modernism in Ross and Knister

Canadian Modernism, like the Anglo-American Modernism from which it derived, was heralded by a literary phenomenon that has been characterized with some degree of authority and accuracy as "Imagism." Not even so coherent a movement as the British, which certainly had its internecine skirmishes, the Canadian derivative of Imagism was practised chiefly by two isolated and hardly recognized poets who in their prime knew nothing of one another, Raymond Knister and W.W.E. Ross. Knister, who gave up poetry altogether at the age of twenty-seven,[1] and Ross, who printed private volumes in 1930 and 1932 and then wrote quietly for over thirty years while awaiting general recognition, came to similar conclusions about the need for a revision of Canadian poetry based on their roughly similar readings in the poetry then being written in England and America. Their resulting canons manifest, undoubtedly, some conscious adoption of Imagist principles, especially in a small core of poems which have become as a result their most acclaimed.[2]

Some injustice has been done to both poets, however, by the focus of critics and anthologists on these core poems; not because other poems that are clearly better have been ignored, but because other efforts they made, other successes that do not fit the Imagist mould, as well as other apparent failures which nevertheless reveal interesting tendencies in both poets, are not generally acknowledged. Both seem, as a result, simpler and more superficial than they truly were and more truly Imagistic even than they desired to be. Attractions revealed in the wider range of their poetry in fact cut deeply against the Imagist grain: to such preoccupations of Aestheticism as fragility, beauty, death, and the rushing by of time. By calling up the complete work of each, suggesting ways in which that work echoes Aesthetic themes, and then disclosing the true nature of their apparently Imagistic pieces in the context of the theoretical relationship between Imagism and literary Impressionism, we can reveal the degree to which Ross and Knister were the beneficiaries of many theoretical and poetic trends of late nineteenth-century English literature.

A variety of analyses point to this unfamiliar conclusion. We may begin simply and profitably by remarking the desire of both poets to create, to capture, or to theorize about highly conventional beauty and ecstasy, a little-noted predilection that must surprise the critic indoctrinated into their presumptive Imagism. The desire is a clearly traditional one; the language in which they express it is usually the introspective, poignant language of Aestheticism, and so tells convincingly against the sharper Imagist diction of visual presentation. Of course, beauty is addressed in Aesthetic poetry in various ways: the speaker invokes "Beauty" as an abstraction, or refers to particular beauty – female, natural, or spiritual – or bemoans the fallen ugliness of his world and struggles with painful memories of something more appealing. Ross and Knister explore the various manners of Aesthetic address with a consistency that betrays more than a coincidence of expression with the earlier school.

Knister, for instance, opens his muted "Autumn Clouds" thus:

Here on the quiet upland
Among the withered corn
Wondering I stand:
Beauty again is born.[3]

A traditional quatrain coordinates an emotional fascination with autumn, a need for natural beauty and the ecstasy it may bring, and a lament for the absence of such beauty in the larger world, since the poet finds "Beauty" not merely apparent, but "born again." The speaker is arrested in a sudden, silent contemplation of natural splendour. The autumnal melancholy of the "withered corn" is confirmed as "The thin light melts and yields, / The torn stalks shiver," but all this imagery of decay is "submerged" by the "pale gold" of the river in the distance, which reflects piercingly the yielding sunlight, "and passes,"

Leaving all no less unspent,
Nor more lonely. And I find,
Long lost, the trees' assent
To sunlight and to wind.

The "assent" of the trees to "sunlight," in autumn, is a surrender to their own seeming deaths, to the loss of their leaves into the winds rising to take them. When the speaker finds "the trees' assent" to their inescapable decay, he means that he finds it for himself, takes their lesson of willing surrender into his own spirit. Certainly the speaker takes more comfort from his vision than a Decadent poet would, yet he uses a strategy very similar to theirs – the blending of vague melancholy, passing time, and autumnal landscape – to reconcile the conflict between his emotions and the vista he has suddenly discovered. Knister's evocative setting is not accidental or decorative, then, but central to a poem in which the speaker is able, by means of a glimpse of "beauty," to intuit the inevitable processes of decay that characterize the passing of time in his rural world.

Such moments of Aesthetic arrest are often employed by Knister to illuminate and extend a personal sorrow. In "Immemorial Plea," for instance, "the rain-filled air / With thunder far away, / And tremor of lightning" carry flashes of painful understanding to the poet in the midst of an emotional upheaval:

What else could I crave, as I sit here
    And hearken all the lore
Of leaves, as each leaf sings its joy in fear –
    Save only you, what more?

Each leaf is rapture in all the tree,
    And you too should be kind;
And after, rise and go through lanes with me,
    Rain-bitten dust, sad wind.   (WC, 39)

Although the lightning has suddenly shown him the earth "all fair ... beneath its play," the speaker perceives only the distance between this glimpse of "rapture" and the necessary corollary of it in his affections, the presence of his beloved. Presumably she is *not* kind, since he tells her that she "should" be; the dreariness of the lanes through which they might pass in his best scenario confirms that the poet's vision has chiefly served to remind him of his own melancholy. Thus, although it moves towards poignant failure, "Immemorial Plea" exploits the same emotional strategy as "Autumn Clouds"; both poems are initiated after the speaker has been stricken with a keen sense of the world's power and beauty.[4]

Knister's general lyric method is obedient to this pattern. His brief poems tend to record moments of beauty and intensity that unfold onto personal horizons previously uncontemplated and then pass suddenly, leaving in their wake the pain of half-understood meanings; a single Knister lyric may capture the whole or any part of this

Aesthetic process. The formula does much to explain an otherwise inexplicable bitterness in many of Knister's lyrics, usually focused on the inattention of a woman, as in "March Wind," a poem markedly reminiscent, in stanza structure and in tone, of certain effects of Dowson's. The natural phenomenon is, once again as in "Immemorial Plea," a storm tossing the trees, and the result is the expected subjective revelation:

> My heart cries out, my heart is broken, Lady!
>   What of after-years, with this deep pain sown?
> Never to forget. But my heart is praying
>   It had not known.   (WC, 46)[5]

But in this case the momentary illumination is too painful for the speaker to bear; it is never articulated in the poem, and the final lines merely express a desire to have avoided illumination altogether. To the extent that it attempts to refuse its spontaneous emotion and knowledge, the poem fails, but its very failure is ironically revealing.

Knister was perfectly aware of his preoccupation with such arresting glimpses and of his inevitable failure to capture them. "Moments When I'm Feeling Poems" refers to poetic inspiration as a time "when beauty creeps like pain" (note the conjunction of abstractions), when he acknowledges "the old futility of art":

> When some forgotten clear slight
> Secret's imminent plangent chords
>
> Come like a full moon's night
> That has been stolen by rain,
> Dimmed grey, radiant and palled.

It would appear that Knister's poetry was often incited just after a vision, or glimpse, or "moment"; but by creating "just after" instead of "during," the poet loses the "light" of the vision, which is clouded over, left "dimmed" and "palled," even if still somehow "radiant" in the memory. The sorrow of this loss is hinted at with "plangent," which prefigures the "pain" associated with "beauty" in the creative instant. The result?

> I know the old futility of art,
> But know as well the ladies and the lords
> Of life are they who, knowing, feel
> No call to blight that sense with words.   (WC, 40)

In other words, the supreme poetic moment can never be recorded, since expression necessarily mars it. As Peter Stevens asked, "Is this the reason that ultimately long before his death Knister gave up poetry?"[6] Knister remarked elsewhere that the "futile" feeling was constant, not specific to this poem's genesis: "Everything I see or hear reminds me of something I must write, and of the impossibility of doing so, consequent upon the well-known brevity of life and length of art."[7] Poems about poetic failure with such philosophical foundations were the specialty of the Decadence, especially when the failure was due to the loss of an original, ostensibly perfect vision.

In such a context, with the speaker transfixed between his glimpses of intensity and the utter impossibility of extending them into his painful private life, or of realizing them at all successfully in his art, the resonance of "The Plowman," Knister's most famous poem, is much increased. The disheartening distance between vision and realization provides the tension of a brilliant poem with no immediately apparent relation to aesthetic difficulties. But so one may interpret it: wrapped in artistic struggle, the poet "care[s] not for skies or upturned flowers," that is, for vision itself, since success, the perfect rendition of vision, is all that matters. Despite all he can do, however, after each effort he knows he will

Look backward
Ever with discontent.

A stone, a root, a strayed thought
Has warped the line of that furrow.

But he remains faithful to his difficult task, urging his "horses 'round again":

When I tell myself
This time
The ultimate unflawed turning
Is before my share,
They must give up their rest.

Someday, someday, be sure,
I shall turn the furrow of all my hopes,
But I shall not, doing it, look backward.
    (WC, 20 [incomplete version])[8]

The poet seeks, then, an unconscious perfection, the work of art achieved without concern, without "looking back." Only in this manner will he overcome the extreme aesthetic self-consciousness that taints each pure vision even in the act of recording. He understands that he has not yet reached his goal, which is why a faint desperation rings in his repetition of "someday," a promise always fading into the distance, ungraspable. That very fragile affirmation counterpoints and ironically highlights the much greater conviction of "Moments When I'm Feeling Poems," asserting the "futility of art."

To be sure, the Aesthetic "moment" need not always lead to such meditations: hence Knister's apparent Imagism. He was occasionally willing to record the "moment" without overtly subjective comment. In a less rural-naturalistic vein, and with a deftness reminiscent of the late nineteenth-century fascination with Oriental art forms, "Woman Reading Poetry" captures just such a "moment":

> Paper like wisps of snow
> On the granite blue of Cat's hair:
> I cut the pages ...
>
> I chanting wake, and you, my Cat,
> Slip silken from my lap; and on the footstool,
> In a lull look up from slanted topaz
> Opening eyes:
> A metal god of China come
> Across seas that reach to music.   (WC, 61)

The exoticism of the images and the free verse form sit uncomfortably with such phrases from the middle of the poem as "selvage of dreams" and "my soul," abstractions that Knister never avoided as rigorously as Pound might have desired. But that form and exoticism catch Knister only half-way away from the refined meditations of Baudelaire's "Le Chat" or Wilde's "The Sphinx," half-way towards the purer feline images of Carl Sandburg's "Fog" or William Carlos Williams's "Poem":

> Viens mon beau chat, sur mon coeur amoureux;
>   Retiens les griffes de ta patte,
> Et laisse-moi plonger dans tes beaux yeux,
>   Melés de métal et d'agate.[9]
>
> Dawn follows Dawn and Nights grow old and all the while this
>   curious cat

Lies couching on the Chinese mat with eyes of satin rimmed with
   gold.   (Wilde, *Poems*, 289)

The fog comes
on little cat feet.

It sits looking
over harbor and city
on silent haunches
and then moves on. [10]

As the cat
climbed over
the top of

the jam closet
first the right
forefoot

carefully
then the hind
stepped down. [11]

The Imagist influence is perhaps responsible for restraining the subjective content of Knister's poem; Wilde and Baudelaire see in their
felines symbols of their own desires, whereas Sandburg and Williams see in theirs forceful autonomous images. On the other hand,
in the vision of Knister's subjective persona, the cat is orientalized,
exoticized, not objective and "American" like Sandburg's and Williams's. The place of Knister's ostensible Imagism begins to be de-
terminable: whenever he is willing to record his "moments" with
little or no comment, he is drawn towards an apparent Imagism;
but the preponderance of his poetry discourses freely on the emotional and spiritual ramifications of his Aesthetic visions.

   This preliminary skirmish with Knister's poetry suggests, then,
that his Imagism arose in conjunction with a large body of work
with a quite different aesthetic philosophy in a highly traditional
form. His passion for the visual appears to have developed first from
an essentially Romantic connectedness with the landscape, fostered
by a steady melancholy that runs throughout his work. Such concerns do not dominate Knister's poetry wholly – we have only
touched a portion of the canon – but they account for certain tendencies within it: moods he desires to capture, or aesthetic implica-

tions that lie hushed beneath the surface of a given image. These concerns are much illuminated by certain references in his private papers, which will be considered later in the present chapter.

In Ross's poetry beauty has demanded different strategies. First, his Modernist poetry reveals a fascination with the incarnations of conventional beauty in the natural world; second, a substantial portion of his work that has been largely ignored, the *Sonnets* of 1932, addresses beauty much more directly and openly, in a tone distinctly reminiscent of the late nineteenth century. Few of these *Sonnets* have been anthologized – only three were admitted into *Shapes and Sounds*,[12] a collection of Ross's work published by Raymond Souster two years after his death – and the others are all but lost to literary history, rejected presumably as the non-Imagistic work of a Canadian Imagist. Contemplation of these twin faces of beauty in Ross's sharply divided *oeuvre* encourages a renegade understanding of this unique poet's achievements.

The brief, often delicate lines of Ross's best-known manner are well suited to transmit his finely tuned aesthetic breathlessness in the face of Canadian beauty; Knister's verse adopts the typically shortened line of the Imagists haphazardly, but Ross uses it religiously, capturing his image with light quick strokes:

One leaf is
floating on
ripples in
shallow
shore-side
water

over the
sand at the
bottom that
shimmers in
sunlight[13]

The narrow focus of the vision – a single leaf in shallow water – is reflected in the sparse, chopped lines that capture it. The poet appears to be impersonal, detached, yet it is his sense of delicacy that infuses the image, his precision of eye that has fixed the scope of the poem. He has not been forced to perceive a vision so monumental that no eye could avoid it; he has instead gone searching for the tiny intimate world of a few inches of shore-line and returned with the poem as trophy. This sensation of the poet's selecting his images is everywhere in Ross's poetry and accounts for the oddly personal voice in his impersonal style:[14]

> We shall be
> lovers of
> all that is
> lovely and
> gentle and
> bold
>
> Fearing no
> death but the
> lapse of our
> souls.   (SS, 34)

The search for the small floating leaf can lead the seekers to something like grace; "death," the "lapse of our / souls," will strike only when the search itself is abandoned, since "Death ... curves / mouldering / out of the / mouths of our / idleness."[15] "Loveliness," "gentleness," and "boldness" effect positive spiritual growth in the "lovers," and it is in such a context that we ought to appreciate Ross's poetic achievement: not as a record of neutral perceptions, but as a panorama offered by one pair of seeing eyes, which seek in that panorama above all the beauty it can offer.

Those who doubt this statement will hunt fruitlessly for images of ugliness in Ross's canon. He is after other images, more conventional in their precise, often delicate loveliness:

> Terror below the surface,
> Beauty above,
> As the exquisite dark trees
> Gaze endlessly at their reflections.   (SS, 17)
>
> The snake trying
> to escape the pursuing stick,
> with sudden curvings of thin
> long body. How beautiful
> and graceful are his shapes!   (SS, 109)

Ross's scattering the abstraction "beauty" or the poetically dead adjectives "beautiful" and "lovely" throughout his Modernist work, a feature strongly against the Imagist grain, is, moreover, a reminder of the lost portion of his canon. Ross divided the volume *Sonnets*, published privately by "E.R." in 1932, into several poetic groups, the most poignant of which is entitled "On Beauty, etc.," a somewhat shuffling designation for a group of poems that are anything but hesitant in their Aesthetic hunger:

> Islands of song, where the shrill veering winds
> Are never known, and never the keen frost
> Has come relentlessly with shivering host
> Of ghostly snowflakes, and where no man finds
> Other than speech melodious from minds
> Attuned to beauty that was never lost
> Or by the streams of dull stupidity crossed
> But yet is living as the light that blinds –
> Would I were there!

Like a true Aesthete Ross yearns for a distant paradise where Beauty is still recognized and praised, where "song" rises naturally from the "attuned" spirit, where such Canadian nuisances as frost and snow never come. But his vision is soon crossed by painful realities, promoting a sestet with exactly that delicate anguish of loss and regret which is so central to Aesthetic poetry:

> ... And yet, where are those isles,
> Where are those archipelagoes of song?
> And who can find them, or do they appear
> But in the fancy's dim and furtive smile?
> Sunken into forgetfulness for long
> Where are those isles that have been so near?[16]

In another sonnet this separation between poet and Aesthetic paradise is all that "inspires" the feeble speech:

> If I am blind, do not encumber me
> With any talk of beauty's trappings dull
> Or anything superfluous else, or full
> Of wind and vain – such things are not for me; –
> Or any tales of islands in the sea
> Or lands of much entrancement, beautiful,
> That are where beauty's residence may be.

The pervasive and fairly subtle irony in the speaker's voice weakens the sincerity of this rhetoric, however, and fixes our vision of the poem above all on the beauty he has lost in his blindness. He now desires only to

> ... move most scornfully among
> The relics of a long since ancient land;
> Why incommode oneself to such extent
> As to see wonders in a simple song
> Or to be wrapped in musing sweet or stand
> Amazed before an empty monument[?]   (*Son.*, 34)

The phrase "incommode oneself" serves to direct the poem's irony more clearly against those who make no effort to perceive the beauty that *is* available to them, those who will not lift a finger towards "beauty's residence." Hence the scorn of the "blind" speaker is for aesthetic sloth, not for "beauty" itself, wherein the whole potency of the poem is centred.

This bitterness, engendered by the distance between the poet and his aesthetic desires, leads Ross in "The Same – 2" (the second instalment of "The Lover Plaineth the Absence of his Love") to express a desolation and wandering melancholy very like that made sacred during the 1890s:

> Empty of life and sad and desolate
> .............................................
> All kindness, beauty gone, and nothing left
> But empty stones to shed salt tears upon –
> So is thy dwelling. Now it stands bereft,
> Like crown of jewels, or rose-bush of its bloom.
> Thy dwelling is as empty as a tomb,
> As cold and as forlorn when thou art gone.   (*Son.*, 62)

The atmosphere is created and enforced by the autumnal allusions and by the hint of death at the end. The fascination and pain of a beauty that has passed mingle with the suffering of the defeated lover, and Ross's sonnet is infused with the vision of the Decadence, although perhaps less evocative of melancholy than many of its precursors. Compare Ross's poem with Dowson's "The Garden of Shadow":

> Love heeds no more the sighing of the wind
> Against the perfect flowers: thy garden's close
> Is grown a wilderness, where none shall find
> One strayed, last petal of one last year's rose.   (*PW*, 73)

or with Symons's "The Street":

> I passed your street of many memories.
> A sunset, sombre pink, the flush
> Of inner rose leaves idle fingers crush,
> Died softly, as the rose that dies
>
> ...........................................
>
> I know not if 'twere bitter or more sweet
> To stand and watch the roofs, the sky.
> O bitter to be there and you not nigh
>
> ...................................................
>
> There was the house, the windows there
> Against the rosy twilight high and bare,
> The pavement-stones: I knew them all![17]

To his credit, Ross's sonnet lacks the indulgent whisperiness of the Decadent lines, but his outcry in "The Same – 2" recalls directly the sentiments of Dowson and Symons. Ross sees his beloved's "desolate dwelling," her rose bushes and tree unattended, the hardness of her floor of "empty stones," and adds the suggestion of death to enforce his Decadent bitterness; all this is made evident in a catalogue of potent images, each of which is intended to add to a cumulative sense of loss, failure, and suffering.

Unlike his Imagist poems, Ross's sonnets are behind his times by some thirty or forty years, but we cannot dismiss them. Ross the Imagist wrote them; he thought highly enough of them to bring them before the public, significantly, two years *after* the publication of his more famous and notable *Laconics*; and they certainly reveal a number of the unrecognized preoccupations of a poet whose better-known verses make us treat him, generally, as a simple poet skilful at a limited craft. When in his Imagist poems we find a hunger for beauty, moments of aesthetic fixation, painful delicacy, or whiffs of looming death – the emblems of Decadence – reading the *Sonnets* can confirm these as the subterranean themes of the modern work. The two distinct manners of verse he explored constitute a more substantial traditionalist-modernist tension in his artistic development than is generally recognized.

We have so far studied both Ross and Knister only to the point of recognizing their preoccupations with beauty and ecstasy, in Knister's aesthetic of lost "moments" and in Ross's delicate, directed eye and in the abstract references of his *Sonnets*. But the pursuit of beauty is only a portion of the Aesthetic program; that generation also appropriated for "Beauty" epithets of impermanence and fragility and usually drew the obvious conclusion, the inevitability of decay and death. If the spirit of beauty suggests an Aestheticism in the Canadian poets' work, these secondary features must be consistent in their poetry as well.

We have already noted that Ross's very choice of poetic form reveals a fascination with refinement to the point of painful delicacy; this form is often used by Ross to render, significantly, images of utter fragility, of beautiful natural creations poised on the edge of destruction. Nowhere is this loaded use of the tiny line so clear as in his "Wild Rose," which unites the form ideally with the sensation he wishes to convey:

Delicate
is the light
petal of
wild rose
    . . . . . . . . . . . . .

Fragile and
delicate,
lightest of
pressure will
unbalance
fatally
    . . . . . . . . .

Delicate
fragile and
apt to be
swept away
suddenly.   (SS, 24)

There is some danger that poetry uniting such delicacy of form and of content will itself "unbalance fatally" and collapse into sentimental wee melodrama.[18] Perhaps "Wild Rose" just avoids doing so. Ross's fascination with those briefest phenomena of nature that hover between serene beauty and imminent destruction reveals a little-remarked element of his poetic personality, refinement to the point of verbal extinction, which pulls him in the opposite direction poetically from the solid building blocks and chunks of thought that inform his *Sonnets*.

Raymond Knister develops similar patterns of fragility in his verse forms. His "Peach Buds" unites such formal fragility with pathetic fallacy, to create a singularly sentimental poem:

As we wait
In the dark,
In Winter's young Spring-rain
Stricken the lashed drops cling.

In dawn, in the wind
We crispen,
Complaining silverly,
Weeping.   (WC, 18)

Delicacy of form and sentiment also governs "Bees," which juxtaposes frail snow-drops and a swarm of insects with a significant concluding regret for passing time:

Snow-drops hang
Dancing,
Lifting and flitting
Tiny
Through the swarm,
Never striking;
Hum about the tamarack,
Drift a little
Toward the cabin window:
Too late.
The honey of frost-flowers is melted –
Too late.   (WC, 24)

The superficial Imagism of these poems, engineered largely by their truncated lines, should not be permitted to obscure the tender delicacy of sentiment that informs them. Ross's and Knister's indoctrination into the tenets of precision and exactitude inherent in Imagism obviously led them to certain similar and somewhat surprising formal habits. While there is certainly a strain in Imagism (particularly under the guidance of Amy Lowell) that tended towards the pretty and the delicate, the original stimulating Imagism of 1912 to 1914 tried for more muscle and sinew and also had the courage to reject much late nineteenth-century sentimentalism, even if it seemed demanded by the Images they wished to seize for the reader.[19] Ross and Knister did not avoid as rigorously their own tendencies towards such sentiments; we have already noted echoes of ghostly Dowsonism in the latter, and in Ross the painful delicacy of a poem like "Wild Rose" strains against the urgings of Pound towards poetic hardness as well as clarity. While such tendencies do not mitigate the force of their more correctly Imagistic poems, they do serve as a reminder that poets who imitate one school of poetry might well be imitating another as well, often less consciously.

In the context of such revealing tendencies, the absorption with death evinced by both poets becomes particularly provocative. Ross tends to refer to death in the abstract, addressing with a mixture of curiosity and fear its properties and colours: hence his poem "Death" is a mere circle of interrogatives:

```
                is it
  dark
  is it
                black
                is it
  black         is it
                dark
  is it         dark?   (SS, 49)
```

Knister on the other hand treats death with a Romantic sense of its terrible relevance to his own individual life, to his relationships with lovers, for instance, and to his place in the earth. A frequently expressed scepticism about his own ability to live life nobly brings to the poet's fear of death a sharp edge, as in the stark vision of "Cedars":

```
          ... we shall remember ...
    ..........................................
    When we quiet our clamour, and, awaiting the echo,
    Choke for the air, and it is not, and mocks us,
    And our head sinks down and we cannot raise it,
    Holding our hand behind us, hoping that life may come and take
       it yet;
    And the soul floats high, and will not see,
    Cannot even smile.   (WC, 37)
```

Most importantly, in the work of both poets, their fixations on death and beauty are entwined in a strange perpetual dance, so that the striking image often leads to thoughts of death, or fear of death to a regret for the loss of beauty. Thus, in "Autumn Maples," Ross records the trees with their "Beautiful / colours though / not the most / varied / hues of the / rainbow," then renders the "Autumnal" atmosphere and concludes suddenly, obtrusively, "Surely this / gay display / cannot be / hinting of / death?" (SS, 143). His wedding here of beauty, autumn, and death produces a poem with Modernistic formal qualities, yet with images that, in their conjunction, are very like those of Decadence. The counterpoint thus created is startling and disturbing. If the reader shifts for confirmation to Ross's *Sonnets*, similar transactions between beauty and death emerge. "The Lake" opens with such a natural scene as might instead have prompted Ross the Imagist:

> A beautiful and shining lake there was,
> Its surface of a smoothness like a mirror
> That has been made and polished without error
> Most carefully, of finest moulded glass.

The octave thus sets up a perfect crystalline image of natural beauty; the sestet brings that beauty to what somehow seems its inevitable conclusion, the interruption of death:

> He looked on it who felt temptation's pull
> To bathe therein although the banks were high
> Snow-covered, cold; this stranger passing by
> The peril of the lake was filled with striving,
> One moment seen in youthful glory diving,
> Then chilled and dead in water beautiful.   (*Son.*, 35)

The striking interrelationships between the *Sonnets* and Ross's better-known Modernist poems become particularly apparent if one meditates upon thematic and visual similarities between the sonnet above and his famous "The Diver." While the Modernist poem brings the diver up from his vision of the "cooler zones," the pre-Modernist sonnet leaves him dead and beautiful after a moment of supreme glory. Clearly the tension in Ross between Aestheticism and Modernism runs deeper than mere formal qualities can indicate, the beauty of death attracting him frequently throughout his career.

Such transactions preoccupy Knister as well. In "Martyrdom," he links the dying of leaves in autumn to an exquisite religious ritual.

Only the less fortunate leaves fall to the rain puddles and rot swiftly on the ground:

Others happier
Far more happy
Winged suddenly
High lifted,
Crucified on the wires,
Swing and writhe
Transfixed on thorns
In immeasurable pain,
Immeasurable ecstasy. (WC, 22)

This mixture of spiritual ecstasy and the pain of martyrdom is vaguely Decadent. In "Martyrdom" the mixture is extreme; in other poems the mood can be quietly grim, as in "Cedars," with its trees "In inebriate frenzy" and its poets who "reel through action and glory" (WC, 37), or poignant and bittersweet, as in the autumnal "October Stars":

Was it the frenzied whisper
Of covert wind to obdurate apple-boughs
(Leaves sheltering no more fruit)
Or the paled sky drawing in,
Or the peal of a shooting star
Across the night?
Or did all these
And the tame apple-smell
Through the wind in your hair
Make me to long
For an end to life? (WC, 25)

The melodrama is not entirely atypical of Knister, as one or two poems cited already may suggest; yet one of his finest poems, "Change," rises above such a sentimental bent to capture a tone of simple, patient resignation to the silence and darkness of death, with some hint of the Imagist's wonder:

I shall not wonder more, then,
But I shall know.

Leaves change, and birds, flowers,
And after years are still the same.

The sea's breast heaves in sighs to the moon,
But they are moon and sea forever

...............................................

You will be you yourself,
I'll find you more, not else,
For vintage of the woeful years

...............................................

I shall not wonder more, then,
But I shall know. (*WC*, 33)

It is in contrast with "Change" that the sentimentalism and decay-fixations of Knister's other "death poetry" become clear. The fact is that when he chose to address beauty and death at once, he did so most often in late nineteenth-century diction, with frequently traditional stanza structures and conventional emotions.

To establish such a beach-head and not move inland, however, seems careless. If the poetry of Ross and Knister reveals in style, form, and theme a series of non-Modernist, non-Imagist tendencies, a fuller examination of their characterization as Imagists is requisite. Criticism that has ignored significant non-Modernist strains in their poetry might also have misread the more modern poetry and leaped to the vague verdict of "Imagism" too hastily. The school of Imagism was not, after all, so coherent, easily defined, or homogeneous as to permit the quick conclusions that have limited the study of Canadian Imagism in the past.

*T*here is no question at all that Imagism influenced Knister and Ross, that there are elements of their poetry that are Imagistic, or that the word has some usefulness in our discussion of their canons. But what manner of Imagism touched them? The Poundian? The "Amygistic"? Williams's Imagism? Did they receive it passively or develop it in directions that we can now delineate? If the latter, how far did they go? These questions lurk behind the conventional assessments of the two poets, but they have yet to be broached, much less answered.

Imagism was a movement always tending away from a nuclear and restrictive definition that was, I shall suggest, the Poundian Image. Only a few poems by Pound, Lowell, and Richard Aldington could be called Imagist if that purist definition were enforced, so it is quite obvious that Imagism must be defined more flexibly in order to have meaning. At a certain point, however, literary terms may be made so flexible as to have no meaning. For instance, a wide range of criticism has proved in recent years that Modernism has striking theoretical and practical roots in primal Romanticism; yet we would be foolish therefore to speak of Modernism as a Romantic variant, in that the latter term would have lost all prescriptive and descriptive meaning. There is a point at which the similarities between two movements become less significant than the differences, and once that point is reached the second must receive a name to distinguish it from the first. Of course, to say where exactly Romanticism ends and Modernism begins is impossible, a task before which we should retreat into a healthy scepticism. The same will be true of Imagism: a certain degree of variation from a purist definition of the school will take us to a kind of poetry that "Imagism" can no longer describe, although we may still wish to speak of Imagistic tendencies or echoes in the derivative verse. One of the difficulties of defining Imagism is that the movement largely defined itself against other literary practice, so that the clearest picture one can generate in turn is usually negative, that is, based on a sense of what Imagism was not. The theoretical advantages of such dialectical definition are clear: by remarking Imagism's revolt against previous schools we establish an historical context in which the polemical and antinomian features of the Modernist pre-school may be highlighted. The disadvantages of such comparisons are, however, more insidious. No movement is pristine in its antinomianism; all literary movements have deep roots in the standards that they think to reject. Conscious distortion or concealment of this truism has led to a view of Modernism and of Imagism that assumes their utter discontinuity with literary history. To restore a sense of balance, then, we must initiate concomitant comparisons with other precursor-schools to reveal Modernism's historical rootedness. In the case of Imagism, we may offer a fortuitous and concise literary comparison to a single precursor-school that reveals both continuity and discontinuity, hidden affinity and conscious rejection.

The school to which Imagism may be so compared, and to which it provides a direct positive corrective, is literary Impressionism, a manifestation of Aestheticism that fixes the poet's attention on moments of visual beauty or intensity in the transient impressions received from the surrounding world. The affinities Imagism maintains with such a school are obvious, the visual emphasis, the submission to perception; the dissimilarities are less so. David Perkins notices both sides of the relation between the two:

there are strong affinities between Impressionism and Imagism, the movement Ezra Pound founded and briefly commanded just before World War I. To Pound, Symons was a personal "god," as he once said, and he was well aware of Symons's poetry and criticism. The famous Imagist statements of purpose by Pound in *Poetry* (1913) offer directions that would, on the whole, apply equally for Impressionist poetry. Both groups of poets strove for direct presentation of the object without discursive reflection ("abstraction," "rhetoric"); accuracy, concreteness, and economy in language without "poetic" heightening or ornament; and rhythms that contributed functionally to the presentation. Both groups tended to write free verse. Both groups reacted against those many readers who valued poetry by the importance of its subject and the scale of its emotion, though the Imagists were more confident in urging the irrelevance of these factors. The differences between the two are generally that Imagism – more militant, self-conscious, craftsmanlike, manifestoed – went further in the shared directions; it reflected Pound's positivism rather than the skeptical, relativistic uncertainties of the Impressionist mind; it typically focused on single objects rather than the Impressionist scape or scene; it tended to dwell on static things, or on motion in a phase of stasis, as opposed to the Impressionist sense of flux. Moreover, there was in the Imagist movement a special emphasis on metaphor as the most effective mode of presentation. This emphasis, which had momentous importance for Modernist poetry, was altogether lacking in Impressionism.[20]

According to Hugh Kenner, "Dowson, Lionel Johnson, John Gray, 'Fiona Macleod' ... had defined a new convention for the short poem; a pictorial rather than a syntactic space holds its elements in relation."[21] While convinced that the Decadents brought the "new convention" to a "dead end" (Kenner, 186), which Imagism managed to avoid, Kenner admits nevertheless that their "aesthetic of glimpses contained possibilities: for note that Symons' 'Pastel,' but for being rhymed, corresponds exactly to what Imagist poems are often supposed to be. It presents something visual, and does not ruminate nor interpret" (183). Kenner also relates the roots of Imagism to Pater's doctrines, in which the moments of life are seized "for those moments' sake," not for their spiritual or doctrinal ramifications. John T. Gage's *In the Arresting Eye: The Rhetoric of Imagism* confirms that descent from Pater and traces it a step farther back, to Wordsworth, whose "spots of time" have often been argued to prefigure Pater's aesthetic "moments."[22] (Of course, Frank Kermode's *Romantic Image* had scouted much of this material long before.)

The relationship between Imagism and Impressionism was, after all, the central bone of contention between Ezra Pound and Ford Madox Ford (then Hueffer) during the first years of their friendship;[23] the older man provided the younger simultaneously with a mentor and a locus of polite attack, which made it appear, to others, that Imagism was pointed as much against the subjectivism of Impressionism as against the verbose gentility of the Victorian tradition. Thus Pound chides Ford in 1912:

His flaw is the flaw of impressionism, impressionism, that is, carried out of its due medium. Impressionism belongs in paint, it is of the eye ... A ball of gold and a gilded ball give the same 'impression' to the painter. Poetry is in some odd way concerned with the specific gravity of things, with their nature ... The *conception* of poetry is a process more intense than the *reception* of an impression. And no impression, however carefully articulated, can, recorded, convey that feeling of sudden light which the work of art should and must convey.[24]

Nascent Imagism, then, attacked Impressionism in order to make room for itself in the literary world, to define its difference from that which had gone before and establish its right to separate consideration. But once success of a kind had come about, as with the publication in March 1913 of F.S. Flint's article on the school, preceded by the poems of "H.D. *Imagiste*" in *Poetry* (Chicago) and "A Few Don'ts by an Imagist" by Pound, the concentration of this attack began to waver. Pound, in his review of Hueffer's (Ford Madox Ford's) *Collected Poems*, considered that "The thing that [Ford] praises is good; it is direct speech and vivid impression."[25] Kindness to a friend may have motivated Pound here more than it had in 1912, but no doubt he was also coming to admit to himself the slightness of the distance between Impressionism and Imagism. Gage reminds us that "Pound cited Ford as the source of imagist principles, and Ford concurred" (7); Michael H. Levenson suggests that "the Impressionist influence on pre-war literary activity was transmitted almost entirely through Ford's interpretation of the method."[26] Pound had in Ford a potent and rather intimidating precursor, and he naturally struggled to establish his own value as a poetic commodity before acknowledging freely the debt he owed. By 1920 he felt able to write, in a letter to Ford, "I take impressionism as the first necessary assault on Fanny Bawn and the Folios. And certainly one backs impressionism, all I think I wanted to do was to make the cloud into an animal organism. To put a vortex or concentration point inside each bunch of impression and thereby give it a sort of intensity, and goatish ability to butt."[27] Thus Pound, after the disillusionment with his school that had set in once "Amygism" had gathered steam, felt less need to defend his own brainchild and acknowledged obligations that later criticism has been slow to perceive.

If Imagism and Impressionism are indeed related by blood, as they appear, then the need to distinguish between them becomes acute, lest the later school suffer the invalidation of derivativism. I will postpone a brief discussion of the doctrines of Imagism; Flint's (i.e., Pound's) three rules published in *Poetry* (Chicago) offer a foundation for most studies,[28] although their vagueness and generality have led many critics to look elsewhere for exact definitions of Imagism, and they will serve the purpose for the time being. Impressionism requires further definition first, especially given that there has been very little critical agreement upon exactly who the Impressionist writers were, much less upon their doctrines.[29]

Impressionism surfaced when Pater licensed the pursuit of "moments for their own sake," without consideration of their value in any other than an aesthetic sense. Such seizing of "moments" is another example of the Aesthetic attempt to submit to and yet to stabilize the Heraclitean flux of which Pater had made so much in his Conclusion to *The Renaissance* and his *Marius the Epicurean*. Thus, against the "direct treatment" of Imagism, Herbert Howarth describes a central premise of Impressionism as "the constant manipulation of rhetoric to capture flow, energy, vibrancy."[30]

[Hauser] says that Impressionism is Heraclitean and makes reality not a being but a becoming ... By virtue of this perception and valuation of the becoming, the movement, the lustre of change, I would agree with Hauser and those who like him regard "transience" as a leading characteristic of Impressionism, or at any rate of its heirs. Movement, say the heirs of Impressionism, is life. (Howarth, 44)

Thus "to discriminate an 'instantaneous' attitude of a horse moving at speed, or a dancer executing an arabesque, of light striking water or mist, was to rejoice at the constitution of things" (Howarth, 43). In order to render the "feeling" of this world in flux, certain stylistic developments had to take place beyond the mere pictorial emphasis noticed by Kenner: "such structural devices as fragmentation of form, the breaking up of rhythms, juxtaposition without subordination, the avoidance of big climaxes, and a general preference for small units" (Howarth, 54) were adopted by the Impressionists as formal and stylistic analogues of Heraclitean evanescence. Light, which had fascinated the French Impressionist painters, became "the soul of impressionist literature" as well,[31] since it created particularly rapid and fleeting sensations of flux, as the sun passes through broken cloud across a landscape, or as a striking face hovers briefly in the outer edge of candlelight.

There is a fundamental contradiction in the Impressionist pursuit, of course: on the one hand the Aesthete seeks to acknowledge quite frankly the lack of solidity and stability in his situation, thereby submitting joyfully to the flux, while on the other he struggles rhetorically against the flux, to stop time, in order to maintain the beauty and intensity he has chanced upon – another example of the fear of natural processes inherent in Aestheticism. Hence a contradiction in the poetry itself: while claiming neutrality to the visual setting and seeking only to record a passive impression of it, the poet brings to the scene such moods and imaginative colours of his own that the poetry inevitably gives off a subjective aroma.

In this sense, the "direct treatment" of Imagism is partially prefigured, partially contradicted in Impressionist doctrine; to the degree that the Impressionist endeavours to be passive, so as to record with the utmost accuracy the natural impression the poet has received, a mode of objectivity is set up within which the poet's personality becomes less significant; but insofar as it is a mood which the poet wishes to record, a mood that can hardly be thought of as rising from the natural phenomena separate from the perceiving soul, the Impressionist is a subjective poet and so provides for Imagism a focal point against which to define itself. Thus, when Ford writes that "the Impressionist gives you himself, how he reacts to a fact; not the fact itself, or rather, not so much the fact itself ... Impressionism is a frank expression of personality,"[32] he accepts that his is above all a subjective mode of poetry and helps Pound to accentuate the differences between Impressionism and Imagism.

For quite some time this served as the sufficient critical distinction between the two, as it did for Stanley Coffman: "While the Imagists carry on certain of the principles of the nineties – insistence upon intensity of feeling (and therefore a kind of subjectivity), denial of values other than those of art, and (in some cases) an emphasis upon beauty – their attitude toward poetry avoids the earlier romantic posturing and returns to exact consideration of the external world."[33] Coffman obviously accepts the Imagists' claims that their presentations of the external world were "exact" – that they rendered meticulously and without "posturing" the visual reality around them. Difficulties arise in any discussion of Imagism, however, when too much emphasis is placed on the "external world" as the centre of

Imagist interest. Gage notes, for instance, that Pound's desire for exactitude was centred, not on natural, but rather on emotional or spiritual phenomena: "Pound literally undertook to make the poet a scientist, and objectivity therefore became a further requirement of imagist doctrine. The imagist poet was prevented from moralizing by his obligation to observe emotional phenomena and record them in concrete terms, as the ideogram was considered to do" (21). Emotional phenomena recorded in concrete terms is a good distance from Coffman's "exact consideration of the external world" and reveals how tenuous certain distinctions between Impressionism and Imagism are: Gage's emotionalist definition of the "objectivity" of Imagism would also serve well to describe the Impressionist's intention.

The doctrinal overlap between the two schools quickly became apparent when Imagism reached its natural limits: the poets who still professed it, those who had aligned themselves with Lowell in the disputes of 1914, were forced to seek newly subjective strategies to develop their doctrines: "To achieve a greater range of emotional experience required making the state of the speaker one of the terms of comparison, which of course also made the presentation more subjective. Although a technical violation of the imagist principle of objectivity, this is the more frequent use of comparison in imagist poetry. It required only the addition of the first person" (Gage, 91). As Gage digs deeper into the contradictions that arose as Imagism sought to prolong its literary life, he realizes an inevitable conclusion: that it is impossible to distinguish "the objective from the subjective in imagist poetry" (130). Thus a significant portion of his excellent study deals with the ways in which Imagist poetry became inarguably subjective, for all its critical associations with objectivity and impersonality. For instance, Imagist techniques are presented as ways of escaping "technique" altogether – of subordinating the creative personality of the poet to the striking relations between the natural objects perceived – yet Imagism in early and late stages is among the most consciously technical schools in literary history (Gage, 44). Similarly, the Imagist's "fear of abstractions" breaks down as the Image is applied to new areas of emotional experience: "When the function of comparisons in imagist poems is to measure the degree of an emotion rather than to specify what it is, it happens that the emotion is nearly always named abstractly, despite, once again, the prescriptions of the theory" (Gage, 96). Imagism was forced to adopt "new" manners of expression that brought it closer and closer to the old style of Impressionism, its devotion to free verse and refusal of traditional verse forms being the last visible distinction between two schools of poetry that are more similar than any other two schools of Aestheticism and Modernism.

Nevertheless, all the parallels one can draw between an earlier and a later school should not obscure the fact that they are distinct in certain inviolable ways. We may not speak accurately of the objectivity of Imagism, but we may say that the semblance of objectivity was a principal desire of its practitioners, although they manifested an occasional subjectivity in their responses to visual stimuli. Conversely, we may postulate a general subjectivity of manner for Impressionism, without forgetting that the most accurate recordings will necessarily tend towards the objective. While it would be generalizing to define Imagism by its presentation of stasis or Impressionism by its accession to the flux, we may cautiously consider that the dichotomy reveals tendencies, probabilities if you will, of the two schools, which help us to distinguish them. Such principles, thus rendered far more relative than the self-proclaimed theories of each school, allow us to proceed towards a cautious and fairly solid dividing line between Aesthetic Impressionism and modern Imagism.

Perkins noted the Imagists' preoccupation with metaphor as one strong distinction from the practices of the Impressionists. This metaphor exists, ideally, without syntactic structures to support it, offering instead the mere juxtaposition of two images that relate to one another in a way previously unperceived, creating one larger Image. Thus the archetypal Imagist poem may require no more than two lines:

The apparition of these faces in the crowd:
Petals on a wet, black bough.[34]

Each image in the Image could have been revealed, of course, in more than a single line; the point is that the conjunction of the two without syntactic explanation produces that "feeling of sudden light" that Pound found lacking in Impressionism, because a relation is suggested between two hitherto unconnected visualizations that reveals new aesthetic qualities in each: "For Pound's Imagism is energy, is effort. It does not appease itself by reproducing what is seen, but by setting some other seen thing into relation ... The 'plot' of the poem is that mind's activity, fetching some new thing into the field of consciousness" (Kenner, 186). Kenner thus places "Pound's doctrine of the Image" at the heart of Imagism, argues convincingly that it is the unique achievement of the school, and suggests that other attributes commonly associated with the school are at best inconsistently adopted and at worst fictitious.

For the Poundian Image to be as central and necessary to Imagism as Kenner suggests, no other significant features of Imagist poetry should have the like distinction of being unforeshadowed by the practices of poetic Impressionism. Their devotion to free verse is an insufficient distinction; certain Impressionist poets had toyed with free verse without waiting for the school of 1912; anyway, we should be sceptical before we rest crucial historical distinctions on purely formal qualities, lest we come to judge movements as no more than shifts of versification. A mere emphasis on the visual also clearly falls short of the mark. In fact no single concept other than the Poundian Image can take as much theoretical weight as necessary to support the distinction between Impressionism and Imagism.

If we add to the Poundian Image such other properties as do seem to retain a limited validity – those relative attitudes to objectivity and stasis proposed above, or "fear of abstractions," permitting occasional lapses – we come as close as possible to a functioning definition of Imagism that does distinguish it from Impressionism in a clear and sharp manner. We retain, at the same time, an understanding that Imagism is descended directly from Impressionism, so much so that it is arguably a fortuitous variation on the earlier school.[35] There will of course be wide variations of Imagist practice that do not follow all the normative implications of the above definitions, but it is safe to say that poets who miss the mark much more frequently than they hit it may be attempting Imagism but have probably arrived at something quite different. With this in mind, we now turn to the poetry of Ross and Knister to interrogate the common view that they represent an Imagist phase in Canadian literary history.

The first curiosity now noticeable in the poetry of both is the near-absence of the Image as Pound's doctrine shaped it. The concept either did not much attract the two poets when encountered, or had never been encountered by them. Ross's closest approximation of the technique is his "Reciprocal," the two stanzas functioning to some degree in the manner of the binary Image:

The shuttle swinging
to and fro;
the piston
of the locomotive
moving smoothly,
powerfully,

into the cylinder,
out of the cylinder;

dancers swaying
in one place;
crows' wings
in lazy flight;
waves on the ocean
up to the shore
and back swiftly
broken and foaming.   (SS, 19)

The placing of three minor images in opposition to the single minor image of the first stanza produces, however, a diffusion of visual feeling, not a compression; and, although the tension between the one mechanical and three natural rhythms is certainly intriguing, each reader must decide whether there results a particular intense relation between the "piston" and the "dancers," "wings" or "waves" that "has to do with the specific gravity of things," as Pound would say, and not their "show." To my mind, the three binary Images theoretically created do not successfully penetrate one another, so that we see something new in each half of each pair: for instance, only birds in energetic rather than "lazy flight" move their wings in a manner arguably similar to the rhythm of the piston. Ross is interested more in the "reciprocity" of these images, in their reflection in some general sense of one another's motions, than he is in their spiritual, emotional, or psychological relations. Moreover, he deliberately contrasts mechanical and natural rhythms so that they will not come together or penetrate one another, but will rather jar visually. The poem, therefore, is at best an approximation of Pound's Image and yet is the only work approaching that form in Ross's published works.

   Knister's one or two poems that most closely approximate Pound's doctrine are similarly diffused. "Consummation," but for its subjective, self-oriented tone, is glancingly like Ross's:

I hear a frenzied windmill whirling in the dusk.
I see the wind's grey steed of doom.
I smell the blown-down apples like a musk.
I taste the black hail-bitten loam.
And touch proud Death within a 'living room.' (WC, 41)

Despite the fact that the effect of the prototypical Imagist poem was to be instantaneous rather than cumulative, the juxtaposition in "Consummation" of four images of natural motion and change with an image of ultimate change, the passing of a life, renders it not unlike a Poundian Image. The final line counters and gives some further meaning to each of the previous four, and to an extent they interpenetrate, enrich, and inform one another. But it is a brooding personality, clearly, that imposes the connections, not the reader's own aesthetic receptiveness that permits their discovery. Similarly, in "Cinquain: Pattern," Knister poses two minor images and seems to desire of them an Image of a higher order:

The sleet
Through warp of wind ...
Is the pattern profoundly weird as these
Sharp guesses to
My heart.   (WC, 45)

But the abstraction, the emotionalism without particularization, of the second image precludes the possibility of the two halves' really enriching one another; the two portions remain distinct, perhaps vaguely alike but refusing to wed. (Similar structures and motives may be observed in his "Reverie: The Orchard on the Slope," quoted in another context below.)

For a start, then, we may speculate that Ross and Knister did not encounter the Image as defined by Pound, or failed to understand it, or understood it but desired to modify it in a direction that veered away from essential Imagism. Both vary the Image, interestingly, by diffusing the form, by posing one image against three or four others, so that the reader experiences above all the effort of juxta-position, rather than the fruit of the juxtaposition, of a number of images. Similarly, many of the Anglo-American Imagist poets de-veloped techniques and structures that had nothing to do with Pound's Image; they found other methods of elaborating the visual focus Pound had encouraged; they sought to embody Pound's basic goals of objectivity, clarity, and brevity, without necessarily living up to the doctrine of the Image, which seemed difficult, impractical, or tending towards a speedy entropy. This gradual development from the pure Image placed a greater emphasis on the subordinate doctrines of the school, the depiction of stasis, for instance, or the appearance of objectivity in presenting subjective phenomena.

Perkins's general distinction between the stasis inherent in Im-agist, and the flux in Impressionist, renderings of the visible world, like all distinctions between the two schools, will break down under analysis of later Imagist practice and, therefore, cannot be relied upon as a normative description of either school; but it has some validity on the Impressionist side, as a glance at Symons's or Wilde's Impressionist pieces, rich with motion and light, will quickly prove.[36] Those elements of Heraclitean flux that are important in Impressionist doctrine (light, water, rhythm) are, however, easier to characterize than the ostensible stasis of the Image. The centrality of such stasis to Imagist practice presumably arises in relation to the claimed objectivity of the school; only the subjective human mind, connecting past to present, perceiving over an extended period, understands and could wish to depict images of flux. Stasis, however, the moment captured independent of all sense of temporality, of all intellection, is the result of objectivity: a flower does not bud and open, for how can the mere eye know that without the subjective memory's assistance? The eye sees a flower frozen, as if it might endure so, and that is what the poem struggles to render. A bird in flight will be caught, snapshot-like, in mid-wingbeat; the whole course of its flight, the arcs and loops and plunges of its progress, suggests time, distance, comparison of past with present, and moves the poem toward the Impressionistic mode.

In "Wild Rose," for instance, Ross clearly tries to render an object at perfect rest, balanced on a fine point of time and left there by the poet. Similarly, his "Winter Scene" discovers the "black of the/ branches and/white of the/snow that is/lying/upon them," over the street down which the poet walks; the image is frozen, not melting or passing; the snow is "New-fallen,/light, not/heavy with/liquid" (SS, 25). A final stanza repeats the image in exactly the terms first used to picture it, and the reader is given the effect that time has stopped, that change has been conquered. "Curving, the Moon" enforces a similar stasis:

Curving, the moon
over the mirror lake;
the new moon
thinly curving
over the lake.

Below, the pine
standing dark and tall,
through its black
topmost branches
the curved limb
of the new moon.

A third stanza repeats and strengthens these images, without altering them by a hair's width; but the fourth, upon which the poem closes, brings in the faintest touch of movement, of transience, which, in the context of the previous motionlessness, is all the more striking: "Is it a breeze?/No sound from the pine,/but on the water/ a long shadow/ripples" (*SS*, 30). Ross deliberately poses against objects at perfect rest a hint, almost sinister, of the inevitability of motion.

Contrasting with such poems of near-perfect stasis, which are significantly few in the Ross canon, is a varied body of Imagistic work that dwells above all on patterns of change, on the passing of time, on this or that firmness passing into frailty, on the shifting of light over the landscape, all of which qualities must make us question to some degree our present understanding of Ross or of Imagism. Thus "If Ice," one of Ross's much-anthologized poems, records not a moment, or a precise visual fact, but a flow, an energy; it is the motion above all that he wishes to render for the reader:

> If
> ice shall melt
> if
> thinly the fresh
> cold clear      water
> running      shall make
> grooves in the sides
> of the ice.

The poem's fixation upon process and life-cycle is made clear: "if life return/after death/or depart not at death,/then shall buds/burst into May/leafing" (*SS*, 47). Regeneration, flow, and the life-giving water are the sources of Ross's interest here: the visible image of ice is above all a transient means of registering those powerful impulses. Refusing the presumptive stasis of Imagism, Ross fixes his sharp eye on the engulfing flux of nature and seizes upon the water as the symbolic messenger of change.

"In the Ravine" works back to the very source of water, the cycle of precipitation that initiates the process of rebirth:

> Filled with melted snow
> to the brim
> the creek      came
> around a bend –
> and disappeared below

around a bend –
ground covered with snow

Thus I stood      the snow
descended        by degrees
into the stream
                    into the stream.   (*SS*, 40)

The "degrees" of change capture the poet's attention, and in their shifting the poem commences. "The Dawn; the Birds'" establishes similar patterns of degree, tracing the movement inch by inch of early light:

The dawn; the birds'
tumultuous clamour
grows as the light
gradually
makes more distinct
the rocks, the trees,
picking out each
from among the grey
.............................

And more distinct
the rocks, the trees,
and brighter now
the early lighting –
when suddenly
all these sounds cease –
a strange silence
and then the sun!   (*SS*, 62)

Remembering that energy, vibrancy, flow, and light are the central characteristics of the Impressionistic mode, the qualities of these poems must be striking to Ross's reader. Light has especially attracted the poet, its play over the landscape motivating a large number of poems, such as "Ripples," "By the Shore," "Moonlight," "Loon," "One Leaf," "Moon," and "Picture."

Note that "Pine Gum," another famous Ross poem, turns entirely on play of light; only a very particular hour of daylight reveals the significance of the image to the poet:

for it is evening;
the air has ceased

its daily stirring;
the light grows dimmer
within the shadow
of the pine,
but ever appears
through the darkness
the ghostly glimmering
of the gum.   (*SS*, 69)

"If Ice" and "Pine Gum," two of Ross's best-known poems, demonstrate visual qualities that are centrally Impressionistic. The play of light, the working of water, and the cycles of nature are so important to Ross's canon as to dominate it; and stasis, the moment of perfect poise, the freezing of time, plays a comparatively minor role. Should we continue to speak of Ross's Imagism, but modify further (and further) our sense of that term? Or should the term, this far distended, be replaced?

In Knister's case, largely because he left a smaller body of poetry, the emphasis on flux is less apparent; nevertheless, when one considers those poems which might by some stretch of the imagination be called Imagist, the same preponderance as with Ross emerges. Not one of Knister's poems depicts any object, scene, or being in a state of rest, with that sharpness and clarity that typify the manner of the Imagists. Stasis, of course, was not described by Perkins so narrowly as "an object at rest," but also as "motion in a phase of stasis," which provides the sensation of unchanging, the suspicion in the reader that the poet desires to capture, even in movement, the fixed potency of certain images. In "The Hawk," Knister's well-known Imagist poem, he captures the image as if by force in four distinct moments of visual poise. Thus he appears to freeze the bird of prey despite its constant motion:

Across the bristled and sallow fields,
The speckled stubble of cut clover,
Wades your shadow.

Or against a grimy and tattered
Sky
You plunge.   (*WC*, 21)

This is as close as Knister comes to the presentation of stasis; other poems involving visible motion tend to delight in the motion, to desire to prolong or further it, rather than to militate against it. Thus "Reverie: The Orchard on the Slope" opens in seeming fixity: "Thin ridges of land unploughed/Along the tree-rows/Covered with long cream grasses," but continues with a powerful rendering of natural process (the same image, now enriched and in flux):

> Row and row of waves ever
> In the breaking;
> Ever in arching and convulsed
> Imminence;
> Roll of muddy sea between;
> Low clouds down-pressing
> And pallid and streaming rain.   (WC, 22)

Notice again that formal properties that might have rendered a Poundian Image in this poem are diffused; the extended image-making of the second stanza cuts against that "feeling of sudden light" that two quick strokes in sudden juxtaposition can give, and the speaker's visual absorption in the scene (confirmed by the title) creates an atmosphere of personal reverie rather than sharp perception.

"February's Forgotten Mitts," while superficially recording an all but insignificant moment of farm life, chooses to render it meaningful by providing a similar background of seasonal progress, of the passing of time, against which the specific incident is almost lost, the last line focusing not the immediate and human but the transient natural content (WC, 17). "An Old Wooden Windmill" fixes with visual delight upon the process of decay that finally reduces all buildings to rot and rubble, juxtaposing the past, when the windmill served a purpose, against the present when it creaks and groans in the night (WC, 24). "The Colt" captures exactly that image mentioned by Howarth as typical of Impressionism – "a horse moving at speed":

> In long lopes he speeds,
> Rising and dipping,
> Down the rolling lane.
> Such beauty, see,
> Such grace,
> Moving (diversely!)
> Never was
> ...............
>
> See the long swift
> Flash and swing,
> Low,
> Of his limbs.   (WC, 51)

"A Road," with its three sections "Summer," "Autumn", and "Winter," delights aesthetically in the visual effects produced by seasonal change upon a stretch of country road. (Compare Claude Monet's various views of the front of Rouen Cathedral: the artistic inquiry is the same.) Knister certainly had the Imagist's eye, the sense of visual sharpness, although he turned that sharpness not to the depiction of fixed or concrete "moments," but rather to the way in which the passing of time, the movement of light and shade, the shift of the seasons, alter each moment's glimpse perceptibly. Change attracted him, and he showed little interest as a poet in any effects of visual stasis to posit against that change.

If a relative interest in stasis or flux is a consequence of, respectively, desire for objectivity or acceptance of subjectivity, we should expect to find some concomitant degree of subjectivity in both Ross and Knister – another turn against the Canadian critical consensus – to support the above claim that both were attracted to images in process rather than at rest. In different ways, and to different degrees, that is exactly what we find: the apparent objectivity of Ross must be carefully questioned, whereas any notion of Knister's general objectivity is dispelled by the most cursory reading of his poetry.

To be sure, Knister left a handful of poems with a relative objectivity of presentation. "The Hawk" is an example; "Lake Harvest," with something of a Krieghoff quality, is another. The personality of the poet does not seem particularly to colour or to alter the material he presents in either poem. To a minor degree, the four stanzas of "The Hawk," with their four manners of visualizing the bird's flight, call to mind Wallace Stevens's "Thirteen Ways of Looking at a Blackbird," in their shifting perspectives, relativism, and implicit subjectivity; but the generally objective quality of Knister's poem must be emphasized, not the lesser ways in which that quality can be disputed. Similarly, "Elm Tree and Sun" should be considered a primarily objective poem, despite the odd ominousness of its conclusion, which imparts a strong sense of a personality creating the poem's mood: the elm tree "draws/And wafts onward/A Breath/ From the void" (WC, 43).

Apart from those few poems that offer such objectivity, the idea of detachment is irrelevant to Knister's poetry; he is clearly a subjective, practically a Romantic poet, whose desire to express his own feelings distinctly controls his approach to natural phenomena. "The Plowman," which exploits an archetypal rural image for purposes of aesthetic confession, typifies this quality in Knister's work. "Martyrdom," "Bees," "Snowfall," and "Sea-Blue Eyes," all with the superficial appearance of Imagist poems (brevity, visual emphasis), serve nevertheless to confirm the strong subjectivism in Knister's poetry and reveal to the reader, not a precise, objective rural poet, but a rural confessional poet, one who poses his own emotions frankly against the landscape or climate in order to elucidate them. Along these lines, Knister quotes twice from Wordsworth in his criticism of "The Poetical Works of Wilfred Campbell," noting that even modern poetry "comes back to Wordsworth, defining the distinction of his own work: 'That the feeling therein developed gives importance to the action and situation, and not the action and situation to the feeling.'"[37] Knister's revealing use of the quotation does much to explain why his own poetry is almost wholly subjective, from the short poems that relate his emotions to sudden visual stimuli, to the longer narrative poems that are soaked in the personal experiences of a farm boy growing up just after the turn of the century. Against such subjectivity Knister can scarcely be said to have struggled, and that accurate portrait of the poet ought to dominate the way in which we approach his canon.

A very different subjectivism is apparent in the larger body of work offered by Ross. A portion of his canon consists of poems wholly objective, brief depictions without comment and without the hints of emotionalism that dominate Knister's; such are "Butterfly," "Winter Scene," "Woods, I Remember," "A Night," and "Young Poplars." "A Night," for instance, pictures

a tall pine
black against
the cold starlight;
its branches outlined
sharply against
the studded sky
with brilliant stars.   (SS, 67)

The next two stanzas, while deepening the focus of the picture, offer no more than visual complication. A perfect objectivity is maintained.

Nevertheless, for two reasons we must question the appearance of objectivity that covers these poems (taking a cue from Gage's demonstration of the subjectivity of the entire Imagist enterprise). First, we ought to be aware that Ross's clear preference for rural images over urban is a deliberate and perhaps an odd choice for a modern poet living most of his life in the city. As noted earlier, the poet chooses his images carefully; they do not "happen" to him, but are selected from a welter of visual stimuli as befitting his treatment and capabilities. Thus an abstract subjectivity lies behind the entire

Ross canon; while he obviously welcomed the call of the modern, he did not explore it to such an extent that it significantly altered the focus of his visual attention. (In the published works no more than a dozen poems explore urban scenes or appear to be aware of modern settings, a paucity that perhaps disappoints us in Ross's career.) In the Foreword to his *Sonnets* – a book which makes a more obvious gesture against the modern – he referred to his Modernist *Laconics* as having "made an explicit effort toward the regional" [ii]; the explicitness of that effort provides, arguably, the subjectivity of the entire Ross enterprise.

A second feature of the poetry that troubles a little the objective surface of these poems is Ross's common habit of imagining actions beneath the visual plane. With the aid of an active and highly personalized imagination, he fills in details that the viewing eye cannot provide. Thus "Night Scene," with its initially objective description, is troubled by images that the objective eye would not have found:

> The lake is mirror-like tonight.
> The trees on the bank
> Dark, beautiful,
> Look down at their reflections.
>
> The water is shallow by the shore.
> There reeds stand dimly seen,
> Among whose roots
> The wary pike lurks, waiting.

The scene then leads, uncharacteristically for an Imagist poem, to abstraction: instead of visual surfaces coming together in striking configurations to produce depths of meaning, Ross literally moves beneath the surface of the lake, imagining a "wary pike":

> Perhaps a splash at the surface,
> Perhaps a swift shadow
> Will show where he pursues his victim
> That cannot escape him.

All action *per se* in the poem is preceded by "Perhaps"; thus the poet brings to his image *what he expects to find*, and the feeling of passive intuition central to Pound's theory of the Image (Gage, 43–4, 82) is undermined. Note that Ross does not see a splash and then seek to explain it; he imagines the pike first (entirely without visual incitement to do so) and then extends his thoughts upon it until they alter the visual scene. Therefore a poem with all the appearances of objectivity moves strongly into the subjective mode, without apparent cause except the need to express some sublimated aspect of the poet's personality. Further, repetition of the first stanza's phrases in the last, in a new order, confirms the oddity of Ross's Imagism:

> Terror below the surface.
> Beauty above,
> As the exquisite dark trees
> Gaze endlessly at their reflections.   (SS, 17)

The juxtaposition of a perceived "Beauty" – unabashedly abstract – and an imagined "Terror" creates the unusual balance in a surprisingly *mental* poem. The images stand only to give the poet something to pierce with his eye, to justify reflection; thus their recording reveals as much about the poet perceiving as about the landscape perceived.

Similarly, "If Ice" depicts the season following the melting of the ice, when "shall buds/burst into May-/leafing, the blooms of May/ appear like stars/on the brown dry/forest bed." The conditional quality of the image must be emphasized: "*if*/ice shall melt," "*if* thinly the fresh/cold clear water." The ice has not yet melted; only the "brown dry/forest bed" (SS, 47) is visible to the poet: the rest is brought to the poem by Ross's governing subjectivism. Again, in "Fresh Leaves," the poet gazes at "leaves/green in the/light of the/ strengthening/ sun," but quickly imagines them "dusty as/they must be/soon when the/season grows/hot and/hotter" (SS, 59). In each of these poems we witness Ross in joyous participation in the processes, the flux if you will, of the world; in fact imposing on the world his own sense of flux when the immediate scene does not create it. (Compare Knister's habit of posing his images against the seasonal cycles of decay and regeneration.) So Ross infuses his otherwise objective poems with a strong human presence: we recognize the poet's voice in the importation of human perception and intellection into the otherwise purely visual incident. This, not ostensible Imagism, is the source of his charm.

In "The Diver," the same subjectivism is at work: Ross sends a subjective persona plunging into the world of received images, dragging down with him a very particular mood. Thus, despite a strong visual focus and an accumulation of images, "The Diver" gains its renowned power because of its manipulation in a subjective way of immediate experience. It is a strongly particularized person who dives, not some abstracted Man; his recording of what he sees and feels is individual, tinged with private emotion, rather than detached and distinct from personal experience. It is a strong and affecting "I" who

> would like to dive
> Down
> Into this still pool
> Where the rocks at the bottom are safely deep,
>
> Into the green
> Of the water seen from within,
> A strange light
> Streaming past my eyes.   (*SS*, 36)

The experience, which never actually happens, is recorded with lyric intensity in order to make it appear to have happened, and thereby to convey the emotions such a plunge might arouse in each of us; and the "hostile" response of the underwater world is no more than a reflection of what the Diver brings with him: "You cannot stay here, they seem to say," the "Things" he sees there; the hypothetical visual experience is enriched with an emotional exchange, and subjectivized.

Ross's subjectivity, then, affects many facets of his Imagistic poetics – it helps him to reject "direct treatment of the thing"[38] in favour of imagining "the thing" in various states, past and future; it helps him to see beneath the surface of his chosen images to find human relevance, human content; it even alters, as he seeks to convey the precision of his mood, his manipulation of formal and stylistic properties.

There are certainly enough openly subjective Modernist poems by Ross (setting aside the *Sonnets* momentarily) to support the above contradictions of his apparent objectivity. "Arrows of Desire," "Lovers," "Over the Water," "As I Left," "View," "Glimpse," "Love's Silver Bells," "The Spring," "Apparition," and "Morning Greeting" – a substantial but still inexhaustive list – are straightforwardly subjective, with very little or no effort to appear distant or detached from the material related. As such they may not seem immediately relevant to a discussion of Ross's Imagism, but it is worth noticing such subjective poetry in the context of that discussion, as it can assist us when we face Imagistic poems with such strong currents of subjectivity to understand that the personality in Ross's poetry is not to be ignored or sublimated by the objective truth of any image. Nevertheless, Ross's subjectivity is neither so pronounced nor so consistent as that of Knister. Ross has a small number of successfully and thoroughly objective poems, for one thing, and he has a strong ability to render essentially subjective material with an effect of objective precision that controls and restrains the personal or emotional content. Still, when we balance the ledgers, Ross's openly subjective Imagistic poems, his subliminally subjective Imagistic poems, his spiritual, supernatural Modernist poems of death, and his traditional late nineteenth-century *Sonnets* constitute a body of poetry heavily weighted towards the personal, the emotional, the reflective. He is only very rarely eager to achieve a thorough objectivity. This conclusion tells against the contemporary criticism of Ross's poetry. We do him less than justice to dwell on his objectivity, when so much of his poetic effort seems to have been spent upon finding new methods within modern forms to record the passing qualities of his own mind.

When we consider the preponderance of subjectivity in both poets, as well as the almost total absence of Images in the sense Pound desired them, and their preoccupation with the flux, with conditions passing into one another, we are naturally urged away from certain conclusions. We must account for features in the poetry of Knister and of Ross that are not strongly Imagistic, that qualify their Imagism to such an extent that the term becomes a difficulty, not an assistance, in discussing their poetry. To go beyond that simple demur, however, is to venture into a wider speculation, by its critical nature far more easily disputed. Although I find reason to speak of their poems as Impressionistic, there may be readers who would still wish to emphasize the obvious ways in which their poetry does not fit the Impressionist mould: for instance, the chopped Modernist form of most of Ross's poetry directly counters the fluid Impressionist sensibility. Can more eventuate, then, from such a study as this, than the questioning of one term (Imagism)? Can a new term clarify matters?

If offered without absolutism and blindness, yes. As it has been a principal weakness of those critics who have found Imagism in Ross and Knister to apply the term with neither sufficient definition nor sufficient study of their poetry, it is not the purpose here to conclude that they are instead Impressionists, as a simple application of that term will not add particularly to our understanding of their work. Let us say, rather, that there are a number of features of their poetry that are generally more appropriate to Impressionism than to Imagism; that they show a tendency, which is consistent and surprising, towards the techniques of the earlier, even as they pursue the later school. But to speak of them as "Impressionist poets" would be meaningless given their situation in the 1920s and the fact that they became, to other more clearly Modernist poets (Smith, Scott, Dorothy Livesay), precursors, pioneers in twentieth-century Canadian literature.

This is why I have deliberately analysed their work *vis-à-vis* a definition of Imagism so pure that only a few poems in the Imagist anthologies could match it: because only doing so clarifies what Ross and Knister have done with the Imagist influence. Only in comparison with a rigorous standard Imagism can their subjectivism and their fascination with process and flux become apparent. To recognize these features of their poetry in no way invalidates their achievements. When we attempt, quite naturally, to characterize Ross's and Knister's adaptations of the initial Imagist impulse, we are bound to remark the Impressionistic tendencies of their work; but we are not bound to choose between the two schools. Their Imagism, I would suggest, was heavily Impressionistic.

When we place these remarks in the context of the other preoccupations we have witnessed in their verse, such as fragility, the passion for beauty, the fixation on death, we should not conclude that they are nineteenth-century poets held over into the 1910s and 1920s, but that in any poet of the 1920s some features of the art of the nineteenth century will play some role, form a significant background to their own achievements. In Ross and Knister this generalization is particularly true. Because they show themselves sufficiently sympathetic to the emotional inquiries of their precursors in the 1880s and 1890s, we must ask whether they had any direct familiarity whatsoever with those precursors, whether they reacted well or ill to them, whether they found Imagism to be an answer to older Impressionist tendencies, or whether the distinction between Impressionism of the late Victorian period and Imagism of the early modern period was not particularly driven home to them.

The fortunes of any two critics who dig through the private papers of these two poets will vary widely. Knister's family has kindly left a good deal of his material to the archivist, from correspondence to plot-sketches of unwritten novels to galley-sheets of his two published novels, *White Narcissus* and *My Star Predominant*. Ross on the other hand has left no unified collection of his private materials, and one must find his letters in the archival collections of other Canadian writers, or in Bruce Whiteman's edition of *A Literary Friendship: The Correspondence of Ralph Gustafson and W.W.E. Ross*. Knister, moreover, seems to have had literature and his ideas of it always on his mind, so that his papers are peppered with intriguing and provoking comments upon poetry and poetic theory that are most valuable.

One of the most striking series of comments in the Raymond Knister Papers concerns his preoccupation with beauty and how it may be fitly appropriated by poetry. He writes, for instance, to Miss Frankfurth (a regular correspondent and a "kindred soul" according to Knister's daughter) in response to some thoughts she had offered upon a biblical passage: "Speaking of understanding, your remarks on the Bible touches [sic] on my pet theory – that we need not understand. We do not understand life, nor great art that is its essence. Enough if we see its mystery and beauty" (11 April 1924, Vic., Folder 84). Eight months later he repeated to her that "The great thing is to find some beauty and interest in life" (22 Jan. 1925, Vic., Folder 84). He seems to have been able to express to Miss Frankfurth theories of art that have not always been critically re- lated to his writings; thus he writes to her, almost three years later, that his forthcoming novel, *White Narcissus*, "does not fall into any special category of novel. But it will have in any amount of roses and moonlight. You won't recognize the me of other work in it" (31 Oct. 1927, Vic., Folder 84). This rather *fin-de-siècle* image of the novel is at least revealing of Knister's intentions for its atmosphere. He also admitted to Miss Frankfurth the Aesthetic sadness we have noted in his poetry, when he wrote to her of "things all men know, that life is slow and yet brief, beauty far-off and yet tormenting" (10 May 1925, Vic., Folder 84). One could not find a more ideally Aes- thetic phrase to capture the artist's suffering, and such frequent references to beauty as the essence of art and of life help us to appreciate those qualities in Knister's poetry that might otherwise be missed, particularly his hunger for beauty and frequent regret that it cannot be found or held for long.

Two possible reasons for his fixation on the nature of beauty may be suggested, with the usual caution that the search for sources must entail. The first of these is the poetry of John Keats, whose Romantic art and Romantic biography appear to have filled Knister with the force of a personal obsession. His fascination with the figure of Keats goes beyond the writing of *My Star Predominant*, a noveli- zation of the life of Keats; references in Knister's letters and other prose make clear the degree to which he steeped himself in the Keats myth before proceeding with the novel. Indeed, shortly before he died he announced to his wife that he felt something of the power and inspiration of Keats in his veins, that he was identifying more and more with the poet who had so absorbed him, an announcement that makes his death a few days later all the more potent a Canadian literary myth.[39] A letter to his former professor, Pelham Edgar, written on 14 January 1930, was very frank about the degree to which he had studied and absorbed the Keats mentality (Vic., Folder 84). An outline for a novel which he was never to begin, tentatively entitled "Via Faust," traces the development of a young writer through various stages, the first of which is climaxed when the artist "Concludes that it does not matter, that life is all sorrow ... wounds of life, continued, but an acceptance of life learned ... he decides à la Keats that the truth about life is its beauty, etc, and grimly struggles to put this into his novels, realistic."[40] (Interestingly, attached to this outline is a note from Minnie Acton-Bond, Knister's maternal aunt, to Dr Lorne Pierce, in whose collection of Canadiana the Queen's Knister Papers are placed, which remarks, "To me, this outline for his novel, written the last week of his life, explains his philosophy of life somewhat" (Queen's, Box 46, Folder 11). If Acton-Bond was correct, the Keats-identification seems to be confirmed.)

The degree to which such a preoccupation with Keats could wed itself in Knister's mind with his other aesthetic explorations (the minor incidents of farm life, the "realistic" detail of his prose and of some poems) is made clear by a typescript of an early version of "The Colt" in the Raymond Knister Papers at Queen's University. In its present form, "The Colt" is a simple piece of rural narrative, tracing closely and with fondness the young pure movements of a colt released into an open country lane. In its earlier version, the following passage appears:

> Could Apollo spare dole
> From beauty's pelf
> Beside him?
> Must not Keats have loved Hyperion
> Before he saw Bucephalus, too late?   ("Extracts," Queen's, Box 45, Folder 8)

The fragment certainly sits uncomfortably in the poem, and we can hardly regret that Knister rejected it in the end; yet the typescript demonstrates how naturally the Keats legend blended in Knister's mind with the images of rural Canada for which he is much more recognized today. The lost passage makes particularly clear that such a fascination with Keats may well have led Knister to fix upon beauty as one central truth of his own art; it could also explain the obscure note of death in his verse, since the marriage of beauty and death, while perhaps difficult to trace exactly, forms a potent part of the

Keats image carried forward by the Pre-Raphaelites and the generation of the 1890s.

Indeed, the latter generation's love of Keats may be one reason Knister referred to it frequently in his occasional critical prose and often with a warmth of understanding that may surprise us in a modern writer. In part it was the Aesthetes' championing of pure, uncommercial art that attracted him; the Introduction to *Canadian Short Stories*, which he edited in 1927 and 1928, briefly leaps its chosen genre to note that

It is a 'standard of living' to which many writers feel called more imperatively than to their professed art. Something of the guild spirit might be helpful. It has been said that the English writers of the Nineties embodied this in a sort; they did not have wives, homes, lands or motorcars, but they did have an inalienable sense of professional integrity, and they brought into being works of real merit, if of a minor order: and from the Rhymers' Club came William Butler Yeats.[41]

Knister's guarded approval here of Art-for-Art's-Sake, particularly in the anti-commercial sense of that phrase, is remarkable; while the quotation does not prove any great familiarity with the writings of the "Nineties," it proves some knowledge on his part of their theories, which other quotations from his prose and from his papers can confirm. As he chides the excesses of Wilfred Campbell, for example, he suggests that "there would have been an improvement even if he had turned a sympathetic ear to the *Yellow Book* school in London which in the time of his youth was engaged in a negation of Victorianism in its chiefest haunt."[42] That word "even" tells us that Knister had his reservations about "the *Yellow Book* school," but he again praises them as a corrective of what he perceives as the real enemy, Victorianism. Here again the degree of Knister's familiarity with specific members of the school can be questioned. By close examination of the papers, however, some more specific encounters with Aesthetic literature come to light. He was quite familiar with the writings of George Moore and the criticism of Arthur Symons, for example (Rev. of *A Modern Book of Criticism*, Queen's, Box 46, Folder 10); he had also written an article on the poetry of Francis Thompson, reason to believe that his knowledge of the decade was specific as well as general. In an article on A.E. Housman's poetry entitled "A Shropshire Lad," Knister contrasted Housman with "the reigning artificial *Yellow Book* school of the nineties, then in the ascendancy with Wilde, Yeats, Symons, LeGallienne as high-priests."[43] This reference, brief and casual as it is, is not proof of his individual acquaintance with any of the writers mentioned (since their notoriety caused their names to be often recited without direct experience of their writings); indeed, the acidity of the comment may suggest that his opinion of the school was rather low, despite his other, hesitantly appreciative comments. Nevertheless, in a roughly contemporary article on the stories of Katherine Mansfield, he comments with remarkable perceptivity that

In fact it is more than coincidental that other writers, and to a degree more explicit, show the spirit of our day as still quite incurably *fin-de-siècle*. It is as if the age took on an added hopelessness on discovering no improvement in itself with the numerical addition to the calendar twenty-five years ago, and had determined to be more aggravatedly *fin-de-siècle* than the nineties.[44]

The comment lacks irony, and if Knister were able to understand modern literature to be the heir of the Decadence (which critics generally took another forty years to do), it seems unlikely that his ultimate opinion of the earlier generation was one of utter distaste. The drift of his comments about them, the number of which is in itself remarkable, is roughly approbatory, although with clear-headed reservations.

One still hesitates to rest questions of influence on such tenuous references. Students of Knister are fortunate, however, in that they can advance beyond the realm of speculation, thanks to the diligence of the poet himself. In 1924 Knister completed a list of the books he had read to date (begun at the age of fifteen); the list, typed and remarked upon by his daughter Imogen Givens, is highly revealing. While it does not by any means "confirm" the influence of Aesthetic literature upon his own writings, it does confirm that he read, early in his creative life, such prime Aesthetic texts as Moore's *Confessions of a Young Man*, Pater's *Essays and Reviews*, Wilde's *Salomé*, Swinburne's *Poems and Ballads*, and Symons's *Dramatis Personae*, in which he would have found, besides "The Decadent Movement in Literature," essays on Rossetti, Maurice Maeterlink, and Emile Verhaeren, and a brief piece entitled, temptingly, "Impressionistic Writing," with references to a wide range of French Decadent writers.[45]

It would be misleading, however, to present the list only in this light. It also includes, of course, the more familiar writers said to have influenced him, Thomas Hardy, Joseph Conrad, Anton Chekhov, and so on. He read these writers later, generally, than he read the Aesthetes and Decadents. There is no reference, moreover, to specifically Impressionistic writings, say, the poems of Wilde and

Symons, or of Ford. Instead the Aesthetic literature he encountered was more of the mainstream and indicates no particular research into the techniques of Impressionism. (On the other hand, there is scarcely any evidence in the list of his having encountered the Imagist poets; although he probably read them in journals only, and therefore would not enter them into a list of *books* read, the list certainly supplies more Aesthetic than Imagist antecedents for the Canadian poet.) In a sense, then, the list can support the present argument in a relative and cautious way. Knister had certainly encountered a wide range of Aesthetic literature, and he may have taken from it his first ideas of beauty, later to be enriched and adapted in the arms of Modernism.

Before that encounter with Modernism, it would appear that he developed a fascination with Keats – the list suggests that he read Keats and the Aesthetes contemporaneously – which kept his preoccupation with beauty alive, reinforcing and validating ideas of art that his later experience of Modernist exemplars might otherwise have overwhelmed. Certainly the study of Keats is a natural concomitant of some sympathy with Aestheticism; it is difficult to imagine that a young artist who approved so thoroughly of Keats throughout his life could ever develop a whole-hearted disdain of the Aesthetes and Decadents who rescued his hero's name and desired to emulate him themselves. Even with the advantage of Knister's "List of Books Read," his youthful negotiations with various artistic influences cannot be ruled upon absolutely; but we may certainly conclude that a central preoccupation of Knister's meditations, his aesthetic of impressions and glimpses, followed lines drawn by both Keats and the Aesthetes, whose mutual influence maintained itself as he moved towards his Modernism.

Much less can be said, unfortunately, of Ross's literary ancestry. Great privacy still shrouds his personal life, and apart from scattered correspondence very little archival material of significant value exists. In his extended exchange of letters with Ralph Gustafson, therefore, one can enjoy some first insights into the workings of Ross's mind; prior to that publication, one could hope at best for a chance literary reference here or there, most of them of little critical value. It is diverting, however, to hear Ross, so long supposed to exemplify Canadian Imagism, firmly deny elsewhere the importance of two central figures of Imagism in his creative development: "'I felt hostile to, and irritated by William Carlos Williams ... felt [my work] consciously ... as antagonistic to the tone and form – if any – of the poems by William Carlos Williams I saw in the Dial,' so that any influence came from 'Williams somewhat adversely, Pound quite adversely.'"[46] This excerpt from a letter from Ross to Peter Stevens is a frank expression of distaste for two of the leaders of Imagism as he first encountered them. Two reasons tending in opposite directions could account for such a comment: either Ross really felt such distaste and consciously tried to veer his poetry away from the Pound-Williams thoroughfare, or he understood himself to have been imitating the Imagists too openly and, in later life, downplayed their influence in an understandable desire to emphasize his own originality. Peter Stevens goes on with the following description of Ross's true precursors: "His early verse arose out of an admiration for E.E. Cummings and Marianne Moore: 'it was these two that really excited me most keenly among contemporary poets (though I was already acquainted with Lindsay, Frost, Pound (a little), Amy Lowell and Sandburg, not to mention the Untermeyers and Sara Teasdale!)'" (45). Stevens later mentions that Ross "was an admirer of Wallace Stevens" as well (49).

One hesitates to make too much of such comments, because of the well-known unreliability and occasional outright prevarication involved when artists talk about their own histories. It is difficult, however, not to notice Ross's creation of an unusual set of heredities: Marianne Moore, E.E. Cummings, and Wallace Stevens, while highly distinctive poets who by no means form a school, do have in common a certain formalism, occasionally bordering on the dandyish and reminiscent of the late Aesthetic manner; Pound and Lowell provide the more clearly Imagist strain; while Robert Frost, Vachel Lindsay, and Sandburg could have provided Ross with a more American colloquial tone and homespun frankness. Since Pound was received "quite adversely" by Ross, one wonders if he did not take his Imagism from the distilled springs of Amy Lowell (who interestingly receives no such denigration); but more importantly, if Ross's assessment is honest, it is revealing to see his clear preference for the most aesthetically sensitive and formally meticulous strain in American Modernism and his downplaying the clearly Imagist training he had received. If the speculations of this chapter have been correct, however, it is not entirely surprising to see Imagism suffer a little at his hands, because Imagism was not, speaking exactly, quite what he himself practised as a poet.[47]

Little can be added to these glancing insights into Ross's thoughts. His piece of critical prose, "On National Poetry," contains scarcely a hint of Ross's own opinions, except for one unusual reference (especially given that the article is supposed to be on Canadian poetry, and modern poetry at that) to an anthology of "pure poetry" edited by George Moore and published in London in 1924.[48] From this book Ross draws a reference to Keats that he employs most haphazardly in the context of his article; the anthology itself, however, is interesting to look at, since the concept of "pure poetry" from French Symbolism has not been much mentioned in the study of Ross's poetry, nor has there been any other evidence that Ross knew anything whatsoever of writers of the English Decadence like George Moore. It is therefore interesting, for those who read Ross's poetry with the Imagistic bias, to imagine him encountering, in George Moore's "Thesis" to the book, the following claim: "we are in these poems at the heart of poetry: because these poems were born of admiration of the only permanent world, the world of things."[49] It is even more provocative to speculate as to his reactions to Moore's brief aside: "art for art's sake means pure art, that is to say, a vision almost detached from the personality of the poet. So perhaps the time has come for somebody to ask if there is not more poetry in things than in ideas."[50] That Ross's rare published prose should refer not to one of his own supposed poetic precursors but to an archangel of the Decadence like Moore is an interesting twist of literary history, but it is proof of nothing. Ross remains an enigma for the scholar of literary influences.

Another curious feature of the Ross jigsaw is his fascination with mysticism and spiritualism, with such phenomena as automatic writing, seances, and the "spirits" lurking in our daily lives. A tantalizingly small amount of critical material mentions this feature of Ross's personality, which is discussed by Peter Stevens (57). That the interest was strong and consistent in Ross is made clear in several of his sonnets, such as "On the Supernatural":

We must affirm the supernatural
However doubtfully we have looked upon
Its bare existence
......................
Angels there are and kindly demons too,
Their throng, removed from faulty human sight,
In the unseen worlds as we should know in spite
Of natural explanation thin and void.   (Son., 18)

The characteristic is more than a biographical tidbit; because we have seen the Ross canon pivot on the distinction between seeing only what is there to be seen, and recording it objectively, and seeing more than what is there, adding to nature preconceptions and visions of his own, his interest in the supernatural, his suspicion of the existence of "spirits," must necessarily colour further our understanding of his Imagism and Impressionism. Such conclusions have a limited usefulness; but it is thought-provoking to consider how many of these briefest glimpses of Ross take us away from Imagism into a world where the mind rules, where images exist as correlatives of spiritual and aesthetic conditions, not only as "facts" in the clear Canadian sunlight.

Despite Ross's and Knister's archival connections with Aestheticism, critical terminology is a heavy weapon, "influence" a particularly loaded word. While it is now possible and necessary to revise our critical understanding of the Ross and Knister canons so that we perceive the tenuousness of their Imagist commitments and recognize the Impressionistic techniques that they have exploited either consciously or unconsciously, the line must be drawn cautiously when the question of "influence" arises. The degree of direct textual affinity between the poetry of Ross and Knister and the poetry of Impressionism is not so exaggerated, and the references to the schools and trends of the nineteenth century made by both poets are neither so thoroughly approbatory nor so entirely familiar, as to make us conclude confidently that such affinities as are inarguable are the result of a direct influence from the Impressionists to the two Canadians.

However, to approach them as Imagists is an equally dangerous critical procedure. Their mutual interest in beauty and in the inevitable fragility that leads to its passing, their fascination with the moods and shapes of death, their rendering of images of flux, change, mutability, their mutual devaluation of visual stasis, and their general subjectivity of approach (in Knister frankly, in Ross more subliminally), all coalesce to form a very different assessment of the two poets from those handed about over the last forty years. These first modern Canadian poets are significantly less "modern" than they are generally thought to be; they were drawn backwards by a generation as well as forwards, into recognition and acclaim from Modernist criticism.

A final word on the whole idea of Canadian Imagism: D.M.R. Bentley, in one of the most penetrating articles yet published on the poetry of A.J.M. Smith (another Canadian poet tangled up with the Imagist story), leads his reader away from those easy assumptions about Imagism that have plagued Canadian literary history with the following disclaimer, quoted at length because of its immediate relevance to the conclusions of this chapter:

It has in recent years become a critical orthodoxy in Canada to claim that one of the archimedean points of Imagism can be located in Hulme's journey in 1906–7 across Northern Ontario and the Prairies. Of his experience in Canada, Hulme later wrote: "the first time I ever felt the necessity or inevitableness of verse, was in the desire to reproduce the peculiar quality of feeling which is induced by the flat spaces and wide horizons of the virgin prairie in Western Canada." From this statement, coupled with Hulme's seminal role in the imagist movement, Canadian critics have been perhaps too eager to reach the conclusion that, in Sandra Djwa's words, *"vers libre* and imagism, [are] particularly well-adapted to a depiction of the Canadian landscape ... " Leaving aside the questions begged by the phrase "the Canadian landscape," ... and granting that free verse may be a fitting form for those landscapes that are conceived of as open, it is still necessary to question the attractive equation, by way of Hulme, of imagism and the landscapes of the Canadian hinterland. For Hulme does not say that he discovered the idea of the image on the prairie but, rather, that he experienced "the desire to reproduce the peculiar quality of *feeling* ... induced ..." by the prairie ... "The flats of Canada," he wrote, "are incomprehensible on any single theory."[51]

"Incomprehensible on any single theory," as well, is the poetry of Ross and Knister, which has too long been taken to manifest trends that are instead significantly distilled in their work. The Imagist influence is not entirely irrelevant, just as Hulme's journey across the prairies is not entirely irrelevant to the development of his later theories, but a healthy scepticism should be invoked before we make too much of the Canadian roots of Imagism or of the Imagist roots of these Canadian poets. We add nothing to our understanding of either by over-eagerness.

## CHAPTER THREE

# Aestheticism in the Canadian "Contemporaries"

The line between major and minor poet has never been so obscured as in this late twentieth century of settled critical relativism, or in this difficult nation, whose most significant poets still struggle to achieve the mastery that earns world acclaim for an enduring voice in literature. The Canadian critic might seem to be faced with a painful choice: to evaluate and rank, then necessarily admit, as Raymond Knister did, that we "have not produced a Keats,"[1] or to suspend judgment altogether, to treat his Canadian subjects on Canadian terms, and thereby to conclude that certain poets are major, others minor, *vis-à-vis* a Canadian experience. The dangers of either position need no recitation: but where is the middle ground? May we speak of certain poets as major, others minor, in Canadian literary history, if we are constantly reminding ourselves that in the literary history of the English language they are, as yet, minor poets one and all?

There can be only one answer: to make of "minor" a neutral adjective, to reduce or eliminate if possible the opprobrium that has clung to it, by recognizing that in the literary cosmos there must be stars among which the planets are recognizable. To be a minor poet is to make a significant contribution to a literature; in our own time, when poets are legion, achieving "minor" recognition is still a successful approach to the pinnacle.

Criticism would benefit from such a shift in attitude. By studying minor artists we may indicate the currents, the trends, the regressions, the forecasts, against which the geniuses struggle and play. In some cases, minor poets provide the "tradition" against which major poets are forced to define themselves, so the study of the new generation is inevitably facilitated by study of the old; this has been the standard approach to Canadian Modernism, to postulate a late-

Victorian "genteel" school of minor poets against whom the important Canadian Modernists defined their revolution. On the other
hand, minor poets may be the precursors of later major poets; by a
precedence of a decade or two a poet may appear to foreshadow
the greatest achievements of a slightly later poet, although with less
talent or worse timing, which keeps him in the rank and file: such
was James Beattie to Wordsworth, the eighteenth-century "Minstrel"
highlighting much in the Romantic genius that looked backward
rather than forward in literary history. Moreover, the minor poets
of a generation may provide confirmation that the perceptions, philosophies, or formal innovations of a contemporary major poet were
truly "of his time," that his achievement was not merely individual
or freakish; they may have intuited the same currents in culture, or
drawn the same conclusions about modern man and modern art as
their greater contemporaries, yet lacked the genius, the ambition,
or the leisure to pursue their course to a major achievement. For all
of these reasons, the greater our knowledge of Canada's minor Modernism, the deeper we may strike with our stabs at understanding
such larger figures as Scott, Glassco, and Smith.

Stephen Spender's not dissimilar postulation of two groups of
writers, the "contemporaries" and the "moderns," in twentieth-
century English literature, has much import for Canadian literary
history.[2] Spender's "moderns" are those who pursued innovations
of form and crises of spirit to seemingly inevitable ends: the liberationism of *The Waste Land* and of Pound's *Cantos* demonstrates in
this view the determination of the two great "moderns" to revise
poetry utterly, to scourge the tradition and forge new conventions
out of their discontinuity with post-Renaissance literary history. The
"contemporaries," necessarily affected by the potency of Pound's
and Eliot's successes, were those who struggled to incorporate them
to some degree with more traditional forms of poetry, or to maintain
a degree of literary continuity with the past, which the "moderns"
rejected. Their poetry therefore tends towards the traditional, but
with certain formal characteristics seized from Modernism: thus one
may read in the "contemporaries" tightly controlled quatrains with
line length still determined by syllabic count, but discover within a
freer rhythm, struggling against the regular metre, that appears
destined to break out of the quatrain altogether.[3] Criticism has thus
far made of these contemporaries the "minor" poets of the twentieth
century, the Betjemans and Larkins who cannot, it presently appears, reign supreme with Pound and Eliot, whatever shocks the
reputations of the latter two may have undergone over the years.

This dichotomy is apparent in the development of Canadian poetry as well; those minor poets of Canadian Modernism who are assumed, if discussed at all, to shore up the Modernist revolution in this country – Finch, Kennedy, and others – may in fact be discussed profitably as the "contemporaries," in Spender's terms, who serve as counterpoints of relative traditionalism against and through which our "moderns" made their way. This distinction usefully illuminates a number of qualities of Canadian literary history that are frequently disregarded. The traditional view of the development of Canadian Modernism has made no room for "contemporaries." Accustomed as we are to speaking of the available facts in Manichean terms, the idea that the Canadian Modernists and the genteel traditionalists were joined in their battle by a third force manifesting qualities of both is not a comfortable one to consider. It is much more convincing, after all, if a vast range of poets can be spoken of as outright Modernists, whose few dissimilarities are much less significant than the general spirit of literary revolution that unites them. Thus we establish a major Modernist revolution in the country, with outposts of activity across the nation, a series of coeval uprisings made inevitable by the sorry state of Canadian letters. The Victorians were routed: the Modernists stood forth.

Certain facts necessarily tell against this dramatic version of the story. There were the genteel versifiers and the Modernists, of course, and they were at odds; but within the Modernist camp there were a number of lesser-known poets who developed techniques and thematic interests that align them with the poetry of the nineteenth century against which they were often trumpeting. The modern qualities of their poetry are of obvious interest and form a vital link between these poets and their more significant peers; but equally so are the non-modern qualities therein, which make us regard them differently if we study the sources of such traditionalism.

To that end I will discuss the poetry of Frank Oliver Call, Frederick Philip Grove, Louis Mackay, Neil Tracy, Robert Finch, and Leo Kennedy in order to demonstrate that their poetry, while arguably modern, is firmly rooted in the technical and emotional attitudes deriving from poetry of the late nineteenth century, and particularly from the fascination with the beautiful and the melancholy that is a central premise of English and French Aestheticism. As in Ross and Knister, we shall discover in these poets concerns with beauty, death, and temporality that converge in a manner strongly reminiscent of Aestheticism, while remembering on the one hand their touches of

Modernism and on the other that to be drawn to Aestheticism was also a valid way of battling the "genteel" Victorian mentality in Canada, as it had been in England. Thus these "contemporaries" walk a line between the two schools that have always dominated our version of the early twentieth century in Canadian literature: more with the "moderns" than against them, but more against them than we have cared to admit.

*F*rank Oliver Call (1878–1956) took his modest place in the Canadian modern firmament largely because of attentions paid to his *Acanthus and Wild Grape* by Louis Dudek and Michael Gnarowski, whose *The Making of Modern Poetry in Canada: Essential Articles on Contemporary Canadian Poetry in English* remarked the Foreword to the book as one of the earliest defences in Canada of free verse.[4] Call claims that

… vers libre, like the motor-car and aeroplane, has come to stay whether we like it or no. It is not really a new thing, although put to a new use, for some of the greatest poetry of the Hebrews and other Oriental nations was written in a form of free verse … The modernists hail this tendency as the dawn of a new era of freedom, while the conservatives see poetry falling into decadence and ruin. *The right view of the case probably lies, as it generally does, between the extremes.* There is much beauty to be found in walking in beaten paths or rambling in fenced-in fields and woods, but perhaps one who sails the skies in an aeroplane may see visions and feel emotions that never come to those who wander on foot along the old paths of the woods and fields below.[5]

Call responds to this development bravely, by endeavouring to write both "Acanthus" (traditional) and "Wild-grape" (Modernistic) poems. His efforts at *vers libre* are a bit droopy, sometimes sinking into flat blank verse, at other times elevated to the level of good, sliced-up prose. The poems in the "Acanthus" section, while indisputably regressive, traditional, unmodern, are the better-crafted: the form, while still in the hands of a limited artist, more comfortably reflects the traditional sentiment and appears to have been longer worked over before appearing in print.

If the traditionalist side of Call's dialectic seems to overcome *Acanthus and Wild Grape*, however, it is not so surprising as the well-balanced Foreword may suggest. Call's attraction to the modern was, at best, intellectual sportsmanship, evidently the result of a spirit of fair play. Later in the same piece he admits "that it matters little in what form a poem is cast so long as the form suits the subject, and does not hinder the freedom of the poet's thought and emotion. And I am old-fashioned enough to expect that beauty will be revealed as well. Out of this union of thought, emotion and beauty, we could scarcely fail to get strength also, which term many modern poets use to cover an ugliness that is often nothing but disguised weakness" (11). Here he more accurately reveals his prejudices: the poet is to create beauty, and thereby aesthetic "strength," and free verse is a good form only if it helps the poet to do so by blending naturally with his "subject." Traditional form may serve just as well; as Call adds, "who could say that one was more beautiful than the other? The carved acanthus leaves upon the column were beautiful because of their symmetry, harmony of light and shade and clear-cut outline, but the wild grape was perhaps more beautiful still in its natural freedom" (AWG, 13). With this formal equanimity "the author has tried in a humble way, to mingle elements of thought, emotion and beauty" (AWG, 13).

Thus we are prepared by the schism in this Foreword to appreciate Call's "wild grapes" as a first fruit of modern doctrine in Canada and yet to recognize other "Acanthus" elements in his poetry that are nostalgically traditional: to consider him, therefore, as in some limbo between the nineteenth century and Modernism, which is where, by chronology and doctrine, Aestheticism lies. Hence the sestet of the first poem in the volume:

> Eternal Beauty, thou wilt not be bound
>   By time-forged fetters, but dost find a home
> Where Gothic pillars rise acanthus-crowned
>   Beneath gray northern spires or southern dome,
> Eternal Beauty, Everlasting Truth,
> Thou hast the secret of undying youth.   (AWG, 17)

We have heard Call's prayer for "undying youth" before, and with it this opening sonnet of *Acanthus and Wild Grape* sets the dominant and most successful tone of his poetic career. He was so committed to abstract Beauty, and in such a manner, that his modernity is called convincingly in doubt, and soon enough by the poet himself; this is his outcry "To a Modern Poet":

> Why will you sing of railways,
>   Of Iron and Steel and Coal,
> And the din of smoky cities?
>   For these will not feed my soul.

But sing to me songs of beauty
  To gladden my tired eyes, –
The beauty of waving forest,
  Of meadows and sunlit skies

..........................................

And though Sorrow may walk beside me
  To the far, far end of the road,
If Beauty but beckon me onward,
  Less heavy will seem my load;

And led in the paths of beauty,
  The world from its strife will cease;
For I know that the paths of beauty
  Lead on to the paths of peace.   (AWG, 42–3)

The poet removes himself from the ugliness of the modern world (and modern poetry) by desiring songs of natural and conventionally Romantic beauty. This is theoretical if not quite brilliant Aestheticism, that "Beauty" should perform as the spiritual redeemer of the world, and needs only a greater emphasis on the poet's "load" of "Sorrow" to pass into the greater obsessiveness of Decadence.

Call's Aesthetic doctrine is not always so explicit, but the "paths of beauty" serve at least as a spiritual backdrop against which his observations, descriptions, or meditations are pinned. In "The Lotus-Worshippers," Call believes that "The ancient beauty-worship wakes and stirs/Within" him, as he watches morning light strike "white lily-buds, whose lips agleam/Whisper the secret of the world-old dream" (AWG, 24). Call is a devoted celebrant of worldly beauty, sometimes with preoccupations that betray the mere late Romantic or Victorian, but just as often with the tone of weariness and longing for release that characterizes the Aesthetic, not the Victorian, response. His "Lake Leman," for instance, gives over half of its length to a catalogue of Aesthetic delights:

My eyes can scarcely bear its glory,
As it burns crimson and scarlet
On jasper and flame-coloured sard,
On ruby, red as sunset flame,
And topaz shot with golden lights.
Like the eternal fire of the distant stars –
Blue, green and white,
Gleam diamond, emerald, sapphire,
Jacinth and beryl,

Onyx and green-banded agate,
And amethyst purple as wild iris-flowers.   (*AWG*, 66)

The catalogue clearly takes its tradition from such long poems as Wilde's "The Sphinx," the endless visual, aural, and olfactory catalogues of Joris-Karl Huysmans' *A Rebours*, and the similar treats in store for the reader of Wilde's *The Picture of Dorian Gray*.[6] Evidently when Call looked to record the beautiful he looked backward – "Back to the glorious years when Beauty itself was God" (*AWG*, 67) – to the indulgent extremes of conventional beauty, despite his modern effort.

Indeed, it is because of this very fixation that the poems of the "Wild Grape" (or modern) section tend to fail; Call does not seem able to change his themes as easily as he changes forms:

Wanton and wild,
Like an unhappy lover
Clinging to the breast of his dead mistress,
The vine clings in voluptuous embrace
About the naked, pallid forms,
And mingles there with the eternal beauty
Of youth and age
And life and death.   (*AWG*, 57)

As Call himself noted, the form must fit the emotion or both will fail, and his "Acanthus" poems had already demonstrated that the necessary container for such traditional contents as these will itself be traditional. Another "Wild Grape" poem, "To a Greek Statue," conquers the paradox a little, but only by approximating the quatrain (note the catalogue again):

Slender and white is your beautiful body,
Gleaming against the gray walls that surround you;
Like hyacinth-flowers beneath the snow sleeping
Is the dream you emprison; –

A dream of beauty that lingers forever,
A dream of the amethyst sky of midnight,
A dream of the jacinth blue of still waters,
Reflecting white temples.

And my dream of beauty and your dream eternal
    Embrace in the moonlight.   (*AWG*, 58)

The rhythms of the poem more adequately complement the emotions Call desires to render; and yet how odd it is to find so highly Aesthetic a vision couched in these diffidently modern lines.

It is no wonder that his last publication, the 1944 chapbook *Sonnets for Youth*, makes no bones about its "Acanthus" orientation; the seeds of the "Wild Grape" are surrendered, and Call now appears reconciled to his traditionalist calling. As if thirsty from his experiments in the Modernist waste land, the poet rushes headlong to the pool of Narcissus:

> ... From that flood
> Of infinite beauty, like a soul parched and dry,
> I drank – woods mirrored in the pool, wild swan,
> And youth's brave, eager turning to the dawn
> Of beckoning life. Then came a startled cry
> Of sudden wonder from your lips, as on
> White flashing wings the swan rose to the sky.[7]

Everywhere in this little volume Call explores his Aesthetic doctrines: in "White Hyacinth" he echoes "A voice that mourned for beauty past and gone" (2); he claims that "beauty only dawns to fade and die" in "Optimist" (3); in "Philosophy" the poet gently chides himself for upholding "the tottering fane of beauty and truth/ Where [his] old gods lay hidden" (4); and in "Immortal" he mourns a young soldier who, with the poet, "once looked on beauty for a fleeting hour" before it (and he) passed away (7). We are not surprised to see the *Sonnets for Youth* conclude with the poet's prayer that "strong as love of life shall grow his faith/That burning beauty lights the face of Death" (8); it would be surprising on the contrary if a poet who showed such consistently Aesthetic tendencies had not sooner or later married "Beauty" with the inevitable interruption of "Death," a conclusion his Aesthetic precursors had reached one by one.

Thus the mid-century, mid-World War *Sonnets for Youth* sit secure in a world where beauty is the sole poetic concern, and the form that best captures it is the frankly traditional sonnet. Call accepted in the end his own talents and specialized poetic doctrines and followed them into the limited acclaim he enjoys today. While few would now insist that Call was a modern poet, it is not often remarked that he was, instead, an Aesthetic poet; towards which judgment critical renderings of his contribution should tend. If he belongs in *The Making of Modern Poetry in Canada* at all, it is as a reminder, ironically, of how deeply the roots of Aestheticism ran in the earliest flowering of Modernism in this country.[8]

A contemporary of Call whom we are still unaccustomed to think of as a poet is similarly instructive in this preliminary survey. Frederick Philip Grove's attempts at English poetry are still much ignored; his reputation rests on his novels and on the startling demonstration in D.O. Spettigue's *F.P.G. The European Years* that Grove was originally Felix Paul Greve and had a European history quite different from the versions he himself offered of his early years. What remains is to exploit these surprising biographical revelations to shed light on our understanding and appreciation of his writings. Forthcoming translations of his German verse (*Wanderungen*, published in 1902)[9] should be instructive of Grove's early development as a poet and reflect interestingly on the major piece of poetry he published in English, "The Dirge," two-thirds of which appeared in *The Canadian Forum* in April 1932.[10]

"The Dirge" is less than impressive poetry, but it is, however well we like it, an unique document in one of the most puzzling and intricate lives of writing yet recorded. Because Spettigue has clarified the various and occasionally intimate relations Greve maintained with the Aesthetic movement in Europe (particularly by translating, studying, and criticizing the works of Wilde, but also those of Pater and Dowson, Gustave Flaubert and André Gide),[11] "The Dirge" is significant in that it adapts to a funereal end many of the conventions of Decadent poetry. Grove the modern novelist, the hard-bitten and ironic realist of prairie and farm life, is revealed by "The Dirge" to have had other preoccupations as a writer that give us a much more intimate and complex portrait of the man than we have yet attained. Greve/Grove thereby provides an unique example of the Aesthetic commitments underpinning much of the activity of Canadian Modernism.

Grove's daughter Phyllis died in 1927, at the age of twelve, during an operation for acute appendicitis,[12] which was naturally a severe blow to the otherwise childless parents, and to Grove especially, who seems to have achieved a comfortable intimacy with his daughter that was not usual in his dealings with others.[13] "The Dirge" is essentially a desperate response to this incident, an attempt by the poet-father to find meaning or comfort after his bereavement. His world had collapsed, its purpose now maddeningly hidden.

The blow fell; we stood stunned – forced to accept
A world subverted and crepuscular
............................................

And we stood sightless, impotent to try

Where we could find, with bleeding tentacles,
Some token known to orient us by.[14]

The poem moves forward by rejecting alternatives of comfort after
the child's death. In Section III, the poet bitterly complains that he
cannot even rail at "the gods" for taking away the child: in a culture
without piety, to "relieve//The anguish of [the] heart by blasphemies" is impossible. The comforting timelessness of art is similarly
rejected as beyond the reach of the modern poet; so are "Faith, Hope,
and Love." Although "of these/Love is the greatest," Love cannot
lift the stone from the tomb and recover the dead girl; thus Faith
and Hope are logically proved to be too weak as well. By considering
and abandoning all traditional sources of comfort after death, Grove
maintains not completely without skill a condition of ultimate despair. The speaker accumulates such feelings of impotence that he
is artistically crucified:

I wish I could one particle preserve
Of what you were; could speak or sing or be
As looked your eye, as bent the telling curve
Of perfect lips parting to smile at me.

Then could I feel I had not lived in vain
Nor wept in vain.   ("FD," 260)

Thomas Saunders, the only critic to examine "The Dirge" closely,
claims that Grove eventually comforts himself with the concept that
beauty is immortal;[15] much as that idea would support an Aesthetic
reading of the poem, the fact is that Grove rejects beauty too: he
desires it to comfort him, but knows that it cannot. The section to
which Saunders refers opens as follows:

I grow a sacred lily on my desk
And watch it as it grows from day to day
And think of you who, cold and statuesque,
Yet beautiful, within your coffin lay.

Thoughts of the myth of Persephone, taken to Death but freed each
year, cheer him briefly, but not wholly or thoroughly; for the myth
to have any force at all over his despair, he must approach it as a
diverting game, a toy that briefly distracts, for as a salve that heals
it is doomed to failure: "Let me accept that story which they bruit,"
he says, "If but for moments and as but a dream!" But "moments,"

as the burden of "The Dirge" guarantees, will inevitably pass and leave the former pain, often stronger. Ultimately this section of the poem rejects the promised rebirth of Persephone and admits that "All know the lot of beauty, that it fades" ("FD," 260). If there is comfort here from the immortality of beauty, it is a weak and twisted comfort doomed to dissolve. The poet suffers a world of inescapable despair that had been foreshadowed from the poem's first line: "Oh, many are the moods that come to me,/Sometimes of hope, more often of despair" ("FD," 257).

The point of this dispute with Saunders is that Grove's response to beauty is in fact Decadent rather than Aesthetic. Were he comforted by beauty, he would reflect the tendency of Aesthetic poetry; the Decadent, on the other hand, is tortured by beauty but knows that it cannot redeem him from his "crepuscular" condition. Grove's harping impotence in "The Dirge" is the genuine Decadent condition, in which beauty merely functions as one more reminder of the poet's terrifying impotence.

Is it surprising, after all, that a writer who had studied and translated Dowson and Wilde and other leading Decadents should, when personal tragedy forced him to poetry once again, manipulate lilies, burials, beauty, and time to nail down a framework of infinite despair? That is what the conventions of "The Dirge" are: not merely the recording of the poet's suffering at the death of a loved one, but a suffering detailed, extended, studied, even caressed, without compromise, amid a certainty that no worldly event so captures human poignancy as the death of a beautiful young girl. The precise comparison I am suggesting would highlight such similarities as exist between certain passages from Grove's poem and some typical images of Decadent verse, such as the following echoes between Dowson and Grove:

We sit and stare as, grey and in grey gown
Each passes by beneath his load and sign,
And others rise and rise, an endless line. (Grove, "FD," 258)

Neobule! ah, too tired
Of the dreams and days above!
Where the poor, dead people stray,
Ghostly, pitiful and gray,
Out of life and out of love. (Dowson, PW, 64)

And I should point to bedded plants and flowers
Such as you loved before you vanished hence;

They hide the mound and trail along the fence
To be an emblem of once happy hours.   (Grove, "FD," 260)

Encircle her head with a clustering wreath
Of lilies and roses and woodland flowers
That she loved to pluck from garden and heath
When the Earth smelt fresh of sweet May showers,
And no sombre shade of sorrow had laid
A pitiless hand on her sunny hours.   (Dowson, PW, 139)

or these, between Grove and Symons:

If I could sleep and sleep and never waken,
And dream and dream of what is not but was,
Then would both hope and faith remain unshaken.

But ah, there comes a point when shadows pause
And when I wake and find myself forsaken
And doubly feel the grief that bores and gnaws.   (Grove, "FD," 261).

Pain gnaws at my heart like a rat gnaws at a beam
In the dusty dark of a ghost-frequented house;
And I dream of the days forgotten, of love the dream,
The desire of her eyes unappeased, and the peace of her
   brows.   (Symons, CW, 1:285)

And we stood sightless, impotent to try
Where we could find, with bleeding tentacles,
Some token known to orient us by.   (Grove, "FD," 257)

Now that this desolating voice has spoken aloud
I look out on the world with blind eyes seeking you
In old familiar places where your feet have been.   (Symons, CW,
   1:313)

Other images from Grove's "The Dirge" mirror certain other emblems of Decadence: autumnal weather, architectural decay, the
impossibility of faith and hope, the cruelties of the mocking masses.
I do not suggest that Grove consciously imitated the earlier school,
as the evidence cannot fully support such a claim: but there are
undeniable similarities between the three voices which suggest that
his probable knowledge of Decadent poetry may have found some
fruition during his later Canadian career.

The Grove poetry that did not appear in *The Canadian Forum* confirms the Decadent tone of "The Dirge." In "The Pool," for instance, he repeats many of his favoured themes:

"Her life was beauty; and that beauty must
"Forever be since once it did exist
"In me, her mirror, whether autumn mist
"Creep up the hills or leaves fall down to dust.

"And beauty, of soul and body, made this love
"For her spring in my heart, a magic flower
"That cannot fade ..."
............................

But suddenly, from the valley's circling rim,
Down ran a breath of wind o'er wood and grass.
The image shivered into shards of glass.
Will thus this mirror shiver or grow dim?[16]

Note once again the poet's attempt to be comforted by thoughts of beauty, and its inevitable shattering that leads him to question the value of his art, his "mirror" of the girl's "soul and body." This traditional theme reappears in "Expression":

Fain would I lift them from the enfolding gloom,
Poor corpses buried ere they were full-born,
Like infants that have withered in the womb,
Of life's first breath, of its first heart-beat shorn.

Thus are these lines which tentative I trace
Abortive efforts brooding to construe
Which, thus I supplicate, may help to brace
This heart of mine its courage to renew.[17]

Notice the ambivalence: although he prays that his poetry will give his heart renewed courage, he recognizes in it a series of "abortive efforts," with which he struggles in a "tentative" way. The prayer seeks comfort, but the novelist knows the limits of his talent in this alien genre.

The major qualification of this Decadent reading of Grove's poetry is that a death had in fact occurred, and of a daughter, not of a lover. Perhaps what strikes us as most obsessive in the poetry of Dowson is that we know the death of the young girl did not take place: Adelaide Foltinowicz, the slender, scarcely glimpsed twelve-year-old of his most haunting poetry, refused the uncomfortable attentions of the poet and ultimately married a man who served with her in her father's public house. This constituted a "death" to Dowson, and he treated it as such with determined grandeur; hence that ring his poems so often have of spiritual hollowness, of having been forced into the gloom and melancholy they so skilfully exhibit. But if the death had indeed occurred, would we be inclined to take more pity on the bitter lover (or father)? Is Decadence, in other words, if based on truly horrid personal experiences of death, misery, negation and intensity, less Decadent? Stendhal spoke of the decadent as "quelqu'un qui se sacrifie à ses passions, mais à des passions qu'il n'a pas."[18] If he is right, does the poet exhibiting the same passions because of personal experience require another critical terminology?

By instinct, by free judgment of human nature, we may say so: with biographical information Grove may look more noble, Dowson more self-involved; but critically we may not. Decadence is, again, a style of art. To distinguish the Decadent conventions of Grove by biographical means from the same conventions in Dowson is unsound. Grove's poetry, forgetting his daughter, and Symons's and Dowson's, forgetting Adelaide, manifest a number of similar images, emotions, and structures of despair, and thus provide the student of Grove with a latter-day Canadian document with forceful links to the literary atmosphere of Grove's early years as Felix Paul Greve, translator of the English Decadents. The hardened prose realist reveals an unfamiliar aspect of his training in "The Dirge," which should serve as a reminder that no man could so entirely obliterate his past that, in moments of extreme crisis, it would lie perfectly quiet and restrained within him.

Grove and Call were born in the same ten years that saw the births of Sandburg, Stevens, Lawrence, Pound, Eliot, Woolf, Joyce and Moore. While they were not, properly speaking, part of Canada's Modernist generation in poetry, they were situated historically to have responded sympathetically to the first uprisings of Modernism in Europe and the United States; and it may be because they were neither young enough to seize upon Modernism fully, nor old enough to disdain it, that they became "contemporaries" of the young poets of the 1920s, shadowy precursors who must ultimately serve as the pre-Modernists in Canadian literary history. But the next generation, of an age with the first major Canadian Modernists, also produced poets who struggled to maintain principles descended from Aestheticism as a valid and effective response to the rigidity of Victorianism in Canada.

One of these was L.A. Mackay (born in 1901), a minor Canadian Modernist who owes some portion of his reputation to the anthologizing mind of A.J.M. Smith. His two publications (*Viper's Bugloss*, by "John Smalacombe," 1938, and *The Ill-Tempered Lover and Other Poems*, 1948) are neither so substantial nor so distinctive as to guarantee the poet his place in literary history; but when Smith included three of his poems in *The Book of Canadian Poetry* in 1943, referring to their "packed classical richness and penetrating satire,"[19] he helped Mackay to the place among the second rank that he enjoys today.

Smith's judgment of Mackay's "classical" poetry has also endured. Mackay's career as a scholar of classical literature reinforces his image as a wit with classical leanings, an expert at the Martialesque epigram and manipulator of tight verbal ironies. These qualities certainly exist in Mackay's poetry; it may be that they dominate his better poems, but the judgment is difficult. Wit, irony, and paradox are not the domain of the classical mind only, nor is Mackay's creativity so concentrated that a single descriptive term can summarize the variety of his writings. A poet who turned from poetry by middle age must have failed to find the voice, style, or inspiration that could have taken him further or materially assisted his development. Thus, we find in what he has published a certain cacophony, a number of alternatives explored and abandoned, that would be suggestive of impending silence. In Mackay, the classical tendency is mitigated by a dissonant tendency towards Aestheticism; the irresolution of the two is apparent in a number of his poems.

"I Often Wonder," for instance, is a rather traditional Decadent poem, with its beauty-drinking poet sitting in silence, rapt in contemplation of the visual object, with a desire to "cheat the hour," to rise out of Time by proximity to ravishing beauty:

> I often wonder what you're thinking
> While I sit there in silence, drinking
> Your beauty in with all my power
> To cheat the envious absent hour.
> Half I attend the thing you're saying
> But always half my mind is straying
> Against those couchant eyes, to wonder
> What thoughts they be that prowl thereunder.[20]

The woman addressed is a hastily delineated *femme fatale*, one of those baleful females with "couchant eyes" who so fascinated the Decadents, particularly in the form of blood-thirsty Salomé.[21] "Stand, Swaying Slightly," with its very similar physical situation, is a little redeemed from the derivativism of "I Often Wonder," perhaps because it is less cautious about its preoccupation with beauty:

> Stand, swaying slightly, thus; and I could look
> At you forever, nor content my eyes,
> You are so lovely: scarcely can I brook
> The transformation to another guise
> Lovely no less ... A slender sunny flower
> That in some far lone hollow sways and swings
> Marking the charmed, unregarding hour
> And dreaming vague delightful nameless things.   (1)

The concluding line is pure abstraction: the pathetic fallacy of the last four lines culminates in a vision of "dream," precipitated by a likening of the intense beauty of the beloved to a very traditional "slender flower." This perception, and the strange hint in the third and fourth lines that the poet is aware of some imminent change in the condition of his beloved or of their relations, make of "Stand, Swaying Slightly" a parallel to the less controlled "I Often Wonder," the two poems typifying the Aesthetic posture visible occasionally in Mackay's poetry.

Nevertheless, the tender emotional conventions of "I Often Wonder" and "Stand, Swaying Slightly" are not frequent in Mackay. More often the lady's refusals leave the poet bitter and spiteful; "Look, I Have Thrown All Right" is the rejected poet's complaint against love, with a degree of bitterness, disgust, and horror that produces violent anathema:

> I have thrown all right to love you into the mire.
> I tell you my love would defile you now by its touch.
> It was scorched, discoloured, deformed, besmirched by the fire,
> The tinsel gilt withered up to a dirty smutch;
> And out of the ashes it was not a phoenix flew,
> But a grimy soot-fouled worm crept out from the pyre
> Lifting a mute and horrible face still towards you.   (10)[22]

The poems are somewhat rescued for the modern period by their extremely direct, violent tone, although the persistence with which the images of dismemberment, deformity, artificiality, and rejection are elaborated to the end bespeaks a Decadent obsessiveness.

Despite the dreamy peacefulness of appreciations like "Stand, Swaying Slightly," and the strange violence in these darker poems,

Mackay is not quite so black and white a theoretician of love as it may seem. He also achieves a note of sorrow and resignation, which often replaces violent suffering in Decadent poetry, to create a vision of pessimism and morbid failure that is redeemed, if at all, only by its gentleness. He still retains in these quieter complaints the passions of the Decadents, but dwells now on their weariness and pessimism, their obsession with finding in the failure of a particular love the failure of all love, all beauty, in the world. In "Now There Is Nothing Left" the failure of love evokes an overwhelming pessimism that reduces life itself to its opposite principle:

> Doubtless we still shall find that we are able
> To call a ghost up, with a little trying,
> And learn, like many more, that life's a cable
> Twisted of tedious, small, unfinished dyings.   (11)

The "sorrow," "broken hearts," and "swindles" of the first stanza lead the poet to this conclusion of *taedium vitae*. The calling up of the "ghost" in the second line of the second stanza is hardly any relief, except that to think of death seems the only alternative to thinking of failed love. The gentle suggestiveness of this poem is repeated in "Moonset," where the beloved stands "Dark in the dark air by the dark lake":

> There is a sober stillness in the air,
> And in your eyes
> Wisdom, that knows the moon now sinking there
> Will never rise.   (71)

The moon *will* rise, although not for these lovers; but their wisdom prevents the mutual tongue-lashings of "Look, I Have Thrown All Right" and wraps them in gentle sorrow. The stanza of "Moonset," pentameters alternating with dimeters, captures ideally the drifting, ethereal quality of the setting and the emotions involved and, again, harks back to the similar form popularized during the 1890s in England.[23]

The varieties of Aesthetic love that Mackay chose to explore serve to prepare the reader for other tendencies of his poetry. For instance, the poet's enraptured contemplation of beauty in "I Often Wonder" and "Stand, Swaying Slightly" gives to such poems as "Luxembourg Gardens" and "Mozart" an appealing sensitivity: we appreciate in these poems the refined aesthetic icons in front of which the speaker stands bemused, and Mackay's lines gain thereby a quality of timelessness, evocative of the timelessness of art that he seeks to represent.[24] In the "Luxembourg Gardens" the poet passes the statues of women of another era and is drawn sensitively into the web of time:

> In your time too, 'tis said,
>   Lovers were lorn, and ladies ill to please,
> Old queens long dead,
>   Standing in effigy under the chestnut trees.   (11)

The alternation of line-length and frequency of liquid consonants in the second and third lines create the deliquescent feeling of the piece and give the ghostly statues remarkable aesthetic power over the reader. "Mozart" records the poet's aesthetic pain at the beauty of a composition and his slipping away into a world of crystalline beauty:

> Ah! could we call those scattered sounds again
> To build such perilous loveliness, as when
> The fleecy trees a million fingers show
> Cupping a crowded bloom of plumy snow.   (63)[25]

As we expect of so apparently Aesthetic a poet, Mackay often interweaves his appreciations of beauty with the transience of life and the nervous intensity of approaching death. One of his much anthologized pieces, "Admonition for Spring," skilfully unites the two; by drawing on the classical myth of Apollo and Hyacinthus for his symbolic framework, Mackay produces a juxtaposition of melancholy, beauty, and death, in a voice of pure resignation:

> Look away now from the high lonesome hills
> So hard on the hard sky since the swift shower;
> See where among the restless daffodils
> The hyacinth sets his melancholy tower.
>
> Draw in your heart from vain adventurings;
> Float slowly, swimmer, slowly drawing breath.
> See, in this wild green foam of growing things
> The heavy hyacinth remembering death.   (60)

The aspirates in the first stanza ("high," "hills," "hard" twice, "hyacinth," carried over to "heart" in the beginning of the second) are left in suspension by the sudden rush of sibilants and fricatives in the second: "float slowly, swimmer, slowly," "see," "foam," and so on, until the "heavy hyacinth" reasserts the aspirate pattern in the last line. This phonetic pattern parallels the pattern of thought, from an essentially visual recording in the first stanza, through a series of imperatives in the first three lines of the second, until the two voices are united in the last line. The final sound of "death" tolls like a bell at the end of a poem with a concentrated and carefully structured melancholy.

The motif of the hyacinth, because of the classical image of the beloved boy dying in the arms of Apollo god of poetry, was a particular favourite of the Decadents. That Mackay should employ it to capture similar emotions of resignation is not unusual, given the other interests apparent in his poems; for instance, "Damna Tamen Celeres Reparant Caelestia Lunae" echoes the resignation to death in "Admonition," confirming the centrality of the theme to Mackay's poetic vision:

Yet daily higher prowls the stealthy sun.
Quick to revenge the ruthless seasons run;
The quiet pine raises her patient head,
The rivers, groaning, toss their tumbled bed,
Crocus and hyacinth consort with men,
And the whole earth awakes to death again.   (72)

To Mackay, the yoking of hyacinths and death seems an automatic metaphor with which to fix the groaning progress of time.

Mackay's fascination with mutability is also evident in "Aubade," in which he announces "the awful death of Dawn," but begs, "Heed it not, love. Sleep on! Sleep on!" (3). In "Elegy" he exploits the abrupt comings and goings of the hours:

Had they but known that eyes were made for weeping,
    Or had they ever guessed
Dreams are a desperate unbelief, for keeping
The heart from rest, while empty Time devours
    The blood and bone
    ............................

Mocking they come, the sleek and rustling hours,
    Oh, had they known!   (12)

The "dreams" (that were comforting in "Stand, Swaying Slightly") are here acknowledged as gestures against the inevitable, illusions by which we comfort ourselves in the teeth of "Time." This is the final component of Mackay's Aestheticism: the fascination with beauty, the linking of it with death and hyacinths, and thus with the sentence of Time's passing, show very clearly that a significant portion of Mackay's poetry has less to do with classical satire than with his immediate literary precursors.

It seems clear, for example, that Mackay was closely acquainted with Wilde's poetry. His "Murder Most Foul," a war satire, alludes casually to a Wilde poem that is not so famous or so striking as to have been in every young poet's mind at the time:

> ... Instead of one, ten lives, are split, [sic]
> And now the victim shares the butcher's guilt.
> The point's familiar, but it must be made:
> Christ died, but not upon a barricade. [26]

Wilde's "Sonnet to Liberty" concludes with the poet's ironic announcement that "These Christs that die upon the barricades,/God knows it I am with them, in some things" (Poems, 25). Once the allusion is granted, it suggests first of all that Mackay knew a good deal of Wilde's poetry, since this is not one of the latter's much anthologized pieces; second it suggests that Mackay had read Wilde frequently or closely, since it is difficult to imagine that at such a point in a satiric poem he would deliberately set out to find a Wilde poem to which he could allude in such an unusual way. The allusion seems to have come to him easily and to have been firmly in his mind prior to the writing of "Murder Most Foul."

Perhaps by coincidence, Mackay's criticism in The Canadian Forum is oddly reminiscent of Wilde's essays and dialogues. One cannot help but mark the Wildean flavour of his comment on the unfortunate Bliss Carman: "I should put it this way: at times, at his best, to the very end of his work, he retains what I think is his genuinely personal note; a sort of shy, awkward, half-inarticulate adolescence, its quick fresh exuberance, the smooth-skinned, soft-fleshed delicacy, and the graceful charm, of one of Donatello's youths." [27] Mackay's article on the Canadian poet James Gay is a deliberate lie from end to end, the whole point of which is that the reader perceive the irony and mock the poet "noticed" in Mackay's column. Wilde would be envious of the writer's nerve. Mackay quotes the following lines from Gay:

> Up, up with your flag, let it wave where it will;
> A natural born poet, his mind can't keep still

..................................................
Not one in ten thousand can compose;
And those that can should be on a good cause
..................................................
The poet is ready to do his duty as nigh as he can
Between his conscience and his fellow-man.[28]

He then remarks, without batting an eyelash, that "It is hardly too much to say that this last utterance contains in striking and epigrammatic form, the whole essence of the moral problem." Mackay's article is beyond doubt a sustained, beautifully controlled exercise in critical prevarication, presumably to the end of demonstrating to the Maple-Leaf School how utterly distorted their tastes had become. (How one would love to have the results of a poll of how many of the *Forum*'s readers took the column seriously!)

Because of these incidents in Mackay's criticism, it is possible to suggest that during that period of his life when he read Wilde's poetry Mackay may also have encountered his delightful critical prose and appreciated those very qualities which appear in his own articles: the tongue-in-cheek understatement, the winking intellectual deceit, the occasional sensuality, the attack on bombast and jingoism. Such readings in Wilde, coupled with many qualities noted in Mackay's poetry, strongly suggest that his poetry contained in it much direct overflow from English Aestheticism.

Another younger Modernist, perhaps less familiar still than Mackay, is Neil Tracy (born in 1905), whose early pamphlet *The Rain It Raineth* contains "I Doubt a Lovely Thing Is Dead," the literary ancestry of which seems fairly evident. Tracy had been blind since youth, and blindness runs as a theme through many of his poems and gives them their unique poignancy; for the sensitivity to beauty, developed during his sightedness, when poised against the darkness of the blind, produces such sensations of loss and patient suffering as to compete forcefully with the complaints of all the sighted Aesthetes and Decadents of the world:

I doubt a lovely thing is dead,
    An inward thing, so clear and sweet;
I come at night and lay my head
    Against its breast, and hear no beat;
    I touch its hands, and feel no heat.

Lo! I have slain a lovely thing,
    For I am blind in soul and sight.[29]

These lines evoke with great restraint the reliance on tactile sensation that the blind must maintain; the death of the "lovely thing" is metaphorically a result of the speaker's blindness, since loveliness must be perceived and appreciated in order to survive. Because he cannot perceive it, the speaker is doomed to mourn the unattainability of beauty, to linger in "loneliness and empty rooms,/With dust and ashes of the past," because he knows he cannot expect any new beauty, however transient, to lift his soul anew.

Tracy's "Prelude IV" echoes this dismal knowledge:

A thing long sought:
Something long held, and lately lost;
Sold for a song, but for a passion bought.

What did its losing cost?
One soul's death, another's shame.

The poet's bitterness is increased in this "Prelude"; he turns from regret for the "lovely thing" to sorrow for his own condition, but with a strength of spirit that precludes self-pity.

Nothing shall turn
To dust save Beauty and Youth;
Gold and gems and words do not burn;
Not an oath shall move;
No truth of your swearing shall feed the flame;
I shall keep your vows in a golden urn.

The powerful irony of "Prelude IV" plays over the concepts of "Beauty and Youth," "Desire," and "faith," to assist the poet in his eventual triumph over the process that breaks down beauty and youth and removes the "thing long sought" from his grasp. The speaker is no longer responsible for the distance between himself and his "loveliness," as he had been in "I Doubt a Lovely Thing Is Dead," which accounts for the power of his position and the relentless conclusions he now directs to his beloved:

No: I planted a seed in the ashes of faith,
A germ in the track of the fire:
A thing that shall feed on your peace,
That shall cling like moss to the bones of Desire;
And the brightness of it shall trouble your sleep,
And the beauty of it shall cause you to weep;

Till you call to me from your bed, over the years and the lands.
I shall come with my urn in my hands.   (19)

There are clues in "Prelude IV" to one of the precursors Tracy
might have exploited in the development of this early verse. "One
soul's death" as a result of the loss of "passion"; the recurrent imagery of "burn," "flame," "fire"; the conjunction of "Beauty" and
"Youth"; the "gems" in the third stanza: these words cluster together, as Pater would have them: "To burn always with this hard,
gem-like flame, to maintain this ecstasy, is success in life" (*Ren.*,
189). The death of the "lovely thing" of the first poem, due to some
intrinsic flaw in the poet, further suggests the presence of an Aesthetic attitude.

Tracy's familiarity with Pater is suggested, incidentally, by his
"Ballade Morale," his variation on the anonymous French medieval
tale of "Aucassin and Nicolette." Pater's *Renaissance* recounts in its
first chapter "Two Early French Stories," one of which is the tale
Tracy adapts to his purposes (by describing, curiously, the two lovers
Aucassin and Nicolette after time has worn away their youthful
beauty). It is possible of course that Tracy encountered the tale
instead in either of two English translations from the museum manuscript (by F.W. Bourdillon and by Andrew Lang) that were published in 1887, but not likely that he had any first-hand familiarity
with the old manuscript that was resting in the Bibliothèque Nationale de France and was little-known until Pater wrote of it in 1872,
apparently intrigued by Swinburne's mention of it in 1868 in his
*William Blake* (*Ren.*, 303). But when we consider the apparent Aestheticism of Tracy's early poems, their concern with beauty and time
and death, it seems probable that Tracy encountered the tale in one
of the various editions of Pater's *Renaissance*.

Tracy's later poems pulled away from the Aesthetic tendency, into
a Modernist voice of wry irony, with occasional moments of confes-
sionalism harking back to the former style. He is virtually unknown
today. He published his *Collected Poems* in a slim volume in 1977,
significantly including none of the poems discussed above, although
these three gave him what little critical notice he has received for
his work. "I Doubt a Lovely Thing Is Dead," "Prelude IV," and
"Ballade Morale," Tracy's most Aesthetic pieces, were chosen by
A.J.M. Smith for inclusion in his *Book of Canadian Poetry* in 1943,
whereby Tracy found himself in the company of his peers; but the
second edition of Smith's anthology in 1947 contains no poems by
Tracy, his excision having been necessary to make room for the poets
of the 1940s who had been excluded from the first edition. Smith's

role in Tracy's career was in this regard rather substantial, and we are reminded, as Tracy himself must have been, of the immense power wielded by the anthologist, especially of a young literature. As with any such selection, the anthologist is as much revealed as the poets he publishes, and Smith's influence over Canadian letters can hardly be over-estimated. That he should choose such Aesthetic poems from Tracy,[30] or should include Tracy at all, is indicative of Smith's own predilections: as is his selecting Mackay's poems for the 1943 edition, or his noticing Robert Finch as the first example of the "dandy" voice in Canadian poetry, or his "rescue" of Leo Kennedy from the pseudonymous depths of *The Montreal Star* in the *McGill Fortnightly* days. Let us turn for now to these others he discovered, Finch and Kennedy, who are too arguably and substantially modern to be considered with the older styles of Call, Mackay, Grove, and Tracy, yet are true to their Aesthetic traditionalism in many revealing ways.

When Florence Livesay, mother of Dorothy, wrote to Raymond Knister, her acquaintance and neighbour, on 16 May 1924, she chanced to mention a young poet she had encountered who, she thought, would interest her correspondent: "We have discovered one man here (for our anthology) who seems to have great promise – has never published anything – Robert Finch, a student at the university" (Knister Papers, Queen's, Box 45, Folder 4). Were sheer prolificity the sufficient measure of a poet's significance, Mrs Livesay would have discovered in his earliest days one of the major poets of Canadian Modernism. Finch's first two volumes, for which he is still best known, were *Poems* of 1946 and *The Strength of the Hills* of 1948, but he had been writing since the early 1920s and through the period of his education at the Sorbonne; like most of the Canadian Modernists, he wrote much of his best known poetry during the 1930s, when the Depression precluded the real possibility of publication. He joined A.J.M. Smith, F.R. Scott, Leo Kennedy, A.M. Klein, and E.J. Pratt in *New Provinces: Poems of Several Authors* in 1936, by which means he was first brought to the attention of the book-reading public, or at least to such little attention as that land-mark received. The 1940s brought inclusion in Smith's *Book of Canadian Poetry* and the publication of his first two volumes, but the end of that decade was also the end of his first active period as a poet.[31]

Finch's style has been characterized, with much accuracy, as "dandiacal" by Smith, who seemed delighted to have found an example of such poetry in the rather puritanical confines of early twentieth-century Canadian literature.

> Mr. Finch is an intellectual poet. Of the six contributors to *New Provinces*, he is the most elegant and the least sensuous. His verse is not without feeling, but the feeling is so carefully husbanded and so fastidiously winnowed that one is impressed with its delicacy and precision rather than with its abundance and strength. At its most intense, it expresses an aesthetic emotion: an emotion which rises out of the effort to compel an order from a given experience. Finch's poems ... illustrate excellently a quality that has not previously appeared in Canadian literature, a quality that may be called *dandyism*.[32]

In 1976, almost forty years later, Smith still spoke of "Robert Finch, whose elegant dandiacal poems I very much admired."[33] Smith does not bother to define his idea of "dandyism" in poetry, so it is not easy to assess the accuracy or value of his private judgment of Finch; but there will be little disputing that he has in mind the style of Edith Sitwell that he affected in his own "A Hyacinth for Edith."

The premises leading to this conclusion are fairly obvious. First, we can safely eliminate from Smith's sense of the word "dandy" here such prototypes as Théophile Gautier, Paul Verlaine, Baudelaire, Swinburne, or Wilde. He had demonstrated sufficient knowledge of Aesthetic literature French and English prior to his first remark about Finch (see Chapter 6) to have called him a Symbolist, Decadent, or Aesthete if that was what he meant. Second, he would surely be hesitant to point out a derivative nineteenth-century bias in one of his fellow *New Provinces* poets, so it seems a reasonable conclusion that he was instead relating Finch to a fairly contemporary trend in poetry, which narrows our focus and points us towards certain literary phenomena of the 1920s. There was, for instance, a vigorous dandyism in the ascendant at Oxford when Finch was at the Sorbonne in Paris – see Martin Green's fascinating *Children of the Sun* for a complete rendering of the scene – which was partly responsible for a few qualities of mainstream Modernism (Sitwell's diction and the nature of W.H. Auden's early style). Among the young men at Oxford at that time was John Betjeman, important in the present context as a second kind of dandy poet from the period. Smith refers explicitly to both Sitwell and Betjeman in his *Poems New and Collected*, and they are clearly the only poets therein (other than those already eliminated) who serve as ready exemplars of a pre-conceived "dandyism." Smith had a youthful appreciation of Sitwell's poetry; his having discovered in Finch a

Canadian version of such a phenomenon would account for the obvious pleasure in his initial statement of the idea. Moreover, even a cursory reading of Finch's 1946 *Poems* shows us that there are some apparent stylistic affinities between Sitwell's early poetry and Finch's.

This is useful information, but we need not limit ourselves to Smith's perceptions, after all. There is more to Finch than imitation of Sitwell and more to dandyism in the 1920s than her poetry makes evident. Smith was not suggesting a relation between two poets only, but between Finch and a school, movement, or tendency of poetry; so we are free to look beyond his own obvious frame of reference. To appreciate fully the aura of dandyism we need to complicate our sense of it further: dandyism was not merely a literary style but also a milieu and a vigorously expressed attitude to life. Keeping the three distinct is crucial to the criticism of Aestheticism, but they must be equally understood if we are to grasp the "dandiacal" nature Smith appreciated in Finch's poetry. To that end we ought to find a poet, preferably a contemporary of both Finch and Sitwell, who gives us a sense of the dandy's place in the 1920s and of the personalities belonging to that place: to meet which criteria one could indeed find no better poet than Betjeman, whose beautifully contrived dramatic monologues call up the golden afternoon of a dwindling and increasingly mercantile empire:

> The scent of the conifers, sound of the bath,
> The view from my bedroom of moss-dappled path,
> As I struggle with double-end evening tie,
> For we dance at the Golf Club, my victor and I.[34]

The droll, self-deprecating, and bathetic voice of this delightfully affected young lover typifies the dandy note in Betjeman, here at its height in verse from the 1940s. His earliest work, first collected in 1932, manifests similar qualities, albeit less masterfully, and so he parallels Finch's own progress from a 1920s apprenticeship to an even and confident tone in the poems of *New Provinces* and his volumes of the 1940s. Despite these parallels, I see no firm evidence that Smith was also thinking of Betjeman when he wrote of Finch; nor does the dandy style of Sitwell find any parallel in the urbane and essentially traditional language of Betjeman. But much of his poetry provides the thematic, symbolic, and contextual analogue of Sitwell's formal and stylistic dandyism; his vision of a tasteful and slightly hollow England rose from the vague post-war malaise that afflicted aristocrat and middle-class scion alike and found particular expression in his gently ironic glimpses of a faltering social order:

Shall I forget the warm marquee
　　And the general's wife so soon,
When my son's colleger acted as tray
　　For an ice and a macaroon,
And distant carriages jingled through
　　The stuccoed afternoon?[35]

Because this highly aesthetic, dandiacal voice is central to Finch's poetry as well, Betjeman offers a useful contemporary comparison that helps to highlight certain of Finch's characteristic effects which might otherwise escape comment. ("Influence" is not a relevant term for such a neutral comparison; I wish to remark Sitwell's and Betjeman's differing relations to Finch in order to elucidate his own poetics, but not to explain those poetics as the consequence of such relations.)

Dandy poetry of the 1920s was fundamentally a product of a post-aristocratic British culture, that is, a culture in which the significance of an hereditary aristocracy is dwindling in proportion to the increasing power of a mercantile, financial, and industrial aristocracy; the concept of the upper class in such a culture is of course not eliminated but fundamentally altered, a procedure occurring in Britain throughout the nineteenth and twentieth centuries. This supposition clarifies the relationship that we often infer between modern dandy poetry and Aestheticism, for the earlier movement had also revelled in the fact of a bygone aristocracy, *via* the medieval splendour of the Pre-Raphaelites, the secular hagiography of Pater's *Renaissance*, and the fallen lords and ladies of Huysmans and Wilde. But the dandy poet of the 1920s recognized that he was cut off from those old sources of cultural power and that they could not be reconstructed merely by wistful art; and in his regret for the old structures or contempt for the levelling effects of the new democracy, he attempted to portray, and so to surround himself with, the decorative aesthetic symbols of the old world: the elegant gardens, the exquisite fountains, the abundant afternoon teas, the precise harmonies of classical music, fine clothes and furnishings, the elegant, perfectly polite conversation between gentlemen and ladies of fashion. But his was no slavish connoisseurship; instead, following the cue of his Decadent predecessors, the dandy poet recognized the humbug behind the social appearances he so fondled and, in order to preserve his integrity, developed a wry tone for addressing that world, teasing and cajoling where he could not bow and respect. Thus he was an accepted outsider in a world of painful elegance to which he wished to belong but from which he was always distanced. Nevertheless, the emulation of those who struggled to maintain the false distinctions of the past left the poet ripe for self-mockery and witty neurosis.

Our archetypal dandy poets, Sitwell and Betjeman, obviously had strong links (the former by blood, the latter by friendship) with the English aristocracy. Betjeman has explored their world more thoroughly than any other poet, at times with poignancy, at other times with pleasant invective, and primarily in the role of an outsider, like the young student in his *Summoned by Bells* who feels that he is the only man at Oxford without an ancestral country estate at which to pass the long vacation.[36] Similarly, when he turned his attention to the slightly less refined world of his parents and his childhood, he invested that lesser milieu with the delicacy, ritual, and exaggerated sensitivity he had imbibed with the aristocratic spirit. The gentle irony that is so central to his poetic vision and voice is the result of his wandering between the two classes, belonging wholly to neither but loving both deeply for very different reasons. Sitwell, perhaps because she was born an aristocrat, felt no need to catalogue the various pleasures of the post-war world of wealth, but launched instead an inspired poetic aimed at undermining that world's image of itself. She developed an iconoclastic language of paradox, wit, and inversion that captured a fervidly artificial world, a kind of refraction of the artificiality of the aristocracy of Britain after the First World War. Down to the single image, artificiality becomes the keynote of her early poetry:

> Oh, the keys we stumble through!
> Jungles splashed with violent light,
> Promenades all hard and bright,
> Long tails like the swish of seas,
> Avenues of piano keys.[37]

In this world of marvellous falseness Sitwell's satire can have its freest rein. The Betjemanesque and the Sitwellian are therefore two quite distinct strains of dandy poetry, the former more elegant and nostalgic, the latter more cutting and biting: if they could be united, a powerful voice would be created for the poet.

Dandy poetry is a recognizable branch of Aesthetic poetry in the modern period for all of these reasons: because it looks back to a lost time when the "innocence" of upper-class life was assured; it longs to recapture the former aesthetic intensities of that life; and because it finds, in the exquisite epigrams of the Decadence, proof that renegade artistic mannerisms can still attract and delight a jaded aristocratic audience.

Dandy poetry, to realize these motives in verse, developed a number of striking stylistic features. The quirky artificiality of Sitwell's verse established a norm for dandy imagery and phrasing that was much imitated by its adherents; indeed, the most famous and direct imitation in Canadian poetry, Smith's "A Hyacinth for Edith," juxtaposes a long catalogue of Sitwellian images with a more traditionally worded triad of couplets at the end, in order to counterpoint and comment upon the dandy manner. The interpolations of poetic diction necessary to that straining artificiality effect another characteristic of dandy verse: such poems tend to thicken with words, polysyllabics pile up delightedly, each noun must have its half-accurate, half-nonsensical adjective and each verb its astonishing adverb. The effect created is often of two poems crowded into the lines of one, of verbal encrustation that turns the surface of the poem into a lapidary marvel. This quality, coupled with the dandy's fascination with line and colour, a fascination that results from his attention to the delicate symbols of the aristocratic world, gives to dandy poetry an intense formalism, related to but beyond a Flaubertian search for *le mot juste* or Wilde's often derivative versification: a sense that form has been frozen in the millisecond preceding explosion, that not one word more could be added without mental danger to reader or poet. This formal intensity also allies dandy poetry with the poetic theory of the Decadents and the chief formal principles of that movement.[38] A final quality, perhaps accidental but very common to dandy poetry, is one of child-likeness; when the quality of verbal play is heightened to this extent and combined with the sensation of being a foundling in a pre-determined, highly constructed world, the result is often a fascination with childhood and a child-like wonder at the shapes, lines, colours, and gestures that give life to that aristocratic world.

If these are the qualities of dandy poetry that Smith had in mind, there is ample justification for his reading of Finch's poems. In the early poetry particularly, the two volumes from the 1940s and the periodical pieces from 1925 on, the dandy voice is heard with increasing skill and assurance. One of the prevalent symbols of this period is Finch's fascination with flowers, with their form and scent, with their colours, and with the personal delicacy that urges a man or woman to pick them. Thus in "The Lilac Gatherer," a little-known poem, he makes the clipping of flowers an intense pseudo-metaphysical inquiry:

There's something I must ask you. Do you know
Why she cuts lilac carefully, why she clips

Here, there, there, here, a spike, a spire, her long
Bright shining scissors uttering quick squeaks
Astonished at their own ubiquity?
.............................................
There's something more in her incessant mincing
Round lilac trees than merely love for lilac
...................................................
Tell me, oh, tell me quick! If a tulip died
Would she kill all the other tulips in the bed?[39]

The flower emblem survives throughout Finch's development: the most cursory reader of *Poems* and *Strength of the Hills* will easily remark the ubiquity of roses and lilies in Finch's world. Anyone, indeed, may write about a rose; but when flowers become a dominating motif in a poet's life work and incite in him some of his most profound and skilful utterances, the reader will necessarily experience a highly sensitive, aesthetically delicate artist. Flowers, in their amoral, purposeless, exquisite beauty, are after all logical symbols of the Aesthetic mentality.

The most significant element of "The Lilac Gatherer," however, is that we see in it the first manifestation of Finch's mature style. The urgency of diction in the third line, with its alliterative and assonantal play, prefigures the techniques of such better-known poems as "The Statue" and "The Fans." As well, the "quick squeaks" of the "ubiquitous" scissors are faintly Sitwellian and produce that odd aural-visual refraction associated with the dandy note in Finch's poetry. Furthermore, the overwrought alliteration of "lilac trees than merely love for lilac" produces sufficient phonic tension and difficulty to create an appropriately pre-explosive effect.

"Normandy Mantelpiece," published in *The Canadian Forum* in 1930, prefigures another visual preoccupation of Finch's later poetry: the capturing of odd, precise interiors, by means of rapid and obviously Sitwellian juxtapositions, the logic of the poem suspended in the sheer force of its verbal technique.

à gauche: biscuit de Sèvres.

Jean-Baptiste, five years old,
Clad in sheepskin, cannot hold
Back a too-suspicious lamb
Confident it sniffs Madame.

au milieu: photo.

Up goes a fireman,
Walrus moustachio,
Hailing a dire man
Pale as pistachio.[40]

The image of the mantelpiece is lost in the free verbal associations, with an intricacy of sound and unreality of imagery that suggest the manner not only of Sitwell but equally of Jules Laforgue (Finch had spent his years at the Sorbonne in the study of French poetry, albeit with an earlier focus than the nineteenth century). The mental progress is absurdist, the only clear sense of interior provided by the "à gauche ... au milieu ... à droite" structure linking the stanzas.

Reflecting this *Symboliste* flavour of "Normandy Mantelpiece" is the roughly contemporary "Headmaster's Drawing Room," in which a queer aesthetic vision stolen by a young teacher renders him incompetent in the real world: after opening the door never to be opened (a common motif from fairy tales, of course), he sees, "Thin-nosed and haughty, a/Heavily jewelled and/Palpably noble dame," who addresses him:

Look at my queendom, she
Said to the timid one,
Ivory fireplace and
Opaline flame, and bears
Cringing, with icy teeth
Blazing, and opaline
Eyes. See my vases, my
Basins of flowers, my
Golden-traced volumes, my
Pictures of apple-trees
Drifting in rosy smoke

.............................

Flowers with decorous
Wit speak in sofas, and
Utter my arm-chairs, soft
Poems to sit on.
I am the queen of all,
Proud and imperious.

After the resulting dismissal of the young man, "Judged quite incompetent," from the school, the "truth" of his vision is ironically confirmed at the end: "the Queen of all" was no private fantasy,

but something higher, the *genius loci* of a secret room not intended
for the aesthetically undeserving:

> Just as I thought, said the
> Drawing-room Empress, as
> Showing her bluest veins
> Ultramarinely she
> Blended in tastefully
> With her blue background.[41]

The blue-blooded lady destroys the unaristocratic intruder, who has
crashed by accident into the world over which she rules, a mystical
relic of an age of wonders. The poem is pure dandyism, and with
it Finch closed the 1920s on an artistic note that has stayed with him
to the present day.

From this point of Finch's development to the familiar *New Provinces* material and the poems of the first two volumes there is not
far to go. Gradually through the early 1930s his range of imagery
extended, and he mastered the possibilities of the dandy style he
had adopted. By the publication of *New Provinces* in 1936, we are in
the company of the Finch of the 1940s, "whose elegant dandiacal
poems" Smith so admired. "Window-piece," from the 1936 venture,
typifies the manner at its best:

> Trees; hands upthrust in tattered black lace mitts,
> enormous brooms stuck handle down in snow,
> the nervous roots of giant buried flowers.
> Old willows in spun copper periwigs,
> and many-fingered firs smoothing white stoles
> beside the drained rococo lily-pool
> whose shuddering cherub wrings an icicle
> from the bronze gullet of his frozen swan.[42]

Notice the implications of class in the imagery of "periwigs" and
"stoles," and how quietly that word "rococo" establishes the mood
of an upper class: note also, and perhaps most significantly, that
the "lily-pool" is in disuse; it is winter, of course, but a strange sense
of failure is evoked in these images of an elegant garden.

These rich patterns of imagery are not, of course, the only virtue
of Finch's work in the landmark collection. He had also mastered
the oddities of syntax and sound glimpsed in "The Lilac Gatherer"
in good time for the appearance of *New Provinces*; consider the concluding quatrain of "Beauty My Fond Fine Care":

beauty my fond fine care, no vaunt collapses
the promise made though sworn perforce in laughter,
memory, beauty, in a unique ellipsis
modulate fact to faith, now, and for after.   *(NP, 3)*

The rich Aestheticism of the poem is certainly worth remarking; it is crossed with the interweaving dandy style to produce a remarkable hybrid that captures the essence of Finch's poetry. The style is never adopted mechanically; despite the complex aural echoes of "The Five Kine," for instance, we can recognize a degree of restraint that was unnecessary in "Beauty":

Pasture of ease, what vigilance withheld
froze the intrepid marrow of your grass?
  The kine were there, fivefold and safely belled,
The wall was there, oh perilous blade of glass,
  sheering denial between pent and wrung,
The soil was there, long, long ago, alas
  so long.   *(NP, 1)*

Such skill characterizes Finch's style at its most rewarding. The patterns of alliteration, assonance, rhythm, and metre that enrich this distinctive style are by no means so haphazard as they may at first appear; but I shall temporarily defer a discussion of their conscious manipulation by Finch, in order to comment further upon the necessary development of imagery and visual richness which took place between the *New Provinces* poems and the volumes that appeared in the late 1940s.

  For one has the impression from Finch's *New Provinces* poems, despite their skill, of a poet with an uncertain sense of his purpose, as if he had not yet found the means to unite a mastered style with the symbols arising from his early development. No doubt this is due in part to the editors' efforts to show the variety of themes and styles tackled by the new poets. But, in this cacophonous collection, the presence of two rather tentative free-verse pieces signals a certain uneasiness, a hovering on the edge of artistic maturity, which prevents the reader's full absorption in Finch's poetry. Nevertheless, such maturity was to inspire the *Poems* of 1946, a volume containing a series of minor masterpieces and (famous attacks by John Sutherland to the contrary) clearly deserving the notice of the Canadian literary community. When, for instance, he applies his recognizable style to his long-established fondness for unusual interiors, Finch renders half-sketched, delicate rooms and blends them with open

air, sunlight, snowfall, or the coming on of night, so that the eye
drifts in and out, nature mixing with interior in haunting harmony,
as in "Petit Lever":

> The drifting curtain is uncurtaining dawn
> Drowsily rising from a night of waiting
> For a gull's cry, shredding its driven sheeting
> To mists that fray from linen into lawn.
>
> What Chinese scroll could be unrolled more softly?
> Time is no object while its servers sleep.[43]

Carried to a complex extreme in "The Smile," such an effect becomes
magical, evoking a world of dreams and wonders in which both the
poet and the reader are hushed:

> The lake has drawn a counterpane of glass
> On her rock limbs up to her island pillows
> And under netting woven by the swallows
> Sleeps in a dream and is a dream that has
>
> Strayed to sleep in the library of space
> Whose ceiling beams are purple over yellows
> And whose blue shelves behind a cloudy trellis
> Wait for tomorrow's volumes of new grace.    (*Poems*, 9)

So technically skilful is Finch's interweaving of interior and nature
that it is difficult at first to discern that in "Petit Lever" the interior
"exists," is part of the reality that he seeks to capture, whereas in
"The Smile" it offers a cluster of metaphors for natural movements
and rhythms and has no presence. It is the sharp eye and unique
style of Finch that can recognize associations between the lines and
colours of tasteful rooms and the shifting forms of the world, and
the perception of those associations is one of the most striking gifts
we are given by his poetry.

As "Headmaster's Drawing Room" suggests, however, it is not
merely the elegant interior that transfixes the poet, but also the
manners and niceties of the men and women who live there; the
blue-blooded lady is one with her setting and is as much the focus
of the poem as her bizarre catalogue of Sitwellian images. Similarly,
in "The Sisters" he evokes the highly precise world of the afternoon
tea, but renders it particularly by half-glimpses of persons caught
up in its refinements:

... sometimes not a word is said,
Yet always the rose on her balcony
Smiles down in lace at the thin bread
And up in grace at the guests for tea.

Invisible fingers pour and pass,
Unerringly the curate glides
On invisible feet, while as through glass
The Visible Presence of Rose presides

In a hat of shadow, a dress of light,
A shawl let fall from the silver sport
Of weaving rain; the fragrant sight
Is ever and never the same in sort.

Throughout the fine social world of the "invisible" tea, the rose
blooms and pours beauty into the air by scent and sight, opening
and closing daily in what seems an immortal round of decline and
rebirth. But the poem soon draws away from the tea, and into a
meditation on the process of time and its relations with beauty:

What deft tool of delicate mettle
Daily remoulds the casual smooth
Coral of each imperial petal
Into this maxim of fadeless youth?

Having initiated this familiar debate, the poem closes on a note of
decay and loss; the rose is prized, acclaimed, and cut from its stem;
the interference of the ghostly appreciators destroys the mysterious
timelessness of the rose's triumph:

Declared unique, a rose as due
Receives a ribbon and a name.
The name dies with the rose. The blue
Ribbon fades on the sapped stem.   (*Poems*, 12)

Thus, into the world of elegant settings and wondrous nature (the
tea, the rose), people of refined taste intrude and bring about demise
and aesthetic failure. The closely controlled irony in the conclusion
of "The Sisters" makes it clear that the poet is, so to speak, outside
of the tea, looking in, partly delighted by the lines of motion and
delicacy he perceives, partly ironic about its pretensions: thus he
mourns the rose, the true source of elegance and beauty.

The poet's dual function as recorder of and interloper in the refined world is heightened and dramatized in "Scroll Section." More direct in its aesthetic purpose than "The Sisters," "Scroll Section" nevertheless poses similar questions by arguing for the elegance and beauty of natural wonders against the artificial, over-determined pursuits of the person of leisure – yet with what fondness Finch poses the splendid creations of a dandified world upon his page:

> Leave kingdom breakers
> to juggle nations,
> and care's broad
> cloud
> to the white hare that with mortar and pestle
> sits in the moon by the cassia tree,
> leave your lacquer trestle
> of puppets, your aviary
> of pets in petrified wood,
> your malachite lion with its ball of brocade,
> your clique to scribble the past
> on dust,
> and with no inlaid saddle,
> no jewelled bridle,
> follow me over the snow in search of plum blossom.

The poet urges the owner of this marvellously artificial collection to come away with him. The poem has already opened with a clear and ironic summation of the owner's predilections: "You who practise the four elegant occupations/tea music calligraphy and checkers." It is against such habits that the poet wishes to militate. After rejecting the dandy collection above, further aesthetic and quasi-ethical suggestions to the owner are in order:

> The leaping salmon rainbows the cataracts,
> the dragon in chase of a pearl skips space
> and the phoenix, alighting, first selects a place
> to arrange its tail. Emulate in a degree these agreeable acts.

These are perhaps odd alternatives to the artificial menagerie that is to be left behind; they are, however, symbolically rather than merely decoratively meaningful, differing from the artificiality of malachite lion and petrified pets by rising from nature and myth, not from lapidary and sculpture. The intention of all this imperative richness is that the addressed owner shall achieve a new art: he or she shall reject "tea music calligraphy and checkers" in order to

> ... paint in ink
> mountains trees creepers clouds
> gorges rivers cascades
> the brink
> of wind, monasteries in mist,
> beauties that have no best,
> that through your purpose a longing be learned, earned,
> the seal of your mind borrowed and not returned.   (*Poems*, 34)

The Romantic naturalism of these artistic ends clarifies the role of the "salmon," "dragon," and "phoenix" – the salmon in its "rainbow" glitter, the dragon and the phoenix as mythic beasts, are half-way towards the "natural supernaturalism" of the final landscapes and half-way away from the artificial constructs of the enclosed and dandified world. In this sense the poem progresses away from the post-aristocratic and back to the naturalistic-Romantic, which redeems and revivifies the "elegant occupations" of true art.

The chief features of these early poems – the perceptions of the child, the elegant and refined interiors, the flashing of artificial imagery, the playing of Art over the appearance of things – form the consistent stuff of Finch's poetry. While he may wander away from the aristocratic world into a world of mere tastefulness, more middle class than dandyish in later volumes, while the willingness to sound childlike may dissipate somewhat and the fondness for odd twists of imagery weaken, Finch's poems always contain a determined elegance and verbal highlighting that arise early in his development, whatever subject he approaches with his fastidious mind. To be sure, the vision of his early verse, captured largely with effects of style, is weakened in later volumes by a more logical manner and a more restrictive syntax. Yet his concerns remain: how may artistic form be used to reflect the meaning the poet wishes to relate or to create and yet remain "pure," free of morality and philosophy and tending primarily towards beauty and wonder? It is not difficult to appreciate the peculiarities of style that permit Finch to toy with the question; he is one of the most stylized Canadian poets, manipulating rhythms and phonics to substantiate his dandy themes in various ways.

Indeed, few poets have made of sheer formalism the virtuoso performance that distinguishes the work of Finch. This quality has attracted most of the attention of critics who have commented on his work: Earle Birney referred to the "impeccability and deceitful simplicity of form" that characterizes his work;[44] Roy Daniells has remarked that "les formes de l'art de Finch ... restent dans leur propre monde d'artifice, un monde brillant, qui est hors du temps."[45] Daniells considers that "L'art de Finch est du rococo sous la forme la plus soumise. C'est un art de surface et d'incrustation, d'adroite marqueterie et d'habile cloisonnement, un vernis crépitant" (91). There is one fundamental reason for these properties, and it is not surprising that A.J.M. Smith, with his remarkable sensitivity to Finch's achievement, hit upon it when he discussed Finch's best-known poem, "The Statue": "The Keystone comedy of the chase is presented with an ironic seriousness, but there is nothing ironic about the seriousness with which the existence of an absolute, meaning-giving pattern of beauty is implied in the whole fable. It is the 'moving stillness' of human art that gives a focal centre around which the fuss and rustle of our confused and meaningless violence subsides into a fruitless and tolerable irrelevance."[46] As the Decadent poets demonstrate so well, when Art is treated as the supreme object of humankind, the surface of the work of art rises in significance in relation to the "depth," or meaning or content, of the work; hence Wilde's comment that "There is no such thing as a moral or an immoral book. Books are well written or badly written. That is all."[47] What the critics have noticed in the formalism of Finch is the result of these principles of art and confirms, incidentally, the relationship of dandy to Decadent and Aesthetic poetry.

The first and most obvious formal characteristic of Finch's poetry to strike the reader is its determined traditionalism. In the modern era, what seems an obvious point always deserves to be highlighted, for the use of traditional forms in the twentieth century is always on the part of a well-read poet a deliberate choice: not necessarily a regression, but a refusal of certain forms of progression popularized in his time. Even in his early periodical pieces, where we might expect the young Finch to have felt most sharply the formal revolutions occurring in contemporary English poetry, there is only a little playing about with form; "The Lilac Gatherer" has the appearance of a sonnet, but it has dropped one of the requisite fourteen lines and turned to blank verse; "Normandy Mantelpiece" plays with absurdist rhymes and irregular line length, the resulting tension shoring up the dandy tone; "Headmaster's Drawing Room" abandons rhyme but holds so fast to a particularly unusual metre (dactylic dimeter) that the effect of traditionalism is cheekily carried off. Each of these early poems, while toying with modern poetics, safely anchors its form by some means in traditional poetics; only then does the poet seem to feel comfortable in dropping a rhyme or varying a highly regularized metre. By the time of the publication of his first volume, however, Finch appeared to have firmly resolved the formal issue; while one may find in *Poems* the rare piece of free verse ("Sea Piece," "Sampler"), the majority of the work is in traditional forms – sonnets, closely rhymed quatrains – with vigorous but regular metrical structures throughout. These forms also prevail in the many volumes that followed.

The formal traditionalism of Finch cannot be over-emphasized. It is in the context of such restrained form that his stylistic innovations are released, in part as necessary resistances to mere derivative traditionalism. Hence a constant tension in his poetry between the traditional container and the modern (in this case, dandy) contents, a tension that produces his particular achievement. A number of stylistic features contribute to the modern pull in this tug-of-war: the encrustation of word upon word so that the surface of the poem seems to teem with verbal life; the abrupt, surprising dandy images arising from such clutter; the manipulation of rhythms hovering between the ultra-traditional and the farcical; a strong sense of phonic possibilities; and the use of heavy internal rhyme and occasional repetition to make the surface of the poem seem closely determined and long worked-in upon itself. Thus "Petit Lever" opens with "The drifting curtain is uncurtaining dawn." The repetition of "curtain" thickens and slows the line, while the [k] and [d] alliteration binds the line together. "Drowsily" from the second line picks up the alliteration and, with two present participles ("rising" and "waiting"), links it to another phonic effect of the first, as do "shredding" and "sheeting" in the third, which also serve as an internal half-rhyme. The fourth line of the quatrain drops these hard consonantal patterns to replace them with fricatives, sibilants, and liquids, "mists," "fray," "linen," and "lawn." The consonance of the last two nouns highlights their passing into one another, also one of the chief visual effects of the poem.

The opening quatrain of "The Sisters" displays not dissimilar techniques:

> There are two sisters, one is a rose,
> And no one knows what the other is.
> The first says go and the other goes,
> Or come and she comes, or that, or this. (*Poems*, 12)

The phonic interweaving of the stanza is impressive. Long and short vowels play against one another; sibilants and nasals run counter to one another: yet how simple, even disingenuous, the stanza seems, as though the entire series of thoughts were uttered *without* thought. Partly this is due to the tongue-in-cheek "or that, or this" at the end, as though the poet could not be troubled to specify; but it is above all due to the metre and rhythms of the piece, which Finch delightedly plays against one another.

Perhaps the opening quatrain of "The Statue" offers Finch's most skilful example of such metrical play:

> A small boy has thrown a stone at a statue,
> And a man who threatened has told a policeman so.
> Down the pathway they rustle in a row,
> The boy, the man, the policeman. If you watch you   (*Poems*, 3)

Here, the free alternation of iambs and anapests creates the primary rhythmic pattern of the poem, with infrequent unstressed syllables floating in to alter the effect now and then. It is no accident that the number of syllables in each line varies so little: Finch purposely pulls towards and away from the formal metre, but hovers close enough that the over-all effect is one of traditional form being toyed with, rather than free form being somewhat regularized. Because of the constant effect of "toying," Finch's metres reinforce the dandy images and sentiments he often wishes to capture.

Many unusual verbal techniques inform "The Statue" as well. Smith referred to "the Keystone comedy of the chase," and that comment captures with remarkable accuracy the visual effect Finch achieves. The rhythms are again responsible, but so are the diction ("rustle," not rush or run), the rhymes ("statue," "watch you"), the peppered indefinite articles ("a small boy," "a stone," "a statue," "a man," "a policeman") that switch to definites in the final line. Consider similar stylistic features in "Bees, Thistles and Sea":

> colour in seas, in the sea, in the sand and sands,
> hours of colour that melt in dissolving dunes,
> dunes before and beyond the beginning of thistles,
> and sky electric pale at the yellow of dunes,
>
> rumour of wave, waves, and a broken waving,
> field of blue grain incessantly foaming to flower,
> fire-blue under a glaze of windy glare,
> white blaze, a blue of ending, a blue smoulder.   (*Poems*, 3–4)

The repetition of "sea," "sand," "dunes," and "wave," with slight alternation by varying between plural and singular nouns, enforces the natural rhythms Finch seeks to capture: by moving from the "rumour of wave" to actual "waves," for instance, he draws the centre of the poem out of the poet's mind and into tangible reality and also creates a sensation of oscillation between the two that mirrors the oscillation of the waves and the rippling of the "dissolving dunes." Other effects of sound assist the latter purpose: "hours of colour" provides a rippling internal half-rhyme, as do "pale" and "yellow," "glaze" and "glare"; "before," "beyond" and "beginning," because of the common first syllable, provide an odd linkage of temporal ideas by sound as well as thought; heavy alliteration ([s], [d], [b], [f]) binds the whole together, the incidence of the consonants once again appearing accidental rather than contrived. All of these phonic features shore up the laborious verbal strategies of the poem and produce the feeling of encrustation that Finch so often achieves. "Bees, Thistles and Sea" is literally thick with words, a thickness increased because of their rich phonic relationships; moreover, the poem, because of such encrustation, attains a kind of timelessness, or what Smith called a "moving stillness": Finch's intense formalism at once releases and restrains the explosive potential of his imagery.

All of these stylistic features help Finch to create an authentic voice for the dandy in his poetry. In the atmosphere engendered by his heavily encrusted style, the dandy images of "Scroll Section" and "The Headmaster's Drawing Room" appear less artificial than they might, more in keeping with the poetic climate one encounters at every turn. In "Turning," we face improbable images like these:

Crystal arches leaping a crystal floor
Where like brown ghosts of fish the oak leaves lay
.......................................................

Through purple waves brown fishes swam in shoals,
Or pondered in blue depths of russet glass,
The trees were azure fountains in a race
To graze the sky or melt into its pools.[48]

But we accept their validity partly because the style Finch has adopted through so much of his work seems to support them. In poems so heavy with repetition and internal rhyme, so rich with alliteration and assonance, with such startling rhythms lounging and bouncing through traditional metres, the pigeons that "pinkly drift on smoky sails" in "Doubt's Holiday" (*Poems*, 4) or the "hippic pinions" in "The Flight That Failed" (*Poems*, 27) appear as images that have chanced together, adjective and noun colliding because of the intense stylistic play of the poems.

When Finch wishes to emphasize the Betjemanesque elegant-nostalgic rather than the Sitwellian ironic-playful, his stylistic abilities support him just as well: by softening the phonic effects slightly and restraining the jollity of his rhythms somewhat, he can capture the precision of an elegant world and render it ghostly or faintly disturbing as he sees fit:

> Here I sit in front of the fire, no light
> But that of the flames flickering on the walls
> While from the radio Petroushka rolls.
> The curtains are drawn over the winter's white.
>
> There are flowers, music is open on the grand,
> The latest books and the newest magazines
> Confuse in an orderly spate the elegant lines
> Of this room that is planned to make this life seem planned.   (*Poems*, 26)

Finch, the Betjemanesque outsider in the post-aristocratic world, is but a "week-end guest" in this refined setting.

A similar restraint of his typical style gives to "Weather" the same ironic wistfulness. An irresponsible and unkind gesture on the part of his beloved began long ago a deterioration of their love, a splendid affair that the speaker now remembers with ambivalent regret:

> ... a turning wind as we were turning,
> Blew one of your gloves onto the water's dither
> Of jarred emerald and your glove's grey hand
> Felt slowly a jewelled passage toward the galleys.
> One is no use alone, you said, and you
> Flung the rest of my gift to the lakeward malice
> Of wind ...   (*Poems*, 29)

Even in the midst of painful memory, the dandy poet dwells lovingly on the "emeralds" and other "jewels" that shone on that "Italian day"; reporting them brings a quality of comfort – the comfort of lapidary art – to his nostalgic meditations. The speaker of Finch's poetry is often such a wry, lightly sorrowing and aesthetically sensitive man; while his poetry is not as immediately similar to Betjeman's as it is to Sitwell's, one might suggest without exaggeration that the two male poets shared the spirit of a distinctive sub-culture of the 1920s. Finch's blending of the Betjemanesque with the Sitwellian moods helped him produce what may be, for sheer uniqueness, the most distinctive body of work in Canadian Modernist poetry.

The theoretical relations that exist between dandy modern poetry and its Aesthetic and Decadent prefigurations are evident in much of Finch's poetry. It is because of these original relations after all that he is so preoccupied with formal matters, since the purification of form and the removal of style from mundane moral claims, which were the cardinal themes of Aestheticism, figure to some extent in the aesthetic thought of all Modernists. We find him, therefore, concerned with the essence of art, desiring a stunning purity from each verbal effort and eager, as Smith noted, to make of art the lapidary "stillness" at the heart of all moving trouble. Thus in "The Reticent Phrase" he asks, "Aptness shall come from whence, reticent phrase,/to tinge precisely your pellucid wave?" (*Poems*, 32). He defines "The Poem" as "A shape to hold the form begun to bloom/In the intensive arbour of the brain/With flower and fruit it could not bear at home" (*Poems*, 33). In "From a Hammock" he calls up visions of the world of dandy imagination,

> That holds both vision and the viewed
> Fixed, in a soundless solitude
>
> Whose brilliant exile, for the heart,
> Is, and not makes, a work of art.[49]

Each of the three poems is concerned with the essence of art, the supreme and distant world where Form gathers enough potency to strike the mundane reader with its splendours. While it is not possible to capture that essence, as Finch's "Inmost" makes clear, nevertheless the effort of approximation is to be valued as the best endeavour of fumbling, creative man. If we are sensitive to these qualities of art, we may appreciate life as a collection of vivid and meaningful forms, which in turn will renew our sense of perception and our devotion to beauty.

Finch knows the dangers of this intense formalism: he refuses to live entirely by forms or to accept them as the sufficient medium of life, since that would reduce all meaning to gesture, all emotion to physicality. Those who live so live at their peril; in "The Painters," from *Strength of the Hills*, he chides the Dorian Grays of the world, content to cover with a formal smile all the evil they do:

A man's life is his portrait. Not till death

He sees his portrait mirrored in the past
With the first brush-stroke vivid as the last
...................................................

The impartial portrait never flatters, good,
Bad, indifferent, it renders trait for trait.

Though the painters fool themselves, they cannot fool "the painted fact/Where every overt and covert stroke is scored." Some people, however, are spared for their good efforts and, presumably, for a sense of the way in which forms may reveal the essence of things: "The many paint their lives as they have spent them./The few spend them as they would wish to paint them."[50] Thus Finch rescues his ideas from dependence on superficies by insisting on the implicit ethical relation between the surface and the substance, even if all we may know and deal with is the form of any action. In this sense, he draws back from pure Aestheticism; nevertheless, especially given the remarkable similarity between the theme of "The Painters" and that of Wilde's *Picture of Dorian Gray*, many of the ideas with which Finch struggles are the best ideas of the Aesthetic spirit.

While he demonstrates, therefore, another example of the many theoretical and practical links between Aestheticism and Canadian Modernism, he does so in an unique way, for no other poet of the Modernist generation has developed so distinctive a voice from the presuppositions of the Aesthetic enterprise. To exemplify a general quality of the English literary mainstream in this way, and yet to turn it to personal advantage, is to fulfill a significant role in a nation's literary history; and it may be that once the Aesthetic background of Canadian Modernism is recognized, the poetry of Robert Finch will be accorded rather more respect and study than the present thin bibliography of criticism of his work can provide.

*L*eo Kennedy's role in Canadian letters is by now familiar: his "discovery" by Smith and Scott while writing verses and answering letters for an "advice to the lovelorn" column, under the name of "Helen Lawrence," in *The Montreal Star*; his contribution to the second volume of the *McGill Fortnightly Review*; his editorship with Scott of its descendant, the *Canadian Mercury*; his publishing a volume of poetry (*The Shrouding*, 1933) before Smith, Scott, Klein, or Glassco had produced one; his development of a Marxist poetry throughout the Depression; and finally his contribution to *New Provinces* in 1936, the landmark publication that signalled the demise of the old school of Canadian poetry. Montreal was the centre of the initial Canadian Modernist movement, and Kennedy sat in the inner circle of that "Montreal Group"; his contribution to Canadian literature, then, while not consistent, is substantial, even seminal. The poems of *The Shrouding*, not surprisingly, show the skill and polished voice of a poet too important to be thought minor, yet lacking the staying power, perhaps the sheer adaptability, to rival the eventual recognition of his confreres.

*The Shrouding* is a difficult volume to see critically and clearly. One can hardly help but wonder at the fixation on death manifested in this work, and wonder if so constant a preoccupation does not reflect a personal condition, a quirk of Kennedy's. It is not entirely an act of critical naïveté to draw serious, even morbid conclusions about the achievement of this poet; some such judgments, one feels, have formed the implicit basis of much misleading Kennedy criticism. Succinctly, the prevailing interpretation of Kennedy's poetry runs thus:

Kennedy was a modernist who sought to replace the sentimental romanticism of the "Maple Leaf School" with objective craftsmanship. Under the influence of the metaphysical and mythic sensibilities of T.S. Eliot and Sir James Frazer, he wrote poems that seek salvation from the winter wasteland of death and oblivion by fusing Christian faith in the resurrection with the myth of renewal found in the order of nature: buried bones are like crocus bulbs awaiting the spring to sprout heavenward.[51]

Presumably the darkness of Kennedy's material – described here by David Latham – prompts a reading of his canon as wholly consumed with death and resurrection; but much, unfortunately, has been elided by such a monotone and essentially religious reading. Death and rebirth from Eliot and Frazer and the Christian resurrection from his own religious background certainly do play striking roles in Kennedy's poetry, but they are not all of it. Christian paradigms of death should not become too handy a means of approaching the text. A.J.M. Smith remarked that "*The Shrouding* is not really a book of death at all: it is a book of life ... the concentration upon physical death is a measure of the value placed upon life and sensation."[52] Kennedy obliquely confirmed this paradox: the well-known current version of his "Self Epitaph," often thought of as an epigraph to the entire volume, runs thus:

His heart was brittle;
His wits were scattered;
He wrote of dying
As though life mattered.[53]

Yet an earlier version of the poem, published in *The Canadian Forum* only a few months before the release of the bound volume, contains an interesting variant:

His heart was brittle;
  His wits were scattered;
He wrote of Life
  As though Death mattered.[54]

Kennedy's sudden reversal of the two concepts reflects the opinion of Smith concisely: to the poet as well, *The Shrouding* may have been a book of life as much as of death, and we might invalidate his own opinions (for what those are legitimately worth) if we dwell with subliminally Christian phrases on all the burials and potential resurrections that dot the book.

Far from morbid and relatively detached from Christian paradigms, Kennedy's poetry consistently weds death, one prime concern, with beauty, an equal and perhaps greater concern, and wraps them both in the decay and flux of time, in such a way as to make his poetry eerily familiar to the reader of Decadent verse. While the death-and-rebirth cycles of Eliot's *Waste Land* are indeed also apparent in any number of the poems, as Kennedy's critics have long been arguing, we should not be surprised to find other poems that speak of death chiefly in relation to the life that has ended, to whatever made that lost life valuable, its intensities, its sorrows, its beauties. (Leon Edel, it is worth remarking, noted in his Introduction to the reprint of *The Shrouding* that a true "Collected Kennedy" would be "an assemblage of his intensities.")[55] When we stand at the graveside, thoughts of rebirth and resurrection are forward-looking, and therefore essentially comforting; thoughts of the dead look backward, producing pain, poignancy, despair. Kennedy was a poet who looked intently in both directions, and the resulting poems are very different in effect.

The first section of *The Shrouding*, "Weapons Against Death," opens and concludes with a pair of contrasting poems dealing with the burial of the speaker's (perhaps Kennedy's?) parents.[56] The first poem, "Epithalamium," captures in images of the mother's burial the past love of the couple; the second, "Epithalamium Before Frost," finds comfort, even joy, by looking forward instead, to when "the first crocus hoists its yellow crest!" Hence the sombre mood of the first and the vitality of the last: the division between the two reflects the dual focus Kennedy maintains in his poems of death. In "Epithalamium," the poet is chiefly interested in the strange emotions of the dead:

> This body of my mother ...
> Is laid beside the shell of that bridegroom
> My father, who with eyes towards the wall
> Sleeps evenly; his dust stirs not at all,
> No syllable of greeting curls his lips,
> As to that shrunken side his leman slips.   (*Shroud.*, 3)

The poem is carefully focused on the burial of the mother beside the father, on their relations in the earth, and evokes with stern poignancy the initial, worldly marriage that destined them to a single grave. The poem rises from this sombre note only briefly, to remark that death retrieves "youth's fecundity" for them, whence arises an ironic "bloom of tansy from the fertile ground": only by the agency of that herb is the reader allowed to escape from the close company of the dead. The herb is not a promise of new regeneration; it is "heralded by no moan, no sound," and it carries the stark, sombre note as the poem concludes. There is no relief here: the gloom is tangible, the coffins nailed shut.

In "Epithalamium Before Frost" the poet's perspective is entirely different:

> Now that leaves shudder from the hazel limb,
> And poppies pod, and maples whirl their seed,
> And squirrels dart from private stores to slim
> The oak of acorns with excessive greed;
> And now that sap withdraws, and black geese skim
> In rigid phalanx over sedge and reed,
> And rime surmised at morning pricks the rim
> Of tawny stubble, husk and perishing weed –
> Now shall I cry Epithalamium!

The first nine lines of the sonnet gaze at the precincts of the grave, and describe a rich autumnal landscape, not with the dreariness inherent in the autumnal theme, but with a vigour captured by active verbs of motion throughout. Then the poet glances down again:

> Over the bed which your two forms have pressed;
> And bid Earth's fertile spirits stir and come
> To winter at your hearth, and make it blessed;
> Until returns the bridal trillium,
> And the first crocus hoists its yellow crest!   (*Shroud.*, 14)

From the landscape he gazes into the grave, but the poet cannot be sombre now. His vision is at this point soaked in thoughts of rebirth and revitalization from the fertility of the dead; the autumnal world merely confirms his acceptance of the processes of time, which religiously weed away all passing life and growth. The obvious affinities of these two poems should not obscure their essential opposition of perspective; that opposition characterizes the *two* significant approaches Kennedy made to death. Properly speaking, only "Epithalamium Before Frost" employs the "mythic method," by using Eliot, as Edel commented, "as Eliot used the tradition."[57] The darker "Epithalamium" is unleashed by a second perspective, one of strange marriages and deathly eroticism, the sources of which are yet to be identified. A number of features common to the poems of *The Shrouding* demonstrate that the kernel of "Epithalamium" is in the English Decadence and that that movement stands in a similar relation to Kennedy's volume as do the methods of Eliot.

For example, "Exile Endured" appears in *The Shrouding* with the following octave:

> What hand shall gather sweetbrier, and what breast
> Shall wear it proudly, does not matter here;
> And where and how it withers, I protest
> Is nothing to me, provokes no dread or fear;
> And how the ragwurt fares, and how goes back
> Into the soil's matrix, and whether grass
> Shall perish by fire or frost, or from a lack
> Of rain, does not disturb me – let it pass.   (*Shroud.*, 48)

"Sweetbrier" and "ragwurt," fairly unconventional images of vegetative beauty if we think of roses and daffodils, are actually the result of emendations from a version of the poem that appeared in *The Canadian Forum* in October 1933, entitled "I Being Afflicted." This version opens with "What hand shall pluck this hyacinth," and the fifth line reads "And how these lilies fare, and how go back":[58] an interesting example of the Modernist Kennedy correcting his more traditional roots. The "hyacinths" and "lilies" of the earlier version presumably came more readily to his mind than the "sweetbrier" and "ragwurt." Posed against the images of decay in the sestet, where "bindweed torn" and "sedge/Blistered by drought" set the tone of melancholy, these more traditional flowers create a different context, one in which traditional emblems of beauty, filled with traditional associations of decay, are made poignant in the gentle rush of time.

"Blind Girl," strangely ironic and poignant at once, captures the image of transient flowers once more in the fingers of death and, in so doing, suggests the extreme aesthetic sensitivity of the poet who records them:

Rain desists, and roses pass,
Petals drift along the grass
Beauty that you may not see
Breaks a certain part of me.   (*Shroud.*, 57)

The poet broken by beauty often chose to seize that sensation from the world of flowers, the too temporary loveliness of their petals apparently furnishing him with the exact sentiment he wished to convey. "Rite of Spring (A Fragment)" involves the floral theme in a complex consideration, now of the inevitability of human death: the poem opens with an anti-Eliotic protest that "April is no month for burials" and goes on to catalogue the month's floral splendours. In the midst of this visual riot, the poet's thoughts turn to death, the death of flowers, of sexual love, of "last year's laurels" – all of which regrets unite in a powerful evocation of the intense mysteries of life, much more than of the gloom of death:

Do not regret the hawthorn spray that mattered
And is now crumbled and piteously scattered
With heat and frost between you and its flowering.
*Do not recall the fragrance overpowering!*
Do not remember the folded hands nor the eyes
Under the violet lids, nor the April bosom
Caressed to a breathless tumult of delight –
Make no dolorous plaint for the spilled bright
Hair, or for the brow too dearly cherished –
All these have perished
With the bent throat, the lips that wooed and flattered.

It becomes apparent that Kennedy's flowers are mourned, like the heights of erotic love, as lost "moments" of intensity caught briefly

by the wandering eye. When he does finally turn the poem from
the lost life to his programmatic thoughts of decay, the flowers and
sex are wedded once more, this time with joy:

> New loves await you with every burst of lilac,
> Do not remember the dead in their lilac shrouds;
> Do not recall their lilac-scented dust!
> Strange mouths await your mouth, and other fingers
> Prepare to touch you with a touch that lingers.   (*Shroud.*, 6)

This oddly horrible *carpe diem* demonstrates the perpetual affinity in
Kennedy's mind of flowers, "strange" erotic love, and death: they
are all moments of intensity captured by the true poet at the point
of vanishing, yet are celebrated because they must vanish: transi-
toriness is the way of all things, and so must be made into poems.
    Kennedy turns the same refined sense of process on passionate
lovers as well; in "A Mirror for Lovers,"

> Paris is now a little dust
>     Shifted by every wind that blows;
> In Helen's lidless eyes are thrust
>     The black roots of a rose.   (*Shroud.*, 26)

"Grandiloquent," with its strongly Yeatsian flavour, envisions a time
when the beloved will "Have shared the cloistered reticence of
death," leaving love-struck girls who are now "seedlings in their
father's reins" to guess at her "beauty long since cold and stark"
(*Shroud.*, 9). The approach to death in these poems is, I repeat, from
the past, a time of beauty, intensity and sensuality that must now
be surrendered, not from a future resurrection that will render *this*
death (as it were) obsolete. Their common point is that the coffin is
an end, not a chance for renewal; Kennedy looks at that possibility
in other poems, yes, but it must be clear that in a good many poems
his concerns are backward-looking, death as the end of certain supreme moments:

> How shall I cry a welcome to the worm my sister?
>
> I have loved pain and pleasure overwell:
> Eyes misted with passion, the lids heavily aswoon,
> The small nails bruising the palms in ecstasy ...
> The long shuddering breath, and the ensuing quiet.

After this potent masochism-hedonism, the "Gravedigger's Rhapsody" ends flatly, no sprouting, no myths.

> Now, quietly, let sand slip over
> The varnished wood; let rubble slide and shift
> Under your heel, Gravedigger.
> Withdraw your cords, and lift
> Soberly your mattock.
>                     Remove your barrow.   (*Shroud.*, 20–1)

This stern vision constitutes a significant portion of Kennedy's death poetry: the smoothing over of life's highlights with the earth of the grave. While he has chosen occasionally to exploit the Eliotic idea of cyclical rebirth, in which all things may come to their second season, Kennedy has shown a marked propensity for dealing with the utter end of beauty, ecstasy, passion as well; which, while it no doubt appealed to some portion of his mind, was not the principal source of Eliot's interest in the burial theme.

Kennedy's attraction to the theme appears rather to have had sources earlier than the Modernist. The first three stanzas of his "Perennial" consist of directions to nature's undertaker, who prepares the earth each year for its passage from winter's death into spring:

> With plaited strands of April grass
> Bind up this heart that splits and bleeds
> As each sharp lilac leaf unsheathes.
>
> Twist growing tendrils round the wound
> That gapes anew at each thin sound
> Of water slurring underground.   (*Shroud.*, 10)

Clearly we are expected to pick up the allusions to burial preparations in the passage, and to liken it to such other Kennedy passages as this from "Gravedigger's Rhapsody":

> Lid the flat staring eye, as pale as ice;
> Bind up the fallen jaw; then fold the palms
> Decorously upon the breast; and thrice
> Intone the mass for purgatorial alms.   (*Shroud.*, 18)

There is little reason to question the distinctly modern tone of irony and quiet objectivity in the poems; but consider similar recitations from the nineteenth century:

> Upon the eyes, the lips, the feet,
>   On all the passages of sense,
> The atoning oil is spread with sweet
>   Renewal of lost innocence.   (Dowson, PW, 77)

Thus Ernest Dowson, in his "Extreme Unction," prefigured the ritualistic motions of the Kennedy poems. Of course, his speech is less direct, his rhythms more languorous, his diction more abstract, which makes him the Decadent and Kennedy ultimately the modern poet. Yet it is interesting that "Extreme Unction" and "Perennial" move towards not dissimilar resolutions, in which each poet prophesies for the corpse, in the months after burial, a resurrection of the soul. In Dowson it is a religious question, clearly:

> Yet, when the walls of flesh grow weak,
>   In such an hour, it well may be,
> Through mist and darkness, light will break,
>   And each anointed sense will see.   (PW, 77)

Dowson's tentative affirmation of the resurrection ("it well may be" falling rather short of faith) is a reminder that the Decadents also attempted some vision of rebirth, especially after their various conversions; although the distinctive uneasiness of such religious poetry does little to mitigate the essentially earthbound and disillusioned quality of their "graveyard" poems. In Kennedy's "Perennial" the burial is only metaphoric, but the result is the same: "Then set the heart aside to heal./It will not feel the shock of pain/Until the seasons shift again" (Shroud., 10). The shift of the seasons brings about the hint, and no more, of resurrection.

   The overlapping of Dowson's "Extreme Unction" and Kennedy's "Perennial" and "Gravedigger's Rhapsody" helps to clarify the conditions in Kennedy's poetry that vary from the critical consensus. His fascination with beauty and ecstasy, passing into silence and corruption, parallels similar concerns in the poetry of the Decadents. The ritual of burial is certainly a favourite of Decadent poetry, one worth remarking in order to see Kennedy's "death fixation" in its proper historical perspective. All that distinguishes the poetry of Kennedy from the Decadent versions of a similar theme is his objectivity, his suspension in most poems of any personal feeling for the dead; whereas Dowson drips with his own regrets, and Lionel

Johnson frequently loses objectivity because (for him) death represents a particular "phase" of the rounded Catholic life, the means by which the devout are released to God. Kennedy's greater objectivity and lesser religiosity account for certain stylistic differences: he is less willing to lull and hypnotize and desires both the sharper phonetic effect and the more painful visualization. The Decadent fixation on visual qualities of frailty and pallor is less noticeable in Kennedy, although he does refer to such funereal items as "the frail/ Blossoms of candles sepulchrally pale" (*Shroud.*, 29), "frail aspen hands" that "swoon" (*Shroud.*, 53), and "more/Star-candles than one might count, fragile and white" (*Shroud.*, 55). Furthermore, Dowson and Johnson are generally uninterested in images of physical corruption, whereas Kennedy can sometimes take the interest too far for the sake of subtlety – a predilection that he himself traces to the rather bloodthirsty drama of the English Renaissance.[59] Nevertheless, a glance at Baudelaire's "Une Charogne" reveals that visions of putrefaction were not entirely alien to the Decadent sensibility.[60]

But it is not a question of exact "parallels" between the funereal poems of the Decadents and those of Kennedy; rather he brings Modernist habits (objectivity, direct speech, greater irony) to a tradition of "graveyard" verse that the Decadents had themselves inherited and extended so that it might incorporate beauty, intensity and frail childhood, their own preoccupations. Kennedy's Modernist doctrine was insufficient to swerve him from these Decadent interests entirely; hence we discover in his poems an unique mixture of Modernist stylistic premises and Decadent spirituality.

With at least one thematic link to the Decadents established, we will not be surprised to find their other favoured themes working in Kennedy's poetry as well. While he is not the kind of poet to address "beauty" with the tone of Call or Tracy, his concern with beauty and its link to death will already be apparent, in such poems as "Blind Girl" and "A Mirror for Lovers." "The Squall," similarly, offers this grim vision:

In weeded reaches under sea are laid
The numbered bones of men, who, unafraid
Discerned the beginning and the end of all
Wisdom, found in the measured, ultimate fall
Of water, their lost clarity of soul.

The corpses give rise to the following inevitable prayer: "Let it be said that Death was beautiful" (*Shroud.*, 32). The Aesthetic concern expressed here is so strong in Kennedy that this line might serve as an epigraph for his entire collection, more aptly than "Self Epitaph," which is less seriously intended. Why should death be beautiful? Because only with beauty in our minds can we hush our fears of death; only by attending to the details of death with the Aesthete's care can we affirm some triumph over it, to the end of expressing our "clarity of soul," our ability to transcend the physical fate of the body.

This is repeated with triumph in Kennedy's "Lament for Summer":

> And now the geese are flown, and now the river
>   Is low, and on its banks brown nettles stand
> Rasping their shrivelled, reedy stalks together
>   While dead leaves pace an eerie saraband
> ..............................................................
>
> Make your lament for swallows skimming lightly;
>   For bull-frogs mouthing lyrics brief and shrill;
> For orange poppies, rain drops falling brightly ...
>   For all the beauty winter cannot kill.   (*Shroud.*, 11)

Compare the imagery and mood of Kennedy's poem with Lionel Johnson's "Harvest," to highlight the Decadence of his manner:

>        ... the flame
> Of delicate poppies, rich and frail, became
> Wan dying weed; convolvulus, astray
> Out from its hedgerows into the field,
> In clinging coils of leaf and tender bloom,
> Shared with the stalks it clung and clasped, their doom.

Kennedy's acclaim of "all the beauty winter cannot kill" precisely parallels the movement of Johnson's poem to its conclusion, "Wherein fresh winds might wave a fresh year's yield."[61] This is not to say by any means that the pursuit of beauty enables us to triumph over death; Kennedy is too modern, too realistic, for such pretensions. The "beauty long since cold and stark" of "Grandiloquent" makes pretty clear the inevitability of death and its corruption; but by searching for the beauty in all process, in Death the ultimate process, we alleviate or derail our fears: we understand death as an ultimate achievement in the search for Aesthetic heightening. This is why (to conclude the point) "Time That Wears Granite

Thin" acknowledges the inevitable triumph of death, but still finds
reasons for exultation:

> Out of this passion and these fears
>    We make an ecstasy,
> Shall sing defiance from the grass
>    When we have ceased to be,
>
> Shall name your beauty on a page,
>    And praise your careful talk,
> And plait a legend from your hair
>    And memorize your walk.[62]

Perhaps it is just such a rarefied sense of female beauty that motivated the little-known poems Kennedy contributed to the second
volume of the *McGill Fortnightly Review*: "Song" therein describes a
beautiful woman (without the least thought of death), drawing her
into a fairy-world of dandy imagery:

> So in some verses one will bring
> Blind pagans sing and dryads dance,
> While an elf trips:
> Besotted Bacchus pours his wines
> In cups of gold from fairy mines
> Wooing your lips.

The absence of the deathly note for which Kennedy is known is a
noteworthy feature of "Song" and of his other two poems in the
journal; "The Oldest Song" closes on a nostalgic Arthurian note after
opening on this nostalgic Romantic one:

> Because your maiden kiss stirred old desire
> When banished memory fumbled at a door;
> The woman heart that seemed a lesser thing
> Called gravely on the wind from a far shore:
>
> I have come home from my dim wanderings
> With tattered sails upon an evening sea.[63]

After a string of rather disjointed thoughts and images, Kennedy
concludes, "You do not know ... but you are Lyonesse." "Romance"
continues the theme: "High Arthur lived at Camelot/When all the

world was young." After experiencing these legends of wonder and might, the poet's unconscious memory is stirred:

So does a man drop heavy head
On yellowed book, and drowse:
Dreaming of good, forgotten things,
Beauty and truth, and Dragon's wings.[64]

The echo of Keats is provocative of further thought. Kennedy's early Arthurian impulse leaves him none too far from the Keats-enamoured Aesthetic poets of the previous century: W.E. Collin long ago admitted that Kennedy's "Daughter of Leda" "without the Myth [i.e., the Eliotic mythic method] would be a Pre-Raphaelite exercise."[65] The *Fortnightly* poems make clear that the Arthurian interest in Kennedy predates his "death fixation," so his interest in figures of folklore as emblems of beauty and passion developed quite independently of, in fact much earlier than, the fascination he later manifested with death. This is merely to say that when we notice a theme of beauty and intensity in Kennedy, we ought not to treat it as a necessary offshoot or inevitable development of the death-principle: on the contrary we must recognize the independent themes of his work that may, if anything, be thought the cause as much as the effect. It is worth remarking that, if one wishes to cast about for the secondary theme of *The Shrouding* (assuming the primary to be death), one can do no better than to suggest beauty itself; which helps us to understand the real complexity of Kennedy's attempt in the volume.

For *The Shrouding*, as Smith said, is not a book of death but of life. Its end is to heighten our appreciation of life, primarily of its beauties, by forcible contemplation of death and the imminent end of all of our aesthetic sensibilities. It is only understandable on these terms and can only be appreciated as more than a quaint or morbid exercise if one understands the characteristically Decadent impulses that also inform the work. Although we still hesitate to admit it, Decadence was not a refusal of all moral thought, but an outcry upon the kinds of moral thought prevalent in the Victorian period,[66] and to exploit the conventions of Decadent literature, even in the 1930s, was still to offer a philosophical position, to suggest alternatives. When Kennedy repudiated *The Shrouding* in later life perhaps he no longer understood this, or perhaps he never had.[67] But the fact remains that *The Shrouding* is redeemed from morbidity because of its intense appreciation of beauty, and that, whether conscious or not, is an Aesthetic stratagem.

The long "Exit Without Sennet" helps to enforce the import of these suggestions. Nowhere does Kennedy more clearly express his opinion of the excesses of death in *The Shrouding*: by exploring the thoughts of a female suicide as she waits for poison to work, Kennedy aligns himself squarely with those who recognize the beauty available to them in the world and against those who turn to death as any promise of release or redemption from suffering. She knows that after she has died

> Lilacs would show again beside the wall
> And form brave clumps in hedges ... daffodils
> Would nod and curtsey in the passing wind,
> Or stand up sparse and tall upon the world ...
> Willows would sway ... frail aspen hands would swoon.
> Time would go on without a pause, the hours
> Heap one upon another with the same
> Persistence ... days grow into weeks, months, years
> Of studied anguish ... only she would not
> Be here to watch the lilacs burst and bloom.   (*Shroud.*, 53)

As the poison works within her, these thoughts gain force and make her death more a torture by aesthetic regret than by spasms of pain.

> What had she done that she must put away
> The rapture and the loveliness, the smell
> Of rain-wet lilac and the shouting birds!
> What had she done that she must go into
> The moist black soil and lie beneath a stone!
> .........................................................
> Dear God, to leave it now!   (*Shroud.*, 54)

No sentimentalism mars the poem; the woman dies, but not before regretting desperately that she had failed to perceive the beauty of life. It is quite apparent that if she had done so, if she had seen life with the eyes of the dying, she would not have killed herself, but learned her aesthetic lesson. "Exit Without Sennet" captures cleanly, then, the burden of the entire book: appreciate these beauties of the world while you can, for you will surely come to this corruption.

For the Modernist principles apparent in *The Shrouding* there is little need to account. Kennedy's Modernism has long been taken for granted, first by his cohorts of the *Fortnightly* and *New Provinces* and later by the few critics who have attended to his poems. His own explanation of the Modernist bias of his contemporaries is typical of the opinions of all the young men and women who banded together in the 1920s and 1930s to change the face of Canadian literature:

The pot-bellied, serene Protestantism of Victorian England which still flourished in Canada during the spruce youth of Edward, and which underlay Lampman's spiritual make-up, causes us [the moderns] to chafe. We are impatient of reading into the face of nature the conservative policies of an Anglican omnipotence. We are principally concerned with the poetry of ideas and emotional conflicts. We have detected ... that all is decidedly not right with the world; we suspect that God is not in his Heaven. Uncertain of ourselves, distressed by our inability to clarify our relationship to these and comparative issues, we do not feel superior to circumstances at all.[68]

So the Kennedys reacted against the peaceful conservatism of post-war Canada and turned to a poetry that would reflect new uncertainties. That is the theory of Canadian Modernism, at any rate; yet it will be clear to the reader that in Kennedy's case the turn was rather to other old certainties, the certainty of death and corruption, the necessity of beauty, the struggle against time. He addresses these not as a modern might – by redefining beauty according to new principles of perception, or by taking individual death as a symbol of the collective spiritual death of the Western world – but rather by postulating a higher beauty that will ease the sorrow of death and can, pursued whole-heartedly, survive the passing of years, by dwelling in the clear souls of men.

One naturally wishes to account definitively for this variation from the program of Modernism in Kennedy's poetry, but it is not a simple task: "Influences acknowledged by Kennedy include Sherwood Anderson, Lawrence, Willa Cather (on style); Wyndham Lewis, T.S. Eliot and Barbusse (on thought)."[69] Patricia Morley's list is not meant to be exhaustive: Kennedy's preface to the re-issue of *The Shrouding* acknowledges other debts, to Donne, Marlowe, Webster, Marvell, Shakespeare, Ronsard, Villon, Frazer, Dickinson, Robinson, Millay, Sitwell, and Yeats, as well as to the other members of the Canadian Modernist movement. (Smith's influence upon Kennedy is self-evident, especially in a poem like Kennedy's "Words for a Resurrection"; that his influence might well have encouraged Kennedy's Aestheticism will become clear in chapter 6.) This impressive list is Kennedy's version of his development, of course, and need not be assumed to be accurate or to exhaust the list of influences upon his writings. It is therefore not too disturbing to find Kennedy making no mention of Aesthetic or Decadent poets. Perhaps it is significant in reverse that *The Shrouding*'s acknowledgments rigorously exclude any artists of the second half of the nineteenth century in England: that period represented the "enemy" to Kennedy, yet it was specifically Victorianism "serene Protestantism," that he wished to overthrow, making no particular references to "effeminacy of style" or "questionable morals," the usual lines of attack against the various schools of Aestheticism.

Indeed, the only reference in his writings to those schools is by no means hostile. In his essay on Archibald Lampman, Kennedy refers to the Decadents as one source whereby Lampman might have sharpened his poetry and purified his style: "I am not indignant because his sonnets give no intimation that he ever heard of his European contemporaries, of the dazzling, decadent yellow book crew, nor of the Americans ... But I do say that, since his own personal aesthetic contribution was insufficient for the purposes of art, he should have broadened his canvas, and borrowed from sources that would have benefitted him more."[70] Kennedy, like Knister, acknowledges the limited salutary effect of the principles of Aestheticism and suggests that Lampman should have welcomed them for the health of his poetry. This is no evidence that Kennedy knew the Decadents particularly well, but it suggests that whatever he knew about them did not utterly alienate him as an artist.

Because with Kennedy's early poetry we enter that part of Canadian literary history where the most radical change came about – in the halls of McGill University and in the streets of Montreal – it is worth sketching in a preliminary way the world in which he found himself as a young poet. Kennedy's own image of the times strikes a typically cheeky note: "The Duke of York Hotel, within easy walking distance of a certain university, is primarily an undergraduate pot-house, a refuge for the ragged and the raccoon-coated. It is in the pleasant atmosphere of such taverns that the doctors and lawyers, architects and engineers of tomorrow forgather, drinking cold beer, talking about their mistresses and their work."[71] The slightly affected voice of the debonair young parvenu should be a reminder that this generation was formed during the 1920s, the Jazz Age, the decade of flappers with shorter dresses and shorter hair, the boom years after the First World War that encouraged a life so high off the hog as to make the tragedy of the Depression seem more a moral punishment than a gross international miscalculation. The *esprit* of the time should not be thought to have passed by Kennedy, Scott, Smith, and the others of the *Fortnightly*: they were on the contrary the droll intellectuals of their liberated decade, certainly not so serious as some portraitists would make them. Beside the graduation picture of Smith in the university yearbook for 1925, for example, where each graduand contributed his favourite expression, Smith's is revealing: *"Isn't she darling!"*[72] What else should we expect of young men with lively minds but that they should seize the delights of their age, engage in its manners of wit and dress and dispute? A second very insignificant piece of Canadian literary history highlights the point: in Kennedy's early letters to Smith, made public in the A.J.M. Smith Collection at Trent University, the tone is the bantering tone of young man to man and perhaps reaches no better heights than when Kennedy, in a moment of eye-rolling abandon, calls Smith, the stern doctor of high Canadian Modernism, "my darling."[73] It is the language of the bloods of their day. Of course they were serious about literature and what they wanted to do with it, but it helps students of the period to remember that these young men were also entirely of their time, and that their early poems were written at a cultural moment when affected diction, overwrought prose styles and droll forms of address were all the rage in the society in which they moved.

The image is important, because it is too easy to imagine the Canadian Modernist revolution occurring in times of high seriousness, when Victorian philosophy and morality needed throwing out and replacing with clean, hard, passionate modernity. This is not the case. There is never only one wind blowing in the literary air: while the elitist traditionalism of Eliot and the technical hygiene of Pound certainly reached these young men and altered them for the better, so too the airs of the Decadence were about: the trial of Wilde was not far behind them, and nothing is forgotten so utterly in a mere three decades. The 1920s tried in fact to recapture the playful abandon of the early 1890s, with their dazzling ladies and elegant wits, and it is in that context as well that Modernism reached Canada. We should not be entirely surprised, therefore, to find in Kennedy certain touches of the Decadence, no more than we are surprised to find his manipulation of certain elements of Eliot's *Waste Land*.

There is no determining proof that Kennedy was directly influenced by Aestheticism. His early medievalism could have come straight from the Victorianism he later derided and might have had no direct link to the more sensuous Aesthetic medievalism of Rossetti and Morris. His interest in Helen and the myth of Leda might have come from Yeats without any absorption of early Yeatsian Aestheticism. He acknowledges no influence from any member of the Aesthetic pantheon and cannot as yet be proven firmly to have had more than a passing acquaintance with its principles or its poetry.

Yet we find in his poetry that passion for beauty, that valuing of intensity as a "weapon against death," and that fascination with death as process that we also find in the poetry of the English Decadents. Even without direct allusions, the parallel stratagems, rhythms, and intonations suggest powerfully that the earlier movement had touched the young Canadian poet. Furthermore, it is only by welcoming these parallels that we can rescue *The Shrouding* from treatment as a morbid exercise, as a less than healthy fixation on death and the eternal.

*I* have not given time or attention to the obvious traditionalism of all the poets discussed in this chapter. They have all employed traditional forms of verse, with fairly conventional patterns of rhyme and little variation from regular metrical structure. Perhaps in the poetry of Call and Grove such traditionalism is unsurprising, given their ages, but the "Wild Grape" section of Call's *Acanthus and Wild Grape* at least attempted to rectify the situation, whether it succeeded or not. The role of Grove as major Canadian modern novelist casts his "Dirge" in a rather more dubious light; perhaps we expect modern poetics of him as well, yet the major poem he has left behind is purely traditional, and less than brilliantly so.

But with Tracy, Mackay, Finch, and Kennedy, another question is raised. Since it has been the business of criticism to make of these poets the middle-guard of the Modernist generation, their heavy traditionalism should trouble us more. Why have they resisted the formal opportunities offered by English Modernism? Where in these poets is the imitation of the form, rather than the sentiments, of that Modernism? Only in Finch is there a quality of playfulness that might have led to the fruition of a real anti-traditionalism, but even he resolves his play into the styles of dandy poetry that were popularized in the 1920s, not into the Pound-Eliot formal tradition. Kennedy's and Mackay's volumes perpetuate a staunch traditionalism, against all the claims of modern practice. Even without any consideration at all of the Aesthetic qualities of their poetry, the critic would seem to be forced to a question which has not yet been answered (hardly even asked): why was Canadian Modernism resistant to the more radical forms created in world Modernism? If the question is asked, and it must be, increasingly, recognition of the Aesthetic inheritance developed by these poets provides one obvious answer.

These thoughts and their implications will be held suspended, however, until further chapters are available to broaden and deepen our perspective. For now it is enough to notice that the lesser poets of the Canadian Modernist generation reveal so pervasive an Aestheticism in their various works that the entire balance of the way we talk about their primary decade must begin to shift. If Ross and Knister manifest a developed strain of Impressionism to balance their Imagism, if Finch, Call, Grove, Mackay, and Kennedy explore in traditional verse implications familiar already to the Decadents of the nineteenth century, and if Scott, Smith, and Glassco confirm this odd feature of Canadian Modernism, how may we speak accurately of this complex generation?

For now, let us acknowledge that in the war between Modernism and Victorianism in Canada there was a third and independent force, an Aesthetic group that offered a prior resistance to Victorian morality and practice and that could encourage more significant poets in Canada who had marked the same targets. As we should expect in this transitional decade, the Aestheticism in these six poets is not invariable: Call leans more obviously towards the Aesthetic than does Kennedy, who displays qualities of the more Decadent manner, which are turned to advantage in the dandyism of Finch; moreover none of the younger poets is so entirely Aesthetic or Decadent that his modernity is quite eclipsed. But because the Modernist qualities in these poets are often acclaimed and the Aesthetic obscured, it is clearly necessary to dwell on the latter in order to restore the balance a little. It may be more impressive for Canada's place in world Modernism to emphasize the ways in which poets adopted Eliot's or Pound's or the later Yeats's principles of poetry, but surely that has been sufficiently recognized to allow further exploration: we simply must seek, in Aestheticism or elsewhere, the sources of those elements in their poetry which are not Modernist, so that we may understand not their successes or contemporary qualities only, but rather the real truths of their art, and the complexities of their common purpose.

Note that Aestheticism has by no means weakened the poems here examined, but provided them rather with certain central assumptions or preoccupations, indeed motivated their creation altogether in certain cases. The general traditionalism and formalism of such poets as Finch, Mackay, and Kennedy are not weaknesses of their poetry, inappropriate to their place in literary chronology, but strengths: each poet was conscious of his craft, and traditional forms seem to have suited admirably the Aesthetic perceptions each has wished to convey. Roy Daniells, writing of Robert Finch, makes the following enlightening remark: "Nous avons supposé dans ces pages que la littérature canadienne a souffert dans le passé de trop peu d'attention à la forme et que les poètes qui montrent d'excellentes qualités de forme devraient être examinés avec un respect tout spécial à ce moment de notre histoire culturelle" (96). Daniells's perceptive comment has been a covert guiding assumption of this chapter. If it is their formalism that distinguishes these poets from mainstream Modernism, it now seems a justifiable thesis that Aestheticism lay behind that formalism and gave them a set of themes, symbols and styles with which to enrich it. They are different poets, and to be respected on different grounds; but if they are to be thought of as a "generation" at all, it can only be because each one of them faced and accepted the potent precursors of Aestheticism and Decadence.

CHAPTER FOUR

# "Brian Tuke" and "Bernard March": The Early Decadent Scott

The generally propounded image of the poetry of F.R. Scott is one of biting satire, wry social commentary, tough-minded metaphysical speculations upon the meaning and purpose of the human species, and accurate Canadian landscapes, all of which meld and enrich one another in the canon of a thinker, a wit, and a prophet. Robin Skelton states that "Scott, like Donne, like Carew, and like Marvell, speaks as a complete man; his passions involve his intelligence, and his intelligence gives rise to passion."[1] Thus Scott is placed with the metaphysical poets, which leads us to expect from his verse startling images "yoked by violence together," "wit," pun, paradox, slashing ironies, invariable evidence of the "complete man" speaking. The barbs of these techniques are turned toward a variety of goals, for "Scott is a satirist and social critic whose tone ranges from amusement through scorn to cold rage. His career as a poet does not show development so much as an increase and diversification of targets."[2] Thus Munro Beattie in *The Literary History of Canada* encourages us to think of Scott's poetry as a weapon against the large global injustices which it is the poet's duty to shatter. Similarly, Sandra Djwa in *The Oxford Companion to Canadian Literature* speaks of Scott's first efforts as having been "targeted" against the outworn tendencies of Canadian verse: "As a satirist in the late twenties and early thirties he helped battle an outworn Canadian Romanticism in order to introduce the 'new poetry' ... In 1925 he collaborated with Smith and Leon Edel in founding *The McGill Fortnightly Review*, an iconoclastic journal of modernist literature and opinion. Scott's attacks on the orthodox were to range widely, but his first broadside was launched against the old poetry and its traditional forms" ("Scott," 743). All of these general opinions help us to recognize the determination and antinomianism of Scott, and to maintain the prevailing image of his poetry as vigorous jousting with wicked giants. With undeniable justice we are encouraged to find in Scott's poetry evidence of the self-deprecating White Knight who has given much of himself to his country.

Since complete recognition of the poet is our goal, however, we are naturally curious to know how such a complex, dedicated character was formed and what the early influences and studies were that led to so remarkable a personality. Sketches of the early years of Scott are rare, so Sandra Djwa's recent biography, *The Politics of the Imagination: A Life of F.R. Scott*, is of invaluable assistance to the critic of his poetry; biographical details have also been scattered throughout the occasional memoirs of his contemporaries, permitting a newly comprehensive assessment of Scott's early development. In preliminary sketches Djwa had already delineated some of the characteristics of the young man: "Here is the kernel of the twenties personality: the serious young man characterized by all of the high moral idealism that accompanied the Canadian response to the Great War. Scott in the twenties is very much in transition: still reflecting the sententious young man he had been, changing before our eyes to a bright young man about town, who wrote debunking verse, condemned Montreal graft, and resented Canadian colonialism."[3] She comments later in the same article that "the sententious young man" expressed himself in Georgian poetry: "it was during the following years, 1926, 1927, and 1928, that Scott was to change from a Georgian poet to a modern poet" (18). In *The Oxford Companion*, Djwa would render this shift slightly differently: "Scott's own career as a poet exemplifies the transition from a Victorian Romanticism to the modern" ("Scott," 744). Elsewhere again Djwa writes that "Scott, who had entered the twenties as a conventional young Victorian, an anglophile, and an aesthete, had become by 1927 a modern, a nationalist, and a socialist."[4] She has now fleshed out these varying conclusions in her biography, repeating the influence of Tennyson and the Georgians[5] and tracing in greater detail the conflict the young man experienced as a Rhodes Scholar at Oxford, between his participation in the Oxford of the "hearties" and his attraction to that of the "aesthetes." The latter gave him a way of looking at Canada upon his return that was not to the country's credit: "Until Canada gets some love of beauty," he wrote in his journal, "her soul will not be right" (Djwa, "Scott: A Canadian," 14).

In Djwa's interpretation in the biography, however, the Aesthetic position would never be wholly embraced by Scott because "it was not compatible with Scott's primary aim. He wanted to be 'great,' but to achieve greatness through the Christian way of service to others" (*PI*, 63). She therefore delineates in impressive detail the development over the next decade of Scott's dedication to social reform, and allows the Aesthetic mood of Oxford to recede into Scott's (and the reader's) idyllic memory. In keeping with this interpretation, Djwa devotes the bulk of a later chapter to a rather slanted sketch of Scott's participation in the *McGill Fortnightly Review* from 1925 to 1927. She credits Smith with an enormous influence over Scott's poetic tastes, as have Scott himself and many others, and presents to her readers a collection of Scott's *Fortnightly* poetry that confirms her belief that the Aestheticism he had flirted with at Oxford had been fairly well cast off by the time he began writing poetry in earnest. The Scott poems she draws from the journal are satiric and Modernistic and so are taken to confirm his turn away from a detached and Aesthetic mood toward a life of social observation and agitation.

Despite the thoroughness of Djwa's treatment, it is at this juncture that she begins to simplify to my mind the process of Scott's literary development, primarily by elaborating only those *Fortnightly* poems that substantiate her interpretation of Scott's socialist conversion. Other Scott poems in the journal reveal a distinct Aestheticism that suggests that the tension of his Oxford days carried well over into the days of the *Fortnightly* and was not so easily dismissed by the Modernism of Smith. These poems tell against Djwa's interpretation of the *Fortnightly* and of Scott's early literary experimentation, and force a re-assessment of the "sententious" and "conventional" young man who nevertheless returned to Canada a "budding aesthete."

Some glimpse of this less familiar Scott may be enjoyed in the various memoirs of Leon Edel, which offer a lively vision of Scott and the young men of the McGill days, emphasizing their youth and vigour rather than their vision and sense of high purpose. Although his memory occasionally lapses, Edel effectively captures the *esprit* of the McGill Movement simply for having been in the various homes, apartments and offices where the *Fortnightly* was engineered. His image of Scott is human and real: "With his sharply etched face he seemed to me as if painted by Holbein; he was an attentive listener, he laughed easily and pleasantly, and he possessed a sharp thrust of verbal wit. He always found some phrase in the [*McGill*] *Daily* or the downtown press, some platitude in a speech, and turned it into the stuff of irony and paradox. He seemed to think in epigrams."[6] Edel gives a clue to the kind of platitude Scott loved to attack when he comments that "Like Bloomsbury – and why not compare ourselves with it? – our main delight was in needling the stuffed shirts, the Victorians."[7] He nevertheless acknowledges that "We lived among belated Victorians; we were touched with Victorianism ourselves" ("McGill Modernized," 113).

Edel distinguishes another shade of the question when he contrasts the individual interests of Scott and Smith: "Scott brought to McGill his sense of the old world, but even more his deeply rooted Canadianism and his belief in the country's liberal future. He was two or three years older than Smith, who was less dedicated to social change than to a vigorous aestheticism and the life of poetry" ("Warrior," 8). Perhaps then Scott's Victorian confidence in the possibility of social reform pitted him genially against Smith's Aesthetic concern with the advancement of art. If we accept this version of events, what must we conclude when we acknowledge with Djwa that Scott's understanding of poetry was minimal prior to his encountering Smith and that it was the efforts of Smith that first opened his eyes to the possibilities of modern (not Aesthetic) poetry?[8] Should we assume that Edel's dates were askew? or that Smith's first preachments to Scott were not about modern poetry after all? Moreover, if Smith's "vigorous aestheticism" challenged Scott and his belief in a "liberal future," how did it sit with Scott's own qualities of Aestheticism, with which by Djwa's account he returned from Oxford? A return to Edel's version is not much help: " ... Smith in turn converted Scott from *The Idylls of the King* and sonnets to the free personal style of the moderns, with the results we all know" ("Warrior," 11). Further mystification: was Scott still writing Tennysonian verse when he met Smith? or Georgian? or Aesthetic? all three? and was Scott's Modernist turn the result of the meeting?

Evidently Scott's friendly disputes with Smith over poetics form an obscure but pivotal point in Canadian literary history. Edel confirms that "Smith and Scott fought, amiably of course, over poetry"[9] and that "There was an endless debate between him and Smith about the Georgian poets. Scott was beginning to emerge from his Tennysonian self" ("Warrior," 11). These extended brotherly battles provide, in a general sense, a useful point of information: too often Smith's Modernist conversion of Scott is reported as though it had been instantaneous, and Scott had been utterly willing to learn from the younger poet and abandon his old ways. Such an analysis presumes a clear opposition between the two and an absence of conviction on Scott's part. This was evidently not the case. To extrapolate carefully from the various reports, their friendship instead included a long discussion of the merits of Modernism (and some form of Aestheticism) as against those of Victorianism and/or Georgianism; not Smith on one side and Scott on the other, but with various points of likely agreement (certain tenets of Aestheticism) and outright disagreement (*Idylls of the King*). We have only to think of our own discussions with friends to realize that few of them progress between black and white, but rather oscillate between various positions, now one, now the other seizing the argument's high ground; now reaching consensus, now shattering it with an incendiary phrase. After such reflection it seems evident that we have not yet sought sufficient accuracy in our rendering of this significant literary debate, which was the basis of an artistic friendship with massive repercussions for the literature of a young, largely unformed culture. The friendship can hardly be sufficiently valued in the history of that literature, nor should the learning and insight of Scott be slighted; it is less than critical to presume that he was smoothly defeated in his poetic preconceptions by Smith, or that he instantly abandoned whatever artistic habits he had imported from England.

Scott's own public version of the first years of his writing life does not much clarify the issues involved in these various fragments of biography. He admits to an utter ignorance of modern poetry prior to his meeting Smith, but casts little light on the nature of his own previous poetry: "I had soaked myself in every form of European culture which, as a student, I could find and afford; I bought the Oxford editions of the English poets in their collected volumes, bound in proper dark blue; I knew something of the Georgians from the little anthology called *Poems of Today*, whose second series came out as late as 1922; but I had not read a word of Frost or Williams or Pound or Eliot, or even heard of *Poetry* (Chicago)" ("Smith: A Memoir," 78). The specific reference to the Georgian poets makes it seem not unlikely that they were indeed early influences upon his poetry; yet later in the same address he notes that when he met Smith he (Scott) "was then twenty-six years old, and encrusted with the *Victorians*, particularly Tennyson" ("Smith: A Memoir," 80; emphasis added). A journal entry from the early 1920s confirms the latter statement, when Scott expresses a greater wish to be Tennyson "than any other poet" (Djwa, "Scott: A Canadian," 19).

At least the terms of these confusions will by now be clear. Scott was writing Tennysonian Victorian *or* Aesthetic *or* Georgian verse prior to his meeting with Smith; he was a conventional young Victorian *or* an Aesthete and epigrammatist; he deplored the lack of beauty in Canadian culture *or* desired to effect political change to improve the human lot of struggling compatriots. Given our modern sense of the infinite complexity of human nature, it is tempting to suggest that Scott was all of these things at once, a claim not incompatible with his well-known breadth of vision and intellectual energy. Where the literary critic should not surrender, however, is in the first tangle, for Victorian poetry simply is not Aesthetic poetry, nor is either of these the same as Georgian poetry: and it is not critically sound (at least not without evidence) to suggest that Scott was a relaxed practitioner of all three indifferently, before he met Smith. What then was the nature of Scott's early poetry? Where lay his allegiance in the days before 20 October 1925, when he first met Smith ("Smith: A Memoir," 79)?

There is obviously no final answer available except in the poems themselves. In the biographical sketches from which the above issues have been drawn, the poems, the point and source of all this speculation, are rarely consulted; Edel does not present himself as a literary critic of Scott but a memoirist, and Djwa asserts Scott's Tennysonian, Georgian and Aesthetic influences but quotes from the *McGill Fortnightly Review* only those poems that show his earliest Modernism. Since this approach has led to palpable confusion, the opposite tack would seem to be demanded: simply to look at the poems themselves and draw conclusions that may be supported by our new biographical knowledge of Scott's first mature decade.

Scott's public poetic career began with three poems from his years at Oxford as a Rhodes scholar (1920 to 1923). The Oxford journal *Isis* published his "Lament, after Reading the Results of Schools," which reappeared revised in the *McGill Fortnightly Review* as "Sonnet: On Reading the Results of the Examinations," "The Problem," reprinted in *The Collected Poems of F.R. Scott*, and "To R.P.S.," left to its obscurity in the *Isis* pages. The first two are light verse, comic recitations of the perils of scholarship at Oxford, with echoes of Keats and allusions to various icons of Aestheticism and incidents of European history. None of the poems gives much promise of the career to come, and they are little more than the inevitable student efforts of an apparently cheerful young man; nevertheless, a discussion of "The Problem," which highlights some useful biographical material, will be significant in a later part of the chapter.

"Song of May and Virtue," his next appearance in print, is a more serious effort and shows the beginnings of Scott's later penchant for translation; it appeared in the *McGill Daily Literary Supplement*, the first of A.J.M. Smith's personal vehicles for publication and infiltration, and it was responsible for their later meeting and joining together under the *Fortnightly* banner:

There is no lady fair and gay
Whose beauty does not fade from view:

Care, age and illness bring decay
On that which once most beauteous grew:
But nought can soil the being who
Shall be my light till life is o'er,
And as her beauty is thus true
My love will last for evermore.[10]

Smith was sufficiently intrigued by this submission from an unknown law student at McGill to invite him to participate in a new
literary venture that became the *McGill Fortnightly Review*. The poem
is interesting in the present context largely because of what Scott
has chosen to translate: "Song of May and Virtue" is "from the
French of Clément Marot, 1496–1544," and exploits those conventions
of beauty, decay, and resistance to time that had been adopted and
revivified by the later Decadents of France and England. Despite its
simplicity, Scott's poem is a useful reminder that the favoured conventions of Decadence are variants of the conventions of literature
generally, insofar as any poet of stature will probably be musing
over beauty, time, and death at some point in his career. What makes
a poem Decadent *per se* in its exploitation of these themes is a greater
emphasis on decay, a crippling fatalism because of the inevitability
of death, a near-neurotic attachment to all things beautiful beyond
the border of mental health, and an intensification of formal properties that support these emphases: lulling rhythms, clustered sibilants, and stanzas in which long full-bodied lines may alternate
with truncated whispers. Thus Scott's poem from Marot is differ-
entiated from Decadence by its second half, in which by some miracle
of Renaissance rhetoric the woman's beauty is judged untouchable
by time, with a witty acknowledgement from the poet that his love
depends rather closely upon her beauty. This levity is not a common
feature of the Decadent's approach to the decay of his beloved.

   The advent of the *Fortnightly*, which soon followed the appearance
of Scott's translation, cannot be thought anything but fortuitous in
Canadian literary history; yet its nature gives rise to many of the
same disputes that whirl around the poetry of the young Scott. Ken
Norris in his consideration of the journal first argues that "it would
seem that the editors sought to ally themselves with the bastions of
tradition and institutionalism," but later on the same page he says
that "The launching of Modernism in the pages of the *Fortnightly*
was put forward as a two-pronged attack: firstly there was criticism
to be levelled at the literary temper of the times ... Second, there
was the new program of Modernism to put forward." In the second
assessment Norris renders the conventional critical image of the

*Fortnightly* and directly contradicts any alliance with the "bastions of tradition." It may be, however, that Norris's first comment, although much less common, is the more accurate. Scott himself acknowledged the traditionalism of the journal in a letter of 30 July 1966 to Raymond Souster, now contained in the Raymond Souster Papers in Toronto:

Your introduction [to *New Wave Canada*] reminds me of McGill Fortnightly days: no one but ourselves had ever written good poetry! It is charming, but as you have found out in our case we were not as revolutionary as we thought. Styles and conceits in verse – dropped lines, wiggly lines, no punctuation, verbal abbreviations, breath pauses, coughs and sneezes etc. – come and go like bustles and bikinis. Ultimately, as every child knows, there is only good poetry and bad poetry. A poet's impact is measured by how much he has to say that is important about man and his essential being, not by his innovations of style, though these may lead to a new dimension of thought and feeling. [12]

Scott's suspicion is echoed in his Preface to *New Provinces* in 1936: "This search for new content was less successful than had been the search for new techniques and by the end of the last decade the modernist movement was frustrated for want of direction" (v). It has so long been the custom to treat the *Fortnightly* as the seed-bed of Canadian Modernism that it is a little disconcerting to hear one of its chief participants denying the thoroughness of its achievements. Nevertheless, a full perusal of the fascinating pages of the journal proves the accuracy of Scott's later judgments, and no poet proves it so clearly as Scott himself.

To be sure, there are a number of poems by Scott in the *Fortnightly* that clearly point towards his later achievements, such as the first version of the famous "The Canadian Authors Meet." Of these Smith has written: "Some of the earliest [Scott] poems dating from the days of the *McGill Fortnightly Review* already have a simplicity of language and an exactness of imagery which are the first fruits of conscious discipline, control, and humility." [13] If truly intended to represent a portion of Scott's earliest poetry, Smith's comments are accurate enough. Thus we find in the *Fortnightly*, besides the early version of "The Canadian Authors Meet," Scott's "Sweeney Comes to McGill," later republished as "Burlap Comes to McGill" in *Overture*, then as "Sweeney" again in the *Collected Poems*; an early version of his "Below Quebec," a landscape of the "Old Song" manner; "Villanelle of Manitou," an early effort at the Canadian landscape in a singularly inapt poetic form; "Snowdrift" and "November Pool,"

brief images attempting once more to capture the delicacies of the
Canadian landscape, appearing with slight emendations in the *Collected Poems*; and "Proud Cellist," which Scott finally reprinted only
in the *Collected Poems*. These poems are generally signed "F.R.S." or
"Bernard March," one of Scott's pseudonyms for the journal, and it
is presumably such writing as this which critics think of when they
speak of Scott's role in the "Modernist" *Fortnightly*.

The poems of "Brian Tuke," however, acknowledged by Smith to
have been Scott's work ("Confessions," 4), have received no attention whatsoever. They are completely unlike any of Scott's later
developments; they are immediately recognizable as pre-Modernist
works; and they are, to varying degrees, Decadent imitations, unself-conscious renderings of the style and preoccupations of the
poets of the 1890s. These poems mitigate severely the idea that Scott
was working out his Modernism in the secure climate of the *Fortnightly* and desperately need to be examined and placed in our critical
estimation of this surprising poet.

"To Beauty" is typical of the poems written by "Tuke" in the
*Fortnightly*:

> Could I, in alien dream or lofty trance,
> Pierce through the clouds that veil thee from my sight,
> I would not feel the lust of utterance
> In my sealed lips, dumb with supreme delight.
> Nor in cold images of word and rhyme
> Born of unsated love, desirous eyes,
> Strive blindly to create the form sublime
> That still evades my deepest ecstasies.
> All longing dies in gazing on thy face,
> All yearning, all wild cries of banishment,
> And could I reach to thee I should embrace
> Eternal silence and divine content;
>     Abandoning these playmates of distress,
>     The proof and feeble prize of unsuccess.[14]

Apart from a certain Elizabethan effect in matters of diction and
form, the sonnet obviously exploits any number of the conventions
and mannerisms of Aestheticism. Its insistent images of "unsated
love" and "wild cries of banishment" strike the true Decadent note,
as does the extended exploration of poetic failure, the suspicion that
the poet's vision is to be realized only in supreme uncreating silence.
Thus a glimpse of absolute "Beauty" would leave him "dumb with
supreme delight," since it is only the "unsated love" of beauty that
encourages him to express his strivings. In this context his poems

become the "playmates of distress," whims and toys that do not satisfy his yearning: they are the "proof" of "unsuccess," the failure of his poet's eyes to glimpse the essence. Absolute "Beauty," then, is beyond the reach of art, and the artist is doomed to perpetual failure. Scott demonstrates in the sonnet his recognition of the central emotive premise of Decadence: that an impassable gulf must always extend itself between the poet and the vision he desires. Scott's diction enforces this impression of Decadence, with its "lust," "delight," "ecstasies," and "longing". These emotions, in the context of his appeal to "Beauty," clearly move the poem beyond the reach of Victorianism, yet draw it back from the relative vigour and activism of the Georgian sonnetteers.

The theme is echoed in another of the "Tuke" poems, "Sonnet [Would I were Angelo, and taking stone ...]," in which the poet desires to abandon his calling altogether, as an insufficiently visual medium, in order to replace it with the skill of the sculptor, in fact of the greatest sculptor of the Renaissance:

Would I were Angelo, and taking stone
Rough-hewn from bold Carrara's mountain brims,
Could shape it to the glory of thy limbs,
So uttering the beauty thou hast shown
That all the multitude of men would own
Thee perfect beyond thought, and when death dims
Thy mortal fires, more than a poet's hymns
Would prove the loveliness that I have known.

The visual permanence of sculpted stone attracts the poet: poetry cannot realize *visually* the beauty of his beloved, which is said to be "perfect beyond thought," in other words, absolute. He therefore seeks an art that will overcome the effects of time, which enters the poem because the "Beauty" now addressed is a living woman rather than an abstracted Goddess: this shift results in the poet's concern with her decay and ignites his passions to conquer it. Thus Scott's emphasis has wandered from "To Beauty," an aesthetic meditation, to "Sonnet," an anxious expression of physical and creative desire, because of the newly relevant intrusion of time.

The sestet of "Sonnet" takes another turn, however, suddenly, when even the permanence of sculpture is found inadequate for the intended rendering:

Yet would I pity those enamoured fools,
Gazing enraptured on that heartless bust
With unappeased desire, hopelessly.

For what thy love can mean is mystery
No stone may tell, though Phidias from the dust
Rise with deft hands to wield the edged tools.[15]

Although Phidias implicitly bests the skill of Michelangelo (in that he is addressed as a final appeal), even his art is insufficient, since the woman's "beauty" is not expressed only in her body but in her "love," which the cold stone can hardly render. Thus art fails the poet once more, this time not only his own but also a second art form beyond his means: in other words the artistic failure created here is endemic, not individual, and it is rationalized by reference to the degree of beauty manifested by the woman. The greater assurance of the poet's thoughts (he is not, after all, a sculptor and therefore is less open to real blame here) gives to "Sonnet" a less Decadent quality than is apparent in "To Beauty," although its "enamoured fools," "heartless bust," and consequent "unappeased desire" bring something of the dis-ease of the first to the second "Sonnet."

"Tuke" was able to come down from these abstract heights now and again, however, to capture rather more real women: equally beautiful and just as much subject to the ravages of time, but breathing more of human life than the first two sonnets can offer. A third sonnet, "Miniature," with its faint dandyism, manages a rather haunting atmosphere that is explicated only by the final four lines, and then only to a degree:

You move so slowly down the room,
Stopping awhile to smell a flower
And pluck a leaf off, or assume

A pensive look before you shower
Your kisses on the Pekinese –
As though you knew he had the power

To share your grief – and then you seize
A chair's back with those thin, strain'd hands,
And gaze towards the distant trees

That fringe familiar meadow-lands.
And none would fancy from your pose
That death had strewn his shifting sands

About your home; and left a lonely rose
Longing to share in that last, dread repose.[16]

Note the exquisite qualities of the woman: her smelling a flower, her absent plucking of a dead leaf, her "assuming" a look rather than merely bearing one, her sense of the "pose": she is imbued with elegance and refinement largely because of her gestures, although nothing in the room suggests wealth or aristocracy, except perhaps the fondled Pekinese. The third stanza refers suddenly to "grief," and her "thin, strained hands" suggest that she is in the grip of an unclear suffering, which is explicated by the final line of the fourth tercet and the concluding couplet. Death is a principle here, an undirected abstraction: the dead one is unknown to the reader – presumably a lover, although one could make a not implausible case that the woman herself is dead, her "room" surrounded with "shifting sands" – and only the general mood of death seems important. That the lady is beautiful is nowhere mentioned, yet it seems inevitable in this setting, as though it were too obvious to mention; certainly in the context of Scott's other sonnets it would be difficult to imagine her otherwise. It is not particularly easy to reconcile the title with the poem itself, unless we assume that the poem is inspired by a miniature: we must otherwise assume that the "miniature" quality is recognizable in the delicacy of the images – the rose, the small dog, the "thin" hands. It is of course merely theatrical on the poet's part to claim that "none would fancy from [her] pose" that the woman had been touched by death – the third tercet makes it reasonably clear – but his insistence on the point reveals the underlying purpose of the poem: the aesthetic qualities of the portrait, its "miniature" refinement as a visual "moment," are posed against the inevitability of death, in an attempt to render poignancy and suffering in a medium of refined attention to aesthetic detail. The structuring of the sonnet by *terza rima* tercets rather than by quatrains reinforces this sense of delicacy; the anticipated strong quatrains pull against the lighter tercets much as substantial death pulls at the delicate refinements of the setting. Thus Scott creates a far more genuine tension than those attempted in "To Beauty" and "Sonnet," by relating earlier abstract themes to an actualized individual, in a poem of some formal sophistication.

Another "Sonnet" by "Tuke" continues this increasing sophistication, now drawing into the scheme a pair of lovers locked in lofty dialogue. The dichotomous terms of their conversation are the poles of all Decadent discourse:

One day you asked me to define delight,
And love being new to me, I said "To feel
The swift oblivion of those who steal
Passion from willing lips – that is delight."

Wonderingly then you whispered "And despair?"
"There comes a time when these material joys
Play truant to the sense, and love employs
In vain his stratagems – that is despair."

Then down long days of deepening intercourse
We fared together, through all ease and pain,
Desire, and coldness, knowing that the force
Of our late love outmatched youth's passionate reign.

And when death sealed thy lips to me, I knew
How false had been my answers – and how true. [17]

The opposition of "delight" and "despair" prefigures a heavy dualism in the third quatrain, between "ease and pain," "Desire, and coldness," and, oddly, "love" and "youth" – which strikes the note of passing time. The rather supercilious poet announces with pleasure his understanding of the terms of love, and the breathless girl he addresses wonders at his wisdom. When the terms become real, however – when "death seals her lips" – the answers are shown in all their cocky assurance as insufficient descriptions of delight and despair, although they touch the surface emotions of those visited by death. His answers were "true" because they dwelt on passion and sensation, which is how the poet particularly feels her absence; but they are also "false": the equivocation arises because there is a hidden object of discussion. Although the beloved asks, essentially, "What are delight and despair to lovers?", the poem itself asks a different question: "what are delight and despair to the bereft lover," in which context the insistent sensuality of his answers takes on a keen and poignant accuracy. The emphasis on passion and sense as the basis of love leads as if by rote to the incident of death, which provokes in the poet that ironic self-punishment that is behind so much Decadent literature. [18]

In the chapter on Scott in *The White Savannahs*, W.E. Collin published a short poem that he attributed to Scott. This poem is not to my knowledge published elsewhere, but would seem, because of preoccupations similar to those of the "Tuke" poems, to be roughly contemporary with them. Entitled "Afterthought," the poem realizes in a particular person, rather as "Miniature" had, the ideas Scott had been developing in the pseudonymous poems of the *Fortnightly*:

The body of this woman, flowering once,
Made beggars of proud men.

The tribute of her loveliness,
And she is mistress
Only to pity and tears.

Dim of eye, with hands
Unattentive to hair,
Stooping at shoulder, her step
Climbing the stair slowly,
She gropes her way to her room
For a brief space to dream
Of towering moments time has overcome. [19]

The concerns of "Afterthought" are patently those of the "Tuke" poems: the passing of a woman's beauty, the triumph of "time," the attempt to capture for art and memory those "moments" that give us the sensation of eluding time's grasp. It differs from the "Tuke" poems by virtue of its totally unrelieved sombreness, the insistence upon time's triumph without qualification, without the hopeful assurance of "Sonnet [Would I were Angelo, and taking …]" or the distancing abstraction of "To Beauty," and by its approximation of free verse. These distinctions are perhaps enough to suggest that it is slightly later than the "Tuke" poems, but they are not so forceful as to mitigate the likelihood of Scott's authorship of the piece. It is curious that it appears nowhere else in the Scott canon, and we must assume that it was provided to Collin by the poet himself – although this would seem an odd action for a poet who had by 1936 largely rejected the themes and symbols of this early manner. By virtue of its parallels with "A Miniature" and its exploitation of the conventions of the "Tuke" poems, however, it seems safe to judge it a Scott work, in which case it is an interestingly modern example of Scott's particularizing and humanizing the abstract concepts of "To Beauty" and the first "Sonnet" quoted.

If the Decadent source of the "Tuke" poems remains at all disputable, a final sonnet in the *Fortnightly*, this one by "Bernard March," Scott's pseudonym for his more familiar landscape pieces, will fairly settle the question. "Decadence" certainly reveals by its title alone Scott's sensitivity to the earlier generation of English poets, but nothing makes so clear his knowledge of their practice than the emblems of ennui, amoral indifference, and vague hypnotic eroticism that he juggles throughout the sonnet:

Passionless one, to whom all days are dull,
Come and intrigue me with your weariness.
Droop round me, as the loose fringe of a dress

Flung on a chair's edge, droops; let languor lull
All our mind's curious life, all questionings,
The futile fancy and the puny prayer,
Till on the idle, unadventurous air
Breathing is loud, and sighs are terrible things.
Why lift the pale tip of a forefinger?
If so much move, you make a right and wrong,
There is a God, and we lose Paradise.
But we hold heaven if only you will linger
In stupid rest, and while my kiss is long
Stare out at nothing with indifferent eyes.[20]

Recalled most powerfully by "Decadence" is Wilde's "The Sphinx,"
with its similar images of languor and exotic atheism:

Your lovers are not dead, I know. They will rise up and hear your voice
And clash their cymbals and rejoice and run to kiss your mouth

..............................................................................................

Why are you tarrying? Get hence! I weary of your sullen ways,
I weary of your steadfast gaze, your somnolent magnificence

..............................................................................................

... Go thou before, and leave me to my crucifix,

Whose pallid burden, sick with pain, watches the world with wearied
   eyes,
And weeps for every soul that dies, and weeps for every soul in
   vain.   (Poems, 305, 307, 309–10)

Scott's sonnet comprehends this Wildean languor until all activity
seems absurdity, until "Breathing is loud, and sighs are terrible
things." One recognizes in the line the affected delicacy of the Decadent. The sonnet places ultimate emphasis on the poet's godless-
ness: any action whatever on the part of his beloved will have eventual moral consequences and is avoided on those grounds as tending
towards a frightening religiosity. "Paradise" and "heaven" are in this
pagan context inverted worlds of ennui and sensuality, in which the
"stupidity" and "indifference" of the beloved make her valuable to
the poet. Moreover, like morality, knowledge and wisdom are in-
sufferable to him, since he desires to maintain a world of perfect
spiritual and intellectual inanition. Ironically, this undercuts even
the eroticism, since to engage in sexual delights some finger would

have to be lifted: the "Decadence," then, extends even to the passions, and the keynote is satiety, not sexuality. Only in such hollow claims is the eroticism manifest: the speaker and his addressed beloved are frozen in an image, imprisoned by their own ultimate languor.

"Decadence," then, by virtue of its explicit imitation of the qualities of Decadent poetry and its acknowledgement of the imitation in the title, proves that Scott knew the poetry of the Decadents sensitively enough to produce so successful an adaptation. But the poem, while settling one issue, raises another, more thorny and with larger implications: as we know Scott at this time, however uncertain his beliefs, to have been no confirmed atheist,[21] and as we know exotic inactivity to have been one quality he never manifested, at least after the age of twenty-two when we first glimpse him, we are urged to treat "Decadence" as an impersonal imitation, a poem from which the poet himself felt quite distant. Once we have gone that far, it is impossible not to go further and ask whether "Decadence," and by extension "To Beauty" and the others, might not rather be parodies of a movement that Scott found amusing. In the context of the *Fortnightly*, which contains the origins of Scott's satiric turn and his unique ability to render the precise Canadian landscape, "Decadence" may seem that much more tongue-in-cheek. The injunction against "lifting the pale tip of a forefinger" is so extreme that the parodic voice is not far off: do we therefore read "Decadence" as proof of an influence upon the young poet, or as an elaborate joke climaxing a number of less than serious poems?

We may respond in two ways. In the first place the extremism of parody, the extension of certain elements of a tradition into irony, absurdity, or oxymoron, is quite lacking in "Miniature" and the "Tuke" poems. Such extremism only becomes apparent in "Decadence," and there only in one or two instances. That so much of metaphysical consequence should rest on the twitch of a finger is an extension beyond even the Decadent norm of youthful languor; but it is a very subtle one, not so emphasized that we may instantly assume a parodic intention. The textual evidence of parody is therefore slim, and it is only in the context of what we know of Scott's nature that we question the approach he made to this kind of material. This need for biographical confirmation is not common in our evaluation of other classic parodies of English poetry. Second, there is no reason to assume that all the Scott poems were contemporary with one another merely because they were published in the same journal over a period of two years. One or the other manner, Decadent or satiric, may have been developed first, for one thing, and come into print simultaneously with the other at Scott's first real opportunity for regular publication. Since the satires and landscapes eventually form part of the canon he approved, we may speculate along these lines that the Decadent material was written at an earlier date – an idea assisted by the nature of the early "Song of May and Virtue." This would make it more plausible for one young man to create two such distinctive manners with equal seriousness and would undercut our tendency to make biographical judgments, by returning us to an earlier and unknown Scott whose personal qualities are less clearly to be relied upon.

There is no conclusive proof, then, that the poems are parodies, beyond the brief extremism of "Decadence," which would not strike us as extreme at all if we came across it in a minor volume from the 1890s. Perhaps a more accurate approach would be to treat the poems as formal exercises, poems written in the manner of the Decadents, which helped the young poet to draw away from an ostensible over-admiration of Tennyson that he has himself acknowledged. Thus we may recognize their Decadent sources without concluding that Scott as a young man was eager to be like the Decadents himself, in his person or in his thinking.

This theory is supported by Scott's consistent use of the sonnet to express his Aesthetic interests. The sonnet was by no means anathema to the Decadent mentality – witness George Moore's *Pagan Poems* or Symons's penchant for the form – but it is not their most characteristic form, perhaps because its solid lines and tendency towards progressive revelation of meaning contradicted the Decadent's desire to record frailties and absences of meaning. Scott's lack of interest in alternative forms, like those of Wilde's "The Sphinx," or those borrowed by Dowson from Verlaine, suggests that his material only interested him so far as to explore it within a form with which he was fairly familiar. This would account for a misperception of the "Tuke" poems as Victorian or Georgian, a pair of judgments we may now suspect to have been based on Scott's medium rather than his message.

Scott has assisted us, incidentally, in treating these poems as serious explorations. In an interview late in his life he commented, "Many of my early sonnets, still unpublished, speak of the concept of absolute beauty – with a capital B – and I couldn't forsake this pursuit."[22] If the elderly poet of eighty-three could not forsake the concerns of a formally conventional sonnet like "To Beauty," it is almost certain that the poems were not parodies, but seriously considered experiments with a genuine literary attraction. "Decadence" may have been merely the logical conclusion of that train of his thought, as it was also the necessary conclusion of Aestheticism;

perhaps this last of the Decadent sonnets was a final twist, the extremism of which snapped him out of the particular convention and left him free to develop the modern features of his other poetry, which now attracted him more deeply.

Two sonnets published in the first section of Scott's *Collected Poems*, early material labelled "Indications," suggest the directions in which Scott chose to move after recognizing the Decadence at the end of his Aesthetic leaning. (I am not suggesting that they are later pieces – the chronology is lost – but that they may best be interpreted as mediations between the Decadent poems and Scott's later work.) In "The Trappists," for instance, Scott exploits the Aesthetic convention of artistic removal from the hurly-burly of the world, but, by uniting that indifferent removal with themes of religion and philosophy, Scott foreshadows his later social concerns. Thus his Trappists seek "to break the accursed spell/of things material," to remove themselves from greed and desire in order to "hold a nearer intercourse with God." Scott comments that "A mind detached and calm ... scarce survives/In our forc'd living," which necessitates the removal into "monastic ways."[23] At first glance "The Trappists" may seem to tell against Scott's social commitments, since their retreat into contemplation is praised by the poet; but the underlying concern of the sonnet is with the state of the world: it is the evil quality of modern life that makes the removal acceptable, even necessary. Thus their removal from "things material" is one response to those problems of society that Scott was later to tackle more directly. Therefore "The Trappists" is poised neatly between the Aesthetic detachment of the *Fortnightly* poems and the social concerns of the more famous work: Scott sees his society for what it is and is repulsed, but what matters above all is that he has seen. The glimpse will not long be avoided.

While less socially concerned, "Sonnet [Once when you gave me a new book to read ...]," in the *Collected Poems*, is similarly balanced. The poet is given by his beloved a book that she believes will strike his sensibilities as strongly as it has hers, since they are so often of one mind; and the poet treats this gift as a chance for detachment.

I took it wonderingly, and sought with speed
A firelit chamber, cunningly designed
For midnight musings, and there pulled the blind
On the night's dark sorrow, paying the wind no heed;
And drew thence unbelieved delights.

That he chooses to "blind" himself to the night's "sorrow" and the drift of the "wind" suggests a moral lesson lurking for the entranced poet. This detachment cannot and ought not to be maintained, because it places the book, that is, the aesthetic experience, above the beloved lender. The spell is broken when

> Upon one page I found your pencil score.
> Then instantly the spell of the tale was gone
> In a surge of the blood, and feeling the volume still
> Warm from your nearness, your hand's benison,
> I stared into the fire, and read no more.   (CP, 23)

The intrusion of emotional depth and sincerity into his detached world shatters the hold of the book and wraps the speaker in thoughts of its lender. This is as it should be; the "surge of the blood" cannot be ignored, whatever the source, for the claims of art. Art must give way to the potency of life; the book must be closed, the love re-opened. The underscoring of the passage shows art "tainted" by life; but everything in Scott's later development tells the reader that the "tainting" is a sign of health. The Aesthete would not agree; but Scott would come to.

These two sonnets suggest that the Aesthetic impulse in Scott's early poetry was not simply rejected for new purposes, satiric, metaphysical, or what have you, but gradually became something larger or was absorbed by more active concerns. This makes it of no small importance to the scholar of Scott's poetry; it is imprudent to ignore a strain in his early work which he developed over a significant period (note that Scott was between the ages of twenty-six and twenty-eight when "Tuke's" poems were published – not an impressionable juvenile) and worked out in a number of later poems. Scott the "budding Aesthete" who returned from Oxford did indeed become the crusader against social injustice, but we would be simplistic to think that the interests were coeval, or on the other hand that the one ended the day the other began. Like twentieth-century Canadian literature itself, Scott's development shows a gradual dissolution of one school even as another took hold, the resulting overlap creating a number of poems which pose, like "The Trappists" and "Sonnet" above, between the two tendencies.

There is no clearer or indeed more blatant example of this than "Sonnet (Written on a May Morning)," which appeared in the *Fortnightly*, signed, interestingly, "F.R.S."; a poem, presumably, he was prepared to defend with his name:

> I do not know what I shall wear today,
> For I have stood long hours before the glass
> Snaring the little frisky thoughts that pass

Over my mind's hillsides, like hares at play,
And following, as each became my prey,
The tiny gleams of laughter and surprise
Reflected in my strange, familiar eyes ...
I do not know what I shall wear today.

Why not bare arms and legs that gleam in the sun,
A fillet of leaves in my hair, flowers in masses
Of startling hues on my body, grass on my feet?
By all the old gods of Christendom
I think this would be good for the upper classes
Whom one meets on Sunday morning on Sherbrooke Street.[24]

How suddenly that more familiar Scott note breaks into this frisky piece! It is small wonder the poem was never republished, the topical qualities of the last two lines dating it quickly and embarrassingly; but it nevertheless contains exactly the creative transition that we have been discussing. This is the voice of Wilde, delighting in "the white feet of the Muses brush[ing] the dew from the anemones in the morning,"[25] the voice of the dandy whose pleasure lies in the shock and splendour of the human form on display. Scott the Aesthete adores the playful, self-absorbed young dandy who can scarcely look away from his mirror; Scott the social critic feels sudden discomfort and lashes out at the "upper classes" as he might have done ten to fifty years later; yet how absurd it is to join the two in a single poem, since the young dandy embodies all of the distasteful qualities of the upper classes Scott desires to embarrass. There, in miniature, is the essence of Scott's problem as a young poet: to turn from the mirror and struggle against the march of the upper classes and to put the struggle into poetry that deserves the approval of the young Aesthete.

Before revealing Scott's answers, we must face a more pressing issue. If we accept, from the obvious derivativism of Scott's "Decadence," that he had some contact with the poetry of the 1890s, we might well wonder where that knowledge was obtained. Djwa's depiction of Scott's Aesthetic interests at Oxford would seem to offer the answer. His two years at that remarkable socio-cultural institution certainly left their mark on the young man, as the "Tuke" poems make evident: what exactly did he find in the prevailing winds of Oxford in the 1920s to encourage that Aesthetic response?

S cott's Oxford was in part like the Oxford of any day, a centre of tradition, learning, and personal growth, with ample op-

portunity for a serious young man from Canada to explore his potential in a setting where so many great men had begun their work.
Djwa reveals, in her description of Scott's Oxford years, a typical
student career of the early 1920s:

He joined the Bach Choir, the Oxford Student Christian Union (OSCU),
and undertook regular military drill with the Officers Training Corps. He
also frequented the Musical Society's Tuesday evenings, where he was first
introduced to chamber music. On Sundays the Scott brothers attended early
service at Magdalen Chapel and, often, morning and evening services at
local churches.   (PI, 48)

In the OSCU Scott encountered many of the seminal ideas of his
personal education: the Union read "the fifth report published by
the Committee of the Anglican Archbishops of England entitled
*Christianity and Industrial Problems,*" R.H. Tawney's *The Acquisitive
Society* and the *Imitation of Christ* of Thomas à Kempis (Djwa, *PI*, 51–
2). Such was the serious and earnest portion of Scott's Oxford years;
but Djwa also acknowledges the "apparently frivolous aestheticism"
that offered, to "the English undergraduates especially," a substantial alternative to the earnest life: and "unlike most of his contemporaries," Djwa suggests, Scott "responded to both" (*PI*, 48).

This other Oxford to which Scott was drawn was less "manly,"
less regulated, and had a more recent tradition behind it: it was the
Oxford of the dandy, of the splendid young man, the Oxford that
had once made room for the coterie of Walter Pater. The early 1920s
saw a pervasive resurgence of the dandy cult at Oxford, which by
no means pleased all undergraduates, but seems by all accounts to
have been a compelling and attractive institution of the University
for a number of years. This is the Oxford of Evelyn Waugh, the
Oxford that brought Charles Ryder and Sebastian Lord Flyte together in that novelist's *Brideshead Revisited* and left its mark on their
disparate destinies. It was a cult of exquisites, wealthy young men
from aristocratic backgrounds who dressed with perfect flair, lived
the grand life of the lords they often were, and made a worshipped
cult of the Aesthetes and Decadents of the century that had recently
ended. It was as much the "real" Oxford as the more staid and
reputable Oxford of Scott's Union, and it has been chronicled with
remarkable insight by Martin Green in his *Children of the Sun: A
Narrative of "Decadence" in England after 1918,* one of the most revealing pieces of literary history yet to arise from the modern period.

According to Green, Oxford Aestheticism during the 1920s centred
on two figures, Brian Howard and Harold Acton, both desirous of

poetic careers, both with Catholic and American blood, both determined to overthrow at any cost "their fathers' mode of seriousness,"[26] an attitude that Green perceives to be the *Zeitgeist* of the
1920s in England: making the war establishment ridiculous by clucking back at the clucking tongues of their elders and by shocking
them where it hurt most, in the Victorian concept of manliness,
which was rejected by the Oxford dandies more quickly than any
other. Like their 1890s forebears, the Oxford dandies tended towards
homosexuality, but now with a studied, flaunting effeminacy cal-
culated to stun an already reeling British morality.

[Brian Howard] was vulnerable also because of his homosexuality – and
because of the aggressive pretentiousness of his style, which won him many
enemies, and because of his malice and malevolence, which left many vic-
tims seeking revenge. He was intensely ambitious and full of talents, both
artistic and social, but he was apparently incapable of application or hard
work. And he was unhappy and self-destructive, and cruelly destructive to
others. Harold Acton had a ... good deal more vulnerability and timidity
in his personality, although in his prime this was concealed by a very exotic
facade. Both boys cultivated exaggerated mannerisms of speech and gesture,
but Harold made use of his Italian and American affiliations to suggest that
he was barely acclimatized in England. He too had plenty of panache, at
Eton and at Oxford, but it was not malevolent. He was essentially teasing,
often protectively kind, typically "amusing." There was even something
preposterous about his panache; as one laughed with him (at British phi-
listinism) one could also laugh at him, and without fearing, as one did with
Brian, some brutal retribution.   (Green, 88)

In every aspect of social life the dandyism of these young men was
evident: in their clothes (Green, 152–3), in their taste in the arts
(largely Modernist-dandyish, with great sensitivities to the ballet of
Diaghilev and the icons of the *commedia dell'arte*) (Green, 26–35), in
their rooms, and in their relations with others. One image of Howard
from the period captures him chasing a pale young undergraduate
from room to room with bird-calls of love, directed in the hunt by
a group of diners round whose table the chase happened to pass
(Green, 160).

   Howard's life ended in suicide in the 1950s, the failure of his way
of life, his poetry, and his exquisite version of England driving him
to the ultimate despair. Acton lived in Italy to an advanced age; he
appears in *Summoned by Bells,* the verse autobiography of Betjeman,
who was himself a rather desperate participant in the dandyism of
the 1920s. In this mock-Wordsworthian poem Betjeman captures

Acton in a few quick lines: " ... Harold Acton and the punkahs wave:/'My dears, I want to rush into the fields/And slap raw meat with lilies.'"[27] Indeed, in Green's judgment, Acton and Howard reappear throughout modern English literature and society, whether in person or by their overwhelming influence on the Oxford men of their day. Betjeman's account makes clear that the middle-class boys could not afford to maintain the high styles they adopted during the Oxford year and that the true Aestheticism of the time was a limited phenomenon: but, in the marks it left on those who desired to imitate it, the incidence of Oxford Aestheticism is argued by Green to have had astonishing results. Without facile psychologizing Green demonstrates that the Burgess-Maclean-Philby spy scandal of the 1950s is linked in many ways to behaviour the three men had learned, principles they had shattered, during years at Oxford and Cambridge dominated by Acton's and Howard's brand of Aestheticism (Green, 321–9); if so, the dandy cult is no laughing matter, more than a mere quirk of British eccentric society. The Aestheticism inaugurated by these two young men reached farther than their own personal circle: all of Oxford was touched by it, for better or worse, and it was most unlikely that any of the men of Oxford in the early 1920s should have failed at least to hear of the desperate antics of the dangerous dandy-Aesthetes. That these could have such extreme political and social consequences as treason and suicide suggests the forcefulness of a mode of behaviour that even the Oxford of Pater and Wilde must have rejected as inimical to pure Aesthetic harmony.

Oxford Aestheticism of the 1920s, then, was not general, but pervasive. It influenced all of Oxford and Cambridge to some degree, polarizing the student body as Scott discovered into the "hearties" – those inevitable manly men who sought to destroy the dandy's assurance – and the "aesthetes," and made every man take up his position somewhere on the scale. This pervasiveness is interesting to the present study in its literary manifestations; the Aesthetic temperament had long been recognized in literature, so Acton and Howard could exercise the most power in that field. They not only desired to be poets themselves – the results painfully failing, almost from the first – but influenced the taste of many young men with an interest in literature at the Oxford of their time; and their taste was, as might be expected, for the Aesthetes and Decadents of the nineteenth century. Indeed, Green suggests that a tradition of English dandyism culminates in the 1920s, since "Similarly the dandies of the 1890s had looked back to those of the Regency ... And the dandies of the Regency looked back to those of the Restoration" (16). Thus Oxford dandyism makes clear the way in which ideas and philosophies of the Decadence were shifted in the 1920s into elements of personal style, much as dandy poetry found formal inspiration in the drolleries and overwrought exoticisms in the conversational and dramatic style of the Decadence. Oxford became, in the rooms of these young men, a museum of the Decadence; they would recite Decadent writings to one another in a quasi-religious ritual in order to support the validity of their own Aestheticism. It is a clue to the remarkable split-personality of the period that Anthony Blanche in *Brideshead Revisited* also chants Eliot's *The Waste Land* from the windows of his rooms and out over the quad, an action that was apparently common with Blanche's prototype, Acton. Somewhere between "Cynara" and *The Waste Land* may be found the essence of this remarkable period (Green, 156).

For at least the final year of his stay at Oxford, this was a formidable part of Scott's student world. He attended Oxford from the fall of 1920 to the middle of 1923; Acton and Howard came to the University in the fall of 1922. This allows a full year of study during which the young dandies established their autocracies and gives ample time for Scott to have discovered their behaviour and tastes. Revealingly, Djwa suggests that it was in this last year that "he became particularly interested in aestheticism and the concept of 'Art for Art's Sake'" (*PI*, 62). He now read Pater's *Studies in the History of the Renaissance* and George Moore's *Confessions of a Young Man* (Djwa, *PI*, 60–1), books that were becoming recognizable symbols of (and a means of proclaiming) a leaning towards the Aesthetic manner. It is conceivable that for his first two years of study he may have missed the Oxonian Aestheticism that was always there, a watered-down post-war variety that Acton and Howard set out to revivify, simply because it was not as powerful as the 1922 to 1925 variety; but it seems highly unlikely that he could have passed his entire final year at the institution without in some way encountering their more powerful influence. Although Scott was a Magdalen man and Acton's and Howard's college was Christ Church, and although Scott was their senior by five or six years, the two dandies were so adept at drawing attention to themselves that the older student can hardly have failed to notice them.

Indeed, as Djwa has shown, one of Scott's poems in *Isis* makes it clear that he was more than cognizant of the whirling dandy-Aestheticism of the Oxford world. The tone of "The Problem" makes it dangerous to draw biographical conclusions from its references, but the poem covers the icons of Oxford Aestheticism so familiarly that Scott surely cannot have been ignorant of its contemporary practitioners:

> No problem can be worse than mine,
> My state is quite pathetic;
> One half my soul's a Philistine,
> The other half's aesthetic.
>
> A pendulum, I alternate
> Between extreme positions;
> Now aiming at the Newdigate,
> Now loathing such ambitions.
>
> I long to tread the realms of Art,
> Yet cling to ways prosaic.
> My spirit is as torn apart
> As priest and worldly laic
>
> ................................
>
> And when an opera is given
> With setting most decorous,
> At first I taste the artist's heaven,
> And then – I scan the chorus!
>
> But these absurdities are small,
> My room relates another:
> Large rowing groups adorn one wall,
> Madonnas grace the other.   (CP, 243)

The "Newdigate" was, of course, the famous literary prize won by Oscar Wilde for his "Ravenna" (and by Matthew Arnold, for that matter, but the context suggests a nod to the later prize-winner). The visual battle between the pictures of "rowing groups" and "Madonnas" captures perfectly the tension that Green has traced at Oxford between the "hearties" and the "aesthetes"; Scott's poem wittily places its speaker at a point of utter confusion between them, so that he fails at both. The poem concludes with a prayer that some kind friend may find a means to reduce either his heartiness or his Aestheticism, so that he may achieve a "golden mean" (as the poem says, "v. Aristotle").

"The Problem" was published on 8 November 1922, roughly a month after Acton and Howard put in their appearances. Scott was twenty-three at the time, not so old that he would necessarily have been offended or shocked by the adolescent boys who were turning Oxford on its ear. But the poem is significantly ironic: Scott is sufficiently distanced from the tension of which he writes to render it laughingly, a fair indication that he felt the tension to be less than crucial to his own development. The most we may conclude from a reading of "The Problem" is that the young Scott was aware of the Aestheticism of Oxford, either from its older form or from the rambunctious dandy-Aestheticism of Acton and Howard, and that he understood the social polarization of the university's student populace.

When we read "The Problem," however, as a comic prefiguration of the sonnets that were to appear four years later in the *Fortnightly*, it takes on added significance. As those poems do not appear to be parodies but rather careful exercises in the manner of the Decadents, and as Scott had read the cardinal texts and had demonstrated in "The Problem" substantial awareness of the behaviour and conventions of nineteenth-century and Oxford Aestheticism, we are equipped with two major requirements of an argument of influence: first, textual evidence of affinity and sympathy with an earlier artist or school and, second, visible reception and appreciation of the earlier artists. Because of the influence thus concluded, Scott's Oxford years are pivotal in his artistic development, bearing fruit in Aesthetic poetry published four years later and in the attitudes with which he approached issues of society and of law. Scott knew the conventions and manners of Aestheticism and Decadence when he returned to Canada in 1923 and thought highly enough of them to publish, at the first opportunity, a group of poems that are their direct result. There can be no other explanation for his "To Beauty" and "Decadence."

Scott is not tainted by this unfamiliar conclusion. He continued his intellectual and artistic development in directions that led away from the frank Aestheticism of some of his youthful poetry, but his admirable social commitment is in no way lessened by our reading that poetry with pleasure and care. This study merely assumes a greater balance between the two aspects of his early development; as he himself wrote, he was both "attract[ed] and repel[led]" by the collegial Aestheticism that surrounded his research in history, and interpretations that emphasize his repulsion from the Aesthetic atmosphere in order to grant priority to his more conventional image as socialist guardian of civil rights are as misleading as the present study would be, if it now concluded that Scott was wholly an Aesthete when young, and largely remained so throughout his career.

*I*t will be obvious to any reader of Scott's poetry that he was not long held by the Decadent conventions of languor, formalism, self-absorption, and detachment. The concerns of a vigorous life quickly eclipsed this brief tendency of his early poetry, and the work that we value today gradually replaced the poems of "Brian Tuke" and "Bernard March." He did not choose to include any of these Decadent poems in his *Collected Poems* of 1981, representing there only those early sonnets that showed a drawing away from the early derivative sentiments. What then is the ultimate significance of a group of early poems whose superficial qualities at least are quickly rejected by the poet as he develops the mature style for which he is considered?

It bears repeating that Scott published these poems when he was between twenty-six and twenty-eight years old. He was not an adolescent struggling through a mass of influences in a flailing attempt to find his own voice, but a mature and directed young man who had chosen a career that resulted in his being called to the Quebec bar only months after the publication of "Decadence." These poems cannot be comfortably dismissed as "juvenilia": "To Beauty," "Decadence," and "A Miniature" must be understood and placed in the light of Scott's development, as a distinct phase of his poetic vocation. There can be no better way of doing so than to recognize elements in his later poetry that seem intimately related to the Decadent leanings he manifests early on, in order to argue that his rejection of those leanings was neither so sudden nor so absolute as previous readings of Scott's poetry would suggest.

Why else would "Overture" have become one of Scott's most noted and appreciated poems? The tension in this precise, careful poem is between the old absorption with questions of art, of precision, of exacting beauty, and a new commitment to the problems of the world, of the evils and values of a democratic vision. "Overture" shows Scott recording the very transition between Aesthetic and social poetry that we have discovered in the pages of the *Fortnightly*, and it becomes even more striking when we have been made aware of the predilections of "Brian Tuke":

In the dark room, under a cone of light,
You precisely play the Mozart sonata. The bright

Clear notes fly like sparks through the air
And trace a flickering pattern of music there.

Your hands dart in the light, your fingers flow.
They are ten careful operatives in a row
That pick their packets of sound from steel bars
Constructing harmonies as sharp as stars.

The extreme precision of the image should be emphasized, as it plays a role in our understanding the poem. For instance, note that the light in the room is not diffused or general, but "a cone of light," suggesting sharp lines of light and shadow, clear distinctions between the artist and his audience. The sonata is played "precisely" – not necessarily with great artistry, but with great technical skill. The notes are "clear," with the sudden exactitude of sparks, and the music, although flickering, is a "pattern." The "hands dart," but the "fingers flow": Scott's proverbial keen eye has noted that the player's fingers move as if independent of his hands, and he chooses to note it, perhaps attracted by the Art-Nouveau-like contrast between strong stark lines and sinuous winding curves. The third line of the second stanza suggests both the metallic workings of a piano and a precise gathering from it of particular notes, creating "harmonies as sharp as stars." Nearly every phrase of these first two stanzas, then, contributes to an effect of such precision and heightened sensitivity that the poet's absorption in the musical performance should be obvious.

But the now classic question arises, as if inevitably:

But how shall I hear old music? This is an hour
Of new beginnings, concepts warring for power,
Decay of systems – the tissue of art is torn
With overtures of an era being born.

And this perfection which is less yourself
Than Mozart, seems a trinket on a shelf,
A pretty octave played before a window
Beyond whose curtain grows a world crescendo.   (CP, 87)

Scott the man of law feels, as if guiltily, the call of issues of such importance that "the tissue of art is torn" by them: issues of decay, war, revolution that make the precise, controlled harmonies of the "old music" seem a betrayal of personal truth and vision. A "perfection" that "is less yourself/Than Mozart" suggests the performer's personal non-involvement, a detachment no longer tenable in the difficult modern world. "Pretty" is now a pejorative adjective, suggesting frivolity, lightness, aesthetic froth; the "octave" it modifies is the piece played, set against a world in "crescendo" that emphasizes its insignificance. (Note that the piece is described by the poet in eight lines, with traditional rhymes, which might constitute very naturally the octave of a sonnet: at the supreme moment, Scott introduces a surreptitious pun. This provides one reason the poem is not a sonnet: although it creates expectations of sonnet-like structure and progress, with an appropriately Petrarchan *volta* at the ninth line, it cannot be completed as one because it is exactly such remote or antiquated forms which the speaker wishes to escape.)

It has been traditional to read "Overture" as indicative of Scott's rejection of artistic detachment and his new commitment to social involvement, to the shaping of human destiny by direct participation in its affairs. [28] This is not incorrect, yet it seems too simple a version of the poem's meaning. That the poet has given half of the poem's length to the precise description of the aesthetic experience, a description, one might add, lovingly attended to, suggests more genuine tension between the two alternatives than the traditional reading implies. Any reduction of that tension disembowels "Overture" of its force entirely. The poem succeeds because the tension between the two is skilfully maintained: we are to be highly attracted to the experience of the sonata, so attracted in fact that the introduction in the ninth line of the larger question should strike us as a painful intrusion, as well as a breath of fresh air. We are to understand, with Scott, the need for social involvement *as well as* the passionate sense of beauty and the breathlessness of great art, for it is the tension he wishes to record. "Overture" would be a far more facile poem than it really is if all it depicted were a battle won.

Certain overlapping of diction and imagery helps to confirm this alternative reading. In the first two quatrains the metallic qualities of the piano's music promote a modern diction: the fingers become "ten careful operatives," the latter noun hardly suggestive of a detached, old-fashioned artistry; the sounds come in "packets," giving the music a more mechanical than organic quality, confirmed by the "steel bars" from which "sparks" fly as the music strikes them. Scott wishes to convey the strength of the instrument, its aesthetic solidity and technical power, and does so with a mechanical diction that helps to create the direct tension of the poem. Conversely, the last two quatrains describe the issues of war and revolution in musical terms: "an era being born" is preceded by "overtures"; the rise of power and struggle of systems is a "crescendo." Although the "tissue of art is torn," it is still a point of reference, a scale of terms against which to discuss meaning. Furthermore, note the general abstraction of the images of modern struggle: "beginnings," "concepts," "power," "decay," "systems." Against the concrete precision of the description of the performance, these words necessarily fall a little flat as evocative language. Moreover, the final stanza brings the two scales of meaning, artistic and social, together once more, albeit with faint negative qualities surrounding the musical, so that the poem in its process of attention opens with the artistic, shifts for four lines to the social, returns to the artistic for three lines, and concludes with a final line expressing social commitment. The progress of thought is hardly from the artistic to the social, with clear-cut demarcations in between: rather the poet turns and turns about, as if uncertain, his attention traversing the two realms with obvious determination towards each.

These stylistic features confirm that "Overture" is to be read as an ongoing tension, a powerful division in the speaker. To be sure, he chooses to align himself with the social: but that is a deliberate choice in the face of painful dichotomies in his own nature. The poet is not one to bewail the tension for page after dramatic page, tossing back and forth between imperfect alternatives: he knows that all human action is imperfect, but he knows as well that some expression of will is the most important of man's flawed alternatives. He therefore chooses a particular course, one which strikes him presently as the most necessary for the good of humankind; but he is not so simple-minded as to present the choice as natural, easy or inevitable. A potent attraction to the formality and "perfection" of art is always operating within his nature, and we are assured by "Overture" that it will be a long-lived and thorough attraction.

Bearing this tension in mind will help the scholar in readings of Scott's other poems. His "Proud Cellist," for example, one of the earlier poems, plays with a similar tension, although realized in different terms, and thus belongs with "The Trappists" and "Overture" as expressive of both the aesthetic and the social predilections of this complex poet. The "Proud Cellist" doubts that anything "Of flesh and blood" can equal the beauty and skill of his instrument; he is absorbed in his art, like the pianist of "Overture," and no doubt they would express similar sentiments had the latter been allowed to speak:

In no woman
Is love lent

So beautiful an
Instrument.

None so lovely
In her moving,
None so wholly
Lost in loving.

Again, as in "Overture," the apparent tendency of the poem – in this case to praise the artistic over the real, over the woman of flesh and blood – is made ambiguous towards the end, as the woman is likened to instrument, player to lover:

A low note dying, and
Not yet dead
Is a lover's hand
Uncomforted.

A low note dying, and
Sunk to rest
Is a lover's hand
Still, on a breast.   (CP, 25)

The images of the dichotomy blend together once more, so that neither musician nor beloved triumphs: a heightened aesthetic tension is maintained with great skill, and the delicacy of the musician's art is obviously highly attractive to the mind and heart of Scott. "Proud Cellist" should be read with "Overture" as a reminder of the poet's complexities.

The peruser of Scott's Collected Poems will find further examples of poems capturing the tension between detached artistic perfection and some form of active social life, whether personal, legal, national, or cultural. "A Hill for Leopardi" allows the poet to escape to a heightened world of sensation where "suns pass, galaxies/Shrink and explode, time bends," and he can escape the day's squabbles: a desirable world that cannot, unfortunately, endure:

Yet it is always the same. A loved voice, a touch,
A phone ringing, and the thrust dies.
Another journey ends where it began
Shipwrecked on ground we tread a little while.   (CP, 134)

So it is that "For R.A.S. 1925–1943" earns its particular poignancy: not merely because the boy died in the war, as so many others did, but "because he wished to write,/And because he had time only to pour/The table of his contents upon the historic water" (*CP*, 107). (Note the allusion to Keats's epitaph.) Thus "R.A.S." – Richard Aird Scott, the poet's nephew, killed in a troop transport on his way to Europe in 1943 –[29] has enacted bravely Scott's recurrent question, his brief life typifying for the older man the battle between the artist and the soldier in each man. Other poems in the collection that should be re-considered in this light are "New Paths," "Archive," "To the Poets of India," "Time as Now," and "Poem Talking to Poet." Some lean towards one side of the question, some another: it is their number, their recurrence throughout Scott's career, that is significant, as further evidence that this question was never as resolved for him as some readings of "Overture" have suggested.

The tensions thus delineated in Scott's poetic development are clearly related to others that developed within the Aesthetic movement itself as the 1890s approached, between Paterian Aestheticism (the removal into realms of art, purposive detachment) and Wildean Aestheticism (the transformation of principles of art into conditions and habits of personal and social life). It should not after all greatly surprise us that Scott underwent such a pattern of development, when we remember that Oscar Wilde wrote "The Soul of Man Under Socialism" as a direct result of his Aesthetic concerns. The "Socialism" Wilde envisaged was above all directed to the artistic and spiritual health of the masses, based on the assumption that an appreciation of aesthetics on their parts and on that of the middle class would uplift their condition and make them worthy of greater rights and education. Scott's choice does not really parallel Wilde's, being more devoted and realistic, but it serves as a reminder that Aestheticism and early Socialism were united in their battle against a common enemy, Victorian complacency, which still controlled the Canada in which Scott grew up.[30] William Morris, like Scott a man of immense and diverse energies, is further proof that Aestheticism and Socialism, while odd bedfellows, can link hands quite naturally and without necessary disdain for one another. We should not be surprised, then, to find lasting dialectics between art and action in Scott's poetry, or to notice other qualities of Aestheticism and Decadence grafted onto his Modernist concerns.

For instance, "Autumnal," a poem from the mid-1930s, exemplifies the Decadent vision of that season as expressive of universal melancholy. In its present form the evocations of this Decadent tradition are restrained:

October is the month of dead leaves falling
Beautifully to lie upon grey rock and ground.

Death curves most carefully from the sky in this season
To lay a memory at the roots of trees.

The setting then evokes a curious emotionalism:

Why do you break a dry leaf in your hand?
Stand still awhile with me and hear
How from old hills the wind
Blows cold ...  (CP, 42)

Something in the person addressed curiously reflects the melancholy
of the setting and produces puzzlement in the speaker. Despite its
free verse form, "Autumnal" works over fairly traditional ground.
But in its original form, "Autumnal" is much more clearly reminiscent of the Decadent tradition. The second stanza is significantly
different:

Leaves curl and die.
All has been said of them that need be said
By the old poets, and all has been said
Of you and me long years ago – how love
That once was young desire, grew pale, and died,
And sank to slow decay, leaving bare limbs
In whom the blood was still. This has been told
A thousand times. Today we understand.[31]

This heavily deliquescent stanza was "cleaned up" by Scott for the
later publication, with the following results:

Leaves curl and die, and dying
Give richly back their store of summer green
To strengthen parent stem, as lovers plant
Their seed for ancestry.
But love itself, life's greenest stratagem,
Though ever new, like leaves, is seasonal.  (CP, 42)

Compared with the early version, the stanza is unrecognizable. What
had been thorough gloom, with a paralyzing sense of literary historicity (the very essence of Decadence), has become a process of
rebirth and regeneration, with love now "ever new" instead of "pale"
and dying. The melancholy diction of the former version – "pale,"
"died," "sank," "decay," "bare," "still" – has become "richly,"
"green," "strengthen," "plant," and "seed." It is obvious that in the

process of revision Scott reacted to the parading Decadence of the earlier version and carefully weeded it out to produce a more modern poem. Thus "Autumnal" exemplifies in a processive way the very tension between Decadence and progress noticed in so many individual poems; the first version arising mainly from the early Decadent Scott, the second created by the modern, progressive poet struggling against his early habits.

The eroticism of Scott's early poems is not pronounced, certainly not as Decadent as the eroticism of, say, Symons, who studied the quality often beyond all artistry. Yet an underlying eroticism is also apparent in his later poetry, in a way which will surprise those of his readers who have come to believe that the unifying characteristics of Scott's landscape poems are precision, clarity, and a distinctive formalism. What actually unites these poems is a likening of the landscape to sexuality – a description of the land in sexual terms – that is so consistent within them as to produce a stunning uniformity. No published study of Scott has remarked the consistency of this quality. This is why "Frost in Autumn," with its archetypal Canadian images, turns suddenly to thoughts of physicality:

> When the first ominous cold
> Stills the sweet laughter of the northern lakes,
> And the fall of a crisp leaf
> Marks the eternal victory of death,
> ............................................
> I cannot bring myself to your embrace.
>
> For love is an impudent defiance
> Flung into the teeth of time,
> A brazen denial
> Of the omnipotence of death,
> And here death whispers in the silences,
> And a deep reverence is due to time.  (CP, 39)

Note that Scott still places human love much where the Decadents had left it: as a distraction from the force of Time, a means of seizing in the midst of the flux a heightened moment of aesthetic splendour which redeems the poet languishing under a sentence of mutability (an alternative rejected here, but still acknowledged). Certainly, he denies the possibility of love in the wilderness, but he denies it on Decadent grounds: Scott recognizes the Decadent "use" of love, which is precisely why he rejects it in a landscape where "reverence is due to time."

This interplay carries throughout the landscape poetry in a number of ways. Sometimes physical love is merely a metaphor for speaking about the given scene, as in "Laurentian":

Where dark fir trees
Thrusting high
To probe the mystery
Of sky

Are tall pinnacles
Erect
That speak familiar
Dialect

Night and thrusting
Dark tree meeting
These be tokens
Of my mating.   (CP, 41)

This metaphor is powerfully developed in "North April," which runs through thirty-four lines of descriptive naturalism, then twists the entire poem round to the following set of images:

A soul-stirring
A blood-coursing
The murmur of frost-free waters breaking
On far seashores

A baring of breasts long covered
A slipping of clothes from the dark earth-body
A coming of nakedness and love
Stark beauty soft-heralded
By warm winds

*We come, we come, naked fields*
*We shall warm you, O dark earth-body*
*We shall clothe you with love*
*We shall cover you with the green fruit of our love.*   (CP, 46–7)

The regenerative powers of human sexuality provide a ripe conceit for the natural cycles of the Canadian landscape. Scott renders both with attention and obviously finds the former particularly conducive to his sensibilities as a poet. Sometimes he turns the pattern around, using the landscape as an appropriate metaphor for sexuality, as in "Will to Win":

> Only a handful of me escaped to the hillside,
> Your side, my sweet and holy inside,
> And cowering there for a moment I drew breath,
> Grew solid as trees, took root in a fertile soil.
>
> Here by my hidden fires, drop your supplies –
> Love, insight, sensibility and myth –
> Thousands of fragments rally to my cause,
> I ride like Joan to conquer my whole man.   (CP, 135)

These examples suggest the erotic manner in which Scott explored his landscapes. To confirm the pervasiveness of the habit, the reader should also consider "Spring Flame," "Below Quebec," "He Walked in a World," "Moment," "Poem [Let us stay a moment ...]," "The Clearing," "November Pool," "March Field," "Union," "Signature," "Message," "A Moving Picture," and "The Spring Virgin Cries at Her Cult." I have extended the list to prove the point: any one of these poems will show the reader a close linking of Scott's ability to render landscapes and his desire to transmit an evocative eroticism. That this metaphor should be so markedly habitual, yet remain unnoticed in Scott's poetry, suggests once again that we have failed as critics to comprehend the complexities of the man: by recognizing an early Decadent impulse in his writings we may become fully alive to the shifting currents of Decadence and Modernism in Scott's poetry.

This is not to say that the eroticism of these pieces is Decadent eroticism, which is so concerned with over-spending, failure to meet one another, and the impossibility of achieving spiritual union through fleshly coupling: Scott's eroticism is steadier, more promising of meaning. Clive Scott has said that one problem common to all Decadents was "how to charge an epidermic experience with profundity";[32] indeed, the Decadent may be defined in part by his failure to do so, which is why Scott's later eroticism is not Decadent. His eroticism found its profundity, eventually, in the depths of the Canadian landscape, and thereby managed to unite itself with the most stirring impulses of his poetry. His consistent concern with that union begins, however, with his initial Decadent exercises; he too faced the "epidermal" problem of the earlier school and was able to conquer it, for which we respect him with perfect justice as a Modernist.[33]

Clearly a recognition of Scott's early Decadent poetics can lead to some valuable insights into poetry that we have studied for decades without, I must suggest, full understanding. When we consider how many of his poems turn on the pivot between detachment and action, artistic removal and social commitment, when we note the consistent eroticism of his famous landscapes and discover his first explorations of eroticism to have occurred in the Decadent mood, we are obviously describing a far more complex Scott than has yet been recognized, a Scott whose Modernism was ushered in by a flirtation with Decadence that bore fruit throughout his poetic career. There are no doubt a number of other poems in the Scott canon that may now be re-read or clarified with this information at hand, but we must content ourselves for now with one more, which will help to put the whole issue into a proper perspective.

Scott's "The Canadian Authors Meet" has long been recognized as a brilliant *tour-de-force* in the Modernist battles against Canadian Victorian poetry of the 1920s. Perhaps some do not yet realize, however, that an extra stanza exists in the first version of the poem from the *McGill Fortnightly Review* in 1927. The present version of the poem ends with a consummate rhetorical question:

O Canada, O Canada, O can
A day go by without new authors springing
To paint the native maple, and to plan
More ways to set the selfsame welkin ringing?   (*CP*, 248)

But the original version went on from here, returning from poetic theory to the room where the meeting of the "Canadian Authors" takes place:

Far in the corner sits (though none would know it),
The very picture of disconsolation,
A rather lewd and most ungodly poet,
Writing these verses for his soul's salvation.[34]

Louis Dudek finds within the original last stanza an odd aesthetic contradiction: "I hardly need to point out," he writes, "the contradiction between an 'ungodly poet' and one 'writing verses for his soul's salvation.' In dreams, Freud tells us, contradictions simply co-exist, and the same is true of poems."[35] Dudek has noted a contradiction that might otherwise have escaped me: but there is, with our present knowledge of Scott's early poetry, a way of resolving it. In all of literary history, which poet could we best say was both "lewd and most ungodly" and "writing for his soul's salvation"? The answer, obviously, is the Decadent poet, who had a keen sense of his own sinfulness and a desperate belief that he could be redeemed in the purifying fire of art. If we remember that "The Canadian Authors Meet" is contemporary with "Bernard March's" poem "Decadence," we have found an insight into the former poem that is not attainable by any other means. The jesting quality of Scott's last stanza, later excised, is, like "The Problem," a reminder that his Decadence was never so whole-hearted or unquestioned as to define his early years; but the fact remains that Decadence is a key, to this and to a number of other qualities of Scott's poetry.

S cott has nowhere acknowledged the Decadence of his early poetry. Smith's reference to Scott's "simplicity of language and ... exactness of imagery which are the first fruits of conscious discipline, control, and humility" in his *Fortnightly* poetry[36] is, very apparently, a half-judgment, a failure to remember or to acknowledge another substantial portion of his friend's work. Scott himself has said no more than Smith on the question, preferring not to republish the sonnets of "Tuke" and "March" when opportunity arose.

Scott's wilful silence naturally makes it difficult to elaborate the particulars of the Aesthetic influence upon him. His later references to the poetry of the 1890s, like Knister's and Kennedy's, are cryptic, tending towards ultimate approval but with many reservations along the way. They are perhaps even more cryptic because Scott was not a literary critic but a man of law. For instance, an address given by Scott in 1928 to a group of Canadian poets makes the following statements:

The nineties arrived, and proved to be yellow. But the *fin-de-siècle* poets – Oscar Wilde, Ernest Dowson, Arthur Symonds [sic] and others – who made a valiant attempt to be new, for the most part only succeeded in being naughty. They caused a disturbance, and that is always a good thing; they brought back to poetry a sensitivity and a subtlety of feeling which the Victorians had lacked; under French influence they came close to writing pure poetry – poetry, that is, of pure music and image rather than ideas. But they had really no new concept of poetry to offer; they left their contribution to our literature, but once their attack had spent itself the course of orthodox romanticism ran smooth ... They left the form of English poetry much as they had found it.[37]

One sees in the judgment the balanced reasoning so typical of Scott: while he acknowledges many weaknesses and failures of the 1890s poets, he admits their efforts, their few successes, and obviously sides with them to a degree against Victorian doctrines of poetry and of society. If such a statement were all we had to explain Scott's landscape eroticism or the tension he toys with between artistic detachment and social commitment, we should be on thin ground; nevertheless, the quotation confirms Scott's knowledge of the poets of the 1890s more thoroughly than anything else he was to write – except, of course, the *Fortnightly* poems.

This address was modified in 1931 for publication in two parts in *The Canadian Forum*. The section above was drastically reduced to the following brief comment: "The yellow nineties tried to be novel and merely succeeded in being amusingly naughty; they gave a jolt to the system, but the course of true poetry [Victorian; an ironic comment] still ran smooth."[38] Scott evidently desired to give less time to the 1890s in the later version, perhaps only from considerations of space. But it is interesting that on the next page of the article Scott draws on the Aesthetic idea of *la poésie pure* to launch the following diatribe: "the poet will create the poem with a complete disregard of its effect upon the official or ecclesiastical mind ... Yet because [this principle] involves the proposition that the poet may write something which is a good poem, viewed aesthetically, and a seditious utterance or blasphemy, judged by contemporary social standards, it is a principle that needs continuous restatement in times of changing beliefs."[39] We can see in the article a shift from the earlier address; in the earlier piece Scott was more verbal about Aestheticism and Decadence, about its qualities and contribution; in the later article he talks less about them, but demonstrates more covert Aestheticism in his critical judgments. His obvious sympathy with the concept of pure poetry, and his belief that aesthetic quality is all that matters in a poem, whether "seditious" or not, demonstrates convincingly that Scott's Decadent education was not suddenly rejected once and for all. The Decadent impulse of his early years is absorbed, a part of it developed, another part cut away, the whole process going underground in the formation of the social thinker and legal philosopher. The above studies prove that it is also there in the later poetry, restrained perhaps, even diffident, but constant nevertheless.

It is now possible to clarify some of the mysteries of Scott's early development that were sketched at the beginning of this chapter. For one thing, if Scott ever wrote Tennysonian or Victorian verse as a young man, it was never published, has never been quoted, and must still be buried in his private papers, public access to which has not been arranged. The same comment applies to his ostensibly

Georgian poetry, a term that might not be irrelevant to, say, "A Miniature" or "Sonnet [Would I were Angelo, and taking stone]," but would hardly express the exact nature of "Decadence" and "To Beauty." If we wish a term that comprehends the entirety of Scott's pre-Modernist canon, only Aestheticism can do justice to his efforts.

Once that is acknowledged, the Smith-Scott debates must be re-examined. There is no reason to deny that Smith turned Scott's talents towards Modernism, but it seems likely that Scott defended himself not (or at least not only) by referring to the Georgians but also to Aestheticism. Smith's own Aestheticism (suggested, for now, by Edel) may well have given the two young men the basis of a literary friendship that appears to have had little else, initially, to ground itself upon. As for the chronology of their discussions, we should note that they met on 20 October 1925, and that a year and a half later Scott's "Decadence" still found a place in the *Fortnightly*. Therefore if Smith "converted" Scott from Aestheticism, it took him two years or more to do it, no doubt because he was not entirely unsympathetic to Scott's attitudes.

What we must conclude is that the discussions of Smith and Scott were much more vigorously balanced between the two minds than we have been led to believe by Scott himself; and that it was not Smith who turned Scott from Victorianism, since Scott appears by all the evidence to have done that for himself by absorbing to some degree the Aestheticism of Oxford in the 1920s; and that the *McGill Fortnightly Review* is not an "iconoclastic journal of modernist opinion," but the production of two dedicated but uncertain young poets on a mutual path to Modernism, which Scott would not reach with any certainty until the journal was quite dead. I will make no attempt to replace one date for Scott's "conversion" to Modernism with another; but it is possible to know when the generally accepted chronology is wrong.

Scott's only acknowledgment of this early poetry is a cautious and secretive one, but it highlights exactly the tension between aesthetic detachment and activism that we have discovered to be central to his life and work. When asked why he had never entered politics himself, Scott replied:

I think that goes into the fundamental reason why I am a poet and not a pure activist ... I wanted the pure thing, and you only find that in poetry. I wanted the life of thought. True, I needed to be in touch with everything that was going on, to be in a group, but not of them. Many of my early sonnets, still unpublished, speak of the concept of absolute beauty – with a capital B – and I couldn't forsake this pursuit. I've seen so many people scurrying to political meetings; I scurried to a good many myself, but I wanted more in my life.[40]

This is the image of F.R. Scott we should explore in our studies: the man tempted towards an absolute of beauty, towards a vision of perfection lodged deep in his spirit, but drawn just that much more towards social commitment, the life of a man of relative action. To say that he was torn between the two would be over-dramatic. The tension existed, and he was sufficiently mature and wise to feel it without being destroyed by it; he went out into the world and changed things, then retired to his study and wrote. In his poetry we see these tensions, and they are particularly highlighted when we consider the burden of his early poetry. That Scott did not remain a Decadent is to his credit as a modern: a Decadent can never form a personal gospel to relieve his ennui and indecision, but it was a personal gospel that drew Scott away from his early susceptibilities and into his present reputation:[41]

> The world is my country
> The human race is my race
> The spirit of man is my God
> The future of man is my heaven.    (CP, 89)

Scott's "Creed" has earned our deepest respect and has drawn clearly the firm lines of his character; the poems of "Tuke" and "March," however, will leave him perpetually young and colourful.

# John Glassco's Post-Decadent Verse

Recent revelations about his *Memoirs of Montparnasse* make it clear that a complete critical understanding of the works of John Glassco is only now beginning to emerge. Until his death in 1981 Glassco was not closely studied; it had been sufficient to note the "bucolic and elegiac" qualities of his poetry,[1] to read his *Memoirs of Montparnasse* as an inspired tongue-in-cheek romp, and to close one eye and wink with the other at the substantial amount of pornography he had acknowledged. But when Glassco died and it became generally known that he had deposited a large collection of manuscripts, typescripts, and correspondence at McGill University and in the Public Archives of Canada, a new determination emerged to understand this enigmatic and perplexing recluse through his writings, ignoring his rather Puckish reputation. One major result was a special issue of *Canadian Poetry: Studies, Documents, Reviews* devoted entirely to his work;[2] another was the publication of Fraser Sutherland's *John Glassco: An Essay and Bibliography* in 1984. Such efforts as these promise to revise our image of Glassco substantially before they have run their course.

Charles Murdoch's article "Essential Glassco" was one of the few works of criticism undertaken on the poet and memoirist before his death and re-discovery. The article served to break new ground, to pose a few questions of Glassco criticism; but if one accepts Murdoch's Glassco whole-heartedly, one will have imbibed a significant distortion of the realities of Glassco's career. Murdoch's Glassco is charming, erudite, witty, a poet of rural beauties and sorrows, and a chronicler of pleasant youth. Despite the substantial pessimism that informs many of his "bucolic" poems, like "Deserted Buildings Under Shefford Mountain," Glassco is said to have upheld significant human values that are ostensibly of comfort: "Success in Glassco's poems lies in finding a permanence, not in cheating death but in finding values which will make a whole life complete unto itself within the brackets of birth and death."[3]

This rather too hopeful view of Glassco's better-known poetry forces Murdoch to misread other poems in the canon. For instance, he claims that the presence of Sancho Panza at Don Quixote's bedside in "The Death of Don Quixote" is a "comfort" to the failing knight (36–7), as though the poem ended on a note of affirmation; the actual lines contradict him: "Only Sancho is faithful unto death/ But in his eyes I discern the terrible dismay/For he sees that mine are at last a mirror of his own."[4] Their meaning is rather more ambiguous than Murdoch suggests. He similarly fails to note the bitter context of the Second World War in Glassco's "The Rural Mail," even though he is fully aware of the poem's having been published in 1940 (32–3); that context, once understood, makes of the poem rather a painful *denial* of human values in the face of "death and waste," wherefrom we cannot even gather "three grains of duty" (*SP*, 9). Perhaps the most disturbing conclusion Murdoch draws is his dismissal of "Brummell at Calais," one of Glassco's most striking pieces. Murdoch finds the poem "distressing and ambiguous" in its "eulogy of the notorious dandy of Regency England"; its conclusion has "something of the cop-out" about it, because "Brummell's tranquility is that of an idiot or animal. In rejecting the unique human faculty of the conscious, the dandy has settled for a lower form of life. He has escaped despair in the same way as those who undergo a lobotomy and is consequently less than a complete man" (35–6). If Murdoch had paid less attention to Brummell's supposed "escape" from despair (much mitigated by his appearance at Calais, where he fled after his fall from royal grace and where the despair of his life was to vanquish him), he might have found an entirely different set of "values" by which to appreciate the figure of the dandy, albeit less apparently Christian ones. It is hard not to conclude that Murdoch's humane preconceptions have limited his ability to see Glassco's poetry clearly; harder still not to think that it was to such criticism that Sutherland was referring, when he noted that "Conventional wisdom had categorized [Glassco] as an elaborate doodler, a *nice* dirty old man."[5]

One example of this approach to a "nice" Glassco has been the attribution of Wordsworthian qualities to his poetry. Glassco was himself responsible in part for such criticism; he had written in *Memoirs of Montparnasse* about his "favourite English poet Wordsworth," who had been "the greatest purveyor of *neat* emotion in the language. It was difficult to enter the consciousness of this cold, reserved man who so mysteriously combined the poet and the prig; but what troubled me now was the recollection that he had stopped writing good poetry after 1798, when he was still under thirty."[6] A phrase like "my favourite English poet" was bound to stay in the minds of the writer's early critics, especially in the days when the statements of the *Memoirs* were taken as reliable autobiographical truth; but in context the phrase has some obvious qualifications. To Glassco Wordsworth's emotion was "neat," which could mean un-adulterated (as in "neat" scotch), but has inevitable connotations of "trim," "tidy," restrained; he was after all "cold" and "reserved," something of a "prig" who kept writing for fifty years after his genius had abandoned him. This is certainly no wondering statement of adoration. Glassco knows his poet well: if he is his "favourite," it is not without such reservations as ought to warn the critic.

Nevertheless, the idea of Glassco's "Wordsworthianism" has been popular. Sutherland himself, who wisely rebuked those critics who had fostered the image of a "cute" Glassco, writes that "When Glassco returned to Canada, he rejected the surrealists in favour of an utterly different poet, Wordsworth. While many critics have noted Wordsworth's influence, it is most pronounced in the unpublished "Invitations," begun in 1934; here, *The Prelude* is the artistic back-drop" (13). Recent criticism has merely tried to consolidate the "Wordsworthian" image of Glassco's poetry. The most frank ex-ample of this effort is John Burnett's "John Glassco: The Canadian Wordsworth."

Burnett quotes Glassco on Wordsworth as "poet and prig," but treats the disparaging reference as mere youthful iconoclasm. He states that "there can be no doubt that his true Penelope was, not [André] Bréton, but Wordsworth,"[7] and that "When Glassco finally abandoned surrealism in his middle years and selected 'someone else,' a consciousness to enter, the model whose 'mantle' he elected to wear was Wordsworth – Wordsworth the poet, but *not* the prig" (3). Burnett locates the centre of the Wordsworthian impulse in the "poems of the Eastern Townships from … *A Point of Sky*" such as "Luce's Notch" and "Ode: The Autumn Resurrection" (3). Other poems which do not manifest the impulse so strongly suffer critically for it: for instance, Burnett notes a contradiction between "Luce's Notch," which prays for freedom from the "lust of possession" (the desire to hoard natural beauty for his own pleasure and use), and the last lines of "A Point of Sky," which seeks to make all human pleasure climax "in one clear flame of longing" (5). The implication is that "A Point of Sky" fails to live up to the Wordsworthian re-nunciation of "Luce's Notch" and is therefore marred. An attitude

not unlike Murdoch's is obviously at work in Burnett's study: there
is a "correct" version of Glassco's poetry, and poems that do not fit
it are variations from a norm, rather than poems in their own right
in an altogether different direction.

The critical pervasiveness of Sutherland's and Burnett's reading
suggests, however, that it is a peculiarly attractive means of approaching Glassco's poetry. The Wordsworthian qualities found by
these and previous critics fall into two major categories: one is a
poetic "voice," a tone or style that reminds them of Wordsworth;
the second is the Wordsworthian philosophy of perception and
imagination, the idealization of the natural world by the perceiving
eye, so that, to use the terms elaborated by M.H. Abrams, the poet
is not a mirror of the world but a lamp that casts light upon it. In
Wordsworth that manner of perception is most famously explored
in *The Prelude*, wherein certain visible patterns, conjunctions of
scene, reflection and emotion, produce in the poet moments of
heightened existence, connection with spiritual powers, and profound participation in the rhythms of nature, which Wordsworth
referred to as "spots of time." In its simplest form, this habit of
vision merely inspirits the landscape:

> To every natural form, rock, fruit or flower,
> Even the loose stones that cover the highway,
> I gave a moral life. I saw them feel,
> Or linked them to some feeling: the great mass
> Lay bedded in a quickening soul, and all
> That I beheld respired with inward meaning.[8]

In its more complex manifestation, the Wordsworthian moment is
an ultimate perception of meaning, the remote ancestor of the Joy-
cean epiphany, with the power to change an individual life fundamentally in a matter of seconds:

> There are in our existence spots of time,
> That with distinct pre-eminence retain
> A renovating virtue, whence ...
> ...........................................
> ... our minds
> Are nourished and invisibly repaired.   (12: 208–15)

Beyond the presence of such "pre-eminent" moments in *The Prelude*,
perhaps the most notable exploration of the theme in Wordsworth
is in his "Ode: Intimations of Immortality from Recollections of Early

Childhood," wherein he regrets the loss of that "celestial light" that "appareled" the visible universe in his youth and early manhood.[9] It is, of course, purely arbitrary whether we speak of the idealizing perception of the poet as the true Wordsworthian note, in which case we should seek analogous "spots of time" in Glassco, or whether the genuine Wordsworthian note is one of regret for their passing. It would seem strange, however, to define the Wordsworthian by a single "Ode" that reflects back on all of Wordsworth's earlier poetry, rather than by the Idealist poetry of his young manhood – which Glassco, we remember, thought to be Wordsworth's only "good poetry."

Of the "voice" of Wordsworth's poetry we find many examples indeed in Glassco's. It is certainly not difficult to note the nuances of syntax and style that link Wordsworth's *Prelude* and Glassco's "Luce's Notch," for instance:

> ... ye brooks,
> Muttering along the stones, a busy noise
> By day, a quiet sound in silent night;
> Ye waves, that out of the great deep steal forth
> In a calm hour to kiss the pebbly shore,
> Not mute, and then retire, fearing no storm;
> And you, ye groves, whose ministry it is
> To interpose the covert of your shades,
> Even as a sleep, between the heart of man
> And outward troubles, between man himself,
> Not seldom, and his own uneasy heart:
> Oh! that I had a music and a voice
> Harmonious as your own, that I might tell
> What ye have done for me ...   (Wordsworth, 12: 18–31)

> ... for still I feel
> That these green fields, these waterfalls and woods,
> These valleys and these winding roads that follow
> Always the heights – no matter at what length,
> Time being nothing to the men who made them! –
> That all these things which now are quite confused
> In a beautiful composite of man and nature,
> So that even old Foster seems to bless
> The farms spread out beneath his weightless shadow,
> That they, who are made to outlast my span of vision,
> And in whose life the glimpses that I gain
> Of the mute, breathing beauty of the world

Stand as a passing moment only, a blink
Between me and the everlasting darkness,
May come to consciousness through me.   (Glassco, *SP*, 43)

One could spend a not unprofitable few days noting a number of similar passages in Glassco; adoption of the Wordsworthian qualities of tone and style is frequent in his poetry and can hardly be questioned.[10] If this were the only Wordsworthian affinity spoken of in Glassco's verse, the point could be dropped, for there is an obvious superficial likeness between Glassco's poetics and those of Wordsworth.

None of us would define Wordsworth or Glassco, however, by those qualities of style that are common to the two passages. It is the second manifestation of "Wordsworthianism" that is crucial to understanding Glassco: that is, do we find evidence in his poetry of that Romantic vision by which plain objects are infused with "light," with spirit, and thereby given a relatedness to the spiritual part of man? What is Glassco's relationship to Romantic perception? The *Memoirs*, to the extent that we wish to take them as evidence of Glassco's own thinking, helps us with the following reference: "I was even then a convinced disciple of Bishop Berkeley – the only philosopher, to my mind, who has grasped the real truth of the appearances of things and the proper role of man in the universe. And now, slightly drunk, I fully appreciated his system. *Esse est percipi*, I thought, and I amused myself by closing my eyes, thus annihilating the visible universe" (106). Given the general fallibility of the information of the *Memoirs*, and the fact that Glassco's narrator is "slightly drunk," this is hardly a reliable philosophical statement from the author. But it does indicate that Glassco was sufficiently familiar with Idealist philosophy to toy with it quite comfortably, so that he would no doubt have appreciated those qualities in his "favourite poet, Wordsworth." We turn to his poetry, then, in anticipation of finding further extensions of these ideas.

What we find instead, repeatedly, is an acknowledgment that some such perception has abandoned Glassco: that once, at some time in his youth or early manhood, he too could bathe the world in an irradiated light of sorts, but he has now lost the ability. He therefore writes poems in which he struggles to reconcile himself to the loss, such as "The Art of Memory":

Wanting the paradisal past's intenser light,
My eyelids burn: this hour's page
Is a blur of words, and every word in flames … Oh then

Alas for all familiar things and thoughts,
For the clear of vanished presences before me,

And for their meaning to me, here and now,
As only pegs and props, characters
In the fable of a being – oh infinitely
Remote: I mean, daffodils in a vase,
Sail on the water, sunlight on the grass.    (*SP*, 28)

The poet names these objects as a sign of resignation to their new
simplicity; whereas his habitual response was to envision them
"Dragging another glory from the dead," he must now treat them
as "pegs and props," objects on the stage, perfunctory manipulables
in a mundane world. The admission forces him, as it forced Wordsworth, to take second-best, a love of the objects themselves, an
appreciation of their *quidditas*, with a gratitude that he had, at least
once, been visited with higher essences: he must learn to "see," once
more,

Items as undiscoverable isles
And leave them so, with the accidental ocean
Laving their lambent whatness – to the sense
Inviolate, beyond geography,

And so much deeper by so far untouched
By hope or hunger. So I do, I do;
So leave them as they were, poised on the point
Of what they are this moment, and so resign
The flowers to yellow and the lake to blue.    (*SP*, 30)

"Luce's Notch" explores, really, a very similar transition:

Release me from the lust of wanting, grant me
This sadness always, continuance of this vision;
Stay with me, sorrow that is not sorrow but
The spring of all delight, of the troubled joy
Wherein I approach the consciousness of things
Yearning and aching always, and so become
Each day more closely bound to what you are.    (*SP*, 44)

The flowers *are* yellow, the lake *is* blue, and it is to those simple
qualities of inherent beauty that Glassco now wishes to be "bound."
He surrenders his old visual "lust," the desire to hold beauty unto

himself, even as he surrenders all but the "lambent whatness" of each "item." Objects cannot be bound to the poet's spirit, or to his vision, by a vast Romantic network, but are rather "undiscoverable isles" that he cannot "touch" in the old way. He can, of course, still love them, can still be bound to them in another, less resonant way, but the Wordsworthian element is gone: Glassco's daffodils rest in a vase, they do not "flash upon that inward eye" as had Wordsworth's.

His "Ode: The Autumn Resurrection" plays elaborately with these ideas, evoking Wordsworth even more frankly in the poem's movement from Idealism to the resignation of Idealism. This "Ode" was originally part of the "Invitations," which Sutherland remarked to bear particularly the influence of Wordsworth, and there is no doubt once again that certain patterns of address and form reflect the earlier poet. Glassco chides himself for his tendency to "look beyond" physical beauty in order to invest it with spiritual light:

> But the world is not enough, the bond
> Of flesh is too much of the flesh;
>          I look beyond
> These colours of the earth, and make this air,
> This yellow sunshine, agents of a mood
> More sensitive to the spontaneous sorrow
> Which such a day begets.[11]

A long series of personal reflections follows, anything but Wordsworthian in their description of the poet's past:

>      While the pacing plaster
>        Cast that is the body's also,
> A dingy clay buggered by the iron bar
>            Of dignity, this too
> Appears again over the heart's horizon,
>        Faithful, undeniable, rearisen,
>        The true, the natural vision
> Of God's own phosphorescent fetish, his ugliest scar
> ................................................................
>
>      For in the night now gone
>      So many impious things were done –
>      Cowardly retreats and base ambitions
>      ..........................................
> – I have withdrawn my eyes from the hills
>    In which was my damnation.   (*PS*, 13–14)

By a process purposely non-rational, these odd reflections lead Glassco to a thorough rejection of Wordsworthian perception:

> Never such skies,
>   Such light, have been before!
>   The purity of earth's naked face,
>   The dear uneven natural grace!
>     Never for me again
> Shall these turn wholly to their former state,
>     Revert to vileness and decline
>     Into an aspect dulled and debased
> By a human vision and a distortive brain.   (*PS*, 14–15)

Instead of such distortion the poet will "Withdraw to [his] own excellence," his poetry, "To labour in the grey-gold light/Only for music and my loves." The natural world is left

> Silent and empty, wild to be sung,
> These naked hills and woods, these inarticulate skies,
>   While the barren hushed expectancy of dawn
>   Is slowly filled by the shrill ecstatic cries,
> The wild insentient annunciation of the birds.   (*PS*, 17)

In other words, the poet discovers a new relationship between himself as a poet and the world with which he is in love; rather than see himself reflected in all the actions and patterns of nature, rather than see his moods in the rain and wind, he acknowledges their divorce from his being, but finds in that new distance the ability to write more truly of the "naked hills," which are now "wild to be sung."

It will now be apparent that if there is a Wordsworthian quality in Glassco's poetry it is the Wordsworth of the "Intimations Ode," since regret for lost vision is his primary note, the vision itself having passed with time. At this point Glassco's critics have tended to rest their case. Before doing so, however, they ought to have given more heed to Michael Gnarowski's warning, as long ago as 1966, against a simplistic approach to Glassco as "a latter-day Wordsworth": "The Wordsworthian traditionalism of John Glassco is neither truth nor fact; it functions merely as poetic stage scenery. Nor is the modernism which he renounced in 1935 really absent from his poetry. The bucolic setting with more than passing sadness in its makeup, the rural image centering on the decrepitude of men or buildings, really serve to mask a pessimism which is the product of personal anguish and distress. And this bitterness, in turn, conceals a modern sensibility and a modern content of thought."[12] Before we accept the all-too-obvious philosophizing of "Ode: The Autumn Resurrection" as particularly Wordsworthian, we ought to be cautioned by those odd references to fetishes, damnation, and buggery, which we hardly expect to find in an intuitively Romantic poet. Wordsworth's "Intimations" Ode is not merely a regret for lost youth, lost vigour of perception, but for a particular kind of youth, for a time of "the glory and the dream," of "celestial light," of "jubilee," "festival," "coronal," and "bliss," a time of gentle, delighted loving-kindness, lambs at play with a "happy shepherd-boy," keeping "holiday" with "the heart of May."[13] Into this pastoral world ideas of "lust," "nausea," "after the ecstasy, the travesty" could never enter, as they have entered Glassco's analogous age of "innocence." It is surely necessary to understand exactly what Glassco regrets, because the essence of Wordsworth's poetry is not in the loss of just any heightened faculties, nor in his attempt to reconcile himself to that loss, but in the nature of the intense perception that preceded it: we should not call the Marquis de Sade "Wordsworthian" for gazing back from prison at a youth of vigorous debauchery, merely because he too referred to it as a time of primal energy and vision.[14] We are forced to the question: if it is the Wordsworth of the "Intimations" Ode of whom we find shreds in Glassco's poetry, what was the youth to which the latter refers? What was the true nature of the poetic past – that of the persona of his poems?

At precisely this point the "Wordsworthian" approach to Glassco breaks down and ceases to serve as an intelligent criticism of his poetry. He obviously imitated the Wordsworthian voice and borrowed some of the bones of Wordsworth's "Intimations" Ode, but the emotional history he chooses to record by manipulation of these devices (which is all they are) is anything but Wordsworthian. If we examine Glassco's complete works, we will see that the past he regrets was a past modelled, not upon Wordsworth's Westmorland and Cumberland, but upon the London of Dorian Gray, the Paris of Verlaine and Baudelaire. Glassco's poetry is the work of an ex-Decadent, who has retired to seclusion in the country after being too long in the light of the *beau-monde*, who struggles to reconcile himself to that seclusion and to the loss of his old indulgences. A distinction can thus be enforced between Wordsworthian devices in Glassco's poetry and a description of him as a "Canadian Wordsworth": the former is an accurate critical judgment, the latter is a sensationalizing attitude to a body of poetry that needs no such foreign validation.

Burnett, to be fair, is aware of this other approach to Glassco's work, for he posits his reading of the poetry openly against the other set of apparent influences upon it when he takes up Glassco's "One Last Word": "Although Glassco's habits of mind and feeling were deeply influenced by the writers of the European Decadence, there is a ring of Tennyson's 'Ulysses' to this passage [the final stanza of the poem] which confirms his true affiliation, his kinship with the high Romantic tradition that descends from Wordsworth to Tennyson" (7). Burnett appears to suggest that his reading of "One Last Word" (and logically of the other poems) mitigates the moods of Decadence some critics have hinted at in Glassco's writings, as though the Wordsworth-Tennyson influence were more significant, pervasive, or salutary. But he does not notice (beyond the allusion to Baudelaire's "Voyage à Cythère") the general Aesthetic philosophy of the poem; witness the first four lines:

> Now that I have your hand, let me persuade you
> The means are more important than the end,
> Ends being only an excuse for action,
> For adventures sought for their own sake alone.   (SP, 94)

Perhaps there is in the poem's conclusion a superficially Tennysonian voice, but the spirit descended from the Decadence runs deeper and has more complicated ramifications. Burnett's reading of the poem is a wishful one.

Against it we may pose a significant amount of evidence that Glassco was directly and heavily influenced by the writers of the European Decadence. In Glassco's Preface to *The Fatal Woman*, a collection of three of his erotic novellas, he wrote that he came "under the renewed influence of Huysmans, Pater, Villiers, Barbey d'Aurevilly and others of the so-called Decadents, and decided to write books utterly divorced from reality, stories where nothing happened."[15] The "stories where nothing happened" must have been particularly inspired by Huysmans, whose *A Rebours* is the archetypal Decadent work, in which sensation replaces action and plot, so that "nothing happens" in the usual narrative sense. Glassco's "Intimate Journal 1934–1961," kept in the McLennan Library at McGill University, refers on 9 October 1935 to his having just finished the Huysmans book, as well as having recently re-read Octave Mirbeau's *Le Jardin des Supplices*, an erotic-psychopathic work from the late nineteenth century.[16] Glassco's completion of Aubrey Beardsley's *Under the Hill*, an erotico-comic version of the story of Venus and Tannhauser that the graphic genius was unable to finish, is also fair evidence that he had steeped himself in the style of the period. In fact, Glassco's part of the book has been acclaimed as a masterful rendition of Beardsley's style, so that one cannot discover the "seam" that joins the two sections.[17] Interestingly, Edel commented to Glassco that he also found in *Memoirs of Montparnasse* similarities "to the excellent prose (1890 – Victorian of course) which is now obsolete." He added that "no one writes as well now."[18]

The reference here to the *Memoirs* opens up a wide range of allusions and parallels in that book to the writers of the 1890s. There is, for instance, the young narrator's opinion that George Moore, then eighty-seven, was "the first writer of the age": "Moore was at this time still my literary god" (*MM*, 10). Glassco has acknowledged that he modelled his *Memoirs* on Moore's *Confessions of a Young Man* (Sutherland, 20); most critics have felt that he far surpassed his teacher. In addition to his praise of Moore there are tempting references to Arthur Symons (29), Frank Harris (121–4), Richard LeGallienne (158–64), and Lord Alfred Douglas (202–4), as well as comments upon Mallarmé, Rimbaud (55), Nerval, and Baudelaire (216), with an apostrophe to Théophile Gautier when the narrator begins his descent into the arms of Mrs Quayle (181). These references show the familiarity of an older Glassco, at least, with the major figures of European Aestheticism.

But the *Memoirs*, we have learned, can never be taken at face value. A gradual accumulation of suspicions over several years culminated in the announcement, first in *The Oxford Companion to Canadian Literature* in 1983, that all but the first chapter had been written in 1963–64, in a ballpoint pen, a device unavailable in 1934 when Glassco claimed to have written all but the first three chapters (Woodcock, 300). The first chapter published in *This Quarter* in 1929, now heavily altered, was the only original work: the balance was written during a second hospital stay in the early 1960s. It appears to have been an afterthought of Glassco's to disguise the time of writing, since certain dates in the ballpoint scribblers (in the Public Archives) had been altered from 1964 to 1934.[19] He did so in order to play upon the drama of a *slightly* older and wiser narrator facing death, reflecting back on a youth of pure pleasure and exultation: Glassco did indeed have part of a lung removed in 1934 (Woodcock, 300), so the facts were matched perfectly with his fabrications. No doubt he had a certain delight in creating the illusion as well; the ramifications of its shattering, however, go far beyond mere academic pleasure.

Close comparison of the holograph manuscript and the final version of the *Memoirs* has revealed an astounding amount of prevarication in the book, utterly destroying its use as a factual record of the period Glassco spent in Paris. Thomas Tausky's "*Memoirs of Montparnasse*: A Reflection of Myself" demonstrates by reference to private material from Glassco's journals and letters that he never met Frank Harris or George Moore, that "Buffy's" conversation with James Joyce was on an entirely different subject from that recorded, that he never had an affair with "Diana Tree" (Kay Boyle, American writer-expatriate of the period), that his relationships with Robert McAlmon and Graeme Taylor apparently involved homosexual encounters, and that Glassco was far less cynical and self-possessed than the worldly young narrator of the *Memoirs* appears (61–6, 70). Philip Kokotailo's Master's thesis, contemporary with Tausky's article and recently published as *John Glassco's Richer World: Memoirs of Montparnasse*, goes over much the same ground and concludes that Glassco's memoir exploited a literary "subterfuge" typical of (what Kokotailo repeatedly calls) the "literary dandies, aesthetes, and decadents of nineteenth-century England and France."[20] These revelations, and their implications for Glassco's theory of autobiography, give new weight to Glassco's description of himself in the *Memoirs* as a "great practitioner of deceit," an "accomplished liar" (38). Presentation poems accompanying copies of the *Memoirs*, sent to Kay Boyle and A.J.M. Smith, refer to the book as a "'loose and lying chronicle'" (Tausky, 61); the evidence of the manuscript bears Glassco's judgment out.

These discoveries have made provocative academic reading for the past few years. But we are still left to deal with a work of art, the final version of which claims to have been written between 1928 and 1934, with a wealth of detail, "fact," and anecdote about a group of characters in expatriate Paris who are of current scholarly interest. It is obvious that each student of Glassco will now have to formulate a critical attitude to the *Memoirs* before proceeding: is one to accept it as in any way revelatory of the "true" Glassco, or is one to take it, ultimately, as a novel, a work of personalized fiction, and make no use of it at all in studying the man's development? Against the latter, drastic choice Tausky would wish to militate. While he acknowledges that "Any interpretation of the *Memoirs* must proceed from Glassco's own definition of it as a 'loose and lying chronicle'" (75), he agrees that "It would be both unfortunate and inappropriate ... if detailed study of Glassco's manuscript were to produce the result of simply discrediting *Memoirs of Montparnasse*" (74). One must discover, then, a way of appreciating the work while remembering its unreliability of detail.

Glassco himself provides us with an appropriate path to follow. Tausky quotes a letter from the author to Kay Boyle in which he speaks of the book in terms we may emulate: "You see, I look on the real value of memoirs as being not so much a record of 'what happened' as a re-creation of the spirit of a period in time. The first approach is so often simply tedious, faded literary gossip, name-dropping, disconnected anecdotes etc. ... The second approach is that of Rousseau, Casanova and George Moore ... I don't compare myself to them, naturally, but my book is in their style" (Tausky, 81). If we too approach the *Memoirs of Montparnasse* as factually inaccurate but spiritually and emotionally revealing, we may learn from Glassco's chronicle without being duped by its prevarications. Along these lines, it is not important that Glassco did not meet George Moore, as the evidence suggests: what is important is that he wanted to appear to have met Moore, to appear to have met Frank Harris, and not only LeGallienne (whom he seems indeed to have encountered) (Tausky, 61–5). The significant "facts" of the *Memoirs* are what Glassco wanted to relate, not what actually happened to him. As a book in which we may find information about Kay Boyle, Robert McAlmon, Morley Callaghan, the *Memoirs* are all but useless biographically: but as a revelation of Glassco's personality, what he might wish to have been, the recent discoveries of the manuscript's disparities actually make of the *Memoirs* a much more revealing and personal text than it might have been. The spirit of Glassco's Paris is very much coloured, for instance, by the European Decadence; whether or not it was so "in fact" is insignificant. What is significant is that the author's memory of it – either genuine or "willed" memory – reflects that state of post-Decadence, and that he was willing to distort where necessary to capture exactly that spirit. As Tausky says, "Anyone in the book, whatever his nominal identity, may be called upon to expound Glassco's Nineties paradoxes" (66).

We may therefore maintain that the *Memoirs* reveal Glassco's youth in Paris, if we rely on the atmosphere rather than the facts of the book. Once this is accepted, it is not difficult to rule on the nature of that youth: the central impulse recorded in the text, the spirit of the times Glassco wished to capture, was pleasure-seeking. The massive consumption of alcohol, the sexual promiscuity and variety, the incessant talk of writing and failure to do any writing, all smack of the themes of the Decadence,[21] as does the antinomian dedication of the young protagonist. John Lauber suggests that Glassco's "quest was ultimately not simply for pleasure, but for intensity of life."[22] We are familiar with that formulation and its sources; "intensity of life" is yet another link between Paris of the late 1920s and the Decadence in Europe. Thus Lauber argues that "The conventional moral pattern of sin, punishment, repentance, redemption is necessarily denied; punishment and redemption are impossible in an accidental universe, there is no repentance, and the concept of sin becomes meaningless."[23] Louis Dudek has claimed that these qualities of the *Memoirs* make clear Glassco's adoption of the Decadent mentality.[24]

However, "Decadent" must, for the literary critic, refer to conventions of literature rather than to patterns of behaviour and morality, so the term ought to be avoided in speaking of the Parisian lifestyle recorded in the *Memoirs*. For consistency's sake we must be satisfied with the word "hedonist," which sums up (if we use it in its richest sense) all of those activities of the book that are similar to certain apparent behavioural tendencies of the English and French Decadence. *Memoirs of Montparnasse* is not a piece of Decadent writing. It lacks the style of weariness, the inflated tragedy, and the inability to rise above a fallen condition that typified 1890s prose. In its ironies, its multiple levels of narration, and its taut, refractive prose style, *Memoirs* is masterfully modern.

Glassco's single effort in the *McGill Fortnightly Review*, entitled "Search," offers a revealing glimpse of the young "Buffy" before those Paris days. The recent sensation caused by the *Memoirs* revelations has made it easy to forget that Glassco played a minor role in the student journal; when we consider the earliest of his publications, we cannot help but be fascinated with what we find whirling in the brain of the seventeen-year-old:

What is it we seek? Is it beauty? Is it honour? Is it happiness? The bubbles go racing through the wine and vanish. We raise it to our lips ... Through the window we see the yellow leaves of the plane-tree, drifting in the autumn breeze. Soon the trees will be stripped and bare. Another will hold this self-same cup, will ask the self-same question: What is it we seek? ... Moments come when, blinded by beauty and ecstasy, we have found it. But alas! they pass ... The artist throws the shadow of his various calf-loves on the screen, and we applaud him, because for a moment he diverts us, and gives us a vague hope that we may stumble across it. Whatever it is, it must be the most wonderful thing in the world, because it is so intensely believed in.[25]

"J.S. Glassco," before Montparnasse, toys with undergraduate knowingness with the themes of Decadence. (That the piece was welcomed in the *Fortnightly* says much, again, about the true nature of that journal.) The conjunction of autumn, sipping of wine, moments of blinding beauty and ecstasy, and the artifice of an artist's "calf-loves" strikes the note that was never to appear again in the public Glassco, the open, out-right imitation of the Decadent manner.

An unpublished poem, however, "Sonnet (On My 24th Birthday)," shows Glassco soon after the Paris period looking back at this young man and his "Search" and feeling, again with the Decadent tone, great regret at his passing. When the poet dwells too much on the passing of day into day, season into season, he is aggrieved, and wishes to recapture the glory of his past:

Then could I wish to charm the youth who lies
Within me dead, to life again and learn
From his dear lips what secrets made him wise,
What beauty wooed his inward ear, – then turn
    My face to Time's, and make a bold assay
    Of him and all the evils on his way.   (Glassco Papers, PAC, vol. 2)

The sonnet captures exactly that dread of "Time's" passing, and the effort to struggle away from its grip, that exemplifies the poetry of the Decadents. We also see here the beginning of the pseudo-Wordsworthian condition: a past glory is mourned, a present blandness struggled against; in such a mood it is small wonder that Glassco found a Wordsworthian superficies conducive to his poetry. But it is also clear that emotions far from Wordsworthian are being mourned: we are face up now with the central problem of Glassco criticism and are forced to begin deeper inquiries into the nature of his poetry.

Criticism has enforced, for one thing, a spurious discontinuity between Glassco's poetry and his prose. Murdoch noted a "very different vision" in the poetry from that of the prose (41); Sutherland noted the "Wordsworthianism" of the poetry but believed that Glassco "found an entirely dissimilar locus for his prose."[26] To bear this judgment out, the prose criticism dwells increasingly on the Decadence, not only as a backdrop for the atmosphere of 1920s Paris, but also as an explanation of the constant stream of pornography from Glassco's pen; the burden of the poetry criticism is that Glassco adopted the Wordsworthian mantle to write his rural poems of regret and sorrowful beauty. This discontinuity does not appear to have troubled anyone greatly; but in John Glassco these elements were certainly unified, in a single person, and that person not a tragic schizophrenic but an intelligent, urbane, and curiously gentle man. Until we can find a critical approach that approximates the personal unity of the man, we have done less than we might.

This is why such care with the "Wordsworthian" ideal is called for and why the terminology of "Decadence" is inappropriate in speaking of the lifestyle of Glassco's Paris. Such terms carry loaded implications that we must be careful not to scatter like critical grape-shot, hoping for a random hit. When the *oeuvre* is scrutinized with the care it deserves, we will no longer need to distinguish between a Decadent memoirist and an "entirely dissimilar" Wordsworthian poet, because the poetry of John Glassco can be characterized no more accurately than by the term "post-Decadent." It is the poetry of a former sensualist who has been forcibly retired to the relative quiet and calm of the countryside and who while there reflects upon that tension between a libidinous, ecstatic past and a mundane and reclusive present that is at the centre of his experience. Thus his poetry manifests the themes of Decadent poetry: decay, the passing of beauty, the inevitability of process, the pursuit of intensity, with a personalizing emphasis upon the "pastness" of his Decadent beliefs, a dwelling upon loss, regret, meaninglessness, and pessimism. This reading of Glassco's poetry will permit us to approach his canon with a unified set of critical tools: to place everything he wrote, with appropriate caution, in the context of the European Decadence, and to admit that that earlier period is the true and fundamental model of his persistent dialectic, central to the *Memoirs* as well, between a past of intensity and a present of unloved peace.

*T*o reflect the past-present dialectic Glassco maintains in the poems, this study of his poetry will be divided into two parts. It is a generally accurate proposition that Glassco's poetry speaks of beauty, ecstasy, and intensity of life as properties of the past, or whose present lustre will quickly fade under the discolouring process of time; and of decay, loss, and bitter failure as present qualities, inevitable results of that past intensity. He is not, of course, arbitrary or thorough in this patterning, but is sufficiently prone to it that it provides a useful means of approaching his canon. In this first section I will study the themes of intensity, ecstasy, and beauty in Glassco's poetry and their ultimate conjunction in visions of sex, which form what we may call the "intense past" of Glassco's poetic world.

An appropriate introduction is the remembered past in "Luce's Notch," since that poem has inspired so much of the Wordsworthian criticism of Glassco's poetry. As we have noted, the past of natural simplicity, celebration, and Idealist vision is the essence of Wordsworth's "Intimations" Ode, but in Glassco's poem the past is referred to in significantly different terms:

In earlier days I thought I knew the spring
Of that ecstatic suffering which is joy,
That sense of being unable to possess

A natural scene, or be possessed by it,
That grief engendered by the desperate wish
To make such moments last forever, to stop
Time's hands and the very passage of the blood,
Freeze every conscious faculty, and then –
In a reversal of the course whereby,
As with the loves of saints, desire itself
Is made through the alchemy of their God's grace
The mode of some diviner discontent –
Let all my shapeless flame of yearning change,
Harden and materialize into the form
Of sensual appetite: in those days, indeed,
There seemed one reason only for this pain:
Its end was in its beginning, it was only
In the same rank as the natural affections,
An aspect of inordinate desire. (*SP*, 41–2)

Glassco is trying to understand why "all things radiant and remote in nature" excite in him, "as ever, a feeling close to tears." His conclusion is that joy is linked inevitably with suffering, since no joy can be held long enough to be appreciated fully by the aesthetic sense: therefore his "inordinate desire" of youth was to stop "Time's hands" and hold for himself all "perfect moments." This presupposes a "reversal of the course" of saintly desire, which becomes diviner than it once was: Glassco's instead becomes grosser and "hardens" into "sensual appetite," a phrase that underscores the vision of his youth achieved in "Luce's Notch."

Leaving aside the obvious implications of such sensualism, our interest must lie in Glassco's real terms of reference, which arise, not from Wordsworth, but from the legacy of Walter Pater's *Renaissance*. Glassco's lost youth was centred, or so "Luce's Notch" claims, upon the Paterian moment, the exquisite millisecond that the young Aesthete wishes would "last forever." Pater's own version of this "suffering which is joy" is similar:

Analysis goes a step further still, and assures us that those impressions of the individual mind to which, for each one of us, experience dwindles down, are in perpetual flight; that each of them is limited by time, and that as time is infinitely divisible, each of them is infinitely divisible also; all that is actual in it being a single moment, gone while we try to apprehend it, of which it may ever be more truly said that it has ceased to be than that it is. To such a tremulous wisp constantly re-forming itself on the stream, to a single sharp impression, with a sense in it, a relic more or less fleeting, of such moments gone by, what is real in our life fines itself down.   (*Ren.*, 188)

In the face of this ultimate temporality, the only intelligent response Pater envisions is to clutch at "moments," to centre our experience on impressions, however brief, because they contain all available meaning and beauty in life.

While all melts under our feet, we may well grasp at any exquisite passion, or any contribution to knowledge that seems by a lifted horizon to set the spirit free for a moment, or any stirring of the senses, strange dyes, strange colours, and curious odours, or work of the artist's hands, or the face of one's friend. Not to discriminate every moment some passionate attitude in those about us, and in the very brilliancy of their gifts some tragic dividing of forces on their ways, is, on this short day of frost and sun, to sleep before evening.   (*Ren.*, 189)

Nonetheless the inherent impossibility of Pater's prescription, to distinguish something exquisite in every moment, leads to the linking of joy and suffering that characterized the persona's mood in "Luce's Notch." He understands that the pursuit of beauty is, after all, only one "aspect of inordinate desire"; as all inordinate desire must come to disappointment eventually, he is left at a later age to acknowledge its passing with nostalgia:

> This madness I have no more. I only see
> Beauty continues, and so do not I.
> I have become an ageing eye through which
> A young man looks again and trembles
> ..................................................
> A man implicit in that careless heart
> Even then when all his idle study was
> To drive about the hills in search of strangeness,
> Seeking he knew not what, and now has found
> Here on this windy height – his wandering loves
> Come home to importune him with sorrow now
> And fill this foolish ageing child of his
> With the sense of what is always failing, fleeting,
> Falling away into the gulf of time.   (*SP*, 42)

The meeting of "beauty" and "strangeness" in the speaker's past, and their mutual "Falling away into the gulf of time," strike perfectly the Paterian chord. The poet's acknowledgement of Pater's influence upon him at various points in his life makes it clear that the speaker of "Luce's Notch" regrets a past that had been not so much Romantic as Aesthetic, and movingly so.

"Ode: The Autumn Resurrection" moves to a conclusion similar to the poet's hope in "Luce's Notch" that the beauties of the natural world may "come to consciousness through" him, that is, be expressed in his poetry. But the renunciations he must make before he can express that hope are rather different in the "Ode." To be sure, he still describes a past of "ecstasy":

> After the foolish twilight comes the light
> After the ecstasy, the travesty –
>   What I have borne and shall execrate
>    In the bliss of returning
>     To loathing and scorn
>     ...........................
>
>   A dream of walking in the grey woods
>   Among the perished trees of an early death;
> I walk my solitary woods and weep:
>   These are the footpaths that I trod
>  In ecstasy and wonder, in the breath
>   Of a universal spring sown deep
>   In the heart of dusty solitudes.   (PS, 13–14, 16)

The present is much viler, however, than the vistas he cherishes in "Luce's Notch"; what he must now come to terms with is the fallen world of man, "God's phosphorescent fetish, his ugliest scar." He has a "horror of the human face/That is the world's foulest tenant" (and this precisely because man's Wordsworthian habits colour and idealize the beauty of the world into something false), and must therefore retreat from mankind into his "own excellence":

>   No longer mine
>  The communal eye of man's distress
> And malediction: I am stripped to the sense
> Of solitary affections, to the cry
> Of my own heart, the secret region whence
>   Their dear and separate life began.   (PS, 17)

Pater's "Conclusion" is once again instructive, for Glassco's withdrawal into his "solitary affections" is typical of the Aesthete's reaction to the absence of beauty in mankind and society, a removal that Pater had presaged:

Experience, already reduced to a group of impressions, is ringed round for each one of us by that thick wall of personality through which no real voice has ever pierced on its way to us, or from us to that which we can only conjecture to be without. Every one of those impressions is the impression of the individual in his own isolation, each mind keeping as a solitary prisoner its own dream of a world.  (*Ren.*, 187–8)

The retreat of the "solitary prisoner," in Glassco a quasi-ethical reaction to aesthetic conditions, is represented in Aesthetic literature by the removal of the hero to distant or exotic locales, where he is free to contemplate as his sense of the Heraclitean flux demands. In Pater we see the Aesthetic removal in "Sebastian van Storck," in *Marius*; Villiers de L'Isle Adam's *Axel* turns on the theme ("as for living, our servants will do that for us," the hero announces from his tower);[27] perhaps in Glassco's own life the issue is addressed when he removes to the Eastern Townships of Quebec, there to seek in peace the ends of his natural aesthetic tendencies.

So it is that the ecstasies of the poet's past are comprehended in Aesthetic terms, and the poet is resolved to face their loss given his Aesthetic, not Wordsworthian, philosophies. From this basic poetic vision Glassco rarely wandered. Again and again we see him bemoan, through one persona or another, the loss of youthful intensity, and then reach for comfort by perpetuating the Aesthetic way of life against the insistence of society that he conform or materialize his sensibilities. Moreover, when Glassco chooses to be specific about the exact nature of these youthful ecstasies, he confirms by a different route the inheritance of Aestheticism that determines the life-patterns rendered in his verse. Alternatives of lust, ennui, sexual inversion, and artificial stimulation crowd the background of his persona's memories, activities much recorded (if little indulged in) by Symons, Wilde, and Baudelaire. In Glassco's "The Puritan Lady," for instance, a highly self-conscious persona records the intensities of her former days:

Now our lust's goal is lost to view:
Think, how in that wavering mood
We broke the spirit's solitude
And deified our flesh and blood,
Threw all our senses into one

Bright chaos of indistinction,
And ran that blind career of bliss,
Tumult, relief and tenderness,
Which led us in the end to this,
This stupor of the eternal part
That looked for all things in the heart!   (PS, 45)

Again, a past in which ecstasy seemed an answer to the "spirit's solitude" (Pater's "solitary prisoner" again) was a "bright chaos," but its present results are familiar: a "stupor of the eternal part," as time, "Who knows so well [her] dubious hours" (44), comes between the "Lady" and her lover. The ostensible Puritanism of the speaker provides Glassco with a set of terms ("lust," "spirit," "flesh and blood," "the eternal part") for discussion of the intense past and its effect on the fallen present, much as Wordsworth's "Ode" had, terms by which the poet reconciles himself to the "light" now "dimmed" upon the lovers.

Intense love was not all that occupied the poet's past. It was one means of libidinous expression, but with it came other, perhaps less healthy, obsessions. In "The Day," the speaker gazes back once again, now to a "sleeping city" unnamed, and recalls, not only the power of love, but also the temptations of madness:

My soul, recall those midnights in September
When the sleepy autumn winds blew, warm and amorous,
Up from the lamplit river and over us,
Thou and I – whom we must at times remember!
When walking through the night we beheld in visions
Of the sleeping city our spirit's firm repose,
Luxurious, perfect, like those flowers that close
On the bees they have first made drunken with fabulous visions –
Thou who keepst yet the divine stain of my tears
Psyche, not subject to the enervate years,
Canst thou alone now escape those terrible guardians
To roam again that ecstatic city of delights,
Madder than those who pass her superb nights
Dancing to the insane music of her accordions?   (SP, 79)

The passage opens peacefully with a warm rush of nostalgia, but lashes out suddenly when the "visions" of the poet are likened to an animal stupor (compare the "stupor of the eternal part" in "The Puritan Lady") leading to addiction, imprisonment, and death. The desperate address to Psyche that follows tears away the mists of nostalgia and presents an ecstatic and hellish version of the same past, in which the wife of Eros is appealed to as a last beauty beyond time's degradations. The "sleeping city" is now a "city of delights," madness intertwines with the "music of her accordions," her "insane" temper licenses the hedonistic atmosphere; it is difficult not to assume, after a reading of the *Memoirs*, that this is Glassco's Paris, with its "lamplit river" and haunting accordions. The madness and insanity in this vision of the speaker's past take him beyond mere sensuality into an uncontrolled appetite, a personal abandon, and a loss of self-definition very like the spiritual dissipation of the poet in Dowson's famous "Non Sum Qualis Eram Bonae Sub Regno Cynarae":

> I have forgot much, Cynara! gone with the wind,
> Flung roses, roses riotously with the throng,
> Dancing, to put thy pale lost lilies out of mind
> ...........................................................
>
> I cried for madder music and for stronger wine,
> But when the feast is finished and the lamps expire,
> Then falls thy shadow, Cynara! the night is thine;
> And I am desolate and sick of an old passion,
>     Yea, hungry for the lips of my desire.   (*PW*, 52)

Glassco's version of this dissipation in "The Day," like Dowson's, does not lead to any repentance; rather it provides him with a model of libidinous behaviour, a system of reverse ethics by which life may be justified and enriched, if only we will live to such a pitch of emotional and physical intensity as he found in his Montparnasse; thus his advice, as the poem concludes, is to

> Give yourself only to love your whole life long
> Give your body, your brain, your heart to whoever may choose you
> Out of the multitudinous forms and faces of being
> ...........................................................
> All that surging and singing, lay your cheek against it
> Open your lips to desire and the liquor of its adoration
> Consider only the human music taking its way to silence.   (*SP*, 81)

Glassco finds, in the madnesses of his youth, the only possible means of "overcoming" time and death: by living as fully as possible we will know, at the moment of dissolution, that somewhere "In the heart of another blooms a miraculous home," so that even though

Their own little day
Serene, new born
The day of their freedom
Dawn quietly without you  (*SP*, 82)

your life will be justified in *their* continuation – not romantically remembering, but actually embodying, the hunger of your soul.

The relatively comforting note that concludes "The Day" was not always available, however, to Glassco's complex spirit. Sometimes ecstasy provokes fears of damnation, especially when it is no longer present to distract the mind: and to the artist the pursuit of material ecstasy threatens artistic damnation, the threat of silence and creative failure, as it does in "The Pit":

Down there was the consequence of ecstasy
Where we fell like Lucifer from a jewelled sky
Plummeting through a passage of bright air
To reach our home, our natural despair ...
                    ... We who had sought to lighten
The terms of Your hard sentence and to brighten
Our darkness by the exercise of art,
To take a load from the all-too-mortal heart,
We forgot our weight in the desire to fly:
We were too drunk those nights, my soul and I.[28]

But repentance, again, is not possible: the poet knows too well that he would not change the past even if he could, and that it has, as "The Day" suggested, given the only meaning to an otherwise undirected life:

Among the white the linen fields
The chastity of something strange
To which the tired spirit yields
And yet my heart will never change.

All that I am I give to you
All I was now belongs to earth
What did I mean, what did I do
What else has justified my birth?  ("The Pit," 33)

Obviously the poet views his past as at once misspent and inevitable, as if he had been predestined upon a circuitous path towards death, whose loud loops and meanderings are all he can provide as the pattern of his life. But the ethical import, if not the gentleness, of

"The Day" also concludes "The Pit," in an address to a beloved who is involved, like the poet, in the inevitable autumn of human process:

But you my final my autumnal love
My infinite desire for whom I am speaking now,
Let me cling to you, dear one, as I hang upon
The cliffs of my departure, lend me your smile,
Stay with me in this night of desolation,
Dear one in whose embrace I come at last
To the final revelation
Of the wicked workman's message and fiat:

*Dear children of forefixed sorrow and certain duty,*
*Accept your meed of hope and pleasure now,*
*Embrace the hour and receive also my loving admonition*
*To do your best and die.* (34)

We therefore find in ecstasy the only possible reaction to death: only by doing our best to seek "hope and pleasure" (the conjunction of which is revealing) can we justify our births and make value in otherwise meaningless lives. Glassco seizes upon past ecstasy, then, as a present lesson, an echoing hedonism with moral ramifications.

This philosophy forms the ethical basis of all of his poetry and serves no matter what the kind of ecstasy lost – sexual, aesthetic, spiritual – to comfort the seeker. "A Point of Sky" puts it most succinctly:

... our pleasure and our death
Are consummated every day:
We are already happy
We are already dying
In the moment of speculation
Which holds the shape of the beauty and terror of the experience,
The haze and the storm,
In the moment which holds all our knowledge
As the poise and strain of pleasure is held in the beloved's mouth,
As her glance in the morning of meeting
Holds the whole history of our passion
Multiplying and making rich the events
That will never arrive.   (SP, 91)

The exquisite intervolvement of passion and death, hope and fear, in this masterful passage reflects the guiding philosophy of Glassco's poetry. Somewhere on these complex scales of "beauty and terror" we can locate the burden of every poem he was written and so can demonstrate the Decadent underpinnings of his verse: what is this melancholy conjunction of beauty, death, hope, and failure, if not thematic Decadence?

The keynote of Glassco's poetic philosophy, then, is intensity of life. Visible and passionate beauty often provides the focus of that magnified intensity; beauty, whether sexual, rural, or spiritual, is the most natural incitement to the aesthetically justified life. Beauty suffers the fate of youthful intensity, of course; it too passes away and leaves the seeker mourning:

> ... all the personal trash that the spirit acquires and abandons,
> Things that have made the heart warm and bewildered the senses with
>   beauty
> Long ago – but that weakened and crumbled away with the passion
> Born of their brightness, the loves that a dreary process of dumping
> Leaves at last on a hillside to rot away with the seasons.   (*SP*, 27)

Thus "The Burden of Junk" links the scrap-yard of "Corby the Trader" with the "foul rag and bone shop of the heart," by treating the memory of beauty and passion as the worthless junk of the poet's soul. In consequence of his reduced present, however, the poet is forced to speak of this systematic abandonment as part of "the seasons," the natural rhythms of the countryside with which he is in tune, as a bearer of goods. "The Burden of Junk" does not explicitly suggest that beauty is only a thing for the young – who knows but that we go on collecting such "junk" throughout our lives? In "Luce's Notch," however, the poet admitted that "Beauty continues, and so do not I": the speaker there is clearly removed from such passions and has quit the manner of perception by which they were discerned.

This is the affliction of the newly awakened Don Quixote as well, in "The Death of Don Quixote": his senses were also "bewildered" by beauty, or rather by his severe hunger for it, for the glamour and nobility of an era that had passed him by. He is a natural spokesman, then, for sentiments which Glassco, it appears, was always seeking to express in one vehicle or another:

> O my God
> I have lost everything
> In the calm of my sanity
> Like a tree which regards itself
> In still water

Seeing only another tree,
Not as when the crazy winds of heaven blew
Turning it to a perpetual fountain
Of shaken leaves,
The image of an endless waltz of being
So close to my heart I was always asking
Why should we not dance so forever, be always
Trees tossed against the sky?   (*SP*, 63)

The beauty lost had seemed "perpetual" and "endless," as youthful beauty will, and led the Don to expect to last "forever" himself; but with age, and the "drubbings" that "Wore out [his] silly casing of flesh," the wondrous flux had to be let go, although the resignation strikes him now as even more idiotic than his former condition:

In any event, as I lie here,
The withdrawal of the vision,
The removal of the madness,
The supplanting of a world of beauty
By God's sticks and stones and smells
Are afflictions, I find, of something more absurd
Than any book of chivalry.   (*SP*, 62)

Glassco would perhaps like to mitigate the unfortunate ending of Cervantes' novel, in which the mad Don whom we have come to love rejects everything we remember him for and takes repentantly to a Christian death-bed. Glassco instead posits his championing of beauty as a chivalrous act against God's world, which has no meaning otherwise: only when "the crazy winds of heaven" stir us to an "endless waltz" are we truly alive. This antinomian drive is confirmed by one of the most significant rhetorical questions in Glassco's work: "Why are we men at all if not to defy/This painted quietude of God's world?" (*SP*, 63).

We are not speaking, then, of quiet, contemplative, middle-class rural beauty, but rather an individualized, rebellious sense of beauty that alters the world, makes of a mere tree a fountain and waltz of being, and militates against the boredom inherent in stasis, in the world-as-it-is given to us by a creator. Like Don Quixote, the modern world has been "abandoned," by an "ingenious creator" who has the "insouciance of a nobleman/The fickleness of an author" (*SP*, 62), to its state of rest, and only restless appreciations and the quest for beauty can make it rich and pregnant with significance again. The theme goes back to the earliest Glassco: his "Search" in the

*Fortnightly* opens, we recall, with the questions, "What is it we seek? Is it beauty?" Rather, the search itself is the point, the perpetual hungering after some vision, however absurd, which is a defiance flung in the teeth of "quietude" and a falsely repentant death.

Glassco is not often one to refer to beauty in this abstract manner, however. He will capture as often as possible images of potent visual force, sometimes more traditionally beautiful, as in the landscapes in "Luce's Notch," often more urban, modern, dark, or twisting, as in the Art-Nouveau patterns of "Belly Dance." But his rendering of beauty in poetry, most often as a remembered passion of the past, never ceased: he clearly considered it the essence of his art, whatever its manifestations. Even an odd, half-cocked poem like *Montreal*, published in 1973, late in his poetic career, centres on the theme: to Glassco all potency in Montreal lies in the past, and the further in the past the better it was. At first he ignores beauty and addresses mere sexuality, by conjuring up an image of Indian culture that is historically questionable but personally revealing:

> Wives and husbands, widows, maidens,
> Young men, old men, little children,
> All ecstatically fucking,
> Groaning, grunting, laughing, yelling,
> Slippery and sweaty bodies
> Bubbling in the holy stew-pot
> Of their ante-Christian darkness.[28]

God's world is obviously defied once more, but this time with more vigour than Glassco had ever permitted himself. His damnation of Jansenism and Jesuitism – of "all that hideous, tight-lipped, pale-cheeked hate/Of man and all his natural members" (*Mont.*, 14) – is absolute and unrelenting.

The sexual iconoclasm of *Montreal* is only part of a larger framework, however, in which the ugliness of the modern urban landscape is assaulted and the beauty of an older Montreal lovingly mourned. In the published portion of the poem this is not immediately clear to the reader; one may note that Glassco's reaction to former mayor Jean Drapeau of Montreal is essentially an aesthetic, not a political or intellectual one (*Mont.*, 26); one may note further references to contractors who "make our city – in the modern fashion –/Not beautiful/But only big, and rich, and dull" (*Mont.*, 26). These references are insufficient to establish the clear theme of the poem, but there is an unpublished portion of the poem in the Public Archives of Canada that makes it strikingly clear that Glassco is remembering his youth in a city of trees, quiet avenues, and elegant mansions, which have been cut down, torn up, and demolished to make way for "bigger and better" styles. The clarity and directness of the passage makes one wonder why it was not published: it was intended to pick up where the last line left off and provides a much more conclusive tone than the present ending:

> The City is a creature man has made
> Not from his love of beauty, but afraid
> Of night and noises in the night: it has
> No other provenance; what of old it was,
> Was all by sport and chance. Oh, therefore sing
> The beauty of aged cities as a thing
> Of purest accident, beside the point
> And all too whimsically out of joint
> With man's most genuine ambition, which
> Is simply to be powerful and rich.
> Montreal's now no place for beauty, so
> Let it accede to ugliness, and go;
> Let it live only in my memory
> That contradicts all that I breathe and see -
> Those quiet, green and shady colonnades
> Of streets all slowly murdered, the dear shades
> Of Guy and Sherbrooke, Bishop and Mackay,
> All as they were under a sparkling sky
> Of vanished seasons and a vanished town
> Now beaten to death ...   (Glassco Papers, PAC, vol. 8: 717–36)

One would like to see this Addendum generally accessible, because it might assist critics who have found in *Montreal* little more than "the shock value of the worst *Tish* poetry" (Burnett, 8) to appreciate the ways in which *Montreal* is, rather, a continuation of themes that preoccupied Glassco all of his life. The poem makes of Montreal a city analogous to Glassco's Montparnasse: a place of beauty and elegance and pleasure now lost to the author forever, leaving nothing but memories and ghosts, unsuccessful evocations of an intense youth. The bizarre sexual preoccupations of the Montreal Indians become more understandable within the context of Glassco's other Aesthetic regrets: they are analogous to the promiscuity of the *Memoirs*, as sex is part of the intensity and pleasure of youth, and the poem would be incomplete without them.[30]

   It would be foolish not to examine further the role of sex in Glassco's poetry: despite its obvious centrality, critical discussion of its manifestations in the canon is non-existent. Glassco's references to sex are frequent, his descriptions of it particularly potent, and their character unites with the spirit of reckless physical abandon that brings so much verve to the *Memoirs*. It is true that sexuality is less a thing of the past to the poet than a constant and omnipresent interest: the past sense is often dropped in favour of direct and immediate descriptions. As a point of meeting between beauty and intensity, however, both of which *are* clearly located in the youthful past, sex and sexuality become the epitome of Glassco's poetic concerns: intensity may be a thing of the past, but the insistent pursuit of it through sex is one pleasure of the irredeemable present.

"The Crows," for instance, a complex hovering between the romantic-love associations of lost youth and the strange, harsh, present-day image of crows that "cry over the rosy snow," begins as one more attempt to deal with memories of power:

> And so she left
> And passed beneath the arcade, passing along, her shadow winking
> On and off, on and off, beneath each florid arch,
> The little heels clacking on the marble
> In the vanished sun and dust
> That is shining and blowing still
> Here in the square with the naked man in the fountain
> And an absence of trees.   (*SP*, 83)

Such memories have already caused the poet to demand of himself, "Why did I come to this city again?" He retraces his steps, then, in a city where love had once run its course; the tendency this imposes to remember images of former potency raises incident after incident to the poet's mind (including a brief rendition of the visit to the house where Paganini died, recorded in the *Memoirs*), until

> By sweet and facile stages came
> The retreat into erotic reverie
> The dream of Arthur,
> That dark Avilion where there is no death,
> Only immortal pleasure in a suspension of time
> As conscience drops into the timelessness
> Where the unconscious lives
> Snug in its cortical layer:
>                 draw back, draw in.   (*SP*, 85)

As the speaker retreats deeper into his own shadows, an image of bizarre sexuality appears at the centre of all experience, emerging as the motivation of the entire memory.

Enter this paradise which is always waiting
For the magician of the self, his royal visit
To a world of adoring shadows
Where lust is the only living thing,
Absolute power and absolute submission
Locked in each other's loving arms
In the darkest room of the tallest house.   (*SP*, 85–6)

We are obviously a long way from the comic orgies and whorehouse reminiscences of *Montreal*, yet the two poems overlap largely. Sexuality in both is potency: whether in primitive ignorance of moral codes, or ritualization of inter-sexual power struggles, the act of sex is a use of the body and soul for intensity, which has ethical undertones: that is, the proper condition of man lies in intensity, and the richest quality of that intensity is sexual. In keeping, then, with his sense of beauty and ecstasy, Glassco reverts to a sexual world that is hypnotic but cannot be redemptive of the present, quite beyond any condition of "grace" or morality. We may regret the passing of such dramatic libido, but as long as we remain faithful to its vision we are saved from boredom and ignorant of passing time.

The strange and intricate relationship Glassco thus adumbrates between sex and the past is nowhere so complex or striking as in "For Cora Lightbody, R.N.," a poem composed upon an incident that occurred during the hospital stay in 1964 that saw the completion of *Memoirs of Montparnasse*.[30] Glassco intertwines the brief attractions of sex with a young nurse and the strange images of a "nightmare" from his Georgian childhood to produce a singularly repellent vision of physical ecstasy:

You are a landscape in the Tale of Terror,
   *Ca.* 1910. Your bibful of breasts secrete
   Those dreamy fields, fens, fells, that sinister street
Of the Georgian nightmare I must live forever,
Where up in the attic, or hunched behind a mirror,
   Now in a cloud, now in a winding-sheet,
   The Thing is lurking; cling your palpably sweet
Lips to mine, softly as all that sugary horror.

Action then takes place, admittedly unclearly; a movement is established in the poem not unlike the suggestive obscurity of Symbolist verse: more by association and irrational response to verbal stimulation than by reading closely and intelligently, we are brought to a point at which the "nightmare" climaxes simultaneously with the act of gratuitous sex:

> ... The dénouement climbs the creaking staircase. – Blood!
>    Shots, screams, italics!
>                          In a spasm like my spending
> The Foul Thing drops; in you, my hospital love,
>    I sink my shaft as in auriferous mud.   (*SP*, 65)

The denigration of the nurse's vagina – "auriferous" can hardly mitigate the force of "mud" – makes clear that the sex act is secondary to the memory: it serves to recall a previously unconsidered intensity, but it has little or no meaning of its own. (Glassco's correspondence bears this out, but offers, unfortunately, no clarification of the Georgian nightmare.) Glassco is once again depicting sex after the true intensity has gone out of it: the act itself is not powerful or to be desired, but by its association with a powerful emotion from the past it may attain a loosely meaningful status.

Before we attribute too comforting a redemptiveness to sex, however, we must remember that Glassco only turns to the nurse because he is shattered by a sense of time's power and horror. The act merely sinks him into the "mud" of oblivion, as any other narcotic might have done. "Villanelle II," with its flat concluding line, also treats sex as a flight from the inevitable, affirming nothing:

>                      Dear, you and I,
> Locked in each other's arms, come let us flee –
> Alas, alas! – that comfortable lie.
> God will desert us when we come to die.   (*SP*, 76)

Against a definite and impending death the best the poet can do is wind himself in his beloved's arms and flee. Sex offers no redemption, nor does it create its own condition of amoral "grace"; rather it is a gesture against death, a determination to die well, and to define a good death by reference to the degree of intensity at which it occurs.

That distinction is crucial to Glassco's manipulation of sexuality in his poetic philosophy. He is not proposing a higher (or even lower) moral order, but is accepting a given moral order: the inevitability of death, the possibility of eternal judgment, the impossibility of knowing whether we are so judged already. Against that order he suggests the best means by which to die – at a heightened moment, in ecstasy, rapt in beauty or sexuality: as he put it in "The Pit," "do your best and die" – simultaneously. Because we will definitely come to death: there is no escaping it, as Glassco, in tune with the Decadents, recognizes above all the triumph of natural processes.

This facing up to the fact of death has not prevented Glassco from describing, with the skill of a tested author of erotica, specific acts of sex. In a sense, "Belly Dance" and "A Devotion: To Cteis" – the former a vision of male masturbation, the latter of cunnilingus – are themselves attempts to overcome the same fear of process, if only for the time it takes to read each poem: Glassco desires to create in his readers the very sexual responses he describes, and thereby leave them "intensified" by the degree to which they have experienced his erotic vision. The most noteworthy feature of both poems, and the quality that makes of them pieces of erotica instead of mere pornography, is the degree to which Glassco has disguised the sexual content: references to the "member" in a "nerveless hand" in "Belly Dance" make the matter of the poem fairly clear, but one can read "A Devotion: To Cteis" once or twice before realizing that it is an elaborate blasphemy that turns the act of cunnilingus into a religious devotion (and vice versa).

"Belly Dance" is disguised primarily by its Art-Nouveau quality, which intervolves a series of lines and twining shapes so strikingly that the independent visual qualities can almost take over from the erotic:

> The corpsewhite column spiralling on slow feet
> Tracing the seashell curve, the figure eight,
> Coldly unwinds its flowing ribbon
> With public motions of the private psalm
> Of supposed woman to the thought of man.

"Supposed woman" calls up anything from transvestitism to homosexuality and forecasts the sexual inversion that is implied in Glassco's vision of masturbation: the latter is here an elaborate dance with one's own image, a sexual devotion to one's own body, a mental image of which becomes, in effect, the partner in the act:

> And like that man of Bierce's wrestling
> In the embrace of an invisible thing,
> Flaps in snakehead-strike doublejointed death –
> An evocation of circumfluent air,
> The adversary in a breath of air.

The Ambrose Bierce allusion assists the strangely satanic quality of "Belly Dance," as does the "adversary," in Hebrew, "sathanas": we are not to appreciate the masturbation as rich personal expression but as a strange manifestation of self-fascination, something snake-like and deathly.

The definition of love that follows invites a dehumanization of the "dancer" and a strange marriage between dancer and audience, as though the masturbation were being viewed:

> Love, that is violence
> Made easy, is here the end of all, a dance,
> And man the viewless form, the animal
> No longer animal but seeing-eye,
> But super-member of impossible man.

As the fantasy of masturbation takes over the poem from the image of the belly dance, the reference to a "super-member" seems natural: a superman is addressed who reflects the mental self-image created by the erotic fantasist. Now that the question of audience has entered, we note in the first stanza the suggestion that these are "public motions" – either the action is observed or "the adversary in a breath of air," the fantasized partner, becomes a kind of invisible audience, as though masturbation were (by this poem's definition, at least) a kind of exhibitionism. Hence the "mirror" required in the final stanza and the interchanging of the "partners" in the act:

> So the man of air supplants the man of bone,
> And it is he who writhes before a glass,
> Before the figure of his only love,
> The viewless member in his nerveless hand
> Working within the adverse air.   (SP, 60)

Here the poem stops, before climax, so that the stimulating is the point; the seeking of fulfilment gratifying the reader, rather than the fulfilment itself. The reader is left with an uncomfortable sense of having willingly witnessed, indeed worked to witness, an act of masturbation, of becoming a voyeur in pursuit of an erotic pleasure. The fascination of Glassco's presentation, the elaborate visual and sexual patterns, pass the erotic burden of the poem onto the reader and involve him in that sexual release that Glassco's other poems have urged upon him in more theoretical terms. "Belly Dance" is, in this sense, a practical example of the sexual theory that we have witnessed elsewhere: we are conjured by the artist into his own manner of erotic vision, trapped by the webs and tangled lines into a participation in outright sexual release such as Glassco's childhood society (and the society of the time that Glassco wrote the poem) would at best not talk about, at worst condemn and seek to destroy.

"A Devotion: To Cteis" uses the poetics of John Donne as "Belly Dance" had used the motifs of Art Nouveau, to involve an elaborated act of oral sex with a religious and sacramental vision, and thereby create a delightful piece of potent blasphemy. "Cteis" is a Greek word meaning "forked" or split into teeth, like a comb or a rake, and the image is our first clue to the sexual content of the poem. When "Cteis" is used as the name of a beloved or of a goddess (as earlier poets had addressed themselves to "Phyllis" and "Amaryllis"), we associate the image of split limbs with the female figure, which association, when united with the first two lines, sketches the image that will dominate the entire poem: "Well, I shall kneel, that the whole world can say/Here is desire too that has come to pray" (*SP*, 68). The lover kneels before a "cloven idol" with "desire": if the idol is flat on her back, we need no more to complete the picture: but Glassco does not wish to hurry the image or the action. Instead further ctenoid images are employed to strengthen the image of wide-spread pairs:

The poles of pleasure in our divided dust
Meet often in their own tropics, lust and lust,
Devotion and devotion, but to join
Either to other is this way of mine.

Thus the poet seeks to unite the split pairs, to join "devotion" and "lust" and thereby complete his partner's sexual needs:

Now when my mouth, that holds my heart, has become
An infinite reverence's ciborium,
Now, when the surcharged spiritual part
Exhales its burden – marvel, O marvel at
This joining, this economy of love
That turns the pious breath, the gesture of
My extreme adoration to a kiss,
As if it were all that could be made of this! (*SP*, 68)

The "ciborium" is the religious object that holds the "body of Christ" during communion: Glassco's mouth holds his "heart" in that "ciborium," which makes the gesture of his "adoration" into "a kiss" – so the image is now locked together. He kneels before a "cloven idol," which lies with limbs spread in front of him; he takes into his mouth some blessed substance, which act of "adoration" is, in fact, a kiss; and the "spiritual part" is "surcharged," overburdened by the degree of passion this "religious act" creates in the devotee. There is no way to put these images together except in cunnilingus; and as if to acknowledge that this point in the poem has made its matter clear, Glassco now drops the disguise and becomes explicit in his narration of "carnal ecstasies" (*SP*, 69).

In the mundane terms Glassco must avoid, the poet seeks to postpone his lover's orgasm, which would leave her "all sensible" in the extreme tactile sensitivity following sexual climax. The poet would not "slip from worshipper into man/A space yet, but remain as I began," still attending to the needs of his goddess rather than satisfying his own male requirements after her pleasure. To do so would make of him an "incubus" – a medieval spirit who came to otherwise chaste women at night and "hung" upon their flesh, leaving them in the morning with inexplicable pregnancies that were no fault of their own – a possible impregnator, a self-seeking lover rather than a devotee. Rather he would "Give [his] lips holiday from the work of words," to arrive at a "Sabbath of silence," only "drifting pleasurewards," not rushing. In fact "A Devotion: To Cteis," like "Belly Dance," visualizes no sexual climax: it is the action of moving towards climax that is captured, the actual release of orgasm seeming fearful, as though it would break the spell, restore a sense of process, and remove the religious sense of meaningfulness that has briefly informed their world. Practically speaking the poet now forgets the "cloven idol":

> As the old speechless misremembered year
> Returns in noonlight, hunger and rage and fear
> Cancelled forever, and as there bloom in me,
> On the bare branches of my cynic tree,
> Like mistletoe run wild, the devotee,
> The lover and the child.   (*SP*, 69)

It sounds a terribly sentimental conclusion until one realizes that the poet is "devotee," "lover," and "child" because of his proximity to the woman's genitalia: he kneels there in devotion, he performs there sexually, and he is in effect "born again," as though rather than entering the woman he had just come out of the womb and was now lying between her legs, fresh masculine life.

The complexity of "A Devotion: To Cteis" and "Belly Dance" is a final signal of Glassco's poetic sexuality. He is clearly not seeking here the presumable genital charge that he transmits in his pornography: he seeks rather to uplift the act of sex, to raise it by linguistic tricks, metaphoric connotation, and elaborate style to a higher plane of activity, aesthetic and mock-religious, and thereby to escape briefly from the mundane and the time-bound. He strives in the two poems to capture above all the sheer passionate intensity of sex, the power inherent in the muscles of the body that can only be expressed in the utter abandon of physical sensation and the "exhalation" of the "burden" of the "spiritual part," the release from mind, spirit, reason, even emotion, in the midst of extreme carnal pleasures. Note that there is no effort to transmit a spirit of romantic love in "Belly Dance," "A Devotion: To Cteis" and "For Cora Lightbody, R.N."; sex is separated from the concerns of love and can thereby be contrasted comfortingly with the other processes of the flesh, which he is concerned to do as a means of cancelling his fear of time. Glassco's sex poems, then, are efforts akin to the general drive of the other poems we have examined: indeed, they are the epitome of that drive, wherein passion, intensity and beauty are united in an act of such pure liberationism that it briefly cancels all the fetters of human life, whether these are social or metaphysical, whether imposed by law or by the universal death-sentence.

Because ecstasy, intensity, beauty and sex are the chief preoccupations of the past to which Glassco refers in his poetry, it is instantly tempting to relate this condition of the poetry to the *Memoirs of Montparnasse*, to speculate that it is his past in Paris that dominates his imaginative being for the rest of his life, and that it is Montparnasse to which he looks when he remembers the special conditions of a life of hedonism and unalloyed sensation. If we had nothing but the *Memoirs* and the poetry on which to base such a speculation it would be critically untenable: but with the fortuitous addition of certain references in Glassco's private journal, it is possible to demonstrate that his sense of a rich past showing up the blandness of a reclusive present does indeed occur as a result of the Paris years, and that it is to those years that he refers when, in his poetry, he evokes the intensities of youth.

The journal, held at McGill University, covers the years from 1934 to 1961: it was deposited with many portions cut away, since Glassco wished to preserve the privacy of certain entries. What he has made available is still highly revealing, and depicts a personality struggling with an intense sense of personal failure and loss. "I have got," he writes in an entry for 8 February 1935, "so that I believe in nothing but sensations, painful + pleasurable" (33); but such sensations seem to come less and less frequently in seclusion, and the resulting nervousness produces some painful outbursts in the years that follow. On 15 February 1936 he notes, "I find myself thinking that I *must* live more intensely: I seem to have been asleep for the past four years, moving among shadows" (55). From the date noted, "the past four years" would involve a period beginning in the mid-winter of 1932, only a few months after his return from France in precarious health. Thus, in Glassco's mind the period of loss and aesthetic inactivity begins when France is left behind. This condition is reflected, he believes, in his inability to write any decent poetry: he struggles with "The Invitations" (59), but recognizes repeatedly that he is not achieving what his youth had promised him; he suffers constant self-doubt about his poetic calling, and at some points the journal reads like the record of a complete personal failure:

No, there is no doubt of it: I am finished, completely. I have turned out a failure in everything I have tried to do: I cannot write, and I have no further interest in lovemaking ... Every day now, as I ride around on the mail, I feel like a dead man sitting behind the horse, quite erect, often well-shaved, sometimes even decently dressed, – but dead from top to toe ... I feel already that I am being welcomed into the confraternity of the lifeless, noting the way the villagers ... greet me now: I am one of them, I feel: we lift our hands to each other in the street, on the roads, with that robot-like gesture that is a kind of password among those who have "entered Death's other kingdom." We are living by force of circumstances, through the pressure of gain, from force of habit. Oh God shall I ever come alive again?   (87)

This spiritual condition was brought on, apparently, by a feeling of surfeit, the ennui that comes after all has been experienced and enjoyed. On 20 October 1946, Glassco enters the following thought: "The principal stumbling block in the way of our [his and Graeme Taylor's] pursuing any new goal, is that we have had the best of everything, – the best youth, best house + horses, best women, best everything. We have extracted the quintessence of all the most desirable situations, + gobbled it down: now our appetite is jaded, crotchety, even sickly" (121).

   This is, obviously, the archetypal Decadent condition: if sensation is the only meaning in life (as he had himself concluded) and every sensation has been experienced – the delusion upon which successful Decadence depends – where is there to go? what room to develop? Writing is unlikely, for nothing can be of value compared to what had been experienced previously, so the pen lies quiet. It was not until Glassco was able to find a manner of poetry that could allow him to express exactly this sense of loss, this *pastness* of intensity, that he was able to overcome the terrible ennui that threatened to destroy him. He found it during the late 1940s, with the results we have recognized: it took him, then, fifteen to twenty years to absorb artistically the chief qualities of his youth and turn them to advantage in a mature art. That it is the period in Paris to which all of Glassco's regret for the past refers is confirmed by these journal entries: and from the conjunction of the poetry, the *Memoirs*, and the journals, a preliminary sketch of Glassco's over-all literary development begins to emerge.

I have suggested that the dominant note of Glassco's poetic canon lies in his opposing a past of intensity, ecstasy, and beauty to a present of loss, regret, unwelcome quietude, and age. Having now traced half of that argument, it remains to examine the other half, to point out Glassco's fascination with decay, failure, and ruin, with the results of time and process, that inevitably follow the building, the passion, the heights of human life. It is already evident that his poems of passion and intensity tend to anticipate ruin and loss: but there is another substantial portion of his poetry that dwells on the ruin itself and appears to have surrendered all thought of the lovely past. This is the other side of Glassco the poet, the other face of the intense hedonist, the face that always looks into the mirror at some point in one's life and reminds one of the truth, that we are born to die, that we live only to fail, that our best endeavours are merely beautiful gestures against calm, unhurrying death.

*I*ntensity, beauty, and sexuality are not commonly discussed elements of Glassco's poetry: decay is. Indeed, it would be impossible to read his poems of rural life without noting their fixation on decay: not one of the Eastern Townships poems fails to depict it, not one finds in the countryside images of growth, recurrence, or fertility that are comforting or revitalizing. Glassco does not present himself as a lover of nature, but rather as an opponent of man, of his machinations and marring of all that is free and natural in the world. Because of his opposition to such human structures, decay occasionally becomes for Glassco a sign of hope, an indication that the progressive genius of man will fail and all his best efforts come to ruin and dust: hence his use of "tottering and attrition" as a source of comfort and a perennial symbol in his rural landscape. Glassco wrote to Jean LeMoyne on 4 May 1964 with a vigour that confirms this quality of his verse: "I really *like* decay, or at least prefer it to improvement. For improvement seems so often to mean cutting down trees, widening and straightening roads, raising speed limits, replacing orchards with asphalt and so on" (Glassco Papers, PAC, vol. 1).

Sentiments like these motivate his reaction to a "Gentleman's Farm": the shine and newness of the city-dweller's renovations to the farm repel him, but he knows that in the end will come failure and a falling away. This is the end of all splendid visions:

> Where all goes well and the pioneer has profit,
> Where the titan's work subserves as in a dream
>     The all too fictive goal,
> And the end is perfect beauty, the blessed vision,
> The working out of a man's reverie
>     Of his own memorial!  (*SP*, 17)

Into this antiseptic world of weekend husbandry Glassco brings the inevitability of process, the "forefixed harvest of man's reverie driven/Into the light of day and life of men": no amount of money can stop the gradual rust, the erosion by rain, the indifference of subsequent generations, that will eventually swallow up the "perfect beauty" created by "the city Columbus" (*SP*, 16) and his whims; time will

> ... bring the same revenge
> On the impresarios of all sacred sweetness,
> Whose eyes shall wake to witness, spring by spring,
>     The sad and stealing change,
>
> Hope battered into habit, and a habit
> Running to weariness – the proof and process
>     Of powers which must equate
> Farmer and Gentleman through their monuments,
> Till time's mathematics of indifference
>     Confound them ...  (*SP*, 17)

The result of that long but inescapable process will be "a common loveliness": a more genuine beauty, not painted and nailed and wired together with subsidies from the city, but the loveliness of nature, centred on the rhythms of collapse and death. In the final stanza Glassco adopts a prophetic voice that serves to delineate the beliefs that will dominate these rural poems:

> See that the wreck of all things made with hands
> Being fixed and certain, as all flesh is grass,
>     The grandiose design
> Must marry the ragged thing, and of the vision
> Nothing endure that does not gain through ruin
>     The right, the wavering line.  (*SP*, 18)

In decay then is truth, the truth of flux and relativity instead of the absolutism of the "gentleman" who buys his visions and guarantees (so he thinks) his profits. For this reason Glassco falls in love with decay: it is the great leveller of all things and will bring to dust the gentleman, the farmer, the pauper, the sinner, and the priest, and all the brief structures they have thought to impose on the imperturbable surface of time.

A similar sense of decay is visible in "The Entailed Farm," in which the quarrel of a previous generation with its parents has led to the gradual taking over of a successful farm by the expansions of nature:

> Where the spring's tooth, stripping shingles, scaling
> Beam and clapboard, probes for the rot below
> Porch and pediment and blind bow-window,
> And the wooden trunk with the coloured cardboard lining
> Lies where it fell when the wall of the flying wings
> Fell down ten years ago;
>
> Where the stone wall is a haven for snake and squirrel,
> The steepled dovecote for phoebe and willow-wren,
> And the falling field-gates, trigged by an earthen swell,
> Open on a wild where nothing is raised or penned,
> On rusty acres of witch-grass and wild sorrel
> Where the field-birds cry and contend.   (SP, 13)

This pervasive decay is a sign to the poet of inevitable truths. The farmer and his son quarrelled over some serious matter, which led the farmer to try to "cheat time's night" by entailing the farm so that the son could not have the freedom of it, leading to its present dilapidation; but that wretched argument, with its dismal consequences, is better than the way "we" – the poet addresses himself and his readers – have dealt with our own fathers, through fawning, or hypocrisy, or over-pleasing, to receive our inheritance free of such "attainder." We "can meet a stranger's eye,"

> With a good face, can answer a question, give a reason,
> For whom the world's fields and fences stand up plain,
> Nor dazzle in sunlight or crumble behind the rain:
> From us, with our hearts but lightly tinged with poison,
> Who composed our quarrel early and in good season
> Buried the hatchet in our father's brain.   (SP, 14)

The verbal equivocations dominating the stanza reflect "our" hypocrisies; "but lightly tinged" is, of course, a bathetic attack; "composing" our quarrels means not only making up with our fathers but also pre-determining the course of our quarrels, planning their intensity and fore-ordaining when they should end, for our own financial safety; "burying the hatchet," a colloquialism suggesting peace-making, is suddenly taken literally as well, with violent consequences for our "triumphant" fathers. The burden of the poem is suddenly foisted upon its readers, and the decay of the entailed farm appears as a symbol, ironically, of the *honesty* of the father-son conflict on the farm: the son maintains his principles without fawning or hypocrisy, and the decay is the result, but that is preferable to the inner decay, the spiritual tarnish that overcomes the hearts of those who avoid such truths and slink carefully away from anything that might disturb their receipt of an inheritance.[32]

Thus the images of decay in Glassco's poems lie at the centre of an elaborate and idiosyncratic symbolism. No doubt Glassco's residence in the Eastern Townships spurred on this love of decay; by his own account in his correspondence, poems like "The Entailed Farm" included actual descriptions of particular abandoned or faltering farms in the Foster vicinity.[33] The consistency with which he renders those ruined farms and mansions, however, bespeaks a quality of the poet's character as well: he would not have dwelt so exclusively on the rural failures had he not been personally attracted to the sense of decay, the inevitability of ending that they represented to him. "Luce's Notch" refers to the "buildings hereabouts" that "Are long in standing, longer still in falling,/And wear for a man's lifetime the final grace/Of tottering and attrition like a crown" (*SP*, 40–1). To Glassco it imaginatively appeared that buildings in the process of crumbling lasted just long enough to reflect a man's crumbling life: so they became potent symbols in *his* poetic imagination of the limits placed by time upon human achievement. He has ironically given them a place in literature that makes permanence of their impermanence, that freezes them forever in a state of affectionate wasting.

Glassco has referred to "Deserted Buildings Under Shefford Mountain," the climactic poem in this series of depictions of architectural decay, as his "best poem."[34] Certainly in the degree to which it summarizes a dominant trend in his poetry, relates that trend to a personal spiritual condition, and captures the entirety in simple, beautiful verse, the poem stands rightly as one of his most popular and successful pieces, a status recognized by anthologists since its initial publication.

These native angles of decay
   In shed and barn whose broken wings
Lie here half fallen in the way
Of headstones amid uncut hay –
   Why do I love you, ragged things?

What grace unknown to any art,
   What beauty frailer than a mood
Awake in me their counterpart?
What correspondence of a heart
   That loves the failing attitude?

The fragile beauty of the buildings attracts the poet because of his sense that the appreciation of beauty is most joyous and painful at once when the beauty is visibly on the point of passing away. It is the Heraclitean flux again, the sense that all impressions are on the verge of disappearing and cannot be held for long, that creates in the appreciator a sense of suffering as well as pleasure. Glassco acknowledges the Heraclitean premise – "the lesson of the straight/ That shall be crooked soon or late/And crumble into forms alone" – and he struggles, in the face of his overwhelming sense of flux, to hold something to himself, to use his inner eye to hold what the outer eye can only briefly glimpse. "Between design and destiny" and "Between God and absurdity" (SP, 19) we live and struggle, neither in time nor out of it, until we feel that we have discovered something that shall endure.

For Glassco it is decay itself that shall endure, and from which he takes comfort: by finding in decay a perpetual and unending source of beauty and desire, he guarantees his stability, for only decay and change have the constancy he needs.

So I, assailed by the blind love
   That meets me in this silent place,
Lift open arms: Is it enough
That restless things can cease to move
   And leave a ruin wreathed in grace,

Or is this wreck of strut and span
   No more than solace for the creed
Of progress and its emmet plan,
Dark houses that are void of man,
   Dull meadows that have gone to seed?   (SP, 20)

Whichever alternative the poet settles upon, he has comfort: there is either "grace" in "ruin," peace from the flux, or (the lesser, but still a sufficient answer) a halting of human progress, which was to Glassco a constant and bitter enemy, as in *Montreal*. The "Deserted Buildings Under Shefford Mountain" have brought Glassco to an understanding of his love of decay and an acceptance of process, which stymies the efforts of self-seeking humankind. He is, to all intents and purposes, alone in this ruined world, removed from the others who cannot understand, who see only eyesores where the poet sees "tottering and attrition like a crown." This isolation is also a portion of his comfort; as Marvell had put it, "Two paradises 'twere in one/To live in Paradise alone."[35]

It would be romantic, however, to assume from "Deserted Buildings" that Glassco's sense of decay and ruin was a constant source of comfort, or that he so loved decay that a glimpse of a weathered shed could lift his mood. On the contrary, decay was often to Glassco a source of despair, when he shifted his allegiance now and then to the world of men. In his "Intimate Journal" he writes,

Just now, these days, I am in such very bad shape emotionally, – nervous, frightened, uneasy, yes – but worse than that is the appearance of the world + all human endeavour = everything is *hopeless*, all endeavour doomed, I cannot see a building going up but I fancy it a melancholy ruin 25 years hence, nor see an old house without imagining the hopes + interests that surrounded its building 25 years ago. A terrible sadness is cast over everything ... These days I find myself repeating Schopenhauer's "The soul is grieved by everything it looks on" with real understanding.   (4 April 1946, 119)

The poet of "Gentleman's Farm" or "Deserted Buildings Under Shefford Mountain" is not in tune with sentiments like these; here, instead, Glassco's sudden concern is with human effort, because like it or not he too must make such efforts, must struggle in the world. Aesthetic removal is all very well, but he must earn his bread and keep his sanity, for which he needs human contact, the company and perhaps the love of others. In such periods of reflection his ruined buildings frighten him with the recognition that all human effort is doomed to fail, that nothing he can do will, in twenty-five years, retain its beauty and potency. To a poet in particular, such meditations must be distressing. This sense of decay as personal threat also appears in his poems, albeit with less frequency: in "The Rural Mail," for instance, the poet in his public capacity has constant opportunities to view local conditions, and they are not heartening. The backdrop of the Second World War adds particular terror to his thoughts of doom, and decay here is not a fitting punishment for man but a terribly unfair sentence for a crime of which he is innocent:

> Scraping the crumbling roadbed of this strife
> With rotten fenceposts and old mortgages
> (No way of living, but a mode of life),
> How sift from death and waste three grains of duty,
> O thoughts that start from scratch and end in a dream
> Of graveyards minding their own business?
>
> But the heart accepts it all, this honest air
> Lapped in green valleys where accidents will happen!
> Where the bull, the buzz-saw and the balky mare
> Are the chosen fingers of God for a farmer's sins,
> Like the axe for his woods, and his calves and chicks and children
> Destined for slaughter in the course of things.   (SP, 9)

Now the promised dissolution of man is feared and avoided, and each item on the farm suddenly appears a potential instrument of punishment – anything at all may be adopted by God as the means of ending human life, since we are all, after all, "destined for slaughter" and nothing more.

This infinitely darker sense of decay spreads out through Glassco's poetry like a brooding poison. It is the deeper decay, foisted upon the reader in "The Entailed Farm," of hypocrisy and smiles; in "The Brill Road" it is the decay of the roadbed, and of the spirit faced suddenly with personal failure:

> Like a mind grappling with its own betrayal,
> Thoughts thinning out, the basis crumbling,
> Rising, rising ever into more breathless air
> And a frailer tenure, while the wind blows,
> The hills darken ...   (SP, 23)

In "The Whole Hog" it is the rotting from generation to generation of the sense of absolute values, which the son (the speaker) finds has failed him:

> See the Portland vase before the Venetian mirror
> In my father's house. It is filled with *honesty.*

The abstraction found its body long ago
In a plant of eternally desiccated leaves,
As my father's demons spoke of his hold forever
On my heart, and mine of the fragile tenure
Of all things ...   (*SP*, 33)

The revealing echo between "The Brill Road" and "The Whole Hog"
– "frailer tenure," "fragile tenure" – serves as a reminder that this
sense of spiritual decay is also conditioned by the flux: as moral
precepts are created they crumble away; as structures are founded
upon which we govern our beings, they are overthrown by new
structures. In the midst of this crumbling, the human spirit itself
becomes "desiccated," unable to find definition, meaning, or purpose.

   This sense of entrapment, of involuntary participation in the processes of time that merely exist to destroy us, motivates "A Point of
Sky," with its typically Decadent vision of *tedium vitae*:

   So it happens, from time to time,
   The suspended sentence falling like a fist,
   The shape of blackness into which we are always moving:
   Not the sudden, shattering terror
   With something of the divine in it, which is
   A certain contact and connection with God,
   But the descent of the terrible clarity of tedium,
   The vision of the true face of our condition,
   The man in the mirror who is always there.   (*SP*, 88)

This is obviously not the same decay that promotes the poet's love
in "Deserted Buildings Under Shefford Mountain." This is the larger
process, which may be a fitting punishment for some, but when it
is understood to involve the poet seems suddenly cruel and desolating – the more typically Decadent reaction to the sense of time.
"When We Are Very Old" also strikes this Decadent note, although
it lacks the self-pity that so often accompanied the fear of time's
touch in the 1890s:

Now nothing matters, and we move towards death
Happy and careless, slaves of habit and error,
Sensual, greedy, selfish, short of breath,
Looking at our faces in the mirror.

What do those faces hold? Myriads of denials.

But the denials serve no purpose: acceptance of the meaninglessness of life is no guarantee that we have understood it or found its essence; instead it merely increases our misery, because

> Now we are dying and have done nothing.
> The world is still the same, the wheels are turning
> Over our dying bodies, and our breathing
> Is almost done, and yet we keep on burning.

No "hard, gem-like flame," but a pathetic afterglow; the soul is like a trick match that cannot be blown out until it is all burned away, but after the first gust of wind the initial brightness is gone. "Burning" is no comfort: it is an almost laughable leftover from youth, "when it really mattered."[36]

This larger and more terrifying sense of time, decay, and loss informs the poems of ecstasy and intensity considered in the previous section. There is no beauty in the decay of the body, as there may be in the decay of architecture: in the flesh it is all rot, seepage, and suppuration, but lumber stands solid and clean, even silvered by the sunlight, until it falls for good. Hence the rage of "Noyade 1942": the interference of the war in private human lives suddenly promotes the workings of physical decay to a blistering efficiency:

> ... the pure and tender thoughts – that take
> Too many tears to keep alive –
> Are stifled, and see: the age's will is done!
> A little sacrilege and murder
> Wreaked on the private effigies
> Of bodies joined and put asunder.
>
> O love that thinks that it could always
> Suffer all things, live on the crust
> Of letters and orgiastic leaves!
> Too soon the pointed bones appear
> Of your beginning and your end
> In this long summer of malison and lust.[37]

Because the war is a vortex of human decay promoted by the "skills" of man, Glassco's bitterness soars. "Noyade 1942" is no mere sigh for the glories of past days, but a pointed and painful attack on the rituals by which we promote one another's "falling away into the gulf of time": man is involved in the process of decay not only as victim but as occasional agent, which is not his natural duty or place;

that is rather to maintain "pure and tender thoughts" of others, whatever the "tears" demanded.

From such a sense of pervasive decay to a disheartening and crippling pessimism there is not much travelling. Pessimism is an attitude to the future, which serves to remind Glassco's reader that the decay in so much of his poetry is of the present: it surrounds the poet in his rural travels, it is revealed to him behind all of man's endeavours, and he perceives its workings in his own body and spirit. Clearly, against the ecstatic hedonism of the past, Glassco posits a present day of loss, failure, attrition, and passing away, which creates the particular melancholy of his poetry: a melancholy that is sharpened by the pessimism with which he views the human estate and the sources of available meaning. Not only does the poet deny the possibility of ecstasy and intensity under present conditions, he also suggests that these shall not return for any of us: no imminent future of triumphant rejuvenation is offered; the future is like the present, only darker and more theoretical:

> For thieves grow rich, and poor men steal,
> And beggars ride the backs of all;
> Mouth to bum and toe to heel
> The generations rise and fall
>
> ......................................
>
> Though God knows what drives on the whole,
> In his foreknowledge lies our grief:
> Slavery is the word of all,
> Rich man, poor man, beggarman, thief.[38]

As he insists in "Didactic," if there is a God who has determined the madness of our lives, the information merely adds the insult of "slavery" to our suffering, an endless round of divine abuse and manipulation leading nowhere: such is Glassco's darkest vision of our fate. He has voiced it repeatedly, as in the speech of the "Second Female Voice" in "The Wild Plum: An Entertainment for Radio":

> There are my tears for you, unlovely child
> .....................................................
> Cracked in the dooryard dust
> With distress for labour while the sunstruck bird
> Raves of his paradise and a golden thrust
> Of wings, your voice shall go unheard:
> No one to answer it or lift Orphean tongue

To your dry headpiece. Oh there shall be prayers
To leaden rails and pictures full of blood,
But never the plum-tree's white fruition
Nor the sweet-savage oracle of the wood,
The garden of the beast grown tame.
No one's beauty and no one's name,
You shall be drawn astray with toys and airs:
Small lonely prism of man, these are my tears.[39]

Religious and spiritual meaning is removed from human vision and can no longer return us to health; paradise is only "raved" about, "prayers" are addressed to "pictures full of blood"; "fruition" and the "oracle" are far away, unable to offer hope. Each of us is a "lonely prism," bending and refracting the true light so that we are dazzled by its component colours but cannot see its unities, its blaze of insight.

In "Utrillo's World" the knowledge of this indifferent God – in this case likened to the artist, who sits "above" his creation, "watching it recede" – leads to the terror and amorality of the wilderness, all the more poignant in the setting of Maurice Utrillo's still, grey Montmartre lanes and houses:

A world of love resolved to empty spaces,
Streets without figures, figures without faces,
Desolate by choice and negative from need.
But the hoardings weep, the shutters burn and bleed;
Colours of crucifixion, dying graces,
Spatter and cling upon these sorrowful places.
– Where is the loved one? Where do the streets lead?

But "There is no loved one." The world of the painter is abandoned to spiritual desolation, the emptiness of inner death, and cannot be redeemed. There is no heaven hanging over it with visions of comfort: to Utrillo "It is the world that counts, the endless fever,/And suffering that is its own and only end." Only suffering defines reality, then: "the loved one" – Christ, if the crucifixion image is there for a reason – has been cast out by "perfect fear" (SP, 54).

We have already seen what Glassco can offer to counter such pessimism: not hope that fate will change its sentence, but only a personal effort of intensity, to live well so as to die well. By understanding and accepting the degree to which ecstasy determined the course of his youth, he can, as we have seen, realize its significance for his present dismal situation; and so has, in one or two gentler

moments, accepted the obvious fact that such burdensome pessimism must, now and again, be relieved:

> Lovers are always children. We return
> To the absolute and else impossible page
> Of the double image where the master passion,
> Written in milk and water long ago,
> Revives under the breath of autumn
> ...............................................
>
> And this is all our happiness today:
> This autumn love that rages like a ram
> Coos also like a pigeon in the eaves.
> But that contract was the stroke of doom:
> Dearest, we have no end at all
> More lasting than this skeleton of desire
> That holds our marriage in its arms. And so
> Kiss me again, and let us share
> The common night of falling stars and apples,
> Trapped animals, broken hearts and the final sigh
> That children heave when the long daylight goes.[40]

That is the best Glassco can do: in the face of the universal death-
sentence, of the necessity of suffering, the impossibility of enduring
meaning, to find a lover who will kiss him again and "share" his
slipping into death, share the pessimism but render it gentle by the
presence of another. This is why in "The Day" the knowledge that
"in the heart of another blooms a miraculous home" (*SP*, 81) strikes
the strongest note of comfort in the poem: only by some form of
human contact – and Glassco does not prescribe or proscribe the
forms – can we lessen the terror of our situation, which is not
changed, only misted over briefly, by the touch of another's flesh.
To seek that touch is, with such a vision of the world, an act of
courage, a brave if hopeless attempt to struggle with fate: as in "A
Point of Sky," when he urges us to

> Fight with both hands against the prison of God
> And against the prison of time and eternal power
> Let not your hands fail nor your desperation weaken
> Against the warders who have shut the sky against you
>
> That my regrets
> May so shine before me

That I shall not sleep, and my eyes open
That I shall not die, and my heart beating
But shall remember always
The point of sky and the meadow
The thing foregone and the thing achieved
So that the beauty of both is united
In one clear flame of longing.   (*SP*, 93)

This time we *are* in the presence of Pater's "hard, gem-like flame": for it is against the devouring flux that Glassco posits an endless longing, an endless struggle towards beauty, exactly analogous to that of his Aesthetic master:

we are all *condamnés*, as Victor Hugo says: we are all under sentence of death but with a sort of indefinite reprieve – *les hommes sont tous condamnés à mort avec des sursis indefinis*: we have an interval, and then our place knows us no more. Some spend this interval in listlessness, some in high passions, the wisest, at least among "the children of this world," in art and song. For our one chance lies in expanding that interval, in getting as many pulsations as possible into the given time. Great passions may give us this quickened sense of life, ecstasy and sorrow of love, the various forms of enthusiastic activity, disinterested or otherwise, which come naturally to many of us. Only be sure it is passion – that it does yield you this fruit of a quickened, multiplied consciousness. Of such wisdom, the poetic passion, the desire of beauty, the love of art for its own sake, has most. For art comes to you proposing frankly to give nothing but the highest quality to your moments as they pass, and simply for those moments' sake.   (Pater, *Ren.*, 190)

A profound pessimism is, of course, the motivation for Pater's "hard, gem-like flame": only in a world of impermanence, where we are all in some sense *condamnés*, is it necessary to get as many pulses as possible into each moment. Glassco shares this belief, with consistent conviction and to such a degree of similarity that we may assume his poetry to adapt, much as his prose *Memoirs*, definitive elements of Aestheticism and Decadence.

Whether Glassco's fascination with rural decay led to his distinct pessimism, or whether a pessimistic nature led him to see more decay than growth in the rural world, is ultimately a question of little consequence. If anything, his early and unflagging sympathy with the philosophy of Schopenhauer suggests the latter alternative. What is important is that the architectural decay in the poetry reflects a strong element of spiritual and emotional decay, which is in turn taken to the extreme of an intense pessimism: the qualities are closely related. When we examine in turn the poems that relate past intensities, the joys of sexual abandon, or the divine "madness" of Parisian accordions, we note that they inevitably foreshadow a falling off, a failure of the intense spirit, a "decadence" in the older man who feels, with the ennui of the "Nineties," that all his best sensations are behind him. Between these two impulses, between the intensity of the past and the decay of the present, Glassco's poetry moves.

G lassco's poetry is not, however, simply Decadent. It is the poetry of someone who has understood the premises of Aestheticism which informed the Decadent school of poetry, and who has marked affinities with those premises; but it is not the poetry of a man entirely subject to the philosophical import of Aestheticism, as the real Decadents had been. He rails against (and enjoys) decay with much more vigour and spirit than they could ever muster, and promotes the pleasures of the flesh with more genuine abandon than such a sensitive and ultimately polite soul as Ernest Dowson could have permitted himself. To the Decadents, sexual contact still had moral implications: by reaching one another's flesh we span the Abyss and achieve a headily romantic union. Glassco has no such sentiments; love and sex are to him merely the best we can do: they do not offer redemption or salvation from the condition of our souls. Their intensity is what matters, not their potential for spiritual oneness with the "Other." The question of Glassco's Decadence is cast in its true light if we compare Dowson's "Terre Promise" with Glassco's "The Whole Hog":

> Ah might it be, that just by touch of hand,
> Or speaking silence, shall the barrier fall;
> And she shall pass, with no vain words at all,
> But droop into mine arms, and understand!   (Dowson, PW, 67)

> Nosing about the world for love and tid-bits
> I am still baffled by the faith-breakings
> Of flesh in season and sonorous language
> That tell me I also am a piece of property
> And rouse only my barking rhetoric in answer.   (Glassco, SP, 33)

Glassco would be entirely out of place in the London of the 1890s, simply because he is, without question, a modern poet, a man of the twentieth century with all his irony, bitterness, paradox, and witty pessimism intact.

To comprehend in a single critical approach the diverse pulls of Glassco's poetry, between Modernism and Aestheticism, between Paterian Aestheticism and open Decadence, there can be no more succinct or satisfying term, to my mind, than post-Decadence. I am not fond of the elaborate over-use of the prefix "post-" in critical terminology and would not wish to be thought to contribute to the welter of "isms" and "post-isms" that surrounds us today. I am positing no movement or school, but coining a description of Glassco that I think fitting. It implies at once Glassco's modernity (since Modernism was, after all, the movement after Decadence) and his descent from Pater and the Decadents, while clearly indicating that he is no mere subject of the earlier school but an adaptor and qualifier of its conventions. As a post-Decadent he looks back to intensity, ecstasy, beauty, rather than struggling to believe in them in the present world, as did his Decadent precursors; and he sees decay, falling away, in the present world, as his Decadent precursors inevitably saw it looming in the terrifying future. Glassco is a post-Decadent by virtue of his acceptance of the principles of the Decadence and, at the same time, of his realization that such principles no longer serve the modern world: we can at best follow them as gestures, private structures, but we are not such fools as to think that they can shield us or the world from man's inherently evil machinations, or from the ugliness that is in the ascendant everywhere.

There is oblique confirmation of this critical approach to Glassco's poetry in his justly famous "Brummell at Calais." As Glassco looks back to the Decadents of the late nineteenth century, so those Decadents had looked back to the dandies of the Regency, for their models of dress, behaviour, and exquisite antinomianism: a line of inheritance that Glassco acknowledges in his intimate, sympathetic, triumphant portrait of Beau Brummell, the greatest dandy of all time, now in the days of collapse and despair following his dismissal from the king's favour.[41] Glassco wishes to know – an inquiry not surprising for the poet we have been discussing – how Brummell has remained in the world's memory, how he has transcended death and time, merely by ultimate foppery:

A foolish useless man who had done nothing
All his life long but keep himself clean,
Locked in the glittering armour of a pose

Made up of impudence, chastity and reserve –
How does his memory still survive his world?

In portraits Glassco sees only the foppery, the "tilted nose" and "full blown" lips, that made the presence of the dandy so striking: but he knows, as experience has taught him all too well, that such personal features can do nothing to stave off oblivion in the public memory, so he still seeks answers. With some sympathy he notes the dandy's fallen condition: his physical "stature" is that "of the Butterfly whose *Funeral*/he sang," and "he has returned to childhood now," "a childhood of sweet biscuits and curacao" in which "Hair-oil and tweezers make him forget his debts." But still Glassco desires to know, "Where is he going as well as going mad?" (*SP*, 56). What are the causes of his later glory? The answer is that he is going (and needs to go)

Nowhere: his glory is already upon him,
The fading Regency man who will leave behind
More than the ankle-buttoning pantaloon!
For see, even now in the long implacable twilight,
The triumph of his veritable art,

An art of being, nothing but being, the grace
Of perfect self-assertion based on nothing,
As in our vanity's cause against the void
He strikes his elegant blow, the solemn report of those
Who have done nothing and will never die.   (*SP*, 56–7)

Could there be a more succinct statement of the philosophy we have drawn from Glassco's poetry than that: that we can only seek "the grace/Of perfect self-assertion based on nothing," the ultimate extension of our pleasures and our powers in the full recognition that these are at best hollow gestures against oblivion? Glassco's Brummell is remarkably similar in his philosophy of life to Glassco's personae, and no doubt the Canadian poet found, for once, some comfort in the notion that those "who have done nothing" can, like the saints of old, "never die." That Brummell's way of life is also his "veritable art" confirms the parallel: in poetry Glassco also struggled against the coming on of night, although he knew, with Brummell, that all was vanity, that his poems would not commute his sentence. His reward is that his "art of being" will also "never die," that he has left behind works that will "survive his world," as Brummell survived the Regency, as the Decadents survived the nineteenth century that killed them.

The real benefit of the post-Decadent approach to Glassco's poetry is that it allows us, at last, to unite our critical vision of the man's artistic career. No longer must we assume that the poetry and prose are entirely different bodies of work, the former Wordsworthian, bucolic, and the latter hedonistic, promiscuous. What is revealed is that *Memoirs of Montparnasse* is a prose record of Glassco's intense, hedonistic, ecstatic past, a record of the spirit rather than the letter; and that much of the poetry looks back to that spirit with regret, a sense of terrible loss, and a desire to recapture if only as a gesture the utter abandon of those times, while the poet sees all around him symbolic assurances that his present life is uniformly one of decay, crumbling, and failure. At times he foists the burden of that decay upon those who deserve it – the gentleman farmers, the fathers and sons who "bury the hatchet" – and is therefore able to welcome it; at other times he suffers its pains himself, like the retired hedonist he is: but decay remains the constant of his later life as that is related in the poetry. Thus the prose *Memoirs* and the poetry can be seen as the different phases of a single scale of personal development, from hedonism to decay, which underscores everything he attempted as a literary artist. Students of the *Memoirs* will already be familiar with this attitude to Glassco, if they have read the book as it demands to be read, as an alternation between a present of physical decay – the hospital stay, recorded in italics – and a past of libidinous wonders. I suggest that these are the fundamental qualities of Glassco's writings, and that their manipulation in the poetry is one more proof of John Glassco's vigorous descent, without embarrassment or concealment, from the Aesthetes and Decadents of late Victorian England.

## CHAPTER SIX

# A.J.M. Smith: Aesthetic Master of Canadian Poetry

If the young A.J.M. Smith had leaped full-grown into Modernism as he and his critics have usually suggested, he would indeed be the most remarkable phenomenon of modern Canadian poetry: especially since Pound, Eliot, Yeats, and Stevens came at their Modernism through the back door, after having spent time writing versions of nineteenth-century poetry, and since they only discovered slowly and with labour that an enormous literary revolution was working through them. While Smith's dedication, craft, criticism, and personal influence certainly combined in one of the most forceful contributions to Canadian poetry yet recorded, he no more started out a Modernist than the great poets of America and England whom he began to imitate after three or four years of apprenticeship to nineteenth-century masters. Like the other Modernists in English, he had a specialized and intimate knowledge of the nineteenth-century poetry he was to reject, by virtue of the attentions he had paid to it in his own creative youth. Nevertheless, as part of what Milton Wilson has called "the Smith legend ... growing up around his 'difficult, lonely music',"[1] Smith's critics have long ignored that early poetry and emphasized instead the way in which he seized upon Modernism when it was made available to him. We remember and value him, after all, as a Modernist, so it has seemed unnecessary to look at the poetry he wrote before he became one. Smith has himself assisted in this obfuscation by stating that his "earliest apprentice verses" were imitations of Pound and Eliot, Stevens and H.D., Aiken and Yeats ("Confessions," 4). With all respect, nothing could be farther from the truth.

Critical ignorance of the influences upon Smith's early poetry has no doubt contributed to the frequent impression that he was, as a poet and as a critic, full of contradictions: for instance, it has been surprising to find a poet who places so much emphasis upon "intensity" also arguing throughout his career for artistic detachment and impersonality, or to find Canada's leading practitioner and theoretician of literary Modernism writing in largely traditional verse forms, and with a marked reliance on traditional themes of love and death. Only recently have we come to the conclusion that we must wrestle further with these apparent contradictions, must distil them to some kind of guiding aesthetic in the light of which we may understand the poet's varied and complex career. As Ian MacLaren has pointed out, "Clearly, we are only beginning to understand and document the complexity of the question of inheritance and adaptation in Smith's poetry ... one suspects that the more we uncover of this nature the less Smith's chameleon nature will strike us as troublesome."[2] The tracing of all influences upon Smith's work will help us to explain aspects of that work which are not explicable by reference to the standard influence recognized to have worked upon him, which is Modernism. Contradictory elements of his career may in this way become evidence of his complex inheritance of various conventions and schools of poetry and serve to remind us of the obvious fact that no poet of Smith's stature is likely to have undergone only one process of artistic influence.

To that end I will discuss Smith's generally unacknowledged early poetry in light of Aestheticism, in order to demonstrate an influence upon his art that is at once distinct from Modernism and yet centrally allied to it. My contention will be that Smith was influenced by Aestheticism before he was influenced by Modernism and that that influence was sufficiently forceful and enduring to account for certain peculiarities of the recognized Modernist canon. The tracing of the Aesthetic influence will also serve to lighten our sense of Smith's contradictions, to increase our appreciation of the healthy complexities of his art.

No such study can be undertaken, however, without coming to terms with the *McGill Fortnightly Review*; that journal is, to most of Smith's critics, the creative birthplace of the poet we recognize and appreciate. The *Fortnightly* has been accorded an unique and powerful place in Canadian literary history; indeed it has been taken with wide agreement as the seed-bed of Modernism in Canada, a journal in whose pages many of our best poets had their starts. Those who will take the time to sit down with the *Fortnightly* and read it through, however, will be surprised to discover a journal with many significant pre-Modernist tendencies as well, not the least of which is the nature of the poetry published therein. While Smith's and Scott's Modernism certainly did sketch its first principles in those pages, there was a good deal published which had nothing whatsoever to do with Modernism, as Scott's "Brian Tuke" poems have already made clear. Since the journal operated under the aegis of Smith, any indictment of its Modernism must necessarily reflect on his own creative development from November 1925 to April 1927. Even without the desire to know more of Smith, a comprehensive study of the *Fortnightly* deserves to be undertaken, because its image as an "iconoclastic journal of modernist literature and opinion" (Djwa, "Scott," 743) is wrong and greatly needs to be corrected. For both reasons, this discussion of Smith's Aesthetic poetry will open with an interrogation of the *Fortnightly*, of what it really established and what Smith was writing for its pages, before moving back to his first poetry in the *McGill Daily* and the *McGill Daily Literary Supplement*.

Some preliminary acknowledgment should also be made that others have touched on the covertly Aesthetic qualities of Smith's later, canonical poems. Milton Wilson once commented that "Certainly you don't have to talk to Smith for long to realize that he relishes the thought of being odd classical man out in a society of romantics ... It's something of a letdown to discover how merely Parnassian or decadent or imagistic his classicism can be. Smith's less diffuse Medusa (in 'For Healing') isn't that different from Swinburne's, his Hellenic swallows from H.D.'s, or even his Pan from Carman's" (11–12). Along these lines Djwa argues that Smith's "Prothalamium" manifests "the late romantic or decadent sensibility viewing the subject matter of the Jacobeans."[3] In Canada late Romanticism is not quite Decadence, but Djwa's comment is provoking. So is Edel's remark, already quoted, that Smith during the *Fortnightly* days was "less dedicated to social change than to a vigorous aestheticism" ("Warrior," 8), a remark significant of the qualities of that famous journal. Finally there is John Sutherland's infamous comment, in the Introduction to his First Statement anthology *Other Canadians: An Anthology of the New Poetry in Canada 1940–1946*, that Smith's criticism and poetry suffered from "that pure aestheticism which, properly understood, is nothing less than the history and tradition of the human spirit wrapped in a papal bunnyhug."[4] (It should be noted that towards the end of his life Sutherland came to equate most of Modernism, but specifically Joyce and Pound, with a "literary decadence,"[5] which suggests that it may have been Smith's affiliation with the first generation of Modernists that urged Sutherland towards his droll opinion.) All of these critics have happened on the real nature of Smith's early poems, but none of them has done so while making direct reference to those poems: the Aestheticism or Decadence they have perceived has been in the recognized canon, a lurking quality that they cannot quite put their fingers on. The key to their suspicions lies in the unread pages of the *Fortnightly* and the other McGill newspapers, in the first works by which Smith defined himself as a poet.

N o doubt because of the attractiveness of the myth, the *Fortnightly* is commonly regarded as the vehicle in which a number of brave young Modernists published their defiance of the Victorian literary scene,[6] while setting Sir Arthur Currie's McGill on its ear, with their flamboyant wit and vigorous opinions. As part of this image of the journal Leon Edel has remarked, "In early adolescence I was made aware of the great struggles of our century: war and famine, and industrial strife. I speak of these ancient things so I may describe the steps by which Scott and Smith came together with two others and myself to publish *The McGill Fortnightly Review*" ("Warrior," 9). Edel's implication is obvious: when faced with the massive problems of their cultural epoch, Scott and Smith responded with the *Fortnightly*. The *Fortnightly* was never intended to have such a social purpose, however; it was above all a student journal, an independent voice from that portion of the university population least represented by the official organs of the administration or by the hearty jollity of the 1920s *Daily*, the intellectuals. They ran it to satisfy their audience, with diatribes at the "hearties," assaults on those who would tamper with the rights of the student theatrical company, and reviews of the contemporary literature that was just beginning to attract their talents. Reference to global, national or even municipal events is extremely rare, and the flavour is very much that of a campus journal. More in this spirit, Edel has written elsewhere that the *Fortnightly* "was, of course, a characteristic product of that decade – down to its menckenisms, its eliot-poundisms, its proustian self-examination and its james joyceing; above all in its serene belief in the sanctity of art and literature divorced from all life, and the unimportance of everything except the editors, the review and the university, in the order named."[7] There Edel has captured much more acutely the spirit of the *Fortnightly*, and it is in that context that the journal must be considered. It was not intended, judging by the editorials, to have national repercussions or to serve as the herald of Modernism in Canada – it was intended to give its editors a chance to speak their active minds, and so they did, not always with Eliot, Pound, Proust, and Joyce as their models.

It was not, after all, City Hall or Ottawa or the monarchy whose feathers the editors wished to ruffle, but Sir Arthur Currie's vision of McGill as they chose to caricature it. Currie had been knighted for his important part in the Canadian contribution to the First World War, and his idea of a university required order and a fair unanimity of purpose. He was a stiffly polite military man with a reported degree of uneasiness in the presence of his undergraduates and preferred to administer at a distance and avoid intrusive contact. When the *Fortnightly* began its run, however, Currie took more active notice. During the years following the revolution in Russia, it was the not surprising habit of loyal monarchists to see the seeds of Bolshevism in much non-institutional intellectual activity. The *McGill Fortnightly Review* had no formal connection with McGill University; it was a private publication, funded by remarkable levels of subscriptions and sales, that merely borrowed the name of the University for its banner. It relied, however, on the campus and the Arts Building for its distribution and sales locations, so it could not risk the full displeasure of campus authorities. It is a lesser-known fact of *Fortnightly* history that the journal was investigated by Currie as a possible Communist organ; he sent a representative to question the editors, but the representative seems to have understood his duty rather curiously, and bought drinks for the entire board, concluding his "interrogation" by poking Scott in the ribs with a wink and telling the others that the Canon's son was "the only dangerous man among [them]."[8] The ironic investigation is revealing of Currie's administrative concerns and the stamp he wished to set on the atmosphere of the campus. It can be difficult to remember that Canada's intellectual climate in the 1920s was still very much in the grip of the moral and colonial dogmatists of the Victorian age; respectful obedience may have been the cornerstone of Currie's pedagogy, but to active minds like Smith's and Scott's it can only have been anathema. To their credit, they chose the route of satire and wit rather than outright defiance and hostility, for the latter would with little question have closed down the *Fortnightly* for good.

In keeping with this sense of a pragmatic editorial conservatism, the literature and essays of the *Fortnightly* are not as radical as critical consensus would suggest. Scott's poems of beauty and Decadence and Kennedy's poems of romance and Camelot do much to mitigate the Modernist flavour for which the *Fortnightly* has been famed.

While poems like Scott's "Decadence" would no doubt have troubled those supporting the established morality of the day, they were at least familiar structures, recognizable as sonnets, which did not call into question the fundamental basis of all literature – as would imitations of *The Waste Land*'s form, or the explicit sexuality of Joyce's *Ulysses*.

Smith's poems in the *Fortnightly* are slightly more radical than those of his confrères. There are early versions in the journal of some of his most acclaimed poems, such as "The Lonely Land," which appeared in 1925 with the subtitle *"Group of Seven,"* and "The Sorcerer," originally "Not of the Dust," also in 1925; "Homage to E.S.," appearing in 1927, was vastly improved by Smith to reach its present form as "A Hyacinth for Edith." But we should not conclude as a result – at least not without careful examination – that the *Fortnightly* was therefore a "modernist" journal. For one thing, the early versions of these famous Smith poems were significantly different from the final drafts, and the difference is, in most cases, between a Romantic early version and a modern late version: which leaves the *Fortnightly* rather more nineteenth-century in its literary values than we are usually led to believe. For another thing, there is a wide selection of Smith poems in the *Fortnightly* that were never graced with book publication; the clear majority of these were abandoned because of a derivative Romanticism or Aestheticism, which made them uninteresting to an older Smith.

Among the material eventually reprinted and now part of Smith's canon, "The Lonely Land," for instance, was altered from a plaintive Romanticism in the *Fortnightly* to its present firm and famous lines. The second and third stanzas reveal the most serious alteration; we are used to the ululation of Smith's present version, in which "ragged/and passionate tones/stagger and fall,/and recover,/and stagger and fall,"[9] but the original image was much more romantically sublime:

Hark to the wild duck's cry
And the lapping of water on stones
Pushing some monstrous plaint against the sky
While a tree creaks and groans
When the wind sweeps high.

This infusion of the landscape with traditional Romantic emotion prefigures the turn in the third stanza of the early version; in its present form the third stanza offers further images of hard, cold landscape, "stony strand" and "black pine," but in the *Fortnightly* Smith was trying to express a mood of the speaker, not chiefly of the land:

It is good to come to this land
Of desolate splendour and grey grief,
And on a loud, stony strand
Find for a tired heart relief
In a wild duck's bitter cry,
In grey rock, black pine, shrill wind
And cloud-piled sky.[10]

Interestingly, after pruning the dramatic emotions of "The Lonely Land," Smith added a climactic aesthetic speculation, twice falling back on the word "beauty" in an apparent attempt to define the visual quality of the Canadian landscape:

This is a beauty
of dissonance
. . . . . . . . . . . . . . . . . .

This is the beauty
of strength
broken by strength
and still strong.   (*PNC*, 50–1)

Thus he sublimates in the later version the Romantic quality of the early version, by tying the landscape to human aesthetic judgment instead of to human emotion.

A similar process altered "Something Apart" in the *Fortnightly* to its present form as "The Two Birds." In the 1920s the poem concluded its woodland meditation with the cry of a "raucous bird," which was "As alien from all these/As the sorrow in my heart." Going in fear of abstractions, Smith rewrote the lines: "As alien from all these/As that other foul bird, my black heart." Similarly he turned the "lush grass" on which he "stretched" in the early version to "needles of pine," a less comfortable and more modern resting place; and "Over the pool and the grass,/Over the grass and the fern" has become "Under the columns of pine/And the gold sun's winding stair"[11] (*PNC*, 40).

"Twilight," destined to become "My Lost Youth" in later years, has been altered from a lulling Romanticism to a mordant middle-aged diatribe, in this case by Smith's addition of a triplet at the end which is "spoken" by the aged poet looking back upon the "youth" who wrote the early draft. In the more recent version the poet refers to "his birthplace in Westmount and what *that* involved" (*PNC*, 102), bringing into the poem an autobiographical flatness that perfectly undermines the aesthetic delicacy of the moment he had shared with the woman involved. Allusions to Yeatsian figures in the early version have become references to James and Eliot, and the final question in the new portion from "memory" closes the youthful scene on an ironic note: "'What happens,' I pondered fleeing, 'to one whom Reality claims?'" (*PNC*, 103). The concluding passage then illuminates the speaker's loss of his early pseudo-romance: "I teach English in the Middle West; my voice is quite good;/My manners are charming; and the mothers of some of my female students/ Are never tired of praising my two slim volumes of verse" (*PNC*, 103). This malicious downturn so undercuts the youthful memory presented in the first four stanzas that "My Lost Youth" is overwhelmed by the cynical jesting of the older persona. But that is only fair; the early version, for all its Eliotism, had been equally overwhelmed by *fin-de-siècle* ennui:

> This poem stole by me in the afternoon;
> This poem and that afternoon is you:
> Twilight gray and rather mournful, song a little out of tune,
> And all the things one should, but did not do
>
> ...............................................................
>
> It is easy enough to recall the body of your death,
> To comprehend with the mind what you meant;
> Not easy to forget the quick catch in your breath,
> How an army with banners suddenly came and went
>
> Before the cloud had descended on your face again,
> And you asked if I'd have another cup of tea,
> And smiled and chatted as if there had been no pain:
> "What's Hecuba to him?" you thought, and stared at me.

The woebegone allusion to *The Waste Land* in the opening line shows Smith working hard to adapt the Eliot influence, and wedding it with the tendency he had shown in other poems to express sadness, loss, desolation and failure. Curiously, Smith's revisions have turned the action of the poem more clearly back onto the speaker; in the early version it is the woman doing the rejecting, at least in her thoughts,[12] whereas in the later it is the poet who flees, unable to cope with the pressing attractions of her "living and beautiful throat." The cynical older persona looks rather more pathetic as a result, and his private irony about his youth is transmuted into an irony of larger life.

Of the other poems in the *Fortnightly* that Smith later revised and republished, only "Homage to E.S." shows such significant change. The first four stanzas of the later version are all but unchanged ("stained" has become "stain'd," the archaism of which suits Smith's emphasis on the artifice of Sitwell's poetry), but with the fifth Smith set to work once more. "I will saw a wooden hyacinth/In the woods' callous plinth" becomes "I'll seek within the wood's black plinth/A candy-sweet sleek wooden hyacinth," in order to complicate the rhythm, remove the Romantic connotations of "callous" woods, and lessen the physical activity on the part of the poet, "seeking" rather less vigorous than "sawing." Once he has his hyacinth, Smith's response is entirely different: in the later version he merely celebrates his discovery:

And in its creaking naked glaze
And in the varnish of its blaze

The bird of ecstasy shall sing again,
The bearded sun shall spring again.   (*PNC*, 14)

In the early version, however, the poet takes the hyacinth away so he can "set it seriously in a made jade vase/Appropriately upon the mantelpiece," a concern with his own behaviour evident in the adverbs of the two lines. The young Smith concluded diffidently: "Or failing this, I'll not go out of doors,/But find my childhood in these poems that are yours."[13] To this an older Smith seems to have objected not because it was a Romantic image – the poet in isolation with his muse – but because it was, to speak bluntly, bad poetry. He altered and elaborated the sentiment:

And fall like cool and soothing rain
On all the ardour, all the pain,

Till I am grown again my own lost ghost
Of joy, long lost, long given up for lost,

And walk again the wild and sweet wildwood
Of our lost innocence, our ghostly childhood.   (*PNC*, 15)

The tenderness of this conclusion suggests Smithian irony; its direct stylistic contradiction of the Sitwellian opening of the poem produces an effect of "different voices" and an odd refraction between the two styles that are quintessentially Modernistic. In so doing, Smith has strengthened rather than weakened the emotional fervour of the *Fortnightly* version, evidently because it struck him as useful emotion.

Such revision did not always prove necessary. Another group of Romantic poems by Smith in the *Fortnightly*, also reprinted in later volumes, was left relatively untouched by the poet when he returned to them. In "Not of the Dust," which became "The Sorcerer," Smith has added light topicality (the reference to "Lachine") and satire ("Father Lebeau," who comes under fire from the voluptuous poet). A few words have also been altered: "cold sea,"[14] for instance, becomes "trembling ocean," a more pathetic-fallacious image; but the essential *emotion* of the poem – a desire to live as "a red gleam in a crystal dish," a kind of sexual-aesthetic removal – has been approved by the later poet and, if anything, heightened by the ironies now directed at the "real world" (*PNC*, 69). Similarly, "Epitaph," with which Smith traditionally concluded his volumes, has undergone little editing: the address to a "Stranger" has been cut, the "stone" has become "quiet," and "moulder here" has become "embedded here" to alleviate the passivity of the early version; otherwise the changes are cosmetic, "comfort of the grass" instead of "comfort from the grass," "me" (*PNC*, 160) instead of "Me."[15] Again, "For Healing," which is in the *Fortnightly* as "A Poem," is all but unaltered: the first four lines in the early version,

> Take in your long arms
> The torso of a wave:
> Stroke its lithe loveliness,
> Let it tenderly lave.[16]

have become, to their advantage,

> Spread your long arms
> To the salt stinging wave:
> Let its breathless enveloping
> Cleanliness lave.   (*PNC*, 38)

But Smith did not touch the essence of the poem, which is a vaguely Petrarchan lament against a beloved who, with "The ache of her fingers,/The whips of her hair," gave the poet great pain. Similar minor alterations have worked upon "Legend," which has merely been touched up to become "The Mermaid," and "The Bird," lightly edited and polished.

These poems have been allowed to stand in an early form which, if we do not wish to call it Romantic, certainly cannot be called Modernist, possibly not even "modern." When we see them in the company of early versions of "My Lost Youth," "A Hyacinth for Edith," and "The Lonely Land" – Modernist poems that required significant revision from a fairly Romantic original – we are forced to acknowledge the degree to which Smith was *not* sure of his modern voice at the time the *Fortnightly* was published, and so to qualify our judgments of that journal's nature. If the very poems Smith chose for his later canon – those which provide our sense that the *Fortnightly* was the first flowering of Canadian Modernism – exist in chiefly Romantic versions in the journal, it is simply inaccurate to speak of the *Fortnightly* as a Modernist journal because of their presence.

I do not wish to elide, however, those few beacons of Modernist art that were actually fired in the *Fortnightly*; they exhibit the real promise of the student journal, but we should once again examine their progress into the Smith canon, in order to observe Smith's own judgments of their *Fortnightly* quality. Three Smith poems constitute his full Modernist breakthrough in the *Fortnightly*; "The Woman in the Samovar," later called "They Say," "Poem," later called "Universe into Stone," and "Pastorale," later "Ballade un peu Banale," attain in early versions the impersonality and irony that were to characterize Smith's later poetry. "The Woman in the Samovar" manipulates with some skill the style of Eliot's Sweeney poems and makes clear Smith's understanding of Eliot's "mythic method" as well:

The woman in the samovar
spreads webs of deft desire
more maculate than jaguar,
and offers them for hire

..............................

She pleads in vain, and stubs her toe,
muttering curses to a parakeet:
the nebula whose name is Joe
excuses awkwardness of feet;

perching precipitously on the roof
he strums Stravinsky on a table-spoon.[17]

Revealingly, it was all this derivative Eliotism that Smith later excised from the poem, choosing to adapt only the last two stanzas of the early version into the brief, direct "They Say." Smith begins with two new opening stanzas, both traditional, the second of which merely reflects and precedes the original "Hero and Leander" stanza in the *Fortnightly*; he concludes with two final stanzas of the early version, somewhat doctored to increase their eroticism:

> That Hero and Leander meet
> By leafy Hellespont
> At corner of each clanging street,
> Before each Christian font,
>
> And feel the bawdy music rise
> Beyond the power of breath
> And stiffen as they close their eyes
> In the heavenly sexual death.   (*PNC*, 87)

Note that formally and stylistically, at least, Smith's revision has made the poem *less*, not more modern; apart from the odd rhythmic irregularity, he has produced four traditional quatrains from what was a singularly, if not originally, Modernist poem. It is interesting, then, that one of the most modern publications in the *Fortnightly* should later have been so altered that its qualities of Modernism were almost entirely removed. Presumably Smith felt that the "mythic method" of the poem was of the essence and did not require derivative stylistic properties to sustain it.

In contrast to the whittling down that took place from "The Woman in the Samovar" to "They Say," "Poem" and "Pastorale" have been extended and elaborated until they reached their present form. The former is a three-quatrain version of "Universe into Stone," a well-known poem of nine quatrains. The final version is much changed from its 1925 appearance. What gives it its modern tone, even in early form, is the visual paradox ("And drop a pebble at our feet/And watch it falling up") and the attack on the "vasty cup//Of idiot infinity," which must be "chisel[led] into kinder things/Than blood and brain and bone."[18] The meaning of this last couplet is unclear in the early version, but "Universe into Stone" expounds it:

> How peace and loving-kindness are
> In many a stony thing,

But not in hearts of flesh and blood
  And not in living bone
That pride and chastity and scorn
  Have withered into stone.

After alteration the poet's desire to *épater les bourgeois* is clearer; against such social convention he posits the validity of art, which he will make with "hammer" and "blade" "Into the likeness of a heart/Of flesh and blood and bone" (*PNC*, 77).

A similar extension of the original "Pastorale" produced the "Ballade un peu Banale," which Edith Sitwell noticed with such arch distaste.[19] Its early version is compact and has the general look of the "Ballade," but it lacks the wit and blasphemous delight of the later poem:

The bellow of the lusty bull
  Astounds the timid cow
That standeth in the meadow cool
  Where cuccu singeth nu,
And holdeth her in mystic trance
  Beneath the timeless trees
While ebon-bellied shad-flies dance
  About her milk-white knees,
And sets her dreaming of the Groom
  That doth attend his bride,
Until she lows for him to come
  And fawn upon her side.[20]

By its final appearance, the "timid cow" had been likened by Smith to the Virgin Mary, who was spared the kind of rape about to be foisted onto the animal by the kindness of "sweet Jesus Christ"; and the entire procedure, with the religious associations it has drawn up, reminds the poet of "Eliot's hippo," the reference that particularly raised Sitwell's ire. The later version is sexually explicit, but subtly so: the bull, as he "Bites rump, bites flank, bites nape," is metaphorically mounting the doomed maiden, not merely tantalizing her; and clearly "He wields" more than "his tail like an iron flail" (*PNC*, 81). The bathetic ironies in both versions of the poem, extended dramatically in the later; the vaguely Poundian "cuccu" in the earlier, and the blasphemies of the later version, make the poem one of Smith's most modern; the *Fortnightly* version is revised, unlike "The Woman in the Samovar," in order to enrich and complicate its modernity, not to lessen it.

Acknowledgment of these three modern pieces allows us to proceed to a cautious generalization: of those *Fortnightly* poems that survived in the Smith volumes, most were derivative and quasi-Romantic pieces that needed more or less alteration, cutting, or extending to become the tougher-minded poems of his *News of the Phoenix* and *A Sort of Ecstasy*. Of the three significantly modern exceptions to this statement, "The Woman in the Samovar" was made more, not less, traditional as Smith worked on it; "Poem" and "Pastorale" retained and improved their modern qualities and are now two of Smith's most striking poems.

This canonical material, however, is not the complete Smith work in the *Fortnightly*. A good many of the poems never reappeared in Smith's later volumes, and they can seem as a result peripheral to the Smith canon. They should not, of course, be forgotten. These uncollected poems may also be divided into the tentatively modern and the loosely Romantic, and the proportion between the two is once again weighted on the Romantic side.

The "lost" *Fortnightly* poems that do strike the modern note only rarely do so with modern prosody. Three, however, are noteworthy for developing modern forms; two of these are the work of an unsure hand, a young poet trying out a style of which he is by no means the master. The subtlety of "Theolog at the Symphony" could be much increased to the young poet's credit:

But after Purgatorial damnation
A golden hoop began to roll
An aureole of final consummation –
Predestined Paradise for Presbyterian soul.

Up silver spirals and a golden wire
The resurrected curve moved on.
But when he thought one centimetre higher
Must cut the corns of God, the moving curve was gone.

The well-bred audience clapped its well-kept claws.
The baton-wielder bowed, acknowledging applause.[21]

The rather sophomoric quality of humour in the poem, when coupled with its strong derivativism and the painfully overdone social comment in the concluding couplet, make it little wonder that Smith did not try to resurrect "Theolog at the Symphony." Perhaps he saw in fairly short order that Scott had bested him in the Eliot-Sweeney game, for the *Fortnightly* published Scott's far superior "Sweeney Comes to McGill" in the same issue.

A similarly undergraduate sensibility mars Smith's "Panic." The poem is riddled with ellipses in an effort to create a sense of broken thought and irrationality; but by the end of the poem (four lines containing four ellipses), the device has worn thin. A satiric grand manner also fails to come off:

Reverberations reiterated
Of thunder
In subaqueous canyons.

Does it disturb the easy slumber
Of the Divine Average
Snoring by his wife?[22]

An effort to achieve a prime Modernist juxtaposition, as though a number of voices were participating in the poem, sounds instead melodramatic and uncomfortably self-conscious. "Theolog at the Symphony" and "Panic" indicate that Smith's Modernism in the *Fortnightly* was quite evidently a new and very tricky thing, a conscious artistic decision rather than a spontaneous development of his innate poetic gift. He was still casting about for a way to be Modernistic without losing the qualities of aesthetic refinement and emotional intensity that had thus far been important to him in poetry.

That he was eventually to reconcile these influences is guaranteed by "Testament," a third uncollected modern poem which shows a Smith much more confident about his new techniques:

It is along the seamed and gnarled
And long-dead river-beds
I take my way – I, molten,
Moulded, hardened into stone,

Rifted with ripples, seamed with sand,
Myself more sun-baked, sallow-seamed
......................................................
Than any god of the desert
Brooding with unwinking eyes.

Smith turns the Waste-Land theme he had imbibed from Eliot to sudden advantage in "Testament," with a poetic sureness – an exacting sense of rhythm, a finer quality of verbal music, tougher images – which "Theolog" and "Panic" entirely lacked. He has also learned to mute his message a little in order to release its full power; "Testament" concludes by uniting the imagery of the desert with the spiritual confusion of the post-war generation, and if the last four lines are still a little too clear in their moralizing, they are at least more poetically subtle, the didacticism grafted more skilfully onto the guiding images of the poem:

> I have kissed my hands to distant trees
> And to the girls with pitchers
> Waiting at the well,
> And I am set upon a pilgrimage
> Seeking a more difficult beauty
> Unheartened by even the most faint mirage.
>
> I am not I, but a generation
> Communicant with trickling sand
> And grey and yellow desert stone –
> The blood and body of our unknown god.[23]

Probably more than any other poem in the *Fortnightly*, "Testament" bespeaks the growing talents of the young Smith; not even "Pastorale" and "Homage to E.S.," which were to lead to such renowned later poems, have the steadiness of purpose and distinction of poetic taste evidenced by this provocative poem, and it is a pity rather than a relief that Smith did not include it in his rigorous selection of his own poems.

After these three the question of the *Fortnightly* becomes further clouded. A number of other "lost" Smith poems have modern themes but explore them in traditional verse, or develop traditional themes in modern form. It is difficult to say, for instance, whether "Here Lies an Honest Man" shows Smith flexing his Modernist ironies or still in the grip of nineteenth-century fixations:

> Chisel this monumental calumny
> Clammily cold and eagerly erect!
> This was no saint. But plain gentility
> Owed some respect
> ........................
>
> But red-eyed relatives gave glozing gold
> For chewing chisellers to eulogize,
> And he who surely would have bid them hold –
> Meekly assenting lies.[24]

The ironies of the poem are distinctly modern in flavour, but the stanza is from the nineteenth century, and the faint romanticizing of the dead man – "no saint," but he would still fight his mourners' hypocrisies if he were able – pulls the poem significantly backward in time. "Chiaroscuro" raises similar issues:

This one was somewhat chary of a smile
And something underconfident it seems:
For he who very seriously dreams
Of death imagines in a little while
That the grinning jaws and the rasping file
Are what even the dearest face's gleam
Will presently become, or at least seem:
This one was somewhat chary of a smile. [25]

The fascination with death makes "Chiaroscuro" seem modern rather in the way Leo Kennedy's *Shrouding* poems seem modern: as if no one but a modern poet would dwell on death to such an extent and record the emotions of the dead with such irony. But the sonnet form, with thirteen of Smith's lines in rough iambic pentameter and a fourteenth close enough to be subsumed in the traditional form, coupled with the familiar warning that the beauty of "the dearest face" will decay, draws "Chiaroscuro" away from Modernism. These poems typify the aesthetic balancing act of Smith's talents at the time of the *Fortnightly*, between traditional tendencies and modern motives, an act which ought to be recognized when we speak of the Modernism of the famous Canadian journal.

Thus "Poem" may appear superficially modern, because of its free verse form and its attack on an indistinct "they" who obviously suffer the disease of the bourgeoisie, but the speaker's own nature is anything but modern:

When I was arrested for drunkenness
They wanted to know my profession.
I answered them, saying:
"I am an Interior Decorator."
They thought I was lying:
They did not know
That I decorate my thoughts
With scarlet scarves
Wound on the loom of dreams,
And paper my mind with purple. [26]

That this prancer should be "drunken" suggests the lurking Aestheticism in the poem; by turning away from reality the speaker is able to delude himself with fabulous visions of colour and line, a resulting smugness setting rather well the superior tone of the Aesthete. It is probably safe to take the poem as a joke, but that is not enough to make it modern.

One might argue, similarly, that his appropriation of blank verse gives to "The Moment and the Lamp" a remotely modern quality, but references to "wizards" and "alchemists" suggest the spiritualism Smith had encountered in Yeats's *A Vision*, the touch of Madame Blavatsky rather than the Yeats of a later day:

> But as it is, it is enough to know
> That in the flicker of a candle flame
> We could, were any skilled enough to read,
> And having read, were bold enough to speak,
> Fathom the dido of the universal flux,
> Matching the moment and the momentary lamp.[27]

Smith has accepted, for the purposes of "The Moment and the Lamp," the spirit of the Heraclitean flux, against which he can only offer a "momentary lamp" to cast brief light. That Pater's rendering of the flux infused Modernism cannot be argued, but Modernism took that flux into its poetics and altered literature radically; it was the nineteenth-century poet who thought, felt, and spoke about the flux in traditional language.

Perhaps for reasons like these Smith's vision of Yeats, "For Ever and Ever, Amen," captures the Irish poet in his tower, in an ideal rendering of Aesthetic removal from the flux of the world:

> Lonely aloft in a turret
> Hewn of the bodiless night
> Sits one who out of chaos
> Has carved a cube of light.
>
> Bent double over his book
> What does he ponder there
> As quiet and as lonely as a planet
> Hung in the silent air?

That nothing "happens" in the poem, no action or alteration of scene, is indicative of the message Smith struggles towards and with which he concludes: "The Is is the same as the Will Be/And both the same as before."[28] Thus the removal of the artist into his private world of contemplation is able to halt the process of time, or at least his sense of process, so that he may conquer artistically without being conquered physically. In this sense, "For Ever and Ever, Amen" prefigures Smith's later "Like an Old Proud King in a Parable," in which he was also concerned with the privacy and primacy of the artistic world.

Yeats is everywhere in Smith's early poems, but it was above all the Yeatsian rhythm that attracted the young Canadian poet, particularly the rhythmic patterns of Yeats's *Responsibilities* from 1914, as in his "That the Night Come":

> She lived in storm and strife,
> Her soul had such desire
> For what proud death may bring
> That it could not endure
> The common good of life,
> But lived as 'twere a king
> That packed his marriage day
> With banneret and pennon,
> Trumpet and kettledrum,
> And the outrageous cannon,
> To bundle time away
> That the night come.[29]

This characteristic rhythm of the middle Yeats is created by irregular alternation of masculine and feminine endings, by the accumulation of syllables in mid-line ("banneret," "kettledrum," "outrageous") to create aural tension, and by the scattering of end rhymes at seeming random. By the time of *Responsibilities*, however, Yeats was moving far from his early Aestheticism; that the Yeatsian rhythms in Smith's early poems almost always indicate a profoundly Romantic mood is therefore striking. With these poems Smith has left all pretence of Modernism behind: the woeful poet struggles to find the words he needs to express an overladen heart, as in "The Cry of a Wandering Gull":

> The cry of a wandering gull,
> And the far cry in the lonely air
> Of the crows in the cool
> Of the evening, share
> With the boom of the tide
> On the hollow shore
> All the sorrowful words I cried
> And thought to cry no more.[30]

Early Yeatsian content as well as middle-Yeatsian rhythms inform Smith's "Leda," his first rendition of the legend that had been brought up to date in the Irish poet's then-recent "Leda and the Swan." Smith has picked up all of the appropriate late nineteenth-century symbols:

> The white wings of a swan
> Hovered over her dream
> That became a dream of dawn:
> An inward gleam
> Of beauty shone,
> Piercing her white body
> As the colour of dawn
> Pierces the sky.

This penetration – anything but erotic in Smith's dreamy rendering – suddenly calls up Troy's "troubled towers," but the poet cannot remain much interested in them; he quickly returns to Leda's beauty, because that is where his interest in the legend lies for the time being:

> And there was blood upon the flowers
> Where wandered one
> Whose swan-like loveliness
> Made old men young
> And filled the young with bitterness.[31]

The struggle against time is evident once more in the second to last line, and the "bitterness" with which the poem concludes strikes an appropriately Decadent note.

Perhaps it is for such reasons that Smith's early "Silver Birch" makes its interesting reference to the very "strange beauty" that was the *métier* of Aestheticism:

> Delicate bender over pools,
> your body is as white and
> as slender as a girl's
> ..........................
> It is you who share
> with some women the power of bending
> beautifully to strange beauty, of
> leaning lightly in hiding hair
> over a wide water or an infinite love.[32]

It is most instructive of Smith's development to compare this poem with the later "Birches at Drummond Point," which undercuts the Romanticism of "Silver Birch" by asking of the trees, "What do they say?/or seem to?" (*PNC*, 48). In contrast with such scepticism, the abstraction of Smith's early "Silver Birch," with the delicacy and slenderness of the visual image and the compact emphasis on strange beauty, produces a highly Aesthetic vision.

Beauty and slenderness unite once more in "Proud Parable," which also foreshadows the concern of the later poet with artistic and emotional "pride":

> I will sit with my love
> in the somnolent window seat,
> and watch for long enough
> the slender rain. And how it
> stings the polished street
> to an intolerable white flash
> of loveliness will parable
> how beauty in the flesh
> from a high elsewhere fell,
> blossoming its bright splash
> to a proud, momentary parable.[33]

That revealing "high elsewhere" promotes the sense of absolute beauty that is clearly hovering over Smith's poem. The formal innovations of the middle Yeats obviously seemed to Smith particularly appropriate for the discussion of certain kinds of emotional and aesthetic intensity: which is why his Yeatsian "Save in Frenzy" argues that one cannot "study a loveliness/Like a lesson in grammar,"

> And that the Holy of Holies
> Of devout sweethearts
> Is inaccessible save
> In frenzy you move.

The union of beauty and "frenzy" and the removal of beauty from all mundane matters, from the "analysing and parsing" of a "lesson in grammar,"[34] suggests the haughty knowingness of the enlightened Aesthete. Indeed, Smith often makes all too clear the nineteenth-century source of these early inspirations, as in the second of his "Two Epitaphs":

> Say not of this lady
> Sleeping here

That she was beautiful, beloved
　And dear
　　............
Only say she had a lover,
　Add that she is dead;
Then go away and leave her –
　Everything is said.[35]

Whether this comes from his reading Dowson or not is irrelevant: it is a poem whose sentiments correspond exactly to those of the Decadent poet, down to the bitter and defeated conclusion of an enforced silence.

Since Smith's preoccupations in these quite unmodern poems are beauty, intensity, and weariness, their remotely modern quality is due primarily to their form, that of the Yeats of *Responsibilities*, whom we now recognize to have been developing in that volume the modern style of his later years. "To Evening," however, is not redeemed from its late Romanticism by even that much: it is a highly traditional sonnet recording the weariness of its speaker in lulling musical phrases, reminiscent of the most soporific of the late Victorians:

Thou modest maiden, blessing the quiet light
That gathers in thy forehead with repose
And gradual coming in of peace, until the vale
And all the neighbour copses and the late bright
Hill and the tall poplar trees in stately rows
Climmer [sic] awhile, and fading, fail,
　Turn thou also on me, a too tired child.

Why such a vigorous young graduate student should wish to express such anemic torpor is not an entirely irrelevant question, for all its heretical implications. In order to conclude the piece Smith is forced to turn his address into a quasi-sexual one, likening the "Evening" to a woman whose "eyes," "breast," "mien," and "hair" "spill about" him,

That the last light fading out of the yellow west
Her peace and gentle loveliness may share
With one whose all desire is only rest.[36]

The liberally applied abstractions of the sonnet should be borne in mind when we read Smith's "Contemporary Poetry," because his attack therein on Victorian diction – on all "the *deems, forsooths, methinks*"[37] – has been lauded as a significant shift in Canadian literary fortunes. We need not discredit the essay or assume that Smith had no idea what he was doing when he published it four months before "To Evening"; but neither should we deny that the poem completely contradicts the theories he was developing. Out of that contradiction Smith emerged, so it must have been a fruitful one.

Smith's poems in the *Fortnightly* reveal, above all, a poet in process. He was not yet a modern poet, but various poems indicate that he was struggling to become one; he was not entirely a nineteenth-century imitator, though many poems suggest that he had the tendencies of that older poetry quite deep in his blood. He tried so many different forms at this time, and worked over so many varying themes, that it is obvious that Smith was casting about vigorously for a defining poetic that would sustain him into maturity and establish his reputation. It is safe to say that the *Fortnightly*, so far as Smith was concerned, was not a journal of Modernist literature at all, but a sounding board that he could use freely as he struggled to define himself *vis-à-vis* nineteenth-century *and* modern literature. To suggest that he was imitating the moderns in his earliest apprentice verses – as Smith himself has done –[38] is to repress or ignore about two-thirds of the truth.

When these facts about Smith's *Fortnightly* poetry are appreciated, and we are reminded of Scott's contributions and Kennedy's Arthurian re-workings, a very different image of the journal emerges. Rather than view it as the herald of Canadian Modernism we must adjust our attitudes and recognize it as the gathering ground of a number of significant poets who *later* established their modern tones, but who at the time of its publication were still firmly linked to the nineteenth-century poetry that they were ultimately to reject. Properly speaking, Canadian Modernism begins somewhere in the *Fortnightly*, yes; as well as in the *Newfoundland Verse* of Pratt and the early volumes of Livesay, the manuscripts of Knister and the ledger-books of Ross; but the *Fortnightly* established nothing. It was a proving ground, and possibly it reveals the halcyon days of a generation: but it was not, by any means, a Modernist journal; it is a much younger publication than that phrase implies. Its role in our literary history cannot be denied, but should not be distorted. We should remember the poetry in it for what it was, the poetry of young men who had not, at that time, a clear or certain purpose for their art.

For similar reasons we should not think only of Smith's "Contemporary Poetry" and "Hamlet in Modern Dress" when we assess the prose of the *Fortnightly*. That a Canadian university journal should produce one of the earliest readings of Eliot in North America is indeed remarkable, but the other prose of the *Fortnightly* reveals it for an isolated and uncharacteristic one. Smith's other, and earliest, essay in the journal, for instance, shows much less the impact of modern poetry on his aesthetic theory. "Symbolism in Poetry" set out to do for Symbolism what "Contemporary Poetry" was to do for modern verse. Smith's knowledge of the Symbolist movement appears to be based almost entirely on Symons and Yeats, which accounts for his rendition of the vagueness of the Symbol: "The element of mystery, indeed, is one that is ever present in symbolism. There is a sense of far horizons, of an undiscovered country, of a beauty we can only signify, not describe ... A certain amount of obscurity, evocation, and suggestion is implied in all symbolist poetry."[39] He quotes from and paraphrases at length Symons's *Symbolist Movement in Literature*, indeed borrowing Symons's analyses of Verlaine for use in his own essay. He discusses "this most musical of the *Symbolistes*" with reference to his suggestiveness, nuance, and underplaying of rhyme, all of which information was available to him in Symons's chapter on Verlaine (12).[40] His attitude to Yeats, whom he quotes at the end of his article, demonstrates that it is still the early, Aesthetic Yeats who attracts him: Yeats's postulation of an autonomous validity for the realm of art was learned, of course, from Pater and was qualified by Yeats in works that have not, as yet, had any apparent effect on Smith. Smith quotes Yeats as follows:

A return to the way of our fathers, a casting out of descriptions of nature for the sake of nature, of the moral law for the sake of the moral law, a casting out of all anecdotes and of that brooding over scientific opinion that so often extinguished the central flame in Tennyson, and of that vehemence that would make us do or not do certain things ... With this change of substance, this return to imagination, this understanding that the laws of art, which are the hidden laws of the world, can alone bind the imagination, would come a change of style, and we would cast out of serious poetry those energetic rhythms ... which are the invention of the will with its eyes always on something to be done or undone; and we would seek out those wavering, meditative, organic rhythms, which are the embodiment of the imagination. ("Symbolism," 16)

It is not altogether surprising that "Symbolism in Poetry" should proclaim such a different poetic from "Contemporary Poetry" and "Hamlet in Modern Dress": as his poetry demonstrates, Smith's thinking was undergoing a series of radical changes, and the other two essays were published a full year after the article on Symbolism. During that year Smith met Lancelot Hogben, a young mathematics professor at McGill with a taste for the modern in poetry, who widened Smith's sense of the modern vision and acquainted him with poets who were consolidating the revolutionary impetus of Eliot. Edel claims that Hogben's having hovered on the periphery of Bloomsbury "gave the *Fortnightly* a kind of indirect pipe-line to British post-war radical taste ... Certainly Hogben gave Smith all the new poetry to read, including a copy of *Prufrock*" ("Warrior," 11). If as Edel says elsewhere this acquaintance was not made until the middle of the first year of the journal's run,[41] Hogben's presence might well account for the sudden shift in the second year towards Eliot and "Contemporary Poetry." In November 1925, it still seemed natural to Smith to quote from Symons, Verlaine, Moréas and Yeats.

Perhaps such indefinite Aesthetic tastes attracted Smith to the work of A.P.R. Coulborn, the junior editor behind the *nom-de-plume* "Vespasiano" and the *Fortnightly*'s rude and paradoxical essayist (Djwa, *PI*, 86). *Les vespasiennes* were public toilets in the parks and *carrés* of Montreal, so Coulborn was making a point with his pseudonym: he intended to urinate on a good deal of conventional thought, with a smug pride in his radicalism that links his style distinctly to the essay style of Wilde. He begins his witty paragraphs with phrases like "If I was a little less wise than I am," and peppers them with politely snide *bons mots*: "I believe Mr Toole is as sincere as I am, and I shall continue to believe this as long as I can." He bothers to point out that he is "a little indolent, and do[es] not always take the trouble to make [him]self clear," suggesting that *fin-de-siècle* languor of the retiring thinker that can be so amusing in Wilde: "If Mr. Toole would like any further instances of the affinity between Christianity and Slavery I will rush to the Redpath Library, which I admit I have not entered for some years."[42]

Coulborn's prose character does not necessarily derive from Wilde, but he reflects so many of the tones of the earlier essayist that it is revealing to find, in an essay entitled "Sentimentalism in Education," an unique reference to the "decadence" of the modern day: of "modern youth" in the abstract he writes, "His interests lie chiefly in exaggerations – sure sign of decadence – license of the sex impulse ... immense enthusiasm for sports ... and so on ad libitum. And the main cause of all these things is that the modern youth has never been taught to control his appetites, whether physical or spiritual."[43] In an article written for the *McGill Daily Literary Supplement* a year earlier, entitled "What Is Art?", Coulborn had argued methodically against Art-for-Art's-Sake and shown a thorough knowledge of its characteristics and premises.[44] Because he sets himself up as an arbiter of any number of issues, the amoral disinterestedness of the Aesthetes would necessarily alienate him: nevertheless he manifests a good number of their prose techniques and shows himself, again and again, an inheritor of the Wildean sense of the essay as a forum for droll wisdom.

"Vespasiano's" themes are picked up by Abraham Edel, brother of Leon, in a pair of articles for the *Fortnightly*. His essay "Decadence," unrelated to Scott's sonnet of the same name, argues against the idea that the modern period is merely another "Silver Age," ultimately concluding that "it only seems so to us" who are in the midst of it: "It may be said that amid this turmoil, this confused mass there is something abiding, something that will delight posterity. Perhaps it was so in Babylon, in Athens, in Rome – in every great centre in any period of history."[45] The essence of Edel's analysis is that a period of Decadence will always follow a period of great activity: "Every period of progress, of real advance in civilization has been inevitably followed by a time of stagnation. It seemed that the intellect of man had been drained and was now devoid of resource – that the effort of creation had overcome this creative power. It is the old question of *fin-de-siècle* ... this much is certain that for every crest of a wave there is a hollow, for every height there is a depth, and that human history is a cursory motion over hill and valley."[46] Edel seems to contradict his own arguments against our being in a "Silver Age" by suggesting that the modern period, following the Enlightenment and the Industrial Revolution, is after all Decadent, in exhausted repose rather than forward vigour. Whatever his conclusions, it is significant in a larger sense that he chooses to address modern crises in the terms of Decadence at all: to him at least, and to "Vespasiano" somewhat, the idea of Decadence was a living and opportune question, not a fad of the past that had become *outré*.

Abraham Edel's dwelling on Decadence provides a context for a second piece he published in the *Fortnightly* entitled "What Is Art?", a dialogue between "Thrasymachus" and "Socrates." Eleven different answers to the question posed in the title are proposed by the thick-headed Thrasymachus and the wily Socrates, and most of them turn on the relationship between Art and Life – whether Art represents Life, or distorts it, or rejects it, or improves its quality. Thrasymachus's first answer, that "Art is Beauty," is quickly dismissed by his opponent in the dialogue, which again demonstrates Edel's rejection of an easy descent into modern Decadence. After a prolonged discussion, and in exasperation with the slowness of his interlocutor, Socrates finally announces ironically, "Then Art is Life and Life is Art, and we have come to the conclusion which if you will remember, I predicted long ago." Thrasymachus struggles against this meaningless equation, but Socrates is given the final word: "I call Art true self-expression, and after all, very few of us are really capable of it."[47] The debate around which Edel has built his dialogue is, of course, the central debate of the dialogues of Wilde: as when "Vivian" says, in "The Decay of Lying," "Life becomes fascinated with this new wonder, and asks to be admitted into the charmed circle. Art takes life as part of her rough material, recreates it, and refashions it in fresh forms ... The third stage is when Life gets the upper hand and drives Art out into the wilderness. This is the true decadence."[48] Although Edel explicitly rejects the popular version of the Aesthetic attitude by denying that Art is Beauty or a mere portrayal of beauty, it seems not unlikely (especially given his other article "Decadence") that he borrowed the terms of his discussion from Wilde as well as from Socrates, or from another late nineteenth-century essayist who had also learned from Wilde.

Certainly the debates of Aestheticism were not distasteful to Smith and Scott, the *Fortnightly*'s editors, as the following excerpt will show. We must imagine the two reading the submission, and discussing its virtues: "'Beauty, that beauty which is perfection, that is the quest of my continual seeking,' said the youth, 'but you, old man, shall I some day become as you are, old and twisted; will my seeking end in this? ...' 'Yes, my son, you, too, will become as I, old and gnarled and not beautiful to gaze upon ... But something will remain ever with you, if you do not weary of seeking your high quest.'"[49] "The Quest," by "Juvenis," may seem so extreme in its imitation of Aestheticism as to be a parody; nothing in the piece, however, no irony or drollery, suggests any attitude but emulation of the Aesthetic. The old man goes on to relate that he, too, was "'a high-hearted youth ... in quest of beauty,'" that he came to "'the edge of a deep wood,'" where there arose a "'vision of loveliness,'" a female bather so intensely beautiful that the erstwhile youth had no choice but to linger in contemplation of her charms. The bather, however, was fearful of this young man: "'Youths have deserted me in sorrow; will you also leave me?' Then I said; 'I shall not desert you, if you will but help me in finding that true beauty which is perfection.' She answered that she would do as I desired, warning me of the sorrow it would cause me" ("Quest," 38). In order to realize the youth's vision of perfect beauty, the woman changes the river to ice and herself to stone, since perfection must be unchanging. Thus she loses "that living, ever-changing beauty" he had worshipped. She loses, to put it simply, the breath of the flux, the vital urgency given to perceptions of beauty when we know that they are changing, constantly passing from one state to another. On this mournful note the old man's tale ends, but the youth has not heard: for "the boy was sweetly sleeping in the long grasses at the old man's feet; and he smiled in his dream" ("Quest," 44).

Significantly, "Juvenis" supplied an Epilogue to the piece that denied it all affiliation with Aestheticism (or anything else). "I was informed," he writes, "that it was strongly 'influenced' by Cabell, Dunsany, Stevenson, Wilde, and Yeats." This he claims to be preposterous: it "hardly speaks well for the critical faculty of our reputed intelligentzia."[50] But "Juvenis" must be set at defiance here. There is simply no model in English or French literature for his "Quest" if not in the fables and daydreams of the Aesthetes: to defend himself by suggesting that he came up with the theme independently and developed it without any influences – as he does in his Epilogue – is merely to say that he had an imagination and a sensibility, not to mention a prose style, so close to those of Aestheticism as to make the difference between them negligible. In this piece at least he was an outright and unmitigated Aesthete, by practically any definition of the term that passes current.

Recall Glassco's "Search" in this context: "What is it we seek? Is it beauty? Is it honour? Is it happiness? The bubbles go racing through the wine and vanish. We raise it to our lips."[51] Glassco and "Juvenis" certainly share a few literary attitudes, and we may presume that at least one member of the editorial board was sufficiently sympathetic to such mannered prose to welcome it in the *Fortnightly*. Such Aesthetic tendencies begin to coalesce in one's mind after reading the journal through and soon demand recognition as a second and significant strain in the journal, thus far either unnoticed or unacknowledged.

If we assume some degree of sympathy to the Aesthetic and the dandyish in the journal's editors, it is not surprising to find them praising the Cambridge men who had come to Canada for a round of debates against the teams of Canadian universities. The debating style of Oxford and Cambridge in the 1920s directly reflected the contemporary dandyism of the universities' students, manifested in brusque tones, affected drollery, and much intellectual grandstanding (Green, 152). Leon Edel in his "Note on the Cambridge-McGill Debate" remarks that "Those who heard the Cambridge-McGill debate could not but be impressed by the wit and attack of the English debaters, the ease and facility of their manner of speech, their seemingly endless capacity to meet at every turn the ponderous arguments of the McGill team, and their ability to sweep these aside with a single thrust, a brilliant epigram." The Cambridge debaters showed "polished wit" and "irony," "which stood like a sharp crystal against the clumsy fumblings of the Red team."[52] It is not difficult to sense in Edel's debaters some of the vigorous dandyism of Harold Acton and Brian Howard who, although from Oxford, made their mark throughout British higher education. This approval of the Cambridge debaters is confirmed by an article entitled "On Having a Shoe Shine," by one "Hugh C.G. Herkelots (Cambridge Debating Team)," in the same issue of the *Fortnightly* as Edel's "Note". The exotic name suggests a pseudonym, which makes it quite possible, given the generally deceptive quality of by-lines in the review, that it was one of the editors who wrote the piece. Whether Herkelots was a true Cambridge man or a winking Canadian, he has certainly felt the touch of 1920s dandyism in his elegant prose: "Many impressions I will carry back from the American Continent when I return to England in December. The sight of New York from the sea, the colour of maple trees in Autumn ... Yet no memory, I think, will be so vivid as that of having my shoes cleaned. In England we are prosaic folks: we never see our shoes cleaned; it is a miracle that happens while we slumber ... Here you have instituted the shoe-shine: you have raised a material necessity to the high level of an adventure." The constant undertone of jest in the piece captures the note of the practised dandy, as does his rendition of the art of the boot-black: "In Quebec my shoes were cleaned by a little Frenchman who danced as he worked and played upon my feet as upon a piano. Had fate been kinder he might have been a ballet dancer or a pianist. Perhaps he is, at night, when the labours of the day are over. But fate has not really been unkind to him. He might have been but an ordinary pianist it may be – but he was a very extraordinary boot-black."[53] Herkelots' article and Edel's warm approval of the Cambridge debaters make clear that the editors of the *Fortnightly* desired to affiliate themselves, by praising and by some imitating, with the brash wits of the best British universities, to mimic their paradoxes and appropriate their mannerisms.

It is important, then, not to overestimate the seriousness of the *Fortnightly* and its crew. They were serious page by page, thought by thought, but the review was for them an outlet for intellectual free play as much as dedication to any cause. It was playfulness, not dedicated Modernism, that inspired Scott's brilliant mockery of the style of Gertrude Stein:

I am becoming very interested in my interest in my interest in your University in its relation to beauty. If you do not mind I will tell you how it all happens. You see I am a follower of beauty follower of beauty and because

I follow beauty beauty is just in front of me. That makes it very beautiful, being so close. Being nearness is contemporary with the quite. Now it seems to me that you have beautiful gates just in front of the college with the college behind and the gates in front. The college is not far behind the gates. So it seems to me that your college is following beauty and that is the most beautiful thing a college can follow. Nothing can be more than the most.[54]

The few images that have descended to us of these men in their youth tend to confirm the lack of high seriousness in their *Fortnightly* days. Edel has said that Smith "valued poetry highly and spoke noble words in its behalf. But he tended to retain that ironic pose of the 'twenties which said 'we shouldn't take ourselves too seriously, should we?'"[55] Perhaps the family background of Smith suggests one reason for such a pose; Edel renders it thus: "Smith belongs to Anglo-Saxon Protestant Westmount in Montreal, and his parents came out of the Victorian world. He was supposed to be practical and material and there he was playing with words, his own, and the words of others, which bring no dividends."[56] Certainly Smith could be serious when the occasion demanded: "he possessed a fund of civility, which meant he said all the polite things; but he was a tempest of poetry and revolt against Establishment hypocrisies." Nevertheless "he invited his friends to tea in formal English fashion" (Edel, "McGill Modernized," 113), presumably because he was not willing to abandon the social niceties that attend upon the hypocrisies of a post-imperial culture. Scott shared these qualities; despite a constant personal decorum and civility, "He always found some phrase in the *Daily* or the downtown press, some platitude in a speech, and turned it into the stuff of irony and paradox. He seemed to think in epigrams (Edel, "Warrior," 11). This conversational habit also appealed to D.C. Adam, one of the editors: he was a bohemian night-hawk who regularly missed his classes because of sitting up all hours with his books, who would arrive on campus in the late afternoon to join the troops. "I still remember," Edel writes of him, "how he flicked the ash of his cigarette and worked hard at coining epigrams – out of Wilde, Whistler, or James Branch Cabell." In the second year "Young Buffy Glassco" joined them; he "had something of a faun in him, with his young vigour, slightly receding chin, and precocious eroticism" (Edel, "McGill Modernized," 117). Edel described Kennedy with much the same tone, as a young man "out of his depth" among the worldlings of the review.[57] Allan Latham, another of the editors, whose life was cut tragically short in 1935 in a motor accident, survives in his numerous letters to Smith, which show a young man developing a refined sense of economics and class structures, who nevertheless had a wildly roving eye and filled a good portion of his letters from Berlin by describing its prostitutes and other opportunities for "free love." His life in Berlin was the very *vie-de-poète* that has always seemed to strike John Glassco away from the rest of the group, involving a good deal of alcohol and varied female company. "I shall be delighted," he writes to Smith in Edinburgh, "to accompany you both [Smith and Jeannie, his new wife] to Vienna, which far excels even Paris in matters pertaining to the genitalia."[58] (A letter from nighthawk D.C. Adam in the same collection of Smith's papers also explores this manner of sexual posturing [April 1927, Smith Collection, Trent, MS 80–005, Folder 1(6)].) Edel has also seen fit to recall "the ease with which [Smith] picked up girls in London coffee shops" ("The 'I,'" 89).

In short, these young men were typical young men. They followed devoted causes, spoke in high praise of all they would do in pursuit of their causes, denigrated the accomplishments of the previous generation, sought to deny their common descent from bourgeois backgrounds, passed libidinous humour back and forth, imitated the styles of speech of those whom they admired, and broke as many rules as they could without being disciplined, expelled, or black-listed. They seized examples of behaviour personal and artistic wherever they could find them: if in the nineteenth century they recognized the means to express a particular attitude, so be it; if in the twentieth, so much the better, for that would make them modern. They were partners in crime more than reconstruction; they charged at windmills rather than lay out their own literary movement. "Like Bloomsbury," Edel adds, "– and why not compare ourselves with it? – our main delight was in needling the stuffed shirts, the Victorians" ("McGill Modernized," 115). For that purpose either epigrams from Wilde or ellipsis from Eliot would do the trick, and they turned their talents to either as the fancy took them. We have in the *Fortnightly* one of the most delightfully alive events in all of Canadian literary history, and to make of it, as so much casual comment has done, the high-minded child of a group of determined young idealists is to disembowel it of much of that life. It is healthier by far to remember that the stern-minded A.J.M. Smith we encounter in his criticism, the principled and humane F.R. Scott who shaped so much of Canadian life, had their wild uncollared youth as well; and moreover that they shared it and poured that energy into the pages of one of the most striking journals yet to appear on the Canadian scene.

Can we continue to speak of the *Fortnightly* as "an iconoclastic journal of modernist literature and opinion?" Iconoclastic, to be sure, but of everything, even of the excesses of Modernism. In quantity the literature in the journal is far more nineteenth-century than modern, when we add to our assessment of Smith the poems of Scott and Kennedy, and Glassco's contribution, discussed earlier in this book; and as for quality, no one will contend, I think, that their modern efforts are significantly better poetry than their Romantic, Aesthetic, or Decadent efforts. The journal was created above all at a point of transition for each of these young men: they had been developing in not dissimilar ways for some years and then chanced to come together to work on an exciting project that demanded the best from them, and in that climate their individual processes of growth were recorded for posterity. That is the attitude we ought to maintain to the *McGill Fortnightly Review*: in its pages we may see, not the first stage of our poets' Modernism, but an intermediate stage between Modernism and an older attitude that preceded it in each poet. Only then will we have fairly rendered the *esprit de corps*, the fine principles, and the lingering boyishness that fill page after page of this marvellous document of Canadian life.

With Scott, Kennedy, and Glassco it is not possible to trace the antecedent stages of this transition. Scott's three poems at Oxford and Kennedy's efforts as "Helen Lawrence" for the *The Montreal Star* are all we have of their earlier work; but with Smith the case is fortunately different. Not only is there the *McGill Daily Literary Supplement*, the forerunner of the *Fortnightly* during the previous year (1924–25), but the *McGill Daily* itself has a number of Smith's earliest poems. Prior to the *Fortnightly* poems, then, we have a good four years' work from Smith's hand, material which does much to explain and elaborate the lingering nineteenth-century qualities of his poetry in the more famous review.

The *McGill Daily Literary Supplement* was established by Smith in affiliation with the campus student newspaper, so that he could have greater editorial control than his regular column in the *Daily*, "The Dilettante," could offer. It ran eighteen numbers, but was cut short before the end of the school year because of a financial dispute between the *Supplement*'s board, headed by Smith, and the *McGill Daily*'s editorial staff. Smith's poems in the *Supplement* show him intrigued with the effects of 1920s dandyism, becoming aware of the demands of modern poetry, but still more tempted by beauty, much as (to a lesser degree) the *Fortnightly* poems were to do. The *Supplement* provides a similar collection, therefore, of Smith's early transitional work, but it is more revealing than the *Fortnightly* because the extremes are so much more marked: a slightly younger Smith was even more vigorous in his search for a sustaining poetic voice. "The Wave," which appeared in the first number and was signed by "Max," demonstrates these tensions succinctly, once again between blatantly Aesthetic content and an obscure urge towards modern form:

Beauty ruffles the darkness.

Strange waves curl,
And lift themselves,
Drench us,
And ebb,
And rise again.

Over our lips ... breathless ...
Over our eyes ... oh blind ...

The ellipses are Smith's. This rather desperate attempt to demonstrate the poet's capacity for ecstasy in beauty, captured in the somewhat incongruous form of free verse, signifies the distance to which Smith would go to try to integrate his various poetic intentions. Thorough and thick abstraction prevents the attempted eroticism from coming through, a point of aesthetics Smith was eventually to learn; a comparison of this poem and such a poem as "Souvenirs du Temps Bien Perdu" from the canon makes clear how far he was to move away from this initial state. But in 1924 he was secure in his love of beauty, to which the poem returns after having metaphorically linked lady and wave:

Murmurous, obliterating wave,
Pour down on me
Thy flood of beauty,
Cover me with
Forgetfulness awhile,
That I may sink into thy surging ecstasy
And loose myself in thee.[59]

The poet seeks to free himself into, or to be swallowed, obliterated, by beauty and ecstasy, so that he may forget the hurly-burly of the material world, the interference between the poet and his vision of beauty and love. Note that Smith's awareness of free verse seems to pre-date his imitation of Yeatsian rhythms: judging by its adaptation into his own work, the Yeatsian influence was not felt at all until 1925, somewhere between the last number of the *Supplement* and the first of the *Fortnightly* (a space of about ten months). Thus in the *Supplement* he had not yet found a consistent vehicle for these Aesthetic sentiments, which Yeats, as we have seen, was later to offer him.

Smith also demonstrates in the *Supplement* most of the other premises of Aestheticism: for one, that beauty must pass and crumble into dust, against which process the poet can only offer a vain lament. His "Hellenica," which in the current form has only two parts, was published in the *Supplement* with four, two middle verses having been excised for the later republication. The first of these lost verses parallels the first of the pair in the canon, revealing "The faint curve/Of Iope's sweet mouth":

Little Anthea twined roses
Over the lovelocks of her hair.
Brambles and dry thorns
Litter that garden now.

Smith appears to have discovered Imagism, but brings to it his own sensibilities, which are still heavily charged with Romanticism and Decadence. The second excised verse strikes the latter note more openly: "They have carved words on marble:/When beauty freezes into stone/Its immortality begins."[60] Smith presumably cut these two parts of "Hellenica" because they were dreamier than the others, more open in their worship of beauty and keen in regret for its loss. Nevertheless, these two lost pieces provide a new context for the remaining stanzas, particularly "Hellenica II" in the present version:

Chloe has gone down the dark path
Into the land of shadows,
And the perplexed ghosts
Of the long dead
Are half forgetful of Lethe,
Half remembering the pale flower
Of the wild narcissus
Blowing in spring.   (*PNC*, 36)

The use of the narcissus, an emblematic flower of the Decadence – and for that matter Smith's emphasis on its pallor, its "half" presence – may now be illuminated in the later version, because "Hellenica II" was originally in the company of two other verses that were much more open in their Aesthetic orientation. Smith's fascination with beauty and its passing from the flesh has not prevented him from rendering the images in fairly austere modern verse, which once again underscores the transitional qualities of most of this work.

"Vain Comfort," in the last number of the *Supplement*, picks up the decay theme once more and makes clear that Smith was attracted to these images throughout the journal's run:

> All dear, sweet things grow gray;
> Time steals the fire from eyes,
> And cracks clear laughter's bell,
> Making of truths sad lies,
> Changing felicities
> To memories.

In this dismaying context the poet has no solutions; he recognizes the superficiality of absolute beauty as a source of comfort for such meditations, but suspects that it is the best he can offer:

> Ah, then, and shall I dream
> Beside a glowing fire
> Of old, far faded things
> Without desire,
> Content with the cold ash
> Of beauty's pyre,
>
> Murmuring that memories
> Are in themselves sweet things,
> Lying that loveliness
> Looked on too long but brings
> Satiety?

The weary and rejected Aesthete may do so if he wishes, but cannot avoid the truth: "False, false/Cold comfort rings."[61] There is of course no proper way to identify these sentiments unless we discuss them as Decadent conventions. Beauty he may have had from any of the Romantics, to be sure; but the bemusement with death, the dusting over of beauty, the obsessive fixation on inevitable process, even the sense of "strange" beauty from "The Wave" and from "Silver Birch" in the *Fortnightly*, mark the Aesthetic and Decadent underpinnings of these Smith poems.

To various degrees and in various ways, Smith's other poems in the *Supplement* manifest the effects of this affinity. "Chinoiserie," for example, from 4 March 1925, is an antecedent of the "Chinoiserie" that one will find in Smith's collected poems, a translation of Gautier. The early version has three parts, only one of which is familiar:

> A princess whose arms were white as new-peeled almonds
>   and whose almond eyes were rayed with lashes henna-dipt
> Looked from a casement in her honourable ancestor's tower
>   of porcelain by the Yellow Sea
> And stretched her arms to reach the moon.

This palimpsest is so close to Smith's later translation (and to Gautier's original, which Smith was to render brilliantly) as to prove Smith's having known the Gautier piece by early 1925. Note the overlapping of images: the "almond eyes" of 1925 are "upward-slanting eyes" in the later version; the "henna-dipt" lashes have become "long nails ... stained with carmine red"; "her honourable ancestor's tower of porcelain by the Yellow Sea" becomes, in the later translation,

> She lives at home and cares for her old parents;
> From a tower of porcelain she leans her brow,
> By the Yellow River, where haunt the cormorants.

In the 1925 version the girl "looks from a casement" and "stretches her arms to reach the moon";[62] in the 1954 version a similar gesture: "From her trellis she leans out so far/That the dipping swallows are within her reach" (*PNC*, 34). The 1925 version is close enough to Gautier's original to prove that Smith knew the French poem by the age of twenty-two. I repeat the point because without it we would have no incontrovertible proof that Smith had encountered the *Symbolistes* directly as a young man. That he read Symons by late 1925 is definite; but he had read Gautier by March of that year at the latest, and found him, obviously, rather to his liking.

In the context of this early Aestheticism Smith's "Poplar Leaves," full of delicacy and trembling emotionalism, is rather more recognizable:

> He found her lips by starlight
> Under the drifting sky,
> In the shadow of the poplar,
> Straight, beautiful and high,
> Her lips moved whispering,
> Tremulous and shy ...

He heard the white poplar leaves
Sigh, and then sigh.

This tale of love is interrupted – not much of a surprise – by death,
which drags the beautiful woman away and leaves the lover muttering "his heart's mute 'why.'"[63] "Poplar Leaves" demonstrates,
rather more than the other Aesthetic poems of the *Supplement*, how
badly Smith needed to be rescued by Modernism. Its dead rhythms
and pathetic fascinations indicate that Smith the Aesthete was a
marked man, who would either change or go to the dogs. As Eliot
had said, young poets need "the historical sense, which we may call
nearly indispensable to anyone who would continue to be a poet
beyond his twenty-fifth year."[64] In Canada in 1925, the "historical
sense" was the sense of a necessary Modernism, and that is what
Smith was to find.

Still, there is little evidence of that final conclusion in the pages
of the *Supplement*. One of Smith's first answers to the dilemma that
faced him was very like the dandyism we have witnessed in Finch.
In "Nocturne" the undergraduate teasing of God – "My, won't God
be cross!" – strikes the dandy note, as does the artifice of the visual
element in the poem – "The stars are gold pin-heads/Holding the
purple curtain of the sky."[65] This artifice is emphasized further in
"Interior":

Firelight and candlelight
Gleaming in polished mahogany
Are moonlight and starlight
Across a water-lily pond.
The fat wife of a prominent banker
Drops a lump of sugar into China tea
With the inappropriate splash
Of a bull-frog plopping from a lily-pad,
Wrinkling the white moonlight
And the yellow starlight
On the lacquered pond.[66]

The lilies, the elegant setting, the intended deflation, and the general
visual artifice are very like certain poems of Finch and do much to
explain why Smith later found the Toronto poet's work deserving
of a place in his anthologies. Dandyism is a Modernist transfigu-
ration of the Decadence, a transitional point between the two periods
with elements of both; so "Nocturne" and "Interior" enrich the tran-
sitionalism of the *Supplement*, as did Smith's other dandy poems in

the *Fortnightly*, and help to complicate our appreciation of his search during this period.

These gleanings from the *McGill Daily Literary Supplement* call into question a number of judgments passed by Scott, Edel, and Smith himself upon its artistic tendencies. Edel, for instance, has said of the *Supplement* that its "verse was modern" ("McGill Modernized," 113) and that Smith's first literary models were Yeats and the Imagists, Eliot and Stevens, Sitwell and Conrad Aiken ("The 'I,'" 89–90). The poems quoted above disprove both these contentions. Smith's own version of this transitional period is somewhat obscured with time as well; in an interview with Michael Heenan, he identified 1921 as the year in which he began to read modern poetry, and claims that before that he read "Tennyson, and Shelley and Keats."[67] No doubt he did read these great poets of the Romantic mainstream: from such paradigms he might have found a part of the program of beauty he was to enact in his early verse; but he certainly did not find in them the intense moaning gloom of "Poplar Leaves" or "Vain Comfort": for that special emphasis on death and decay he must have looked elsewhere. In "Confessions of a Compulsive Anthologist" Smith had an even more extreme version of the facts: there he claimed that "Ezra Pound, Wallace Stevens, T.S. Eliot, Yeats in his middle period, Conrad Aiken and H.D. ... [were] the poets whom [he] deliberately began to imitate in the earliest apprentice verses [he] printed there or four years later in the *Literary Supplement* to the *McGill Daily* and the *McGill Fortnightly Review*" (4). I presume that Smith's inaccuracy here is a result of lapsing memory – after all, fifty years had passed – and a context of informal reminiscence. What must be emphasized in these passages, however, is that the entire period is a matter of chronological doubt and that we may well hypothesize, despite the principals' statements to the contrary, that Smith had been reading Aesthetic or Decadent poetry as well, and not only Théophile Gautier's.[68]

Other items from the *Supplement* tend to confirm this hypothesis, by suggesting that Smith had encountered English Aesthetic literature before the journal began its run. "The Quest for Beauty," for instance, is an editorial from the issue of 22 October 1924, which bibliographers presume to be by Smith. Its prose style is purposely elaborated in imitation of the style of the 1890s, to the end of leading the reader astray. With perfect solemnity the editor asks if the poor confused reader had thought "Beauty" had passed away, fled from the haunts of men: "Did you think that Beauty had shaken the dust of cities from her feet, and retired into the lonely places among mountains, streams and trees? That she had gone from amongst us unlamented and unpursued save by the poets, the painters and yourselves? That no bright lamp was illumined any more before her shrine?" With a quick glance the reader would believe himself in the company of a singularly unself-conscious Aesthete. But the tongue-in-cheek editor turns the piece around and foists the joke upon his readers, by announcing that "Beauty" has not passed away, because American "girls" are still pursuing her by all the arts of make-up known to modern woman; he proceeds to lecture Canadian "girls" upon the art and encourages them to take it up themselves, so that young Canadian men everywhere may continue the noble "quest for beauty" upon which they were formerly launched.[69] The aesthetic mimicry and the turn of wit certainly do suggest the hand of Smith, who would indeed be the most natural editorial writer for the *Supplement*. Most important to note is Smith's lampooning of the Aesthetic prose style, which suggests that very turning away from nineteenth-century models for which the *Supplement* and the *Fortnightly* are known; but the passage also suggests Smith's distinct acquaintance with the affectations and conventions of Aesthetic prose, which he has rendered with devastating accuracy.

This suggestion is supported by a reference in Smith's review of Michael Arlen's *The Green Hat*, which appeared on 28 January 1925. Smith is clearly disgusted with Arlen's products: "And Mr Arlen's style is at the best an affectation, at the worst a bore. It is modelled on the painted prose of the literary bloods of the nineties ... There are traces of Dowson's studied melancholy, of George Moore's affected impropriety, even of Oscar Wilde's artistic banalities. And we must conclude that the author of The Green Hat is something of a poseur. His work certainly cannot hold a candle to that of Max Beerbohm or Aldous Huxley."[70] Again, Smith's attitude to the Aesthetic prose style is one of clear distaste. He demonstrates more than a general familiarity with the school, however, by referring to specific features in the works of three different writers, all cardinal figures of the Decadent movement. The likelihood is that he had read them himself; that he picked up these judgments from lectures is unlikely, given contemporary attitudes to the Decadents; if from discussions with others, we may at least conclude that the discussion of Decadent writings was current and that Smith participated in it. It is interesting that he should compare the three, and Arlen, unfavourably with Max Beerbohm who, while a cordial enemy of the Decadent movement, was distinctly of its time; interesting moreover that one of Smith's early *noms-de-plume* was "Max." A surface distaste for Decadent prose does not, therefore, entirely alter the suggestion in this passage that Smith knew the writings of certain of the Decadents beyond mere generalizations, and that he did not so entirely hate them as to root out all their influences from his own sensibilities. He was the author, let us not forget, in this very issue, of "Vain Comfort," lamenting "beauty's pyre."

Moreover, let us remember that Smith accepted for a late issue of the *Supplement* a first poem from Scott, "Song of May and Virtue," that states, "Care, age and illness bring decay/On that which once most beauteous grew," and was so impressed with it that he contacted Scott and asked him to co-edit the new *Fortnightly* with him. He also welcomed a poem by Goodridge Macdonald with heavily Aesthetic undertones: the speaker of "Lately at Evening" is rapt in pursuit of beauty – "the imperial wonder of her flame/That burns to music even in thy name."[71] He was also the patron of "Vespasiano," who was first given room in the *Supplement* before graduating to the *Fortnightly*. As editor, as reviewer and as poet, Smith's role in the *Supplement* shows us a young man who was keenly aware of the questions of Aestheticism and Decadence, who could express disdain for those schools and yet imitate them in verse; it shows us moreover how much the aesthetic questions of the day in Canada were, even after three decades, the questions with which Pater and Wilde had wrestled. In the minds of these young men, and especially Smith, Aestheticism was the distinct literary past, the important movement immediately preceding their own undefined activity; though they battled and derided the Victorians, the Aesthetes maintained a powerful grip on their literary imaginations. Whenever the Canadians chose to name the enemy, it was Victorianism; they appear to have recognized in Aestheticism a rather shamefaced older cousin with whom they were necessarily allied in that battle.

Although these suggestions are based only upon the nature of the *Fortnightly* and the *Supplement*, the earliest Smith poetry confirms their drift: his verse in the *McGill Daily* shows an even more direct and undisguised Aestheticism, without that sense of transition that is evident in the later journals. A reading of these poems will make quite clear that Smith was to arrive at Modernism from what Edel called "a vigorous aestheticism," not (as he claimed) from the Victorian sympathies of a Tennyson or the primal Romanticism of a Shelley. Their existence is so generally unknown that even Scott has expressed an opinion that Smith's "earliest verse" lies in the *McGill Daily Literary Supplement* ("Smith: A Memoir," 79); and Smith the Modernist might well have preferred people to think so:

Let us dig a deep grave for Love –
For Love is dead, you know –

Seek we a willow bank
And there lay him low

.............................

We will cover him with roses
  Entwined with white lilies
And bitter-sweet forget-me-not
  And daffodillies.

And we will cross his frail, pale hands
  Like flowers on his breast.[72]

Published in the *McGill Daily* on 6 December 1922, when Smith was an undergraduate of twenty, "To an Olde Tune" reveals a poet emerging from the trite conventions of late Romanticism, who has realized to some extent their weakness and frailty, which results in a delicate weariness in the imagery of the verse. The image of burial, and the recitation of funeral preparations, was (as we have seen with Kennedy) a standard ploy of the Decadent.

Other Smith poems in the *Daily* are more explicit about their Aesthetic content. They maintain the trite imagery of "To an Olde Tune," but work it into a poetry almost entirely motivated by the young Aesthete's hunger for beauty. One of these is "When Thought of Her," printed on 31 January 1923:

All dreams of beauty I have felt or known,
Like scent of flowers on a quiet wind,
Come flocking to do homage at her throne
Where I have crowned her, deep within my mind.

And there all loveliness is clothed with her,
The spirit Beauty corporate is there,
And throbs alive should she but smile or stir,
And wantons in the tresses of her hair.[73]

The most striking feature of the poem, apart from its obvious Aestheticism, is its setting in the poet's "mind": his sense of beauty needs no direct correlative in the outside world, since he is able to idealize his beloved sufficiently to remain content with a mental image. We have already had occasion to note the "solitary prisoner" of Pater, the mind keeping its own "dream of a world," assembled

from those fleeting impressions that pierce through to its consciousness: this is the epistemology of "When Thought of Her" as well,
as the title itself indicates. The poem is Aesthetic rather than notably
Decadent; its essentially promising nature – the poet experiences
beauty as a blessing, not as a promise of loss or sickness or decay
– strikes it off from the *fin-de-siècle* fixations that are more current,
for instance, in Smith's "Conditional Mood." Note again the location
of beauty in the poet's consciousness, rather than in the outside
world:

> If I could liberate the thoughts that press
> My burning brain, the unknown ecstasies,
> And thirsty cravings after loveliness,
> Mysterious promptings, longings, prophecies,
> And half-glimpsed visions of a finer life
> That thought will bring to be, when love intense
> Shall smooth a peace upon our present strife,
> Building the city's walls to music, whence
> Radiant peoples throng – if this could be
> I'd raise Utopia with a youthful rhyme,
> And burst upon the world, so joyous, free,
> And musical in song that bird nor chime
> Nor any music or of earth or air
> For ecstasy with that song would [compare].[74]

Smith has penned a standard Aesthetic poem, beginning with images of uncontrolled passion and mental pressure: "Burning brain,"
"unknown ecstasies," "thirsty cravings after loveliness" supply the
*fin-de-siècle* context above all, but so, in a different manner, does
Smith's vision of an Aesthetic Utopia. The odd alliance of the Aesthetic movement with early Socialism led to a good many such visions of beautiful societies, the most notable perhaps Morris's *News
from Nowhere*, the least plausible Wilde's "Soul of Man Under Socialism." Smith's Utopia is obviously just such an Aesthetic culture:
his desire is for "radiant" people, not necessarily well-fed, educated,
or happy, and the very walls of the city are to be like "music." These
things would be achieved if he "could liberate the thoughts that
press" – that is, the poem is about the poet's difficulty writing poetry
and in fact turns on the impossibility of his creating something
meaningful. Nothing in the poem suggests that he is about to (save
the poem itself), which is the reason for the very tentative and
somewhat wry title, "Conditional Mood." The grammatical reference

reminds the reader how much this vision is a thing of the poet's mind and how little likelihood there is of any remote realization of his dreams.

"When Thought of Her" and "Conditional Mood" set Smith apart from merely Romantic antecedents. No such dramatic pursuit of abstract Beauty, nor any sense of the pressure suffered in such a pursuit, can have come from a study only of Shelley or Keats, and, since it seems unlikely that at this early and imitative stage Smith should have happened upon such Aesthetic fixations on his own – that is, recognized that Aestheticism was the natural outcome of certain principles of Romanticism – there seems no choice but to conclude that at some point in his early years the poetry of the Aesthetes had reached him and perhaps (judging by "Conditional Mood," with its "pressed" and "Burning brain") that of the Decadents as well.

"Beauty Dead" helps to solidify this latter suspicion, even as it foreshadows the death-preoccupations of a later Smith and of the future friend, Leo Kennedy. A faint eroticism is attempted in the poem – there is mention of the woman's "breasts," no small risk in the context of Currie's anxieties over his students' publications – and that eroticism leads the poet to capture her in decay, locked underground:

> Yet, poor unfortunate, under the tangled grass
> Long centuries she has lain alone, and known
> No movement save the stirrings of decay
> Dividing twitching flesh from crumbling bone.[75]

If such imagery is a further indication, as with Kennedy, of Smith's having read the Decadents – it at least confirms his personal affinity, at the age of twenty, with their spirit – it adds another level of complexity to Smith's youthful Aestheticism. While his emphasis on beauty tugs the early poetry towards the Aesthetic mode, there is a concomitant interest in decay that makes the images and conventions of Decadence appear attractive to the young poet. The coincidence of the two concerns is, really, further evidence that he had been reading Aesthetic literature thoroughly before approaching Eliot and the moderns.

"Humouresque," published 21 March 1923, is the first visible example of Smith's effort to reconcile Aesthetic concerns with the formal liberation and experimentation typical of Modernism. One would call its verse neither "free" nor "blank," but the quality of irony towards the conclusion calls in a satiric, and not far from a modern, note:

> He
> Had always
> Been a lucky one:
> The girl he loved
> Refused him, so he always
> Kept her fresh-eyed beauty
> Safe from ravagings of Time,
> And lived with her in one close
> Corner of his brain, and kissed her lips,
> And pale white hands, and dreamy hair.

Note the retreat of beauty into the brain again and the image of the young Aesthete content to live with such dry mental eroticism. But Smith directs the poem in such a way that we see him rise above his Aesthetic persona for once, making him the hero of a diatribe against materialistic love:

> The man she married saw her dreamy hair
> Become a night-mare, and her red lips
> Crack, and white hands coarsen. Close
> Though he held her, thieving Time
> Crept in and stole her beauty,
> And after that stole love.
> And yet her husband knew
> That Time compounded
> Interest in her
> Wealth. He, too,
> Had always been
> A lucky
> One.[76]

The process of time is acted out once more upon the beautiful lady: but the Aesthete is spared because he has chosen to worship beauty as a thing of the mind and spirit rather than of the flesh: he has abstracted it and is therefore above its vagaries. In contrast to the relative purity of the Aesthete, those who hunger after money and are indifferent to beauty are attacked and shown to lack the spirituality of their opposites. The contrived form of the poem tends to confirm this reading: as the Aesthete withdraws and builds up his private image of beauty, the lines lengthen and the poem increases in visual force; as the money-hungry husband takes over the lines are chopped back. "Humouresque," then, shows Smith to have been highly conscious of his Aesthetic alternative and places such poems as "Conditional Mood" and "When Thought of Her" in a slightly different light. In "Humouresque" we see him manipulate the premises of Aestheticism dramatically, rather than deeply and fervently expressing them; his Aestheticism is a pose here, a convention, not a commitment of spirit. This dramatic quality in his early Aestheticism made him ripe for education by Modernism, which provided him at once with an equally determined set of aesthetics and a new focus of intellectual commitment.

We cannot conclude, however, that he was already turning towards modern poetry in the *Daily*. "Humouresque" is only one poem, and against it must be weighed all the others he published in the student newspaper. For several months after the appearance of "Humouresque" he continued to publish late Romantic, Aesthetic, and Decadent poems in the *Daily*. Some of these, like "At a Fireside," merely make the standard references of an Aesthetic poem: "Musing, without desire/Of loveliness foredone,/On beauty's pyre."[77] But one of them, "In the City," published in the same issue as "Humouresque," elaborates and works over the Aesthetic context to such an extent that we are allowed to see Smith's early speculations vigorously at play. He knows by now that the Aesthetic attitude leaves too much of life unconsidered, but he is not fully able to reconcile himself to the necessary change of mind and heart. He therefore tries to find in the cityscape, and in the faces of the city's poor, something of the old "Beauty" he had always worshipped. It is significant, of course, that he does not abandon "Beauty" altogether in favour of social commitment: that was to come later; this first step may be seen as the beginning of a process of maturation that culminated in such later poems as "The Bridegroom" and "The Common Man." Since "In the City" shows clearly the turn from Aestheticism that was to occupy the following years, and the first "typical" modern concern in Smith, for the poor, for the urban waste-land, and since it clearly confirms that he was pulling out of a strongly Aesthetic youth into Modernism, it deserves quotation in full, despite its uneven quality and ponderous length:

I have got no wealth store
Of silver dollars, bills or
Stocks or property or land,
But only dreams that I command

To habit me to my desire
And minister to Beauty's fire
That's flaming somewhere deep behind
In the darkness of my mind.

I am doomed for lack of cash
To plunge into the metal crash
Of the iron city's toil,
Seeking Quiet in the turmoil,
Seeking loveliness in mud,
Life in brick and stone and wood,
Seeking kindness in the beat
Of the noisy city's street.

I have found these under trees,
And in boats upon the seas,
On high hills and level spaces
When the clouds run merry races,
When the sun comes with the rain
To the watcher's most great gain:
But in the city shall I find
Beauty, living, quiet, kind?

Thus I pondered on my perch
In the office ere the search
Through the flaming town began
For the loveliness in man.
Fire and iron and steel and smoke,
Were trees and clouds. Clamour broke
From every car and motor truck
Lurking forward through the muck.

There was not any bird to sing,
Nor tree to catch the whispering
Of the little frightened wind,
And all the people to my mind
Were pale and peaked, or brutish, coarse,
With some dark taint of hog or horse –
Gum-chewers, spitters on the walk,
Careless, insolent and loud of talk.

"O Christ," I cried, "give me thine eyes
To see, thy heart these mysteries

To understand. Help me to find
A beauty not within the mind.
What is behind these faces hard,
And this dull dirty stifling yard,
These narrow streets and filthy hovels,
And these poor men who work with shovels?"

And all at once, it seemed I heard,
Like voice of some sweet singing bird,
Audible thought that pierced the brain:
"Injustice, poverty and pain
Are here! Swear now on oath to set
The cause of pity first, forget
All beauty but the loveliness
That lies in fighting this distress."

And now, like one a little queer,
To whom the Grail has come too near,
I walk about dark gloomy ways,
The worker, beggar, outcast praise,
And find in some dull dusty street
The loveliness of seas that beat
With roaring radiance on sands
Of burnished gold in old far lands.[78]

"In the City" shows Smith struggling with a major work, a poem
that would unite the various strains of his artistic personality in an
extended process of visual and abstract thought. Between the poles
of beauty and reality the poet is torn and finds, ostensibly, some
means of easing the tension by the conclusion. He has been living
too much in the pure mind, which is once again the seat of beauty
to the poet, and as a consequence is becoming increasingly unfit for
human company, finding only ugliness when he is forced to consort
with the average men of his day.

The tension exists, according to the first stanza and the opening
of the second, because the Aesthete lacks "cash" (no doubt the colloquialism struck the young poet as forceful and modern): that is,
he recognizes that one cannot merely pursue beauty all one's life if
one wishes to eat, be sheltered, have children and clothing, unless
one is guaranteed an independent income that can overrule these
intrusions. Perhaps the poet has recognized that most of the Aesthetes one encounters in literature are lords or the scions of ancient
families, whose refined sensual explorations are licensed by inher-

itances; he on the other hand must "plunge into the metal crash" of the city, not necessarily to work or to strive, but to find "Quiet" and "loveliness" in "mud," "brick," "stone and wood." But these properties of concrete reality affront him severely; accustomed as he is to finding beauty in romantic settings (as the third stanza makes clear), "Fire and iron and steel and smoke" hardly seem promising. That the town should be "flaming" as he begins his search suggests Hell rather than Pater's flame: the poet descends from his "perch," the seat of Aesthetic removal, into the torture of the city and what Smith was later to call the "refining fire" of good poetry. The poet peppers his poems with modern images, cars and trucks, muck and mud, because he desires to render for the reader his distaste for all he saw; but his most revealing and pivotal vision is that of working men, to whose grim ways and features the poor young Aesthete is ill-accustomed. Note that his reaction is an aesthetic one: it is their "pale and peaked" looks, the "taint of hog or horse" in their bearing, that revolts him, not their poverty, their hard labour, their terrible need for a better way of life. These "gum-chewers" and "spitters" are uncaring and insolent to the refined passer-by, and it is an aesthetic reaction, not a reaction of pity or concern, that precedes and initiates his prayer.

The appeal to Christ exposes the essentially Christian nature of the values for which the young poet reaches. He desires to surrender his eyes, that have always fed on beauty, for the eyes of Christ, which are filled with pity, sorrow, and caring. Interestingly, he is sufficiently aware of his own problem to pray for "a beauty not within the mind"; in other words, the speaker desires to be free of a sensibility that we have seen Smith claim for himself in poem after poem. But he proposes a conundrum: he still desires to see *behind* the faces, to find deeper meanings than honest human eyes can offer. The deeper meaning, of course, is social injustice and the class system of western society: this gives the poet something upon which to fix his attention, a real and sufficiently substantial evil to draw him away from aesthetic daydreaming. Thus he is assigned to "forget/All beauty but the loveliness/ That lies in fighting this distress."

The last stanza, however, shows how unready Smith was to take on the new commitment, at least in his poetry. Although he claims to have been altered by the word of "Christ" – assuming that that is who spoke to him - and now "praises" "The worker, beggar, outcast," he still voices his new motivation in essentially Aesthetic terms: what he now finds in the "dusty street" is a "loveliness" that can only be described in images very close to those Smith had rejected in the third stanza. What he finds is "the loveliness of seas," their "roaring radiance" as they strike the "burnished gold" of sands in "old far lands." Beauty, then, is unaltered: it is defined by Romantic imagery, by escape, by something other than what the simple eye presents to the poet. There is, moreover, no evidence in the poem that the speaker will take the action that "fighting this distress" would require: rather he will sing the praises of the poor, a creative kindness for which they would not likely spare much thanks. (If "praising" the poor means writing poems about them – a reasonable interpretation – it was rarely to happen: for all his Modernism Smith usually avoided discussion of the poor and downtrodden in his later work.) I assume that Smith failed to notice the contradiction in the images of the last stanza, or he would have tried to alter them; which suggests that the conventions of nineteenth-century poetry were too deep in his blood, in 1923, to be rooted out with a word from Christ.

Towards the end of Smith's participation in the *Daily* and his establishment of the *Supplement* as a separate organ of the newspaper, a new note is audible in his poems; from January through to the end of April 1924, and at the beginning of the next academic year, he published primarily light satiric squibs, among them "A Hymn of Hate," "Ye Epicure Wisheth for Himself a Merrie Yuletide," "Kindness to Animals," and "Epithalamium." Without wanting to stretch too much into the realm of speculation, one must wonder if the burden of Smith's Aestheticism were not becoming too strenuous to maintain: a satiric focus would be a fairly natural result, as he sought to become more hard-bitten and ironic than his earlier dreams of "Beauty" had permitted him to be. If this is true, the satiric note was by no means triumphant; the poems that were published in the following year in the *Supplement* still make clear a degree of Aesthetic sensibility battling against the pull towards satire and modern realism. On the whole the Smith poems in the *Daily* reveal a poet with a strong penchant for Aestheticism, some touch of Decadence, and an occasional, tamer late Romanticism. It would be incorrect to think, merely because of a sudden satiric turn, that he had by early 1924 rejected his Aestheticism, or that his poems in the *Daily* already bear the seeds of Modernism. A comment he made on Yeats in November 1923 sums up his *Daily* attitudes fairly well: he congratulated the Irish poet on his Nobel prize and remarked that it was a relief to discover that the expression of pure beauty was still regarded more highly than the forced efforts of the modern realists.[79]

To those who would respond to this early poetry as "juvenilia" and therefore doubt its significance, the first defence must be to agree that it is, of course, juvenile poetry. Not an example exists but is derivative, hardly another exists that is not, to put it bluntly, limited poetry. It is not like the poetry of the mature poet; its manner was rejected by him in the next five to ten years, almost utterly; and its vacillations of technique show the indecision of a young and undetermined artist. All true: by any definition this is the Smith juvenilia, the work we look at with antiquarian or encyclopaedic, not aesthetic, interest.

That it is insignificant must be disputed, however, and for a number of good reasons. First, an examination of his poetry makes clear that Smith was not writing modern poetry in his "earliest apprentice verses," and was not reading only Tennyson, Shelley, and Keats before reading Eliot, H.D., and Pound. Second, it suggests by reason of close affinity that Smith was for a time inspired by and an imitator of English Aestheticism and Decadence, an entirely new attitude to his creative youth. Third, as the following will show, various attitudes of this early Aestheticism were maintained in his poetry and his criticism throughout his creative life, and acknowledgement of their initial force will help us to recognize Aesthetic features of the later work that have not previously been recognized. Fourth, the acknowledgment of Smith's early Aestheticism demonstrates that he too underwent an influence from a nineteenth-century school of poetry that a large number of other Canadian modern poets were to experience, which is merely to say that in yet another way Smith was at the centre of the development of the modern literary tradition in Canada. With this kind of critical impact these poems, juvenilia or not, deserve the attention and recognition of any scholar who desires to understand the man's career. In light of these conclusions it is possible to see that career as a long and complex pull away from an early Aestheticism towards satire, realism, and eventually Modernism, a development that had by no means completed itself even in the *Fortnightly*. Aestheticism was the mask behind which the young Smith first decided to challenge the Victorian spirit in literary Canada, and it was natural that he should progress from there to adopt the next real challenge to that spirit, which was Modernism.

Nevertheless, we are still in the realm of textual affinity: Smith's poems manifest strong Aesthetic qualities, but before an influence may be granted there must be clear opportunity as well, evidence that indicates that he *had* encountered the poetry of which we find echoes in his work. We will obviously not find admissions on the part of the poet: nothing he has written about his own development recognizes these Aesthetic poems in the *Daily*, and the evidence must necessarily be presented counter to the prevailing image he has himself fostered. Nevertheless, a significant number of references suggests his familiarity with Aesthetic poetry, and demonstrates that he had ample opportunity to study and imitate its sentiments and characteristics.

*I* have already mentioned Smith's reference, in October 1924, to "Dowson's studied melancholy," "Moore's affected impropriety," and "Wilde's artistic banalities," and the reader will remember that Smith opposed to their styles the finer qualities of Max Beerbohm's pen. That he could ape their styles so skilfully suggested some degree of familiarity with their writings. In addition, in the editorial "Quest for Beauty," he quotes from Dante Gabriel Rossetti's "Sonnet 77: Soul's Beauty," regarding "That Lady Beauty in whose praise/Thy voice and hand shake still."[80] It is also clear that Smith must have had some knowledge of Gautier's poetry, since he loosely translated, at the age of twenty-three, portions of the French poet's "Chinoiserie." Smith's reading in English poetry in 1922 also ran towards the Aesthetic: a borrowing card for the volume of J.C. Squire's poetry held in the Maclennan Library of McGill University, signed "July 25 1922 – A. Smith"[81] still sits in the back of the volume. Squire was described by John Betjeman, in the Introduction he provided for the volume, as a modern descendant of the Aesthetic school, one of those who had sought to retain Aesthetic principles in the twentieth century. That Smith should have felt the need to explore such a poet is revealing.

In addition to these references Smith's knowledge of Arthur Symons's *Symbolist Movement in Literature* is made abundantly clear in his first essay for the *Fortnightly*. In the essay he quotes from Moréas and Verlaine; he would also have found in Symons's pages studies of Gautier, Baudelaire, Villiers de L'Isle-Adam, Mallarmé, Huysmans, Rimbaud, and Laforgue. Smith's evident knowledge of Symons's volume is revealing in itself, since it was also the book that introduced Eliot to Laforgue and the other *Symbolistes*. From that discovery Eliot was to move towards the style of *Prufrock and Other Observations* and draw some of the conclusions that led to *The Waste Land*. A text that contributed so forcefully to the formation of Eliot's style can hardly have failed to affect the indefinite tastes of a young and still isolated Canadian poet. That the impact was a favourable one is attested to by the fact that he read further in Symons: his thesis on Yeats makes use of Symons's *Studies in Prose and Verse*, in which he would have found criticism of Pater, Morris, Dowson and Wilde as well.

Because of these elements of Smith's reading, it is possible to appreciate an unusual correspondence Smith kept up in 1925 and 1926 with one Bill Card from Lincoln, Nebraska. Card ran a portion of *The Daily Nebraskan* at the time that Smith was editing the *Supplement* and somehow happened upon a copy of the McGill journal that terrifically impressed him, especially the poems of "Vincent Starr" – one of Smith's favourite early pseudonyms. He wrote to "Starr," himself using the pseudonym of "Claire Montesrey" under which he appeared in the *Nebraskan*, and for a pair of letters back and forth they maintained this deception without enlightening one another, Smith presumably thinking he was writing to a young woman. When the secret was let out they began to discuss literature and their own artistic careers, with some revealing tendencies demonstrated. The entire collection of letters – all, unfortunately, from Card, for Smith's seem to have been lost to posterity in his correspondent's hands – is contained in the Smith Collection at Trent University (MS 78-007, Box 1, Folder 1), and reveals their personal and literary styles. Card, for instance, announces unabashed that his favourite poets are Keats, Swinburne, Rossetti and Morris and that his favourite dramatist is Wilde (1925). He sends a few poems of his own to Smith, which are very like Smith's, delicate images of beauty, faintly Decadent visions of death and loss. A further affinity is found between the young men when Card adds to his list of favourite writers "the incomparable Max" (1925) – Beerbohm, of course, also a favourite of Smith's. In relating all of this information Card continually adopts a style of address that is very Wildean, which may be accounted for by his dramatic tastes: he adores the pun and paradox and speaks from the lofty heights of a superior aesthetic thinker: "I too have written triolets," he announces ponderously to his correspondent (which suggests perhaps that Smith had sent him some triolets of his own, or admitted to such a predilection [1925]).

By 1926, however, Card had to admit that he had stopped writing, in the face of various career pressures and aesthetic failures (26 Feb. 1926); by 1926, of course, Smith had begun his progress towards Modernism, and so appears to have found "a way out" to which Card was not open. One would desperately like to have Smith's letters to Card to complete this fascinating glimpse of the world of young literary men in the mid-twenties; but Card's letters alone indicate how much the Aesthetes and Decadents were still in the air of Smith's time; that a young writer like Card, with such Aesthetic tastes, should be so forcibly impressed by the poems of another young man over a thousand miles away as to seek him out and engage him in correspondence bespeaks in Smith a recognizable Aestheticism.

This is enough to demonstrate that Smith had done a fair amount of reading in the literature of Aestheticism and Decadence prior to his days as editor of the *Fortnightly*. But I have not yet incorporated what must be ranked as one of the three great influences upon his poetry, that of Yeats. In later years, Smith was to write an essay on Yeats, a poetic tribute to the poet upon his death, and a number of poems in the Yeatsian voice: but in the mid-twenties we have no better access to his attitudes to the Irish poet than in his Master's thesis, held in the Rare Book Room of the Maclennan Library at McGill.

In general, Smith's early approach to the Irish poet is by no means that of a modern critic. Throughout the volume he expresses warm approval when Yeats's poetry renders intensity, ecstasy, beauty, hypnotic rhythm, dim, vague imagery, all of the qualities that Pound was rigorously to denounce in his employer as he urged him towards the modern style of the later years. Smith the Master's student says of *The Wind Among the Reeds*, Yeats's volume of 1899, that "No other volume before or since has reached such a high degree of perfection and maintained it throughout."[82] Smith had certainly encountered such middle volumes as *Responsibilities*, since he discusses them later in the thesis, so we may assume that he was, in 1926, more impressed by the early, Celtic Twilight Yeats than by the toughening poet of the 1910s. Clearly his attraction to the older poetry is due to those qualities which hark back to Aestheticism: Smith writes that Yeats's nature "had been made more refined and sensitive by a delicate aestheticism" (*Yeats*, 6). Typical of his judgments is the following on Yeats's love poetry:

It is in the treatment of love that Yeats' poems show most clearly the peculiar beauty of his genius. The passion in them is rooted in a spiritual intensity that recalls Dante. They are a perfect union of spiritual and earthly passion, of sacred and profane love, a marriage of Heaven and Hell. Sometimes it is of a living mistress he sings, sometimes of "the divine beauty, pure and clear and unalloyed, not clogged with the polutions [sic] of mortality," most often it is difficult to tell of which, because the poem could be laid at the shrine of either. Some again have a white flame of rapture in them in which all that is of the earth is refined as in an alchemist's furnace, until pure spirit alone remains. (*Yeats*, 53–4)

This ethereal Aesthetic critic is a far cry from the stern doctor of Canadian poetry who was to emerge in the later 1920s, 30s, and

40s. Note in the final sentence Smith's warm approval of a poetry that does away with the gross things of the earth in favour of a "flame of rapture," or "pure spirit": a principle unacceptable to the later Modernist and deriving from the heart of his Aestheticism. For these reasons Smith recognizes in another Yeats poem "the old theme of the passing of beauty, of the inevitable toll of the years, the dimming of the eye and the failing of strength (*Yeats*, 68).[83]

Another noteworthy quality of the thesis is the information it provides about Smith's awareness of certain other writers. His knowledge of Rossetti, for example, is confirmed in the thesis and shown to be deeper than a single quotation in the *Supplement* could indicate; in fact he demonstrates a more than adequate general knowledge of the principles of early Aesthetic poetry (6–7). He casually mentions James Whistler's *Nocturnes*, the paintings that are the essence of English Aesthetic art (70), and he refers once or twice to Wilde, because Yeats cited his compatriot in *A Vision* (95). Smith would also have found references to Wilde and the "tragic generation" in Yeats's early autobiographical piece, *The Trembling of the Veil*, from which he draws extensively. Perhaps most interestingly, he discovers in the later Yeats "the cold, hard, crystal-clear gemlike flame ... a higher type of beauty" (99–100). His manipulation of Pater's famous phrasing is much too close to be anything but an easy allusion, which suggests that in some previous studies, or as part of his work on Yeats, Smith read Pater's Conclusion to *The Renaissance* (if nothing else by that writer) and came to terms with its philosophies. Yeats had not quoted the phrase in *The Trembling of the Veil*; we may assume that Smith had hunted out Pater either on his own or from other references to him in the autobiography, and may assume that Smith encountered the doctrine of the "gemlike flame" by 1926 at the very latest. (The "flames" in Smith's early poetry suggest an earlier encounter, somewhere between 1920 and 1924.) Of course, even without direct mention of Pater, to respond as warmly as Smith does to Yeats's early sensibilities is tantamount to approving of Pater.

That the twenty-four-year-old Smith should have responded so enthusiastically to Yeats will hardly seem surprising in the context of his own early poetry. Yeats offered the young poet an example of a great man who had been heavily influenced by Aestheticism, yet had faced its inevitable contradictions and found for himself a direction away from the failure its influence portended for the latecomer. Although Smith is not comfortable, by 1926, with the volumes that show Yeats breaking free from his early Aestheticism, undoubtedly he recognized in Yeats's poems one solution to the problem he was facing, the problem we recognize behind the increasing number of satiric pieces in his 1924 poetry. Smith was faltering as a poet, as Bill Card had faltered and then failed altogether: Yeats's example, by demonstrating the potency of certain modern poetic doctrines, may well have helped the young poet to accept Modernism, to admit the necessity of realism and objectivity even if it was not immediately amenable to his nature. In 1939 Smith was to speak of Yeats in precisely these terms:

The measure of Yeats's powers can perhaps best be gauged by considering the very heavy odds against which he had to struggle and the triumphant success he finally won. He had to free himself from a number of clogging encumbrances, such, for example, as the poetic diction of the 'nineties, and escape from the cloistered aestheticism of the disciples of Pater. Yeats, indeed, was the only poet of the "tragic generation" who succeeded in creating permanently interesting poetry out of the rather enervating poeticality of the *fin de siècle* and survived to become a strong and healthy influence on the best poetry of the succeeding generations.[84]

It is not too speculative to suggest that Smith was subliminally acknowledging the "strong and healthy influence" of Yeats's example on his *own* youth, and expressing gratitude for the path Yeats had blazed away from the poetic death that lay in an early oppressive Aestheticism.

Given the evident Aesthetic tendency of much of Smith's reading and of his early poetry, one of the most famous comments he made in the three essays published in the *Fortnightly* takes on much added significance. At the end of "Contemporary Poetry," published in the second year of the review, he makes a cryptic reference to Aestheticism that is neither so direct nor so simple as most of his readers have found it. Smith winds up his discussion of the moderns with a reference to their sense of form, their desire to create new techniques with which to express the consciousness of the new age:

This preoccupation with form has led some critics to see in the works of the ultra moderns the symptoms of a deep decadence. The dislike exhibited by these poets, they say, for didacticism, for the moral aim has led them to take the safe course, and to keep not only morality but meaning out of their poems. If you read some of Eliot's Sweeney poems, or Edith Sitwell's *Bucolic Comedies* you may at first think that there is a good deal in the charge. If, however, you have had any experience as a reader of poetry, and you come to the test with an open mind, I think you will find it easier to admit that there is beauty in such poetry than to discover in it a logical meaning. More than once someone has spoken to me of a poem. "I don't understand altogether what it means – but I like it; it sounds well; there is beauty in it." Perhaps they were only being polite. But if that is the case, the fact that such a remark is considered to be a compliment rather than an insult shows that even in the popular mind Beauty, (that is, form), is considered to be more important than the idea or the logical meaning, (that is, than subject matter). In other words, though most people loudly disclaim it, in their hearts they really think that what you say is less important than how you say it. A fallacy, of course, but if they did not think thus when wishing to be complimentary they would say: "I don't think there is any *beauty* in your poem, but I understand and admire its *sentiments* very much." This, however, would be considered an affront.

Now this popular idea that form is more important than content, of course, is just as absurd as the professorial conception of the supreme importance of right-thinking and the comparative insignificance of right-expression; and, as a matter of fact the discussion of the relative value of form and subject matter is one, that should never have arisen; because, in poetry, at least, these two things should be merged into one – a single and complete artistic whole – form the body, and content the soul: the one but the visible manifestation of the other.

But what, then, are we to say when the beauty of a poem appeals to us, while its meaning is somehow hidden? Simply that our faculty of aesthetic appreciation is more fully developed than our understanding – that we are become, God help us! – by natural right, a member of that despised sect – the Aesthetes.   (32)

Those who approach this passage honestly in search of Smith's final opinion on the question cannot, I think, claim that it is even remotely clear. There are five stages of thought in the passage: Smith first refers the reader to criticism that equates Modernism with Decadence, because it disdains the didactic aim and consequently avoids meaning altogether. In the second phase Smith assumes that his reader will find Eliot and Sitwell (for example) beautiful sooner than they will find meaning in their poetry. In the third phase Smith proposes that in the popular mind Beauty is more important than Content, because of private conversations he has had in which a poem was discussed as beautiful only – which was enough to justify it. In the fourth phase Smith suggests that such an idea should be replaced by a realization that form and content are inseparable; and in the fifth he concludes that we are more open to Beauty than to meaning in modern poetry because we have learned the lessons of Aestheticism.

Clearly this is not intended as a logical proof wherein premises lead inevitably to a single clear conclusion. Smith circles the relationship between form and content, scarcely explicating and often contradicting his own apparent opinions on the issue. His distaste for the opponents of Modernism seems fairly clear; but why he should argue against them by proposing that many will find beauty in the poetry, rather than meaning – which is basically what the critics are saying, that Modernism is a kind of Decadence – is even beyond guessing. The "If, however" that initiates this second phase suggests an imminent countermanding premise: we are offered instead a variation on the first false premise. This odd construction leads Smith into a digression to prove that the reader's response to such poetry as Eliot's Sweeney poems and Sitwell's *Bucolic Comedies* is typical of the way people in general respond to poetry: in other words, people in general will approach modern poetry as the critics have done, as formal constructs justified autonomously from their "meaning." In the fourth phase he attacks the straw-man critic set up in the second and third, by positing that "form and subject matter ... should be merged into one" – which can hardly be conceived of as an answer to the critics of the "ultra moderns" addressed at the beginning. Nevertheless, let us admit that there is no logical thread here and try to move from the fourth to the fifth phase, for the final striking comment concerns us most. Suddenly instead of "you" who perceive beauty more easily than meaning, it is "we" who do so.[85] We can assume that this is mere rhetoric and that Smith (since he assumes a position above all the contention) does not mean to convict himself literally of such an opinion. "We," then, in the sense of his audience, Canadian intellectuals, society in general, have developed our sense of "aesthetic appreciation" at the expense of our sense of "meaning" and "understanding," which means that we have turned, without knowing it, into Aesthetes – a fact that Smith renders with a distinct ironic flourish.

The "God help us!" and the word "despised" in this passage have led its readers to assume without much hesitation that Smith was attacking the Aesthetes outright, that this is another example of his modern sensibility setting the nineteenth-century poets on their ear.[86] But the presence of such phrases in the *Fortnightly* does not guarantee an atmosphere of attack. First, it is very easy to imagine Smith or Scott writing an editorial that ended, "we are become, God help us! – by natural right, a member of that despised sect – the *intellectuals*." I effect the substitution only to highlight the irony in the sentence. Smith lays it on too thickly; in the context of the "iconoclastic" *Fortnightly*, this phrasing is no assurance of disdain. Second, I would draw attention to that curious phrase "by natural right"; no one but Smith could explain its exactly intended sense, but it does seem to suggest that our descent into Aestheticism has been either inevitable or logical or deserved, rather than foisted upon us by misguided critics and wrong-headed poets. Third, there is no insistence anywhere in the passage that meaning really is available in the modern poets he cites: he half-incriminates his own understanding with his rhetorical "we," and he does, after all, say that those who can find more beauty than meaning in such poetry do so only if they have "experience as a reader of poetry" and "an open mind." In other words, the Aesthetes – defined at the end as those who perceive beauty more readily than meaning – are the ones with "experience" and "open minds" – and what more could one ask for in a reader?

The point need not be insisted upon in either direction – Smith's equivocations suggest that we should not seek an ultimate and clear resolution of the passage. I would only suggest that Smith's reference to the Aesthetes is a much less disdainful and unequivocal one than it is generally thought to be, and that the confusions in this famous passage make clear in an entirely different manner how uncertain Smith still was of the value of Aestheticism *and* the claims of the modern. This climactic reference to Aestheticism in his early prose demonstrates once more the complexity of the development Smith underwent in the mid-twenties and, in its vacillations, suggests that very tension between Aestheticism and Modernism that we have seen in so many facets of his early writings.

In all of these references, from his allusions to individual Aesthetic writers to the sense of Aesthetic doctrine he displays in his allusion to Pater and in the passage above, it is apparent that Smith had a much wider experience of nineteenth-century poetry than his own mention of Tennyson, Shelley, and Keats would suggest. He had, it would seem, ample opportunity to have learned from the Aesthetes and Decadents as well. It would be ideal, of course, to say exactly when Smith read Rossetti, in what context he read Pater, how far he had looked into the "studied melancholy" of Dowson, and so to demonstrate direct links of cause and effect between his readings and his writings of Aesthetic poetry; but the results cannot be so scientifically gratifying. Given the strong textual affinity with Aestheticism demonstrated in a number of his early poems and the knowledge he shows of Aestheticism and Decadence in prose references, it seems entirely reasonable now to postulate that Smith was influenced by Aesthetic poetry early in his life, from at least 1921 onwards, and that Aestheticism, not Modernism, was the poetic school he chose to imitate in "the earliest apprentice verses" with which he began his career. It would be comforting to have Smith's admission to all of this, but he has not provided us with the pleasure; as it has never been the critic's business to take the word of the artist he studies, his silence cannot, I think, shatter the significance of so much and such intriguing evidence.

*T*he later fruits of Smith's initial Aestheticism are various. On the one hand it made him quick to recognize the Aesthetic qualities of other poets: the "dandyism" of Finch,[87] the "feverish emotionalism of the aesthetic movement" in the early D.C. Scott,[88] the "Baudelairism and Verlainism" of Emile Nelligan (Introduction, xl), the influence of Swinburne and the Aesthetic poets on Archibald Lampman, Charles G.D. Roberts, and William Wilfred Campbell (Introduction, xxxiv), the Pre-Raphaelitism of Francis Sherman,[89] and Bliss Carman's role as "a *fin-de-siècle* aesthete turned out of the overstuffed boudoir into the almost equally overstuffed out doors."[90] This latter reference is particularly interesting, since according to F.R. Scott Smith as a young man disparaged all Canadian poets except Carman, whose talent he acknowledged (Scott, "Smith: A Memoir," 81). It also helped him to appreciate the French-Canadian poets Paul Morin and René Chopin, exponents of "the aesthetic and exotic school" (Introduction, xli-xlii), and to find room in his anthologies for such Aesthetically inclined modern poets as Tracy and Mackay.

Aestheticism also developed in Smith into a set of artistic principles that could be used to evaluate and to govern all poetry. The principles of intensity, craft, and detachment for which he is renowned are directly related to his Aesthetic indoctrination in early youth, for they are, very apparently, the theoretical poetic principles of Aestheticism. We can in effect watch these principles unfold in Smith's most noted essays, taking our departure from his "Symbolism in Poetry" in 1925, and noting its praise of Aesthetic and *Symboliste* preoccupations; moving through "Contemporary Poetry" and "Hamlet in Modern Dress," as Smith begins to work his Modernism and his Aestheticism together; from these early pieces move to the famous "Wanted – Canadian Criticism," in *The Canadian Forum* in 1928, in which Smith expresses the following prescriptions for Canadian poetry: "Nowhere is puritanism more disastrously prohibitive than among us, and it seems, indeed, that desperate methods and dangerous remedies must be resorted to, that our condition will not improve until we have been thoroughly shocked by the appearance in our midst of a work of art that is at once successful and obscene."[91] Wilde's intonation is lacking in the newly inspired young Canadian, but Aesthetic principles are common to both: to battle the oppressive Victorian mentality, poets must create, above all, "obscene" art, something counter to the moral order that will shock the public even as it forces them to realize what good art really is. I am not proposing that Smith read Wilde for the ideas; merely that they share them. And they share others; Smith adds, "The idea that any subject whatever is susceptible of artistic treatment, and that praise or blame is to be conferred after a consideration, not of its moral, but of its aesthetic harmony is a proposition that will take years to knock into the heads of our people."[92]

The Aesthetic source of this kind of literary antinomianism is clear; more important is the fact that Smith has found a way of allying the modern and the Aesthetic causes, which was his necessary purpose throughout the 1920s, by playing up their common sense of high art, craft removed from the understanding of the masses, and disconcern for moral questions. All he now needs to do is to claim that these principles come first from the modern school, and he has completed his intellectual shift to the modern position. This was certainly effected by 1936, when Smith wrote the preface to *New Provinces* – a draft that never appeared in the book because Pratt and Finch in Toronto found it too vigorous in its denunciation of all past poetry in Canada. In the "Rejected Preface," under which title it was published in 1963, Smith shows that he has turned away from old Aesthetic themes to play up an aristocratic and modern sense of form: "The most popular experience [in Canadian poetry] is to be pained, hurt, stabbed or seared by Beauty – preferably by the yellow flame of a crocus in the spring or the red flame of a maple leaf in autumn."[93] Although Smith's own lust for "Beauty" drew him to neither crocus nor maple leaf, it is nevertheless true that this part of the "Rejected Preface" has significant ramifications for the poet Smith himself had been. What he describes is not so far from the poetry he used to write – and it may be that the vigour of his denunciation of such poetry was due to his recognition of his own antecedents. Nothing could be more important to him, as he prepared the volume in which his poems would first be gathered, than to make a clean break with the Aesthetic past, to emphasize his modernity and cut himself away from the nineteenth century; it is significant of the value of his early poetry for Smith criticism, that this prose passage takes on such added weight in the present context. Smith continues his self-assault: "The Canadian poet, if this kind of thing truly represents his feelings and his thoughts, is a half-baked, hyper-sensitive, poorly-adjusted and frequently neurotic individual that no one in his senses would trust to drive a car or light a furnace. He is the victim of his feelings and his fancies, or of what he fancies his feelings ought to be, and his emotional aberrations are out of all proportion to the experience that brings them into being. He has a soft heart and a soft soul; and a soft head" (7).

Smith has turned his favour on the practical man, the man who can do things in the real world as well as write poems: those who are only good for aesthetic labour are not much good at all. The Depression context ought not to be forgotten; like so many Canadian poets, Smith's experience of the Depression affected his private situation and his sense of public responsibility and helped him draw away from an aloof, restrained, indifferent Aesthetic style. Thus he suggests, in a passage that has seemed to say so much for his modernity, that

Detachment, indeed, or self-absorption is (for a time only, I hope) becoming impossible ... the artist who is concerned with the most intense of experiences must be concerned with the world situation in which, whether he likes it or not, he finds himself. For the moment at least he has something more important to do than to record his private emotions. He must try to perfect a technique that will combine power with simplicity and sympathy with intelligence so that he may play his part in developing mental and emotional attitudes that will facilitate the creation of a more practical social system. ("Rejected Preface," 9)

The sense of social commitment expressed in this essay has often enough been taken as typical of Smith's Modernist dedications. Of greater present interest is the hesitation in the expression of the ideas: the abandonment of "detachment" is not the condition of all modern poetry, or a necessary feature of good poetry: detachment is merely something that cannot be afforded given the present world situation. Smith's small parenthesis, "for a time only, I hope," sums up the diffidence with which he calls for an end to artistic detachment. Social commitment is necessary "for the moment at least": the entire recommendation is clearly temporary in Smith's mind, a forced attitude, not an integral part of the Modernist program. This reading of the passage is reinforced by the fact that Smith had just offered a definition of "pure poetry" that is based entirely on the principle of detachment, or impersonality: "A theory of pure poetry might be constructed on the assumption that a poem exists as a thing in itself. It is not a copy of anything, but it is an individuality as unique as a flower, an elephant or a man on a flying trapeze ... Such poetry is objective, impersonal, and in a sense timeless and absolute. It stands by itself, unconcerned with anything save its own existence" ("Rejected Preface," 9).[94] Smith's affection for such principles is clear, and it explains the uneasiness he felt about his call for an end to artistic "detachment" on the next page. Certainly the latter word was to surface again and again throughout his critical career. What the "Rejected Preface" indicates is not a thorough-going Modernist routing the enemy, but a man aware of his own Aesthetic leanings, but determined, because he knows its immediate necessity, to encourage the engagement and commitment of modern poetry. In the *New Provinces* context his understanding of "pure poetry" appears to be in keeping with Modernist doctrine, as, indeed, pure poetry was – Smith sees it in Imagism – which allows him finally to cite Modernist roots for his pet doctrines of detachment and craft as end-in-itself. He has made the leap neatly and has found the common ground between Aestheticism and Modernism. When we realize that he wrote the "Rejected Preface" only two years before the passage on Yeats's turn from Aestheticism in "A Poet Young and Old," it becomes clear that Smith had completed his own journey and followed close on the heels of his Irish master.

Another term that Smith has inherited from his Aesthetic youth is "intensity." One could write an independent volume merely by recording each appearance of the word in Smith's criticism and poetry, and the volume would begin in January of 1923 with his "Conditional Mood." By the end of the 1930s, the time of the "Rejected Preface" and the article on Yeats, Smith had found in "intensity" another focal principle that could unite the demands of Aesthetic poetry and those of Modernism. Thus his "Canadian Poetry: A Minority Report," one of the most justly famous trumpet-calls in all of Canadian literature, makes of "intensity" an all but absolute standard of criticism. The absence of "intensity" in the poetry of Charles Heavysege relegates him to the lower ranks, and an occasional "intensity" raises Finch to the expression of an "aesthetic emotion" and above mere playful dandyism ("Canadian Poetry," 133, 137). His final advice to young Canadian poets, which certainly bears repeating, harps on intensity as the most necessary quality of new verse: "Study the great masters of clarity and intensity – Dante, Chaucer, Villon, Shakespeare, Dryden … Read the French and German poets whose sensibility is most intensely that of the modern world – Baudelaire, Rimbaud and Rainer Maria Rilke ("Canadian Poetry," 138). It is paradoxical that in the "Minority Report," which makes so much of poetic intensity, Smith also praises W.W.E. Ross's *Sonnets* which, as we have seen, lack intensity and express more often than not significantly Aesthetic emotions; and that he should comment that the poetry of Audrey Brown "has been incomparably better done by Keats and the Pre-Raphaelites" ("Canadian Poetry,"

135). Comparison with Audrey Brown is hardly praise for Keats, Rossetti, and Morris, but it does indicate that Smith still recognized those poets for offering models of poetic correctness if not exemplars of modern tough-mindedness. Even in 1939, Smithian "intensity" had some significant complications.

That Smith's tendency to express poetic doctrine in terms descended from Aestheticism was life-long, and not merely the business of his first two decades, is made clear in the 1954 essay, "Refining Fire: The Meaning and Use of Poetry." Thirty-five years after his initiation into the poetic world in the arms of Aestheticism, Smith was still arguing that it was the craft, not the "meaning" of the poem, that gave it value:

Yet it is not, I would like to maintain, the nature of the experience, or the moral respectability of the emotions that produced it or rose out of it, or even the immediate, practical, sentimental consequences that appear to flow from it, that make a poem good rather than bad or valuable rather than dangerous ... the value of a poem lies in the intensity with which an experience has been encountered, and the accuracy with which its consequences, good or evil, delightful or painful, have been recognized and accepted. It is the integrity, the clarity and the completeness with which an experience is met, whether it is trivial, harsh, ugly, magnificent, or delightful, that counts in the evaluation of a poem's goodness but also of its usefulness. The nature of the experience, as such, has nothing to do with the genuineness or goodness of the poem, and no preconceived opinion can postulate the special conditions under which the right intensity of pressure will be generated.[95]

An experience must be realized intensely, and its tendency towards good or evil is irrelevant to its artistic virtues; it may be "trivial" or "magnificent," so long as its "delight" or "pain" has been accurately recognized. This is essential Aestheticism. Any number of Aesthetic documents can be shown to prefigure Smith's statements in 1954, but let us be content with one that Smith knew, Pater's Conclusion to The Renaissance: "Great passions may give us this quickened sense of life, ecstasy and sorrow of love, the various forms of enthusiastic activity, disinterested or otherwise, which come naturally to many of us. Only be sure it is passion – that it does yield you this fruit of a quickened, multiplied consciousness. Of such wisdom, the poetic passion, the desire of beauty, the love of art for its own sake, has most. For art comes to you proposing frankly to give nothing but the highest quality to your moments as they pass, and simply for those moments' sake" (Ren., 190). Pater values both "ecstasy and sorrow"; Smith wants the consequences to be recorded whether "delightful or painful." In Smith the "completeness with which an experience is met" reflects Pater's concern that one's "moments as they pass" should have "the highest quality" possible. Pater's injunction "Only be sure it is passion" prefigures Smith's belief that "the value of a poem lies in the intensity with which an experience has been encountered."

What are we to say of such critical tendencies in Smith's essays? Merely that his Modernism was heavily informed by the principles of Aestheticism, and that we may find in his later development the fruition of his initial artistic training. That Modernism borrowed many theoretical principles from Aestheticism has been the premise of a number of critical studies, a few of which have been mentioned in the Introduction; therefore it is no surprise that a prime Canadian Modernist should also have entwined his Modernism with the lingering doctrines of Aesthetic theory. By doing so he merely confirmed the degree to which Modernism had been rooted in the late nineteenth century and the fundamental accuracy of his own understanding of that school. Smith appears to have recognized soon enough that Modernism and Aestheticism were not entirely incompatible and to have developed out of Modernism those very features that most suited his already Aesthetic temperament. He encountered Aestheticism, by all appearances, by his nineteenth year at the latest, possibly when he was still in high school; but he encountered Modernism as an undergraduate and graduate student at university, by which time he had developed entirely new methods of appreciating and understanding literary doctrine. That his Aestheticism in early youth, which was primarily thematic – concern with beauty, decay, time and such – should have developed, after collision with Modernism, into a primarily formalistic Aestheticism – concern with detachment, autonomy of the art-work, irrelevance of morality – may be accounted for by the greater intellectual latitude he enjoyed by the mid-twenties. When he read Modernism, the graduate student could absorb poetic theory as well as poetry itself, and doubtless those aspects of Modernist theory that were closest in nature to his previous poetic practice were highlighted for him from the start. We may suggest, although speculatively, that some such process accounts for the kind of Modernism he was to develop for himself.

Smith's turn away from Aestheticism was much sharper in his poetry than in his criticism. As the claims of Modernism grew upon him he winnowed away those poems subsisting on abstraction, dream, and beauty and drew into his sense of poetic diction a toughness and directness that did much to dispel the old sensibility. He turned to new themes, learned new techniques (especially those of the Metaphysicals, whose poetry became by the late 1920s a chief inspiration), and moved by degrees towards a Modernism less touched by Aesthetic fixations. The process of this modernization and the results in his poetry have been the business of Smith's critics from the beginning, and I will not attempt to recreate it. Rather I will point out in the later poetry some of the surviving qualities of Smith's early Aestheticism, in order to suggest a degree of continuity between his first poems and those of his middle and later years.

One of the most striking features of Smith's poetry for a reader of any persuasion must be his translations. They are numerous and eminently skilful, the results of long labour and great care. Eleven of the one hundred and twenty poems in his *Poems New and Collected* are translations; of those eleven, seven are from poets who are related, either obviously or by Smith himself, to French Aestheticism: "Le Vièrge, Le Vivace et Le Bel Aujourd'hui" and "Cantique de Saint Jean" by Mallarmé, "Chinoiserie," "L'Hippopotame," and "Pastel" by Gautier, "Perdrix" by Paul Morin, and "Le Vaisseau d'Or" by Emile Nelligan. See also his translation of Tristan Corbière's "Petit Mort Pour Rire," in *The Centennial Review*.[96] Of these many translations, "Le Vièrge, Le Vivace et Le Bel Aujourd'hui," "Chinoiserie," "Pastel," and "Perdrix" manifest exactly that haunting Aestheticism that Smith himself had attempted in his early poems, and "Le Vaisseau d'Or" shows Nelligan heavily under the influence of Baudelaire. Smith's "The Hippopotamus" and the "Canticle of Saint John" reveal Gautier and Mallarmé in rather more modern form, but note that "Cantique de Saint Jean" is from *L'Hérodiade* of Mallarmé – his version of the story of Salomé – and is therefore further evidence of Smith's continuing exploration of prime Aesthetic imagery. What is significant about these poems in the present context is the Aestheticism of the poets Smith has chosen to translate. At least one of the poems was the result of a request,[97] which may suggest that others were as well, although there is no clear indication: at any rate, Smith has demonstrated a remarkable ability to translate Aesthetic poetry, which we may attribute not only to his sensitivity to poetic form and language but also to the Aesthetic practices he had himself developed as a young man.

The principle of intensity in Smith's poetry (as opposed to his criticism) is obviously far-reaching. In the majority of his poems he attempts to render, not a reflective or meditative experience, but an intense, passionate moment at the heights of life. To prove the point would merely require a list of Smith's tables of contents from the various volumes. In a narrower sense, however, intensity may be shown to function in his poetry as a principle of action towards which Smith urges his readers, either by example or by direct encouragement. Such a principle particularly accounts for the drift of his eroticism, which Smith uses primarily as an agent of intense vision, a means of fundamentally altering in one fell swoop the course of a life or a civilization. His later Leda poem, "The Adolescence of Leda," takes the young girl from "the tedium of the afternoon," which she spends "sewing or dreaming or reading," into the sexual potency of myth and destiny:

Now watch! to please the girl his snowy plume
  Like a pure flower in the shaggy green
    Rises and rustles – Stifle your clownish laughter!

See, she lies panting in the mossy gloom
  Of tunnelled boughs – but no, the willows screen
    All that portends, now and hereafter.   (PNC, 84)

The visualization of the erotic moment is carefully avoided (to which we may compare the relatively graphic nature of Yeats's "Leda and the Swan"). Instead Smith wishes to emphasize the shattering of Leda's world – her sexual panting alters her entirely from the rather prim girl around whom the poem unfolds. Thus the erotic moment is employed to turn a single human spirit (and, as we know from the myth, an entire civilization) in an entirely different direction from that in which it had tended, as the result of "the intensity with which an experience has been encountered."

For similar reasons "Far West" explores the awakening sexuality of a young girl whose emotions become more breathless as she watches an early western. The girl's fantasies eventually take control of the poem; the "cowboys" are visualized in increasingly sexual terms, the Freudian image of man-on-horse providing a cinematographic parallel to the young girl's desires:

In the holy name *bang! bang!* the flowers came
With the marvellous touch of fingers
Gentler than the fuzzy goats
Moving up and down up and down as if in ecstasy
As the cowboys rode their skintight stallions
Over the barbarous hills of California.   (PNC, 93)

The potency of this moment is all Smith wishes to capture: he refuses to comment on it, since "A poem is not the description of an experience, it is itself an experience, and it awakens in the mind of the alert and receptive reader a new experience analogous to the one in the mind of the poet."[98] Smith wishes to transmit his sense of intensity to the reader, by a visualization which shifts from the movie screen to the entirely stimulable imagination of a young girl.

No Smith poem so strikingly reveals this need for human intensity as his "To the Christian Doctors." In a passionate defence of the untamed human spirit against all the chains and fetters of religion and civilization, Smith touches the essence of his belief in intensity of life:

> Send not the innocent heart to find
> In civil tears denials of the blood
> Or in humility feign kinglihood.
> 'Twould filch his character away and bind
> Him spiritless, whom Holiness designed
> To swell the vein with a secular flood
> In pure ferocious joy, efficient and good,
> Like a tiger's spring or the leap of the wind.

The ceremonies of confession, humility, and absolution, Smith suggests, are bonds upon the free spirit, which only does as it must and cannot be truly fettered within. Intensity is associated with "blood," therefore with birth, with death by violence, with the rhythms and forces of nature, the "tiger's spring" or the rising wind. This is no simple atheism: Smith suggests that "Holiness" itself "designed" the human spirit for exactly such intensity and must be displeased by all that restrains it. Thus in the sestet he directs the "Christian Doctors" to

> Let the wind, then, or a beast of the wood,
> Whose savage fire is self-consuming, blind,
> Match his quick flame: though in its human mode
> Like theirs in force, it is unlike in kind,
> Whose end it is to burn sensation's lode
> With animal intensity, to Mind.   (*PNC*, 23)

Smith's favourite "metaphysical" formulation, that "feeling" should give rise to "thought" and vice versa, which he derived from Eliot's famous statements,[99] provides the background of the concluding lines; yet the "flame" imagery is interesting, and, since he knew the equally famous phrasing from Pater's Conclusion to *The Renaissance*, it is perhaps not surprising that this archetypal treatment of human intensity should draw upon such symbolism to complete its vision.

Intensity in Smith may also be expressed in formal properties, intensity of word-play, for instance, or of rhythm; Smith develops these particularly in his extension of the early dandyism in the *Supplement* and the *Fortnightly*. "A Hyacinth for Edith" and "Three Phases of Punch" are two poems that survived the cutting away of his early work, and they are two of his most dandyish. The imitation of Sitwell in the former and the images of Punchinello, from the *commedia dell'arte* so popular in the 1910s and 20s, in the latter allow Smith a good deal of room for verbal play. This formal intensity was to continue in later work as well, sometimes in purely linguistic structures, as in "The Tin Woodman's Annual Sonnet to Ozma of Oz at the Approach of Spring":

> Soon will the glitter of green and neon-glow
> In the showcase of bulbs and birds' eggs list
> In electric letters buds and bubs kissed
> Into stardom all a green week or so.   (*PNC*, 104)

At other times, as in "Poor Innocent," Smith's entire vision is dandified:

> It is a gentle natural (is it I?) who
> Visits timidly the big world of
> The heart, and stares a little while at love
> As at a plaited and ringleted paleblue
> Seascape, whence escapes a new, untrue,
> Refracted light, a shade or two above
> The infra fringe beyond which does he move
> He moves unsurely in an air askew.   (*PNC*, 71)

The linguistic intensity in which such visions involve him is obviously conducive to his poetic nature and derives, to my mind, from the early dandyism he learned in the mid-twenties, towards the end of his Aesthetic phase, as well as more generally from the doctrine of intensity associated with that phase. It also contributes, by virtue of its contrivance, to his idea of the poem as an aesthetic object independent of morality and meaning: we are more likely to treat the poem as such when we are faced with such blatantly artificial language.

Artificiality is, of course, another feature of Aesthetic theory. The taste for the artificial swung widely in the late nineteenth century, from those who merely preferred the art of man to the art of nature, to those who found in the artificial a new twist of pleasure and stimulation.[100] In Smith the touch of artifice is felt above all in his

298 Aestheticism and the Canadian Modernists

stylistic qualities, as in the dandyism just noted, the strange syn-
tactical inversions of "The Wisdom of Old Jelly Roll," the purposively
false images of "Noctambule," and the qualifiers that riddle "My
Lost Youth." He himself admitted freely that "there is much here
[in his *Collected Poems* of 1962] that is consciously contrived."[101] A
similar perception led Leon Edel to remark that in Smith "Artifice
is everything: the made jade vase is the thing; crafting poetry (as
we say in current *argot*) is like making a chair or a table, one must
simply do it well" ("Worldly Muse," 205). We may thus relate "artifice" as a poetic doctrine to Smith's strong sense of craft: the latter
is not merely a matter of dedication, but a cause and consequence
of his sense of artifice. "That is the function of the poet with respect
to his poems," Smith has said: "He is a craftsman, and for a great
part of the time he is a conscious craftsman" ("Self Review," 22). As
such the poet is aware of his tools and materials and can manipulate
them to seem either carefully constructed or thrown together as if
by chance. Smith, the "odd classical man out in a society of romantics" (Wilson, 11), has chosen most often to stress the contrivance
of his poems, so that the reader is not hypnotized or lulled but
constantly nudged awake and faced with the poet's obscure visions.

Concomitant with a strong sense of artifice, we usually experience
an aloof impersonality in a poet: those who feel strongly the need
to express themselves, their personalities, rarely pause to do so with
an effect of contrivance and artificiality. Aloof Smith has certainly
appeared, and the impersonality and objectivity of his poetry are
practically legend in Canadian literature. Detachment was a constant
focus of his aesthetic theorizing, as the essay passages above will
indicate; Smith himself summed up this element of his poetry in
1962 by quoting Rimbaud: "As Rimbaud said, *je est un autre*, I is
another" ("Self Review," 23). Smith's hands-off attitude to his poetry
immediately presents us with one of the most noticed contradictions
of his poetic career: how can a poet who urges us to intensity and
passion, who wishes us to greet our experiences with clarity and
integrity in our poems, also desire, from himself at least, a relentless
and withering objectivity, an immense suppression of the subjective
vision, to be rendered in poems of sheer artifice and conscious contrivance? How can we reconcile such vastly divergent aims?

The element of detachment in Smith's essays and poetry is not
difficult to trace, if rather extensive. It should be noted that his initial
understanding of Modernism did not include the idea of impersonality: according to his first impression, modern poets had "turned
aside from the world ... probing with the best instruments they can
forge the wounds in their own subconsciousness" ("Contemporary
Poetry," 32). But by 1936 and the "Rejected Preface" he had so

absorbed the idea of Modernist detachment that he was trying to free himself from it, as we have seen. This he was unable to do; by 1962 he had to admit to his "conscious contrivance"; already in 1961 he had developed the entire notion of detachment into a guiding theory of Canadian poetry in the landmark article, "Eclectic Detachment: Aspects of Identity in Canadian Poetry." While Smith claims in the article that his phrase has nothing to do with impersonality, the necessary creative cold-bloodedness that chooses among the various forms of world literature so dispassionately seems to imply a certain lack of urgent self-expression. [102]

Edel has commented that "The flight from intensity of emotion is to be seen in his very first poem in the *Collected Poems*" ("Worldly Muse," 205). As in the two later volumes, this first poem was "Like an Old Proud King in a Parable," which has been the centre of so much Smith criticism that it must be placed in context here as well. In the poem Smith opposes two visions of poetry, one typified by the "fat royal life" surrounded by "fawning courtier and doting queen," the other by "northern stone" and "the cold goddess Pride." He seems to make clear his desire for the latter alternative in the poem's structure, but the choice is deliberately obfuscated in the middle by the poet's announcement, "O who is that bitter king? It is not I." (Note the similarity to Smith's quotation of Rimbaud above.) In other words, the "king" who escapes to the "meadow in the northern stone" is not Smith the poet: only an image, an exemplar, to the poet. The poem thus proposes and yet questions the possibility of a poetry of detachment, in that the poet writing seems as yet unequal to the aesthetic challenge implied in the parable.

In fact, the parable itself is more ambiguous than it might appear. The king, once he went north, "breathed a palace of inviolable air/ To cage a heart that carolled like a swan." The crucial image here is "cage a heart," which can mean, alternately, restrain a heart, stifle its "carolling," or capture a heart, put it in its proper place, whence it might still sing through the bars. The ambiguity is only clarified when the poet, recognizing that he has not yet imitated the aesthetic removal of the king in his parable, prays to a "Father" to let him

    ... die
From this fat royal life, and lie
As naked as a bridegroom by his bride,
And let that girl be the cold goddess Pride:

And I will sing to the barren rock
Your difficult, lonely music, heart,
Like an old proud king in a parable.   (*PNC*, 12)

The poet's version of the king's "northern" life clarifies the issue of the caged heart: if he can mimic the king's removal from the "fat royal life" he will be able to sing the "difficult, lonely music" of the "heart," in other words, will express himself subjectively.[103] It will be "barren" and "proud" poetry, shaped like stone and "difficult" and "lonely": but it will still be subjective. It now becomes apparent that the first alternative of poetry, that of the "fat royal life," was never described: except by associating it with "fawning" and "doting" and "hollow" and "gilt" we cannot specify its characteristics, as we can with the restrained music of the heart, the better alternative. But we may assume that it is a poetry of lush subjectivity, of huge and rich emotionalism without restraint and order, full of decoration and rhetoric and empty of life and art. In other words, it is the poetry of Smith's early years, as yet unmatured by a sterner view of life.

In "Like an Old Proud King in a Parable" Smith argues for a degree of detachment, then, from the absolute authority of the subjective voice. Smith is not yet prepared to advocate its utter abandonment, but he would like to restrain it somewhat, which in the coming years he was increasingly able to do. It is revealing that Smith should use a parable of aesthetic removal in order to capture these ideas: he has adapted a common motif of Aesthetic literature and used it as a means with which to express a further shift towards Modernism. Edel is obviously correct in his assertion that the poem shows Smith's first "flight from intensity of emotion," but his statement needs qualifying. As has already been suggested, "intensity of emotion" is a cardinal feature of Smith's poetics. Edel's point would be more accurately phrased "flight from his own emotions," from the sentiments of Arthur Smith. With very few exceptions it would be sheer folly to read Smith's poetry as the expression of the man himself: the emotions are intense, but they are ostensibly the emotions of others, from myth or from the modern world, who are unconnected with the poet. So even as he flew from intensity he flew toward it: he could not abandon it altogether, so he found a way to import intensity into his later verse without suffering the labels of Aestheticism that might have hounded him had he continued in his original mode. He thus achieves both detachment and intensity, the two in no more contradiction than are the surface fragmentation and the underlying thirst for spiritual order that characterize Eliot's *Waste Land*.

Smith's only other poem to render poetic doctrine explicitly is "To a Young Poet." The speaker urges a protegé to "find/In the stern, autumnal face/Of Artemis" some "device" that must be entirely "alien to romance." Worship of Artemis – whose association with the moon provides the link to poetic inspiration – invites her "cruelty," but that very quality makes of the poetic "duty" a state of "grace." Only Artemis's "votary" can achieve – and this is Smith's point – "the worth of a hard thing done/Perfectly, as though without care" (*PNC*, 21). The emphasis of criticism has been upon the word "perfect," thus relating the poem's doctrine to Smith's sense of craft, his drafting and re-drafting poems until they are as complex as possible. But "as though without care" suggests another kind of attitude, an indifference, great art created with a wave of the hand, which has not been noticed in the poem. Why should "perfection," the highest goal of any pursuit, be "without care?" Scott has offered the following thoughts on the passage: "The hard thing done perfectly, as though without care, but only seeming so because of the immense care taken – that is an aesthetic principle exemplified in Arthur Smith's work. The word 'elegant' is one that fits. Today that word has an objectionable sound, suggesting something at once affected and a bit dandified, but in a Smithian context it is restored to its true meaning of grace, propriety and refinement – something chosen with taste" ("Smith: A Memoir," 84). But it is not the elegance that is "dandified": it is the desire itself, to appear to have created ultimate art without even trying, without appearing to have laboured or even wished to succeed. In the context of Smith's early Aestheticism, and the Aesthetic principles that many of his key essays maintain, it is not unreasonable to suggest that the idea of "perfection without care" descends to Smith from the affectations of the Aesthetes and Decadents, and that it is an essential part of his contrived, artificial, and occasionally perfect poems.

Here we have the answer to an earlier question as well. It is possible to understand Smith's championing detachment and intensity at once only if we see it in the context of Aestheticism: for it was the Aesthetes who loudly desired intensity of life; but it was also the Aesthetes who sought to remain aloof and impersonal, to treat the work of art as an autonomous object in which their personalities played no part. Thus Pater could tell the individual that "To burn always with this hard, gem-like flame, to maintain this ecstasy, is success in life" (*Ren.*, 189), but caution the artist that "Art ... is thus always striving to be independent of the mere intelligence, to become a matter of pure perception, to get rid of its responsibilities to its subject or material" (*Ren.*, 108); Wilde could claim that "Art never expresses anything but itself" ("Decay," 313), that "The highest art rejects the burden of the human spirit" ("Decay," 314), while telling the artist that "Art is the most intense mode of individualism that the world has known."[104] Thus Smith faces another version of the Decadent dilemma: we desire on the one hand to enjoy the bewitching pleasures of the modern world, to plunge into sensation and experience, and on the other to remove ourselves from the ugliness of the world, retreat to Parnassus and dream only of perfect art. Detachment and intensity in Smith are manifestations of his essentially Aesthetic nature; they may be explained when we have come to terms with his earliest poems; and they are not, ultimately, contradictions but complements of one another in the mature poetic he developed after the experimentalism of the 1920s.

To confirm the utility of these findings to Smith criticism, and by way of summary, I offer a final reading, of Smith's "Nightfall," with the provocative subtitle, *"fin de siècle."* There have appeared no readings of this poem, yet its obvious delineation of poetic theory, in the context provided by the subtitle, demands that it be given serious consideration. The poem is a riddle of sorts: how may we arrive at an interpretation that addresses the images of the poem and incorporate that interpretation with the unusual subtitle? One of the most important keys we have is the very particular setting:

All day within the winding gardens
I have paced, and in the maze,
And on the stones beside the waterlily pond;
All day the shadow on the dial has moved
A little farther on its little round;
All day the clouds have wandered
Over the crystal, over the fragile sky.

The "winding gardens," the "maze," the "waterlily pond," and the presence of a sundial definitely suggest an aristocratic estate, and the apparent leisure of the speaker as he wanders through this refined setting adds to the effect of independent ease. Note the precise sounds that add to the sensation of refinement and indolence: the liquid [w] and [l] throughout, the gentle half-rhyme of "paced" and "maze," the [s] and [sh] of "stones," "beside," "shadow," "crystal," the [f] of "farther" and "fragile," and the repetition of "little," which produces the effect of delicacy enforced by such words as "crystal" and "fragile." The realization of the setting is purposively gentle, almost sentimental; but note the importance of time's passing, implied in the poet's repeated glances at the sundial. All this refinement seems, in brief, to be poised in the moments before transition.

The speaker attributes to himself a number of "fancies" that are in some way analogous to this setting: the precision of his language, again, assists us towards a particular interpretation. As he wanders in the estate he is neither thinking nor reflecting, quite, but letting his mind stray where it will:

As idle fancies in me too have trailed
As idly through my sky, and been but clouds
To hide the clearer sky, or light
That only serves to hide a star.

Quite "as if without care" Smith has loaded the diction of the lines towards a particular meaning. The two repeated words, "idle" and "hides" (connected moreover by their consonance), suggest a degree of condemnation, as well as deception, a covering over of some truth. The clouds of the sky are like his fancies, which also cover a "clearer sky" – the suggestion is that "clearer" is better – or like light of a lower kind that "hides" a star. This diction of deception and indolence also illuminates the earlier lines: note now the "winding gardens," suggestive of sinuosity and confusion, and the "maze," a place in which one is easily lost. There is some degree of judgment lurking in the poem, a sense that this refined setting is somehow wrong, that it hides something "clearer" and starlike that should be visible. The interposition of the sun-dial, with its warning note of time, heightens the dramatic confusion lurking in Smith's diction.

The second and last stanza is brief and (visually) to the point:

But now the milkwhite flower fades,
Is drooping, and the dark leaves fall;
The stars are moving in the waving glades
Like words of poems, crisp and sharp and small.  (PNC, 65)

After their obfuscation in the first stanza, the "stars" are visible now, despite their being framed by the silhouettes of branches. The "milk-white flower" is a lily that he has picked from the pond, a typically Aesthetic gesture. Since it was picked, taken up by the self-involved speaker, the flower now "droops," fades away, and is swallowed up into time, even as the day itself disappears in the fall of night (hence the poem's title). Note that we have shifted quietly from memory in the first stanza to present tense and perception in the second.

Something else has shifted as well: suddenly, with the last line, the nightfall vision is "like words of poems," and of a particular nature, "crisp and sharp and small." After the "winding" and the "maze" and the "idle fancies" of the first stanza, these adjectives clearly intimate that the "poems" are to be contrasted in our minds with the aristocratic setting: that is, the "poems" of the second stanza should call up free associations with poetry in the first, poetry that is full of "idle fancies," "winding gardens" of imagery perhaps, poetry that "only serves to hide a star." In fact the entire poem is about poems: on the one hand a complex, loaded, twisted and convoluted poetry that hides a pure light, and on the other a poetry that *is* the pure light, the "stars," rendered "crisp and sharp and small" by precise language.

What "Nightfall" records, apparently, is the end of the nineteenth century, the "*fin de siècle*." Poetry of rich and luxuriant language that captures the "crystal" and "fragile" moments of exquisite life, always with connotations of wealth and ease, has been left behind; poetry of crispness, to the point, without grandeur, and therefore able to catch the light, has replaced it. The *fin-de-siècle* may be located in the poem, as it were, between the two stanzas: as the speaker passes from memory to present tense, so do we pass from poetry of the nineteenth century to poetry of the twentieth. We therefore leave behind the "winding gardens," the "maze," the "crystal" and "fragile sky," for a purer darkness that nevertheless allows us to see the stars. We do not hide our meanings in the dense foliage of Victorian English: those "flowers" have "faded" and "drooped," and the "dark leaves" have fallen. Now, through the bare branches, we see clearly: the modern poetic, by pruning language to its most essential elements, allows the star-light to reach us.

We may argue with Smith's rendering of either century's poetry, but that would be to avoid the point: "Nightfall" captures, hauntingly, not only the transition from Aesthetic to modern poetry, but also Smith's development from the poetry of his youth to the poetry of his manhood. He too had turned the corner, had passed from the first to the second stanza by way of the *fin-de-siècle*; and I would argue that "Nightfall" is his tribute to that change, in fact his only acknowledgement of the true apprenticeship of his earliest poems. For their celebration of idleness, convolution, delicacy, and fragility, they had to be abandoned, so that with a purer language he could touch the highest light; but note, by way of conclusion, that he remains in the garden: this is a Modernist who knows, by personal intimacy, the nature of the poetry he is leaving behind and who will continue to make use of its virtues even as he skirts its dangers.

Once the idea is accepted that an early thematic Aestheticism in Smith's poetry was altered and absorbed into a later formal and theoretical Aestheticism, it will go a long way towards explaining the essence of the man's poetry. Eli Mandel once remarked that "Somewhere A.J.M. Smith speaks of the 'value of calm analysis and objective appraisal' but since his own gift is for impassioned and intense speech and writing, I have often wondered whether that phrase concealed some sort of reservation, some coolness toward his subject at the time."[105] George Woodcock has commented that Smith's "gathering of the poems according to manner and mood rather than time emphasises his remarkable sustenance of both emotional intensity and the lapidary craftsmanship he has always sought."[106] I know of no better means of reconciling these and other "contradictions" in Smith's canon than by reference to what we may call his Aesthetic Modernism. To the degree that there was tension and opposition between those two periods we may expect to find contradictions in Smith; but to the degree that they overlapped and assisted one another, we may justly recognize that in him were combined the visions and doctrines of Victorianism's two greatest enemies.

O f the poets thus far considered, Smith's development of his Aesthetic inheritance is the most complex and fruitful. He neither rejected Aestheticism outright, as for the most part Scott did, nor did he continue to accept it with open arms, as John Glassco later welcomed the themes of Decadence. He has, whether by conscious silence or faulty memory, never recognized the Aestheticism of his early poetry, and yet its effects may be felt in some manner in everything he wrote. Aestheticism has given him principles of craft, artistic perfection, impersonal detachment, poetic intensity, which were to form the essence of his later doctrines: but the gift was not, perhaps, gratefully received. Certainly Smith's status as a leading Canadian Modernist would not encourage him to discuss at any length his initial Aestheticism, especially in the climate following 1947, when John Sutherland's vitriolic attack presented Smith as a reclusive, autocratic exile whose "pure aestheticism" marred his vision of Canadian literature; and no doubt after that time memory did lapse somewhat: the initial poems were forgotten and left comfortably buried in the *Daily* and the *Supplement*.

Having now recovered them, the present examination raises a number of issues. Since Smith was for two or three decades the leading anthologist of Canadian poetry, we must wonder if his Aesthetic leanings did not colour his readings and lead him to promote poets inclined to his own way of thinking. Certainly Sutherland thought so: it was Smith's inclusion of people like Finch, Mackay, and Tracy in *The Book of Canadian Poetry*, at the expense of such poets as Irving Layton, Louis Dudek, and Raymond Souster, that initiated the strong reaction against Smith's standards and set afoot a conflicting current of Canadian criticism that openly devoted itself to crushing the Aesthetic spirit as an unhealthy overgrowth from the nineteenth century.[107] Studies of Smith's anthologies may be able to support Sutherland's claims rather than disprove them, another possibility for work in the future. As Edel once commented, Smith's "has been an aesthetic Canada" ("Worldly Muse," 212). It will take time before we accept the validity of that comment and perceive fully what it has meant to our nation's literature.

In the meantime we must recognize Smith to have been a more complex individual and poet than we generally admit. In a way, our belief that he rushed into Modernism as a young man and never left it has made of him a rather colourless figure, a unidimensional literary crusader with only one good cause in his blood. He was indeed devoted to that most important cause of twentieth-century Canadian literature; but he came at it from a direction that shows up his complexity as a poet and his catholicity of literary taste. His old pursuit of absolute "Beauty" should remind us that his generation was not only bowled over by Eliot but also gazed back to the haunting, other-worldly figures of Aestheticism and Decadence and that some agreement between the two had to be reached. No one, not even Eliot himself, Smith's prime Modernist, had failed to be touched by some form of European Aestheticism, so it should not surprise us that Eliot's Canadian disciples were influenced by Aestheticism as well. The influence, however, is not the ultimate point: what matters is that Smith, like the other poets of this study, was influenced by Aestheticism *in such a way that it contributed to his modernity*; they arrived at a Canadian Aesthetic Modernism that proves their dedication as artists, as Aesthetes, and as socialists. Perhaps they suffered as a consequence some of the inevitable limitations lurking in Aestheticism, but they also created a particularly formalized and beautiful hybrid of Modernism that cannot be ignored in English literary history. If any one poet was more responsible than the others for that fruition, it was Smith. The evidence makes clear that he came to Aestheticism before most of the others; who knows but that he may have encouraged their own absorption of the Aesthetic influence? Fine tuning is required for such a suggestion; dates, lists of books read, and personal journals must become publicly accessible; but we have in the meantime every right to speak of Smith's Aestheticism and look for the development of it in his vision of Canadian letters. Of Smith's "To Hold in a Poem," which sums up many of his literary aspirations, Edel has said that

The operative word ... is "austere," and when you have austerity then the word ecstasy – the ecstasy within these lines – is indeed qualified. It leads me to the conclusion that Smith is an austere, sometimes even a "frugal," poet: and his wit, his liveliness, as well as his asperity, break through his frugality. Such is the ambivalence, the mystery, the beauty of what he has created. I hope I am not being too obscure if I say that this peculiar mixture is a distinctive Canadian quality and a subject open to the deepest exploration. I suspect it derives from a small population in a wild land preserving its quest for beauty, and learning austerity in the process. ("Worldly Muse," 213)

Learning austerity while on a quest for beauty – I can think of no better way to define at a glance Smith's Aesthetic Modernism. I hope it is not too presumptuous to suspect that he would himself, when all the battles and arguments were over, have appreciated the idea: that he would want to be recognized as a poet whose adoration of beauty, while it underwent many a sea-change, lived on within the aging man until the last poem was written.

## CHAPTER SEVEN

# Conclusion: Speculations

Aestheticism, if we approximate the end of the English movement and the beginning of Canadian Modernism, say from the trial of Wilde to the creation of the *Fortnightly,* lay dormant for some thirty years before it had a significant and pervasive influence on an entire Canadian literary generation. The need for this estimate may not be immediately clear, but I presume that the scholar who is interested in the foreign influences upon Canadian poetry will also have a general interest in the schema of Canadian artistic inheritance and will consequently be curious to know if any patterns exist by which we can generalize cautiously about Canadian culture's absorption of European artistic precedents. In this study I have shown an artistic inheritance that comprehends, interestingly, both a delayed influence, Aestheticism, and a contemporary one, Modernism. In general, the poets considered have received the former before arriving at the latter influence, the archetypal example of such a progress being A.J.M. Smith's.

This over-lap of influences is worth noting because many scholars of Canadian literature acknowledge a "time lag" in the Canadian adoption of European models – whether that "lag" be fifty, thirty, or fewer years. D.M.R. Bentley has expressed the idea with the most appropriate sense of its limited application:

It has frequently been observed that literary developments in Canada lag behind those in the major literatures and that Canadian literature as a whole has had virtually no impact outside Canada. From these observations, which, needless to say, are of a descriptive not a prophetic nature, it follows that Canadian literature is derivative and relatively uninnovative, that in world terms it is a minor literature ... This is not to say that Canadian literature, any more than British architecture, is lacking in distinctiveness or distinction. On the contrary, the forms and techniques that Canadian poets have imported ... do not become obsolete and cannot be superseded, so long as there are gifted poets to transplant and to vernalize them with intelligence and creativity in physical and cultural environments as distinctive as those of Canada. Canadian poetry, though its forms and techniques are imported and though it has not, so far, produced innovations of the major kind that affect the course of poetry elsewhere, is yet a distinctive body of literature by virtue of the talents of its authors and by virtue of its uniqueness.[1]

In one sense, the influence discussed in this book bears such a theory out, lending special credence to a three-decade "lag" in trans-Atlantic cultural inheritances. In another sense, it fruitfully and fundamentally complicates our earlier sense of such a "lag," by showing that the poets receiving the delayed influence received at roughly the same time, say within three to five years, a much more contemporary influence, from Imagism, Pound, Eliot and the Modernists. While my conclusions prevent, therefore, any simplistic application of a "time lag" theory, they do lend support to a qualified and relative version of that phenomenon.

Those with little time for discussion of a "lag" (who will not much enjoy the next few pages) usually feel that it betrays a colonial critical mentality that we should by now be well rid of. Common sense suggests however that the contemporary critic need not be colonial to speak of colonists. To deny the "time lag" on grounds of critical bias, therefore, is to close one's eyes to some fairly evident truths of our literary history. If we reach back into the nineteenth century for corroboration of the "lag," we find, for example, the frequently remarked influence of the Aesthetic poets upon the Confederation poets, especially upon Lampman, Roberts, Scott, and Carman. Of course it is difficult to say when Aesthetic poetry ends and Decadent begins, so the "time lag" of such an influence is difficult to measure. The earliest such poetry was Morris's *Defence of Guenevere* in 1858; the latest significant Aesthetic publication was, to my mind, Rossetti's *Poems*, published, incidentally, well after they were written. (Swinburne's second volume, *Songs Before Sunrise*, appeared in 1871, after which time he began his rather awkward descent into the tamer poetry of his later years.) It seems fair, then, to speak of the heyday of Aesthetic poetry as the period from 1858 to 1870. If we again take the "end" of the movement as our mark, we may say that the influence of the Aesthetic poets upon the Confederation poets in Canada took from 1870 to about 1893 or 1895, the dates respectively of Scott's *The Magic House and Other Poems* and of Lampman's *Lyrics of Earth*.

Thus the postulated influence shows a "time lag" of about two-and-a-half decades. Such an estimate does not take into account Roberts's first two volumes; the Aesthetic influence upon his poetry has been argued chiefly from its impact on his volumes from the 1890s on,[2] and similar questions about his *Orion and Other Poems* (1880) have not yet been answered. It is not my intention to debate them here; when we examine the pervasive impact of Aesthetic (as opposed to Decadent) poetry, so far as that impact has been charted at all, we are compelled to remark a delayed absorption of the influence.

Such delays appear earlier in the century as well. Charles Sangster's *The St Lawrence and the Saguenay* of 1856 is said to be "modelled on Byron's *Childe Harold's Pilgrimage* [1812–1818] and Wordsworth's *The River Duddon* [1820]."[3] The influences seem legitimate, so we may say that Byron's early poetry took roughly forty years to reach Sangster, and Wordsworth's later poetry roughly thirty-five. Earlier still is an archetypal story of Canadian influence: that of Oliver Goldsmith's *The Deserted Village* (1770) on his grand-nephew Oliver Goldsmith's *The Rising Village* (1825). Here is a rare case of influence that needs no further substantiation; and we may say that the inheritance manifested required the passing of some five-and-a-half decades.

This is however where problems arise, problems that emphasize the caution demanded by all such dramatic reasoning. The family resemblance between the two Goldsmiths is an essential one; but if we take from the earlier Goldsmith the contrast of a village with urban and commercial viciousness, as well as the skilled practice of rhyming couplets, we cannot look only to his grand-nephew for his influence upon Canadian poetry. For one thing we must consider the way in which the elder Goldsmith influenced Thomas Cary's *Abram's Plains; A Poem* (1789); while acknowledging in the preface to the volume a cardinal debt to "Thompson" (that is, James Thomson), Cary also remarks that "Before [he] began this Poem [he] read Pope's Windsor-Forrest and Dr. Goldsmith's Deserted Village, with the view of endeavouring, in some degree, to catch their manner of writing."[4] Bentley's recent edition of *Abram's Plains* confirms the influence of Goldsmith,[5] making clear our need for care in any quick sketch of the Canadian reception of *The Deserted Village*. It would be useful to raise the same question with regard to J. Mackay and his *Quebec Hill; or, Canadian Scenery* (1797), the rhythms, imagery, and sentiment of which would appear to have been inspired to some degree by Goldsmith. (I am raising a question here, not affirming an influence.) In other words, while the most obvious and essential influence from Goldsmith's *The Deserted Village* certainly shows up in the younger Goldsmith's book in 1825, it is unsound to claim simply that his influence "lagged" for fifty-five years.

Acknowledging so much with regard to Goldsmith forces us to ask similar questions about the other "time lags" sketched above. Tracy Ware, for instance, has remarked the influence of Byron (specifically his *Beppo*) on George Longmore's *Charivari* of 1824, a cultural "lag" of only six years;[6] John Richardson's *Tecumseh; or, The Warrior of the West* of 1828, certainly a less successful poem than Sangster's, nevertheless clearly adopts the Byronic sensibility as well as the Byronic *ottava rima*;[7] and the *Literary History of Canada* suggests Byron's influence on William Fitz Hawley's *The Unknown, or Lays of the Forest*, published in Montreal in 1831,[8] and on Peter John Allan, whose *Poetical Remains* were published in 1853.[9] All of these Canadian heirs of Byron published their works before the appearance of Sangster's better-known *The St Lawrence and the Saguenay*. Similarly, before we can rest with a "time lag" in the absorption of Rossetti's and Morris's influence, we ought to consider their possible influence upon the lyric poetry of Isabella Valancy Crawford. John Ower has remarked, albeit briefly, exactly such an influence, specifically by relating Crawford's "The Lily Bed" to Robert Buchanan's infamous attack on Rossetti and his "fleshly school of poetry."[10] Between Buchanan's essay and the composition of Crawford's poem a mere five years passed – a significant truncation of our original measurement of the Aesthetic "lag." To take Ower's point to its immediately relevant conclusion: where should we now "locate" the full Canadian influence of those Aesthetic poets: in the work of Crawford, of Lampman Roberts and Scott, or in the early poetry of Smith, Scott, and Kennedy?

On the basis of such interrogation the "time lag" idea begins to look a little shabby, to be sure. So will any general argument that helps to clarify vast fields of information when faced with the details that it has tended to exclude. Such details do not, however, invalidate the idea itself, merely its present interpretation. We eliminate the present problem if we acknowledge that we are speaking not of scattered influences but of fundamental or canonical influences; it then becomes accurate to notice a certain lapse of time between the end of major European literary movements and their pervasive and general absorption into the Canadian literary mainstream. The lapse has involved, generally, from three to five decades, with shorter lapses apparently becoming common as the nation's literary consciousness advanced. This delay tells us about Canadian cultural development, our susceptibility or resistance to foreign examples, and our adaptations of foreign inheritances. It confirms our suspicion that Canadian culture has matured in this century by reducing the importance of foreign influences to its own literary development and suggests that a part of our intellectual progress was to discover foreign trends more quickly and absorb them more easily and confidently as the nation developed. Critical expression of the idea should always take into account its theoretical nature, and we should remember that we simplify purposely – not naïvely – when we manipulate such patterns. Ideal discussions of Canadian artistic inheritance will acknowledge, then, that despite such general patterns there are instances of individual artistic achievement that warn us not to treat this visible "time lag" as an element of some mythical "Canadian psyche," but rather as a fairly useful critical framework in which we can sketch important ideas of cultural and artistic enrichment in Canada.

For similar reasons it is insufficient to conclude, in the present case, that Aestheticism strongly influenced Canadian Modernism, since that formulation reveals only a part of the story. What is particularly significant is that the poets who showed the Aesthetic influence most strikingly also turned to Modernism with the most dedication and complexity. In the interests of fruitful complication, the final summation of the influence discussed here should include a reminder that I have been speaking of modern poets from the start, poets whose most significant inheritance came not from Aestheticism but from Modernism. To have found a second and prior influence upon their poetry is no small thing. But the result of that influence is a strain we may best call Aesthetic Modernism; these are still modern poets. The theory of the "time lag" too often suggests that we have adapted foreign literary models thirty to fifty years "late," without absorbing any concomitant contemporary influences; and, because we are not keen to address the issue directly, this terminology of cultural retardation has persisted. Once we accept the fact that cultural delay has been a part of our patterns of inheritance in Canada, we may feel more keenly the need for a more neutral description of the phenomenon. Despite the "lag" involved here, by the end of the 1920s most of these poets had turned to Modernism from Aestheticism, producing a beautiful hybrid of the two, which stamped their Modernism for the rest of their careers. The idea of being "late" is hardly the point; our lateness here permitted a stronger contemporary influence, Modernism, to be redirected in a striking and unique way.

How many of the other "time lags" hazarded above could show a similar hybrid if we were no longer exercised about the "lateness" of the inheritances? In what ways were Goldsmith, Sangster, Lampman, Roberts, Carman, Scott – and all gradually influenced Canadian poets – utterly contemporary as well? Leaving these aside, few poets would fail to reward such examination. What compound of influences, both gradual and immediate, produced the intent aesthetic speculation of Dudek's *Europe*? What more powerful influences overwhelmed the available Aesthetic model in Livesay and Klein, necessitating their exclusion from this study? How far back towards Decadence can we trace the libertinism, pessimism, and sense of spiritual exhaustion in the Beat poets, whose influence on Leonard Cohen seems arguable? Once we have recognized those elements of our poets' work that place them deeply in and of their own milieu (the business of traditional Canadian criticism), and add to that a sense of the more gradual influences upon them from foreign models (my purpose here), we will have, to my mind, an appropriate sense of the role of literary influence in Canadian studies.

This approach will do much to explain the "two Modernisms" in Canadian poetry. Anyone glancing at the poets of the 1920s, and at those of the 1940s, will be able to make certain immediate comparisons: whereas the earlier poets show a tendency to subject matter drawn from myth, landscape, ritual, and "objective experience," the later poets tend towards a poetry of ironic realism, urban life, and class-conscious historicity; whereas the earlier poets tend strongly towards traditional forms and seem to have elaborated few of the Modernist formal breakthroughs, the later poets welcomed more openly the formal revolution and shaped their verse accordingly; whereas the earlier poets tend to voice a detached and hence Aesthetic poetry, the later poets create a poetry that is committed, visceral, and often angry. Now the questions arise: how may we account for these sharply differing versions of Canadian Modernism? Why have they divided the inspiration of *The Waste Land* between them? How are we to respond to the poetic wars that took place between them in the early 1940s? Where lies the "real" Modernist movement in Canada (since these two never really reconciled themselves into a single compelling movement)?

If the poets of the 1920s have produced an Aesthetic Modernism as a result of hybrid influences upon their developments, the poets of the 1940s have taken up the gradual influence of high Modernism and altered it to reflect their own contemporary situation as young men and women of the Depression, soon surrounded by a cataclysmic World War. Two of them, Layton and Dudek, had cultural backgrounds that might well predispose them to a distrust of the Anglo-Saxon literary inheritance. No doubt the poetry of protest

that arose in England in the 1930s, partly as a result of those contemporary conditions, urged their acceptance of a Modernism substantially different from the Modernism of their immediate Canadian
forebears. Theirs was a delayed Modernism shaped by contemporary
forces that they could not ignore, just as the delayed Aestheticism
of the 1920s poets had been shaped and strained by the demands
of Modernism until it produced their most famous works. That they
were hostile to one another is natural, given that each generation
brought to the Modernist impulse antithetical tastes, the first for
Aesthetic, the second for committed and realistic poetry. Only by
recognizing each generation in a context larger and more complex
than inherited literary Modernism can we understand the Modernists in this country; and such recognition can only come when we
grow sensitive to the multifarious ways in which influence, whether
cultural, artistic, or political, whether mediated by time or immediate, has shaped Canadian literature from first foundations onward.

The Aesthetic influence also accounts, most probably, for the puzzling traditionalism of the Modernists studied here. As they had
learned to various degrees the principles and practice of Aestheticism (a delight in pure form, a strong desire to create beauty, an
overwhelming sense of the literary tradition that preceded and
threatened to overshadow them), they maintained such principles
when they turned to Modernism, so that they tended to produce
poetry that reflected Modernist themes, imagery, and diction in
relatively traditional forms. Note, once again, how much of the
Aesthetic poetry by these young men was written in sonnets; some
of the poets obviously had a significant attachment to the form,
which was confirmed rather than eroded by their Aestheticism, an
attachment which often survived their indoctrination into Modernism.

The Canadian parallel to the inarguable Aesthetic inheritance in
Joyce, Pound, Eliot, Woolf, Stevens, and the other Modernists will
now be apparent, but with an essential variation on the American
and English models. Fascinatingly, the Canadian Modernist poets
themselves provided the Aestheticism that so many critics have suggested to be a necessary preliminary to Modernism. So necessary is
Aestheticism to the birth of Modernism that, in a country where no
significant Aesthetic period had existed, one had to be created before
Modernism could occur. The Canadian example also suggests that
the influence of Aestheticism upon Modernism is largely a practical
one; while the theoretical arguments of Morse Peckham, J.E. Chamberlin and Jacques Barzun do much to explain the reasons for such
an affinity, it seems clear that the influence itself is transmitted
largely through the painstaking imitation and eventual adaptation

of Aestheticism by a younger generation looking for practical models for their creative needs.

Such a theoretical explanation is not entirely satisfying, however. If we ask why Aestheticism so particularly affected an entire generation of young Canadian artists, and at a distance of more than thirty years, we need a more complete answer than a claim that Aestheticism inevitably prefigures a Modernist revolution. Several other possible reasons can be suggested. One factor, without doubt, was the cultural sensibility of Canada from 1900 to 1925. Although Victoria had died in 1901, Victorian Canada had lived on, a fact upon which memoirists, historians, and literary critics are in essential agreement. The most severe literary proof of this is a group of intensely minor poets from that period, now referred to derisively (though not always fairly) with such labels as "The Maple Leaf School," a group who perpetuated a soaring patriotism, love of a tamed Canadian wilderness, and attachment to Britain's sustaining breast through thick and thin. (A severe danger of such labelling is the temptation to put all non-Modernists into the school, muddling bad traditionalists with good traditionalists, patriots with poets.) While most of the poets studied here admitted to having read next to nothing of previous Canadian poets, the evidently weak spirit of contemporary poetic creativity in Canada appears to have permeated their consciousnesses and provided them with an appropriate locus for attack: a process of self-definition and antagonism that we can witness in Scott's "The Canadian Authors Meet," if we remember that the poem was actually begun at a meeting of The Canadian Authors' Association attended by Smith and Scott.[11] This unfortunate literary atmosphere no doubt contributed to the fairly sudden development of Canadian Modernism. Although he was speaking of American poets, David Perkins has expressed exactly this idea:

In fact, if we ask why the development of the Modernist mode was chiefly by American poets, one reason is that American poets had no strong, innovative, and rebellious avant-garde movement among their immediate predecessors in their own country. After 1900 English poets reacted against the Aesthetic-Decadent-Symbolist-Impressionist poems of the 1890s and returned in some ways to the traditions of English Romantic poetry ... American poets, on the other hand, grew up during the predominance of a traditional poetry that was second-rate. Naturally they eloigned themselves from it, and with fewer misgivings and greater boldness because it was visibly weak.[12]

Smith, Scott, and Glassco, if we substitute them for the Americans considered by Perkins, reacted in a similar way to the "second-rate" poetry they intuited around them. But they did not move to Modernism immediately, again because the possibilities of Aesthetic poetry had not run their course in Canada. They therefore responded to the contemporary poetic blight by drawing first upon the most potent weapon against Victorianism that they could see at the time.

They did not need to read poetry, after all, to feel around them the oppressive Victorianism of "modern" Canada. For one thing, mid-1920s McGill would appear to have provided them with consistent examples of the Victorian mentality, and as energetic undergraduates they no doubt responded with some fairly typical debunking, deflating, and disrespect. When such undergraduate antinomianism occurs in a poetic personality, in a period of formality and ultra-decency, the result may well be a poetry of Aestheticism, a poetry that could call into question the very foundation of an autocratic university by postulating the individual's right to private ritual, sensation, beauty, and intensity. This is very much what had happened at Oxford at roughly the same time. The so-called "McGill Movement" was more therefore, than a coincidental band of young intellectuals who happened to gather at a Canadian university; it was, beyond doubt, a movement shaped in part by the authorities of a particular university, a movement demanded by the morality and expectations of a cultural system that had disappeared, leaving its heroes from former wars to run its pedagogical institutions.

To make matters worse, home life appears to have offered our poets little relief: another contributing factor in their Aestheticism, no doubt, was their common descent from Victorian bourgeois families. Smith, Scott, and Glassco at least spent their childhoods with many of the privileges and the burdens of a formal and established class. While their descriptions of their childhoods are few, they are telling: Glassco, for instance, describes "that home of Mother's + Father's. What a dreadful place it was! Graeme says that one's respiration changed whenever one entered it; when one was in that ghastly atmosphere of constraint, worry, pettiness, selfishness + malice. Thank God I haven't had any nightmares about it: those dark-panelled walls, leaded windows, thick stair-carpets, period chairs and all the rest of the opulent, fake furnishings"(23 Aug. 1935, "Journal," 37). Edel has written of Smith's childhood with less horror, but just as revealingly: "intensities weren't polite in that world of his childhood. To have temperament, to rage at inequities, to show strong feelings – one didn't do such things. One was supposed to indulge in a cheerful kind of humbuggery, a tea-party gentility … with a poet it can sometimes provide such strong defences that he becomes an endless 'converter' – all is metamorphosis.

Smith's strong feelings are channelled and fragmented into the pictorial and the suggestive, into a highly civilized wit, into delicate intellectual symbols" ("Worldly Muse," 202–3). Scott's childhood, while typically recorded with little of the distaste of the above comments, depicts a fairly similar background: "I was born into the upper middle class, a child of the rectory, but we never had any money. I wasn't born financially upper class, but with certain traditions of the upper class. The Scotts were a good, well-known family."[13] Little of this personal material has reached the various canons, but we should remember Smith in "My Lost Youth": "I thought of my birthplace in Westmount and what *that* involved,/– An ear quick to recoil from the faintest 'false note'" (*PNC*, 102), and Glassco in "For Cora Lightbody, R.N.," which recalls the above journal entry with its "Georgian nightmare I must love forever" (*SP*, 65).

We simply do not have enough real biographical detail to draw literary conclusions from these post-Victorian sketches; but if their general tenor is accurate, it is not difficult to see that such a conventionally structured childhood and education, whatever the real degree of parental love and professorial understanding, might well have contributed to an adolescent fondness for Aesthetic and Decadent poetry. Bourgeois Victorian morality, rendered particularly hollow by the reports of the Great War – a shock not administered to the equally bourgeois and Victorian childhoods of the Confederation poets – could best be responded to with a poetry that was at once sensual, delicate, intense, and irreligious. Presumably these young poets had enough perspicacity to see that they could not express such ideas by surrendering to the prevailing literary atmosphere of 1900 to 1925, so they went a step further back, and found a temporary sustenance in Aestheticism.

The fact that they had one another's support was a fourth important factor in nourishing that Aestheticism. Smith clearly influenced Kennedy and Scott and may have had some effect on the early Glassco (certainly on the later); that he was also the first to imitate the poetry of Aestheticism may well suggest, as I have occasionally argued in the preceding chapters, that he played an important part in the wider transmission of that influence. One might argue that Smith's influence extends to Finch, Mackay, and Tracy as well, given what I have remarked of his peculiarities as an anthologist. Smith also kept up a substantial correspondence with Raymond Knister, the study of which might lead a future critic to hypothesize about the way in which they may have altered one another's perspectives. Scott, moreover, had been under the tutelage of F.O. Call at Bishop's College in Sherbrooke, Quebec;[14] one wonders if the counsel of the older man contributed at all to Scott's desire to go to Oxford, or to his reception there of the newer Oxonian Aestheticism. In short, like many of the Confederation poets before them, one of the striking features of the first-generation Canadian Modernists is that they learned from one another in their youth and had the pleasure and encouragement of an established group of friends: no small contribution, no matter what one's difficult endeavour.

They had, finally, one advantage the Confederation poets did not have in their youth: the chance of early European travel. Mackay and Scott were Rhodes Scholars in the 1920s; Finch spent two or three years at the Sorbonne; Smith travelled to England in 1918 and to Scotland for his doctorate at Edinburgh in 1927, and one can hardly forget Glassco's trip to Paris and its importance in his artistic development. As a generation, then, they show an international ease that no previous Canadian generation had shown; perhaps the resulting cosmopolitanism of their natures made their various Aesthetic readings particularly rewarding and meaningful. Speculation, indeed; but some combination of this and the other factors mentioned above must have contributed to the coincidental influence of Aestheticism on an entire generation of young Canadian artists.

By welcoming that influence they encouraged a strain of Modernism that will come to be seen as a stabilizing and salutary feature of the Canadian literature of the twentieth century. This will necessitate a revision of our attitudes to Modernism, of course, until we value the more traditional strain of Canadian modern poetry equally with the more experimental. Malcolm Bradbury has remarked that in critical assessments of the twentieth century "It is ... more important to suggest the general climate of change, which is perhaps best recognized by identifying an oscillation between modernism and a changing native tradition that is rather less experimental in character and more realist in disposition. The oscillation is in fact present throughout the period in most western countries, and the disposition towards extreme experiment has in few traditions been total or absolutely continuous."[15] To adopt such a broad-minded and tolerant sense of this century's literature is necessarily to welcome and to appreciate the Aestheticism of the Canadians, since that Aestheticism would appear to have encouraged them to maintain a strong sense of the formal tradition. Perhaps that is the real Canadian contribution to international English Modernism: our poets found a middle ground between the extremes of experiment and conservatism, a ground that bears the fruits of each and skirts many of the attendant dangers. Such vast national characterizations are always, of course, the mere recreations of scholarship; but I suspect that in this case they are not entirely out of place.

A final question, which must remain unanswered: why have these poets (Glassco excepted) not spoken of what was, by all the evidence, the earliest influence upon their writings? There are two alternative reasons: either they have forgotten the influence, or they have sought to conceal it. The former possibility would be quite natural, given the passage of years before they began to reminisce about those early decades; the second would also be quite natural, although less than candid. After all, their acclaim in Canada came for their Modernism, at a time when Modernism was still generally considered to be hostile to the Decadent mentality. To have admitted at such a juncture that they had themselves toyed with Aesthetic themes when young – some of them, moreover, maintaining the interest beyond their twenties – might have tainted their achievement, especially since one of them, Smith, had just been charged with a "pure aestheticism" by the later generation. The early poems of Scott and Smith were still buried in the *McGill Daily*, the *McGill Daily Literary Supplement*, and the *McGill Fortnightly Review* and, by all appearances, were unlikely to be excavated in their lifetimes (as indeed they were not) – in which case, why reveal a truth that seemed to have so little to do with their present status?

Still, there is not a shred of real evidence that any of these poets deliberately concealed the Aesthetic influence that had worked upon them. As a result, it is a matter of mere charity, at least until further information becomes available, to presume that the years had clouded their memories and left their Aesthetic days comfortably secreted away in their unconscious histories. Because of that process of forgetting, and because all but a few of the subjects of this book are dead, the evidence must be circumstantial: there will be no confessions now.

I believe, however, that each poet would be pleased to admit to such an influence, once faced with the fact that Aestheticism has provided the Canadian Modernists with their peculiar originality. Hermeren argues that one of the fruits of the study of literary influences should be a sense of a poet's originality, that is, the way in which he was *not* influenced by material known to have been familiar to him.[16] My postulation of an Aesthetic influence upon Canadian Modernism has so demonstrated the originality of the Canadian poets, in the following sense. If the present image of Canadian Modernism were true: if these poets imitated Modernism from the start, and if typical Modernism were all they produced, where is the originality? What exactly are we to respect – their ability to read the latest poetry and imitate it? Surely not; but that is exactly the respect offered by the current version of early twentieth-century literary history in this country. But when we recognize that to such a forceful influence as Modernism the Canadians added the tenets and rewards of a prior Aestheticism and maintained in various ways that Aestheticism deep within their Modernist practice, and as a result refused certain Modernist formal opportunities, we have acknowledged a significant Canadian original, a particular strain of Modernism that I have called Aesthetic Modernism. Creative originality is, at root, the ability to make startling new combinations (a formulation of which Smith would have approved); the true creativity of these poets resulted in a strain of Modernism produced by no other nation with such consistency and forcefulness. That is no small achievement. It is, to my mind, Canada's true contribution to the poetry of the twentieth century; and it demonstrates an ability to make valuable connections, to maintain unfashionable forms, to forge new meanings out of foreign links and foreign chains. Our modern literature is richer for it, our continuity with the literature of the past greater, and more fruitful, than most of us had imagined.

# Notes

1 See, for example, Bentley, "Archibald Lampman on Poets and Poetry"; Brown, *On Canadian Poetry*, 114–15; Parker, "Bliss Carman"; M. Ross, "'A Strange Aesthetic Ferment'"; Stephenson, "The Bitter Sweet Rose."

2 Most recently Philip Kokotailo has acknowledged the influence of Decadence on Glassco's prose, in *John Glassco's Richer World*. Despite Kokotailo's thorough exploration of the discrepancies between Glassco's manuscripts and his published memoir, his tendency to elide the differences between the various schools of Aestheticism and Decadence promotes a simplified version of Glassco's inheritance of Aesthetic techniques.

3 Djwa, "F. R. Scott," in *The Oxford Companion* 743. Further references to this work ("Scott") appear in the text.

4 Pater, *The Renaissance*, 188. Further references to this work (*Ren.*) appear in the text.

5 Appropriate qualifications of the purity of this idea in Pater may be arrived at by considering his *Marius the Epicurean* and his "Sebastian van Storck," one of the *Imaginary Portraits*; in both narratives the hero, despite a life-long determination to live by the principles of aesthetic removal that I have enunciated, commits an act "in the world," which climaxes his life. This does not of course fundamentally contradict my version of the Aesthetic principle; note that both heroes die as a result of their taking action and are therefore no more "of the world" than before.

6 These definitions will be seen to build upon a number of the standard critical perceptions of Aestheticism and Decadence. For instance, the contradiction they describe in the Decadent position is delineated at

length by R.K.R. Thornton in *The Decadent Dilemma* and is stated succinctly in his "'Decadence' in Later Nineteenth Century England":
"The Decadent is a man caught between two opposite and apparently
incompatible pulls; on the one hand he is drawn by the world, its ne-
cessities, and the attractive impressions he receives from it, while on
the other hand he yearns toward the eternal, the ideal, and the un-
worldly. The play between these two poles forms the typical Decadent
subject matter"(26). A.E. Carter has similarly noted that "this fusion of
the artificial and the modern which is one of the identifying marks of
decadence united two fundamentally opposed ideas: a hatred of modern civilization and a love of the refinements modern civilization made
possible. Since decadent sensibility never resolved this contradiction,
the movement suffered throughout its lifetime from a sort of literary
schizophrenia" (*The Idea of Decadence in French Literature*, 6).

7 Buckler, "*Marius the Epicurean*: Beyond Victorianism," 280, 282.

8 It is interesting to consider how often Aesthetic poetry addresses or
meditates upon abstract beauty (that is, "Beauty"), especially given
Pater's warning in his Preface to *The Renaissance*: "What is important,
then, is not that the critic should possess a correct abstract definition
of beauty for the intellect, but a certain kind of temperament, the
power of being deeply moved by the presence of beautiful objects"
(xxi). The degree to which the contemplated beauty becomes abstract
may thus provide a clue to the aesthetic astuteness of the poet; if he
follows Pater, he will avoid such apostrophes.

9 Wilde's "Wasted Days," in *Poems*, 244, and Lord Alfred Douglas's
"Rejected" and "Jonquil and Fleur-de-Lys," in *Collected Poems*, 55–57,
39–45, have overtones impossible to dissociate from the poets' sexual
preferences. Further references to Wilde's *Poems* appear in the text.

10 Rossetti, *Works*, 3.

11 Dowson, "Saint-Germain-en-Laye 1887–1895," in his *Poetical Works*,
102. Further references to this work (*PW*) appear in the text.

12 The formal distinction holds, generally, for the other Decadents: consider, for example, the way the form of Wilde's "The Sphinx" attempts a sinuosity and indirection exactly analogous to the spiritual
drama the poet seeks to capture. The speaker of "The Sphinx" is, in
effect, seduced by his Aesthetic visions and introverted to an extreme.
Little of this formal contrivance will be found in the poetry of Rossetti
and Morris; for Swinburne in this context, see below.

13 Peckham, "Aestheticism to Modernism," 225. Further references to
this work appear in the text.

14 Chamberlin, "From High Decadence," 597. Further references to this
work appear in the text.

15 Barzun, *Use and Abuse of Art*, 47.

16 Barzun, *Use and Abuse of Art*, 46.

17 See, for example, Bizot's "Pater and Yeats," Blissett's "Pater and
Eliot," Csengeri's "T.E. Hulme's Borrowings From the French,"
Greene's "Jules Laforgue et T.S. Eliot," Kenner's *The Pound Era*, Ker-
mode's *The Romantic Image*, Meisel's *The Absent Father*. Curiously
enough, analogous articles dealing with various "Modernist" aspects
of the Aesthetes have generally been less successful; see, for example,
Bassett's "The Uncanny Critic of Brasenose," Beckson's and Munro's
"Symons, Browning and the Development of the Modern Aesthetic,"
Dellamora's "Pater's Modernism," Green's "Oscar Wilde's *Intentions*,"
Stanford's "Arthur Symons and Modern Poetics." These studies strain
to find a reverse-chronological influence, in effect, and are unable to
do so convincingly.

### CHAPTER TWO

1 A subject discussed at some length by Peter Stevens in "The Old Futility of Art."
2 The idea that Imagism forms a strong element of modern Canadian
poetry was not a mere idiosyncratic quirk of A.J.M. Smith, who
treated Ross as an Imagist in his *Oxford Book of Canadian Verse* in 1960,
and gave general currency to the idea; ten years later, Philip Gerber's
article on Ross ("The Surface and the Terror") was based on an assumption, not a proof, that "W.W. Eustace Ross [was] the Canadian
Imagist" (46). In 1976 Sandra Djwa argued in her "'A New Soil and a
Sharp Sun'" that "Imagism … returned to Canada variously: through
the *Dial* and *Poetry* (Chicago) to W.W.E. Ross, through Carl Sandburg's Chicago poems to E.J. Pratt, and through the influential modernist anthology *The New Poetry* (1917) to A.J.M. Smith and F.R. Scott"
(7). The assumption was made still more comprehensive by the publication one year later of Bernhard Beutler's *Der Einfluβ des Imagismus
auf die Moderne Kanadische Lyrik Englischer Sprache*, a wide-ranging text
that discusses the influence of Imagism upon such diverse poets as
Knister, Livesay, Dudek, and the TISH poets. In 1980 Don Precosky,
with particular inaccuracy, wrote in his "Ever with Discontent" that
"the imagist influence is obvious" in Knister's poetry (4), that Knister
"took his cue from the imagists"(6), that "the forms of Knister's poetry
were derived from the imagists"(5); this despite the caution of Peter
Stevens, who in 1965 had already questioned the solidity of Knister's
Imagism ("The Old Futility of Art," 45ff.). The few other articles noticing the two poets are brief studies assuming their Imagism and reading their poems as such.
3 Knister, *Windfalls for Cider*, 40. Further references to this work (*WC*)
appear in the text.
4 While it is not the major point at present, note the steady traditional-

ism of both poems. In "Immemorial Plea," a long third line in each stanza troubles the tight balladic structure only enough to draw attention to it; and the only variation from perfect rhyme in both poems is that very Victorian visual rhyme of "kind" or "find" with "wind." To be sure, the traditional form seems a natural choice for the fairly traditional meditations Knister wishes to record; but all this is only to confirm that the thunderstorm and "quiet upland" function traditionally as well, as a glimpse of intensity which initiates poetic reflection.

5 Knister wrote to Miss Frankfurth (11 April 1924) that "March Wind" had pleased him more than anything else he had yet written in verse (Knister Papers, Victoria College Library, Folder 84). It is curious that this should be so, since "March Wind" employs a stanzaic form almost identical to the prototypical Dowson stanza, as in "*Ah, dans ces mornes séjours* ... " (*Poetical Works*, 59):

> You would have understood me, had you waited;
>   I could have loved you, dear! as well as he;
> Had we not been impatient, dear! and fated
>     Always to disagree.

"April Love" and "Venite Descendamus" in Dowson's *Poetical Works* reveal the same stanza, as do a number of his other poems. There is no proof of an influence here, but Knister's formal choices are worth following up if we want to understand his creative development.

6 Stevens, "The Old Futility of Art," 51.

7 Raymond Knister to Miss Frankfurth, 27 March 1925, Raymond Knister Papers, Victoria College Library, Folder 84. Further references to this collection (Vic.) appear in the text.

8 See also *The Collected Poems of Raymond Knister*, ed. Livesay, 3.

9 Baudelaire, *Oeuvres*, 109.

10 Sandburg, *Complete Poems*, 33.

11 Williams, *The Collected Earlier Poems*, 340.

12 The three sonnets included were "The Nimble Fish," "The Pythagorean Basilica," and "On the Supernatural."

13 Ross, *Shapes and Sounds*, 68. Further references to this work (*SS*) appear in the text.

14 This does not, of course, in itself undermine his Imagism; Gage argues that Imagism is in general a subjective poetic disguised as an objective poetic (*In the Arresting Eye: The Rhetoric of Imagism*, 131–63).

15 Compare Pater's analogous statement that "Not to discriminate every moment some passionate attitude in those about us, and in the very brilliancy of their gifts some tragic dividing of forces on their ways, is, on this short day of frost and sun, to sleep before evening" (*The Renaissance*, 189).

16 Ross, *Sonnets*, 30. Further references to this work (*Son.*) appear in the text.

17 Symons, *Collected Works*, 1:149. Further references to this work (*CW*) appear in the text.

18 A useful comparison may be made between this collapsible quality of "Wild Rose" and the painfully ethereal style and structure of Dowson's "Fantaisie Triste" (*Poetical Works*, 192); both poems approach a formal and stylistic over-determination from which they are but narrowly rescued. See chapter 1 for a similar response to Dowson's "Saint-Germain-en-Laye 1887–1895."

19 See Pound's "Status Rerum – The Second," 39–40.

20 Perkins, *A History of Modern Poetry*, 1: 59.

21 Kenner, *The Pound Era*, 180. Further references to this work appear in the text.

22 Gage, *In the Arresting Eye*, 15–17. Further references to this work appear in the text.

23 See Lindberg-Seyersted's *Pound/Ford*, xii–xiii.

24 Pound, "The Book of the Month," *Poetry Review*, March 1912, 133; quoted in Lindberg-Seyersted, *Pound/Ford*, 10.

25 Pound, "Ford Madox Hueffer," quoted in Lindberg-Seyersted, *Pound/Ford*, 13.

26 Levenson, *The Genealogy of Modernism*, 49.

27 Ezra Pound to Ford Madox Ford, 7 Sept. 1920, quoted in Lindberg-Seyersted, *Pound/Ford*, 43.

28 Flint, "Imagisme," 199. The principles were, of course, written down for Flint by Pound; see Perkins, *History of Modern Poetry*, 1: 333.

29 Brown, "Symposium on Literary Impressionism," 55–6.

30 Howarth, "Symposium on Literary Impressionism," 41–2. Further references to this work appear in the text.

31 Kronegger, *Literary Impressionism*, 42.

32 Hueffer [Ford], "On Impressionism," *Poetry and Drama* 2 (June 1914), 169; quoted in Coffman, *Imagism*, 114.

33 Coffman, *Imagism*, 91.

34 Pound, *Selected Poems*, 35.

35 In light of these speculations it is diverting to note that Richard Aldington, one of the two poets to whom "Imagisme" was first announced by Pound, called Pater's *Renaissance* "one of the most civilized books which appeared in England in his lifetime" and warned that "the intellectuals of this century had set out to burlesque Pater's ideas by applying them too literally" (Aldington, ed., *Selected Works of Pater*, 18). The reader of Pater's aesthetic theory "cannot help noticing that Pater is the origin (so far as England is concerned) of aesthetic views which are held to be peculiarly modern" (25).

36 See, for example, Wilde's "In the Gold Room" (*Poems*) and Symons's "At Dieppe II: On the Beach" (*Collected Works*).
37 Knister, "The Poetical Works of Wilfred Campbell," 444–5.
38 Flint, "Imagisme," 199.
39 Givens, "Raymond Knister: Man or Myth?", 9–13.
40 Knister, "Notes for 'Via Faust,'" Raymond Knister Papers, Box 46, Folder 11, Queen's University Archives. Further references to this collection (Queen's) appear in the text.
41 Knister, Introduction to *Canadian Short Stories*, xiv.
42 Knister, "Poetical Works of Wilfred Campbell," 445.
43 Knister, "A Shropshire Lad," 425.
44 Knister, "Katherine Mansfield," 430–1.
45 Knister, "A List of Books Read by J. Raymond Knister from September 1914 to Mid-1924," Raymond Knister Papers, McMaster University Library, Folder 14.
46 W.W.E. Ross to Peter Stevens, quoted in Stevens, "On W.W.E. Ross," 43. Further references to this work appear in the text.
47 The letters of Ross to A.J.M. Smith contain few surprises of this nature. He neither praises Imagism nor seeks to bury it; nor does he speak of E.E. Cummings, Marianne Moore, or Wallace Stevens, perhaps for the simple reason that Smith had been instrumental in promoting the view of Ross as a Canadian Imagist, thereby gaining for him both recognition and a place in the *Book of Canadian Poetry* in 1943.
48 Ross, "On National Poetry," 88.
49 G. Moore, ed., *Pure Poetry*, 7.
50 G. Moore, ed., *Pure Poetry*, 10.
51 Bentley, "Not of Things Only, But of Thought," 39–40.

CHAPTER THREE

1 Knister, "Canadian Letter," 377. Knister attributes this view to a hypothetical "professor," but his sarcasm about those who oppose the professor's judgment, as well as the tenor of his own comments, makes clear that he is in substantial agreement with this view of Canadian poetry.
2 Spender, *The Struggle of the Modern*.
3 I have found Charles Hartman's discussion of *vers liberé* in his *Free Verse: An Essay on Prosody* (113–20) particularly helpful in the development of these ideas.
4 Dudek and Gnarowski, *The Making of Modern Poetry in Canada*, 4.
5 Call, *Acanthus and Wild Grape*, 10–11 (emphasis added). Further references to this work (*AWG*) appear in the text.

6 Dorian "would often spend a whole day settling and resettling in their cases the various stones that he had collected, such as the olive-green chrysoberyl that turns red by lamplight, the cymophane with its wire-like line of silver, the pistachio-coloured peridot, rose-pink and wine-yellow topazes, carbuncles of fiery scarlet with tremulous four-rayed stars, flame-red cinnamon stones, orange and violet spinels, and ame-thysts with their alternate layers of ruby and sapphire. He loved the red gold of the sunstone, and the moonstone's pearly whiteness, and the broken rainbow of the milky opal. He procured from Amsterdam three emeralds of extraordinary size and richness of colour, and had a turquoise *de la vieille roche* that was the envy of all the connoisseurs." Wilde, *The Picture of Dorian Gray*, 217–8.

7 Call, *Sonnets for Youth*, 2. Further references to this work (*SY*) appear in the text.

8 One cannot help noticing another preoccupation of Call's poetry, one which is best quoted rather than described. In "Hidden Treasure" Call refers to a "sun-browned boy" (*Acanthus and Wild Grape*, 31); "Visions I" has "slender shepherd lads" (*Acanthus and Wild Grape*, 67); the "slender" youth of "Wild Swan" feels "the swift-coursing blood/Tinge-ing [his] cheeks" (*Sonnets for Youth*, 2); in "White Hyacinth" the youth bends "a slender form" over a bowl of hyacinths (*Sonnets for Youth*, 2); "Sceptic II" depicts "the white statue of a Grecian boy/Whose body [is] scarce lovelier than your own," that is, than the boy's to whom the poem is addressed (*Sonnets for Youth*, 5); "Immortal," to a dead soldier, includes a reference to his "strong young body" and then eight lines later to his "strong lithe body" (*Sonnets for Youth*, 7). The only conclusion to be drawn from the homo-eroticism of these images is that it is of a kind for which Wilde in his trial would have been condemned. Call's adulthood long preceded society's current toler-ance of such imagery; if we remember that fact, the images add to Call's poems a further quality of Decadent poetry: the fascination with teasing eroticisms not permitted by society, with any kind of "love that dare not speak its name," heterosexual or otherwise.

9 Spettigue, "Frederick Philip Grove," 326.

10 Parts of "The Dirge," together with other Grove poetry, exist in type-script at the Elizabeth Dafoe Library, University of Manitoba, and have been edited and published by Terrence Craig ("Frederick Philip Grove's 'Poems'" and "Frederick Philip Grove's 'The Dirge'"). I will nevertheless quote chiefly from *The Canadian Forum* publication, not by any means to slight the very valuable work of Craig but because the *Forum* material seems to me more coherent, more selective, and more balanced than the typescript. Craig himself acknowledges this frankly, admitting that the "arrangement [in the *Forum*] can be seen as an im-

provement on the tediously long and repetitive typescript arrangement" ("Grove's 'The Dirge,'" 56). I also presume that *The Canadian
Forum* publication met with Grove's approval, even if it is not the result of his own editing, and has fair authorial validity as a result.

11 Spettigue, *FPG*, 100–18.
12 Pacey, ed., *The Letters of Frederick Philip Grove*, 67.
13 Saunders, "A Novelist as Poet," 237.
14 Grove, "From *The Dirge*," 257. Further references to this work ("*FD*")
   appear in the text.
15 Saunders, "A Novelist as Poet," 240.
16 Craig, "Grove's 'Poems,'" 81.
17 Craig, "Grove's 'Poems,'" 65.
18 Quoted in Bradbury and MacFarlane, eds., *Modernism 1890–1930*, 137.
19 Smith, *Book of Canadian Poetry*, 30.
20 Mackay, *The Ill-Tempered Lover*, 2. Further references to this work appear in the text.
21 In Wilde's *Salomé*, of course; but see also Symons's "The Dance of the
   Daughters of Herodias," *Collected Works*, 2:36–40, and his "Studies in
   Strange Sins," *Collected Works*, 2:274–85; as well as Mallarmé's "Les
   Noces d'Hérodiade," *Oeuvres Complètes: Poésies*, 450–73; and the painting by Gustave Moreau, "L'Apparition," in the Louvre.
22 Compare the sentiments expressed in a number of Symons's poems,
   such as "Love's Hatred":

   > I have flung down a plummet in Hate's well:
   > I hate you worse than any words can tell.
   > With every little nerve I hate you so,
   > My body aches with it. (*CW*, 1: 310)

   and "Idealism":

   > I know the woman has no soul, I know
   > The woman has no possibilities
   > Of soul or mind or heart, but merely is
   > The masterpiece of flesh: well, be it so. (*CW*, 1: 207)

   Mackay's venom is typical of the Decadent whose "idealistic" visions
   have been undermined by a reality of rejection.
23 As mentioned in chapter 2 regarding Knister.
24 Poems about works of art constitute a minor genre that has roots in
   the Aesthetic movement; see Prince, "The Iconic Poem and the Aesthetic Tradition."
25 An interesting comparison may be made between F.R. Scott's "Overture" and Mackay's "Mozart," particularly if we relate the degree of
   aesthetic absorption expressed by both poets. Note that Mackay
   wishes to recapture the emotions inspired by the music of Mozart,

whereas Scott wishes to understand Mozart's music in light of the "world crescendo." Scott's poem reflects transition and growth, Mackay's, arrest and regret.

26 Mackay, "Murder Most Foul," 314.
27 Mackay, "Bliss Carman," 182–3.
28 Mackay, "James Gay," 457–8.
29 Tracy, *The Rain It Raineth*, 14. Further references to this work appear in the text.
30 "Ballade Morale," "I Doubt a Lovely Thing Is Dead," and "Prelude IV" are, incidentally, the exception rather than the rule in Tracy's book. Smith has chosen, with presumable deliberation, Tracy's most Aesthetic efforts and ignored his simply Romantic pieces: an interesting glimpse of the anthologist at work.
31 It was not until 1961 that he published again, with *Acis in Oxford and Other Poems* from the University of Toronto Press and *Dover Beach Revisited* from Macmillan. *Silverthorn Bush and Other Poems* appeared in 1966 and was followed by another period of silence; in 1980 a flurry of publication began with *Variations and Theme*, followed by *Has and Is* in 1981, *Twelve for Christmas* in 1982, and his most recent book, *The Grand Duke of Moscow's Favourite Solo*, in 1983.
32 Smith, "Canadian Poetry: A Minority Report," 136–7. Further references to this work ("Canadian Poetry") appear in the text.
33 Smith, "Confessions of a Compulsive Anthologist," 5. Further references to this work ("Confessions") appear in the text.
34 Betjeman, *Collected Poems*, 106.
35 Betjeman, *Collected Poems*, 52.
36 Betjeman, *Summoned by Bells*, 109–10.
37 Sitwell, *Collected Poems*, 9.
38 Compare Symons's description of Decadent style: "an intense self-consciousness, a restless curiosity in research, an over-subtilizing refinement upon refinement" ("The Decadent Movement in Literature," 866–7).
39 Finch, "The Lilac Gatherer," 272.
40 Finch, "Normandy Mantelpiece," 169.
41 Finch, "Headmaster's Drawing Room," 283.
42 Finch, *New Provinces*, 4. Further references to this work (*NP*) appear in the text.
43 Finch, *Poems*, 6–7. Further references to this work appear in the text.
44 Birney, "Poetry of Robert Finch," 7.
45 Daniells, "Earle Birney et Robert Finch," 95. Further references to this work appear in the text.
46 Smith, "Turning New Leaves," 42.
47 Wilde, Preface to *The Picture of Dorian Gray*, ix.
48 Finch, *Acis in Oxford*, 43.

49 Finch, *The Strength of the Hills*, 51.
50 Finch, *The Strength of the Hills*, 97.
51 Latham, "Leo Kennedy," 406.
52 Smith, "Leo Kennedy," 37.
53 Kennedy, *The Shrouding*, 41. Further references to this work (*Shroud.*) appear in the text.
54 Kennedy, "Epitaph for Myself," 185.
55 Edel, Introduction to *The Shrouding*, [xvi].
56 The dead couple in "Epithalamium" is implicitly identified when the speaker refers to "my mother" and "my father"; in "Epithalamium Before Frost" the couple is explicitly identified in the epigraph reading "for J. & E.K."
57 Edel, Introduction to *The Shrouding*, [xiii].
58 Kennedy, "I Being Afflicted," 27.
59 A claim remarked by Stevens, "Leo Kennedy's Poetry," 42; of course such mock-Elizabethan titles as "A Mirror for Lovers" confirm Kennedy's familiarity with the period.
60 Baudelaire, *Oeuvres*, 105–7.
61 Johnson, *Collected Poems*, 79–80.
62 Kennedy, "Time That Wears Granite Thin," 14–15.
63 Kennedy, "The Oldest Song," 10.
64 Kennedy, "Romance," 21.
65 Collin, *The White Savannahs*, 279.
66 Kennedy's section of *The Shrouding* entitled "Outcry Upon the Times" is interesting in this light. Modernist and Decadent assumptions about the culture in which they live are, not surprisingly, almost identical.
67 Kennedy's repudiation of the volume is remarked by Peter Stevens, in "Leo Kennedy's Poetry" (35–6) and by David Latham in "Leo Kennedy" (406).
68 Kennedy, "Archibald Lampman," 303.
69 Morley, "The Young Turks," 68.
70 Kennedy, "Archibald Lampman," 302.
71 Kennedy, "The Future of Canadian Literature," 35.
72 *Old McGill 1925*, 47.
73 Kennedy to Smith, 5 April 1928, A.J.M. Smith Collection, Bata Library, Trent University, MS 80–005, Folder 1(6).

CHAPTER FOUR

1 Skelton, "A Poet of the Middle Slopes," 41.
2 Munro Beattie, "Poetry 1920–1935," in *Literary History of Canada*, gen. ed. Klinck, 2: 244.
3 Djwa, "F.R. Scott: A Canadian in the Twenties," 13. Further references to this work ("Scott: A Canadian") appear in the text.

4 Djwa, Introduction to *On F.R. Scott*, x.

5 Djwa, *Politics of the Imagination*, 62. Further references to this work (*PI*) appear in the text.

6 Edel, "The Young Warrior," 11. Further references to this work ("Warrior") appear in the text.

7 Edel, "When McGill Modernized," 115. Further references to this work ("McGill Modernized") appear in the text.

8 Scott himself acknowledges the debt in "A.J.M. Smith: A Personal Memoir," 12, 16. Further references to this work ("Smith: A Memoir") appear in the text.

9 Edel, *The McGill Fortnightly Review*," 19.

10 Scott, "Song of May and Virtue," 3.

11 Norris, "Beginnings of Canadian Modernism," 58.

12 Scott to Raymond Souster, 30 July 1966.

13 Smith, "F.R. Scott and Some of his Poems," 29.

14 "Tuke" [Scott], "To Beauty," 20.

15 "Tuke" [Scott], "Sonnet [Would I were Angelo, and taking stone ...]," 64.

16 "Tuke" [Scott], "A Miniature," 13.

17 "Tuke" [Scott], "Sonnet [One day you asked me to define delight, ...]," 30.

18 Consider the emotional masochism in Dowson's "Exile" and "A Last Word" (*Poetical Works*), in Symons's "Amoris Victima" (*Collected Works*), in Johnson's "Consolation" and "To Passions" (*Collected Poems*), and in Wilde's "Apologia" (*Poems*).

19 [Scott], "Afterthought," in Collin, *The White Savannahs*, 192.

20 "March" [Scott], "Decadence," 39.

21 J. King Gordon attests to the keenness of his religious inquiries at Oxford in "The Politics of Poetry" (17–18). Scott's own description of his beliefs at the time suggests a fairly devout albeit curious mind ("F.R. Scott: Discussing Oxford Study Group on Christianity," 84).

22 Wayne and Mackinnon, "Quill and Quire Interview: F.R. Scott," 18.

23 Scott, *The Collected Poems of F.R. Scott*, 22. Further references to this work (*CP*) appear in the text.

24 "Tuke" [Scott], "Sonnet (Written on a May Morning)," 11.

25 Wilde, "The Critic as Artist," 355.

26 Green, *Children of the Sun*, 12. Further references to this work appear in the text.

27 Betjeman, *Summoned by Bells*, 94.

28 But see Elizabeth Brewster's "I of the Observer" for an acknowledgment that the poem is at least more complex than it at first appears.

29 Son of William Bridges Scott, the poet's brother, whose name is in *The*

*Canadian Who's Who (1938–39)* (605). In this entry Richard Aird Scott is
listed as William's third son. In *Who's Who in Canada (1945–46),* one
son is said to have been "killed in action" (676). This information,
given Scott's title and the speaker's affection for the boy, makes the
identification a secure one.

30 Compare, along these lines, Scott's "Charity" and Wilde's statement
that "charity degrades and demoralises. Charity creates a multitude of
sins" (*Soul of Man,* 275).

31 Scott, *Selected Poems,* 23.

32 C. Scott, "Symbolism, Decadence, Impressionism," 217.

33 Germaine Warkentin in her excellent article on "Scott's 'Lakeshore'
and its Tradition" has difficulty approving of two lines in the poem;
after the poet's return from his archetypal dive into the depths, he
notes "a secret anguish in our thighs/And mermaids in our memories." Warkentin finds little relevance in the lines; but the "anguish"
of the thighs is obviously sexual, and the reference to "mermaids in
our memories" is surely an allusion to Eliot's "Love Song of J. Alfred
Prufrock": "We have lingered in the chambers of the sea/By sea-girls
wreathed with seaweed red and brown/Till human voices wake us,
and we drown" (*Complete Poems and Plays,* 7). The haunting memory
of "the mermaids singing, each to each" is part of the spiritual burden
that lames Prufrock; thus the allusion in Scott's poem to the imagery
of Eliot is a reinforcement of the tension in "Lakeshore" between the
primeval, secret urgings of our unconscious past and the duties of the
daily world. I suspect that a refusal to recognize Scott's eroticism has
led Warkentin to sublimate the obvious sexuality of the "secret anguish" and to miss the allusion to Eliot; sensitivity to his eroticism
and its sources, on the other hand, strikingly highlights the lines and
their purpose.

34 Scott, "The Canadian Authors Meet," 73.

35 Dudek, "Polar Opposites in Scott's Poetry," 37.

36 Smith, "F.R. Scott and Some of His Poems," 29.

37 Scott, "Modern Poetry," 76–7.

38 Scott, "New Poems for Old," 297.

39 Scott, "New Poems for Old," 298.

40 Wayne and Mackinnon, "Quill and Quire Interview: F.R. Scott," 18.

41 I am grateful to Louis Dudek for this formulation of the problems of
the Decadent thinker.

CHAPTER FIVE

1 Woodcock, "John Glassco," 301. Further references to this work appear in the text.

2 No. 13 (Fall–Winter 1983).

3 Murdoch, "Essential Glassco," 33. Further references to this work appear in the text.

4 Glassco, *Selected Poems*, 63. I quote chiefly, though not exclusively, from this edition, as it is accessible and is Glassco's last compilation of his poetry prior to his death. Further references to this work (*SP*) appear in the text.

5 Sutherland, *John Glassco*, 7. Further references to this work appear in the text.

6 Glassco, *Memoirs of Montparnasse*, 71. Further references to this work (*MM*) appear in the text.

7 Burnett, "John Glassco: Canadian Wordsworth," 2. Further references to this work appear in the text.

8 Wordsworth, *The Prelude*, (1850) 3: 130–5. Further references to this work appear in the text.

9 Wordsworth, *The Poems*, 1: 523.

10 It is difficult not to point out, however, that Wordsworth extends his sentence's syntax by adducing apostrophes, to "Ye brooks," "Ye waves," and "ye groves," thus proving by a cumulative process his vision's (and his own) centrality to the whole of nature; whereas Glassco extends his sentence by thrusting in a mass of confused subordinate material, which so diverts his syntactic intention that he must twice repeat his original subject in a simpler form: "That these green fields ... That all these things ... That they ... ," in order not to lose the sense altogether. Wordsworth's complex sentence ends with the fact of a past relationship between himself and nature; Glassco's with a prayer that such a relationship might come about in the future.

11 Glassco, *A Point of Sky*, 12. Further references to this work (*PS*) appear in the text.

12 Gnarowski, "John Glassco: A Note," 13.

13 Wordsworth, *The Poems*, 1: 523–9.

14 As he does in a letter to Mme de Sade, 20 February 1781, in *The Marquis de Sade: Selected Letters*, 79–80.

15 Glassco, Preface to *The Fatal Woman*, ii.

16 Glassco, "Intimate Journal," 9 October 1935, 47. Further references to this work ("Journal") appear in the text.

17 Edel, "Glassco and His Erotic Muse," 111–12.

18 Leon Edel to John Glassco, 6 October 1969, John Glassco Papers, Public Archives of Canada, vol. 1. Further references to this work (*PAC*) appear in the text.

19 Tausky, "*Memoirs of Montparnasse*," 60. Further references to this work appear in the text.

20 Kokotailo, *John Glassco's Richer World*, 9.

21 Compare Symons on the young writers of *his* time who wanted to be thought of as Symbolists, Decadents, or Impressionists: "These terms, as it happens, have been adopted as the badge of little separate cliques, noisy, brainsick young people who haunt the brasseries of the Boulevard Saint-Michel, and exhaust their ingenuities in theorizing over the works they cannot write" ("The Decadent Movement in Literature," 866).

22 Lauber, "Liberty and the Pursuit of Pleasure," 63.

23 Lauber, "Liberty and the Pursuit of Pleasure," 70.

24 Dudek, "A Decadent in Canada in the 1970s? Yes!", 40.

25 Glassco, "Search," 73.

26 Sutherland, *John Glassco*, 13.

27 Villiers de L'Isle-Adam, *Axel*, 249.

28 Glassco, "The Pit," 32–3. Further references to this work appear in the text.

29 Glassco, *Montreal*, 8. Further references to this work (*Mont.*) appear in the text.

30 And they prefigure, among other things, the sexual initiation of the speaker: the name of "Jeanne Mance," one of Quebec's saintly and heroic ladies (and the name of the street on which the poet lived while composing *Montreal*) is dear to him, "For on that street that bears her blessed name/There stood, when I was young, a stately house/Pre-eminent in the houses of ill-fame/Of our metropolis; there did I lose/My too-long tried virginity. O bliss!/I was fourteen" (12). Noticing the Wordsworthian echoes of the passage (which are somewhat subtler than the allusion to Marvell), Glassco seeks to undercut them quickly: "Jeanne, these are the thoughts that lie too deep for tears." He is thus linked to the sexually liberated Indians, and both are involved in the web of his regretful aesthetics, which have taken Montreal away from him and left it in the hands of builders without any sense of beauty or refinement, making necessary his retreat into the countryside.

31 Glassco's correspondence fills in the details of the encounter: see his letters to Elma von Colmar, 3 and 15 Nov. 1961, in the John Glassco Papers, McGill University Archives, Box 2.

32 These references to inheritances from fathers have, by the intimations of the journals, direct relevance to Glassco's personal situation. The *Memoirs'* young narrator is constantly temporizing with the demands of his father, maintaining a sweet face and taking as much as he can get; in the journals Glassco refers frequently to money worries that can only be overcome by the injection of parental funds, which will not be forthcoming without certain binding conditions attached. Glassco's distaste for these proceedings is evident and adds another dimension to the reading of "The Entailed Farm."

33 Glassco to Elma von Colmar, 4 August 1956. "The Entailed Farm," for instance, is "Julia Wheeler's place." John Glassco Papers, McGill University Archives, Box 1.

34 Glassco, "Intimate Journal." A note to this effect in Glassco's handwriting is inserted between pages 107 and 108, pages that link the decay of "Deserted Buildings Under Shefford Mountain" with the sense of decay in his own life, recorded on 4 April 1946 (119) and quoted below in another context.

35 Marvell, *The Complete Poems*, 101.

36 Glassco, "When We Are Very Old," 258.

37 Glassco, *The Deficit Made Flesh*, 17.

38 Glassco, *The Deficit Made Flesh*, 57.

39 Glassco, "The Wild Plum," 108.

40 Glassco, "The Heavenly Boy," 88

41 Moers, *The Dandy*, 29–31.

## CHAPTER SIX

1 Wilson, "Second and Third Thoughts," 11. Further references to this work appear in the text.

2 MacLaren, "The Yeatsian Presence," 64.

3 Djwa, "Of Metaphysics and Dry Bones," 29.

4 Sutherland, "Mr Smith and the Tradition," 10.

5 Sutherland, "The Great Equestrians," 115.

6 See, for a recent example of such well-meaning myth-making, Morley, "The Young Turks: A Biographer's Comment."

7 Edel, *"The McGill Fortnightly Review,"* 19.

8 Edel, "When McGill Modernized," 116. Further references to this work ("McGill Modernized") appear in the text. Edel, "The Young Warrior," 12.

9 Smith, *Poems New and Collected*, 50. Further references to this work (*PNC*) appear in the text.

10 Smith, "The Lonely Land," 30.

11 Smith, "Something Apart," 23. Note that the echo of Yeats ("winding stair"), which Smith used in three different poems, does not appear in this version from 1926. As he was only writing his Master's thesis on Yeats in 1926, and would not have fully absorbed his influence as yet, the change is significant of Smith's ways of learning from other poets. The three poems employing the echo are "The Two Birds," "Song: *made in lieu of many ornaments*," and "To Henry Vaughan," all in *Poems New and Collected*.

12 Smith, "Twilight," 45.

13 Smith, "Homage to E.S.," 34.

14 Smith, "Not of the Dust," 3.

15 Smith, "Epitaph," 30.
16 Smith, "A Poem [Take in your long arms …]," 78.
17 Smith, "The Woman in the Samovar," 15.
18 Smith, "Poem [Let us invert the world, and laugh …]," 23.
19 Sitwell, *Aspects of Modern Poetry*, 34.
20 "Starr" [Smith], "Pastorale," 73.
21 "S." [Smith], "Theolog at the Symphony," 2.
22 "S." [Smith], "Panic," 36.
23 Smith, "Testament," 56.
24 "Starr" [Smith], "Here Lies an Honest Man," 42.
25 Smith, "Chiaroscuro," 57.
26 "Gard" [Smith], "Poem [When I was arrested for drunkenness …]," 47.
27 Smith, "The Moment and the Lamp," 15.
28 Smith, "For Ever and Ever, Amen," 23.
29 Yeats, *Collected Poems*, 123.
30 "Starr" [Smith], "The Cry of a Wandering Gull," 12.
31 Smith, "Leda," 7.
32 "S." [Smith], "Silver Birch," 51.
33 "S." [Smith], "Proud Parable," 65.
34 "Starr" [Smith], "Save in Frenzy," 58.
35 Smith, "Two Epitaphs [ii. Say not of this lady …]," 79.
36 "Starr" [Smith], "To Evening," 73.
37 Smith, "Contemporary Poetry," 31. Further references to this work appear in the text.
38 Smith, "Confessions of a Compulsive Anthologist," 4; Heenan, "Interview with A.J.M. Smith," 74.
39 Smith, "Symbolism in Poetry," 11. Further references to this work ("Symbolism") appear in the text.
40 Symons, *Symbolist Movement in Literature*, 214–7.
41 Edel, "*The McGill Fortnightly Review*," 22.
42 "Vespasiano" [Coulborn], "To My Counterblasters," 30.
43 "Vespasiano" [Coulborn], "Sentimentalism in Education," 13.
44 "Vespasiano" [Coulborn], "What Is Art?", 2.
45 A. Edel, "Decadence," 78.
46 A. Edel, "Decadence," 77.
47 A. Edel, "What Is Art?", 43.
48 Wilde, "The Decay of Lying," 301. Further references to this work ("Decay") appear in the text.
49 "Juvenis" [pseud.], "The Quest," 38. Further references to this work ("Quest") appear in the text.
50 "Juvenis," Epilogue to "The Quest," 44.
51 Glassco, "Search," 73.

52  Edel, "Note on the Cambridge-McGill Debate," 23.

53  Herkelots, "On Having a Shoe Shine," 21.

54  Scott, "Gertrude Stein Has Tea at the Union," 62.

55  Edel, "The 'I' in A.J.M. Smith," 86. Further references to this work ("The 'I'") appear in the text.

56  Edel, "The Worldly Muse of A.J.M. Smith," 201. Further references to this work ("Worldly Muse") appear in the text.

57  Edel, Introduction to *The Shrouding*, [xiii].

58  Allan Latham to A.J.M. Smith, 9 November 1927, A.J.M. Smith Collection, Bata Library, Trent University, MS 80–005, Folder 1(4). Further references to this collection (Smith Collection, Trent) appear in the text.

59  "Max" [Smith], "The Wave," 4.

60  Smith, "Hellenica," 1.

61  "S." [Smith], "Vain Comfort," 1.

62  "Starr" [Smith] and M'Ing, "Chinoiserie," 3.

63  "Max" [Smith], "Poplar Leaves," 1.

64  Eliot, *Selected Essays*, 14.

65  "Starr" [Smith], "Nocturne," 1.

66  "Starr" [Smith], "Interior," 1.

67  Heenan, "Interview with Smith," 74.

68  Although this statement runs counter to the standard version of Canadian Modernist pre-history, that standard is itself rather more obscure than it may initially appear. As evidence of this note the varying accounts of Smith's first encounter with Harriet Monroe's anthology *The New Poetry*, in which he first read the moderns. In "Confessions of a Compulsive Anthologist" Smith places the encounter in 1920, by claiming that he published his first imitations of the moderns "four years later in the *Literary Supplement* to the *McGill Daily*" (4); in his annotations to Sandra Djwa's article, "Of Metaphysics and Dry Bones," he says that he was reading "Monroe and Henderson in the Westmount Library while still in high school in 1921" (Smith Collection, Trent, MS 81–019, Box 1, Folder 12); he repeats this date in the interview with Heenan, but later corrects himself and says, "I probably got it [the anthology] in 1922" (74). Scott on the other hand says that Smith came across *The New Poetry* at the age of twenty-two, which would be in 1924 or 1925 ("Smith: A Memoir," 80). The edition of *The New Poetry* quoted in Smith's Master's thesis was issued in 1923, which may suggest that he read it no earlier than that year. To show how unreliable all this information is, I refer the reader to Edel, who claims that Smith read Eliot's *The Waste Land* at the age of eighteen – at least a year before the poem was published ("The 'I,'" 88). It may seem petty to split hairs about the

338 Notes to pages 267–80

exact date, but, if Smith read *The New Poetry* as early as he said he did, we can argue that it had no appreciable influence on his poetry for three to five years. Judging by the development of his poetry from the *Daily* to the *Literary Supplement* to the *Fortnightly*, Scott's date is the most accurate; but acknowledgement of this date would have forced Smith to recognize and speak about his first four years of poetry: material he evidently had no desire to acknowledge at all.

69 [Smith], "The Quest for Beauty," 2.

70 "A.J.M.S." [Smith], "Another Belle Dame sans Merci," 4.

71 MacDonald, "Lately at Evening," 4.

72 "S." [Smith], "To an Olde Tune," 3.

73 "S." [Smith], "When Thought of Her," 3.

74 [Smith], "Conditional Mood," 30. The *Daily's* version contains an anomaly: the sonnet's fourteenth line is printed as "for ecstask [*sic*] with that song would," and it has a fifteenth: "For ecstasy with that song would." At first dismaying, the typographical error in the *Daily* is not too difficult a puzzle. "Conditional Mood" is obviously a Shakespearean sonnet gone wrong, as the rhyme scheme of the first twelve lines suggests. This leaves us three stray lines and, as we need only two to complete the sonnet, we may assume that the fifteenth line is merely an accidental repetition of the fourteenth and therefore strike it off. This leaves a standard concluding couplet meant, presumably, to rhyme *gg* and complete the form. By scanning "for ecstas[y] with that song would" we conclude that another foot is needed to complete the line's iambic pentameter, so we want either one word or two, something to rhyme with "air" and fit the sense of the poem. Since the last five lines (from "I'd raise Utopia" onward) set up a contrast between the poet's song and the music of "bird," "chime," "earth or air," the only likely word for the blank space is, it would seem, "compare." Thus the music of earth or air would not, the poet claims, compare "for ecstasy" with the song he would write. The poem, by all apparent evidence, was meant to conclude: " … so joyous, free,/And musical in song that bird nor chime/Nor any music or of earth or air/For ecstasy with that song would compare." My gratitude to Louis Dudek for his help with this textual re-creation.

75 "S." [Smith], "Beauty Dead," 3.

76 "S." [Smith], "Humouresque," 3.

77 "T.F." [Smith], "At a Fireside," 3.

78 "S." [Smith], "In the City," 3.

79 Smith, "The Poetry of W.B. Yeats," 3.

80 Rossetti, *Works*, 100.

81 There was another "A. Smith" registered at McGill during 1922, according to the calendar for that year; but as he was in Applied Phys-

ics, and as Smith quoted from Squire's *Essays on Poetry* in his thesis on Yeats, it seems safe to assume that he was the borrower of the volume.

82 Smith, "The Poetry of W.B. Yeats," 51. Further references to this work (*Yeats*) appear in the text.

83 This Aesthetic critical taste is substantiated in the thesis when Smith moves on to the later, less abstract, more modern poetry of *The Wild Swans at Coole* and *Michael Robartes and the Dancer* (1919 and 1921). This poetry, admits the young scholar, is "extremely difficult" even after long study (79), especially, we may add, to a young man attracted to the "flame of rapture" in Yeats. Smith clarifies his opinions when he admits that "in concluding what I feel to be a rather unenthusiastic account of this later work, I would like to speak of the very special quality of their beauty" (99). This beauty, it is obvious, justifies the poems somewhat in Smith's eyes. His rendering of Yeats's development is interesting to us as a revelation of Smith's own tastes, which correspond quite naturally to the Aesthetic poetry he was writing at the time of his thesis research.

84 Smith, "A Poet Young and Old," 255.

85 This shift, unnatural in print, may be due to the fact that "Contemporary Poetry" was originally an address given at McGill on 2 December 1926. See Burke, "A.J.M. Smith," 306–7.

86 See Morley, "The Young Turks," 69; Burke, ed., "Some Annotated Letters of Smith and Knister," 104; and Norris, "The Beginnings of Canadian Modernism," 60–1.

87 Smith, "Canadian Poetry: A Minority Report," 137. Further references to this work ("Canadian Poetry") appear in the text.

88 Smith, "Introduction" to *The Oxford Book of Canadian Verse*, xxxviii. Further references to this work (Introduction) appear in the text.

89 Smith, Introduction to *The Book of Canadian Poetry*, 25.

90 Smith, Introduction to *The Book of Canadian Poetry*, 25.

91 Smith, "Wanted – Canadian Criticism," 600–1.

92 Smith, "Wanted – Canadian Criticism," 601.

93 Smith, "Rejected Preface," 7. Further references to this work appear in the text.

94 That Smith's doctrine of impersonality is inspired by Eliot in no way contradicts the idea that his spirit of detachment is essentially Aesthetic; even ignoring the degree to which Eliot's "impersonality" was an Aesthetic concept, we should recognize that his early Aesthetic leanings must have primed Smith for the reception of Eliot.

95 Smith, "Refining Fire," 354.

96 Smith, "A Little Death to Laugh About," *The Centennial Review* 15 (1971): 426–7.

97 Leon Edel to A.J.M. Smith, 12 Feb. 1961, A.J.M. Smith Papers, Thomas Fisher Rare Book Library, University of Toronto, Box 1.
98 Smith, "Refining Fire," 353.
99 Eliot, *Selected Essays*, 287.
100 See, for example, Wilde's preference of man's art to Nature's in "The Critic as Artist," 379–80; and Symons's passionate defence of make-up (and hence of artifice in general, his real point) in his "Preface: Being a Word on Behalf of Patchouli" and "Maquillage," *Collected Works*, 1: 95–7, 107.
101 Smith, "Self Review," 26. Further references to this work appear in the text.
102 I do not say so lightly, recognizing the vehemence of Smith's utter rejection of any sense of "impersonality" in the phrase he had coined. For an expansion of the point I must refer the reader to my "A.J.M. Smith: The Poetry of Eclectic Detachment," 115–21.
103 Compare his roughly contemporary comment in a letter to Raymond Knister, 12 Feb. 1927: "For myself, I am trying to write poetry, which is quickly becoming more subjective and more obscure" (Burke, ed., "Some Annotated Letters of Smith and Knister," 116).
104 Wilde, "Soul of Man," 270.
105 Mandel, "Masks of Criticism," 17.
106 Woodcock, "Two Aspects of A.J.M. Smith," 112.
107 See, for example, Dorothy Livesay's "Review of *News of the Phoenix and Other Poems*," and Pádraig Ó Broin's "After Strange Gods"; in a wider sense all the social realists of the 1940s, not Sutherland alone, presented a massive affront to the Aesthetic sensibility.

CHAPTER SEVEN

1 Bentley, "A New Dimension," 2.
2 See Ross, "'A Strange Aesthetic Ferment,'" and Stephenson, "The Bitter Sweet Rose."
3 Latham, "Charles Sangster," 727; see also Bentley's "Through Endless Landscapes," 17–18.
4 Cary, *Abram's Plains*, 2.
5 Bentley, Introd., in *Abram's Plains*, ed. Bentley, xxiii.
6 Ware, "Longmore's *Charivari*," 17–20 passim.
7 Duffy, "John Richardson," 703.
8 Klinck, "Literary Activity in the Canadas 1812–1841," in *Literary History of Canada*, 1: 144.
9 Cogswell, "Literary Activity in the Maritime Provinces 1815–1880," in *Literary History of Canada*, 1: 136.

10 Ower, "Crawford and 'The Fleshly School of Poetry,'" 275–81 passim.
11 Djwa, *Politics of the Imagination*, 91; Edel, "The Young Warrior," 14; Shore, "'Overtures of an Era Being Born,'" 34.
12 Perkins, *History of Modern Poetry*, 1: 100–1.
13 Wayne and Mackinnon, "Quill and Quire Interview: F.R. Scott," 18.
14 Scott, Preface to *Poems of French Canada*, ii.
15 Bradbury, *The Social Context of Modern English Literature*, 73.
16 Hermeren, *Influence in Art and Literature*, 321.

# Bibliography

PRIMARY SOURCES

*Call, Frank Oliver*
POETRY AND PROSE
– *Acanthus and Wild Grape*. Toronto: McClelland and Stewart 1920.
– *Sonnets for Youth*. Toronto: Ryerson 1944.

*Finch, Robert*
POETRY AND PROSE
– *Acis in Oxford and Other Poems*. Toronto: University of Toronto Press 1961.
– *Dover Beach Revisited*. Toronto: Macmillan 1961.
– *The Grand Duke of Moscow's Favourite Solo*. Erin, Ont.: Porcupine's Quill 1983.
– *Has and Is*. Erin, Ont.: Porcupine's Quill 1981.
– "Headmaster's Drawing Room." *The Canadian Forum* 10 (May 1930): 283.
– "The Lilac Gatherer." *The Canadian Forum* 5 (June 1925): 272.
– *New Provinces: Poems of Several Authors*. Ed. F.R. Scott. Toronto: Macmillan 1936: 1–12.
– "Normandy Mantelpiece." *The Canadian Forum* 10 (Feb. 1930): 169.
– *Poems*. Toronto: Oxford University Press 1946.
– *Silverthorn Bush and Other Poems*. Toronto: Macmillan 1966.
– *The Strength of the Hills*. Toronto: McClelland and Stewart 1948.
– *Twelve for Christmas*. Erin, Ont.: Porcupine's Quill 1982.
– *Variations and Theme*. Erin, Ont.: Porcupine's Quill 1980.

*Glassco, John*
POETRY AND PROSE
– *The Deficit Made Flesh*. Toronto: McClelland and Stewart 1958.

- "Extract from an Autobiography." *This Quarter* 4 (Spring 1929): 198–210.
- *The Fatal Woman: Three Tales.* Toronto: House of Anansi 1974.
- "The Heavenly Boy." *Saturday Night*, Dec. 1980: 88.
- *Memoirs of Montparnasse.* Toronto: Oxford University Press 1970.
- *Montreal.* Montreal: DC Books 1973.
- "The Pit." *The Tamarack Review* 62 (1974): 31–4.
- *A Point of Sky.* Toronto: Oxford University Press 1964.
- "Search." *McGill Fortnightly Review*, 22 March 1926, 73.
- *Selected Poems.* Toronto: Oxford University Press 1971.
- and Aubrey Beardsley. *Under The Hill.* New York: Saint Martin's 1974.
- "When We Are Very Old." *Queen's Quarterly* 82 (1975): 258.
- "The Wild Plum: An Entertainment for Radio." *The Canadian Forum* 40 (Aug. 1960): 108–9.

ARCHIVAL MATERIAL
- John Glassco Papers. Department of Rare Books and Special Collections, Maclennan Library, McGill University, Montreal.
- John Glassco Papers. Public Archives of Canada, Ottawa.
- "Intimate Journal 1934–1961." In the John Glassco Papers, Department of Rare Books and Special Collections, Maclennan Library, McGill University, Montreal.

*Grove, Frederick Philip*
POETRY AND PROSE
- "Frederick Philip Grove's 'The Dirge.'" Ed. Terrence Craig. *Canadian Poetry: Studies, Documents, Reviews* 16 (Spring–Summer 1985): 55–73.
- "Frederick Philip Grove's 'Poems.'" Ed. Terrence Craig. *Canadian Poetry: Studies, Documents, Reviews* 10 (Spring–Summer 1982): 58–90.
- "From *The Dirge*." *The Canadian Forum* 12 (April 1932): 257–61.

*Kennedy, Leo*
POETRY AND PROSE
- "Epitaph for Myself." *The Canadian Forum* 13 (Feb. 1933): 185.
- "I Being Afflicted." *The Canadian Forum* 14 (Oct. 1933): 27.
- *New Provinces: Poems of Several Authors.* Ed. F.R. Scott. Toronto: Macmillan 1936: 15–25.
- "The Oldest Song." *McGill Fortnightly Review*, 17 Nov. 1926, 10.
- "Romance." *McGill Fortnightly Review*, 1 Dec. 1926, 21.
- *The Shrouding.* 1933; reprinted Ottawa: Golden Dog 1975.
- "Song." *McGill Fortnightly Review*, 3 Nov. 1926, 6.
- "Time That Wears Granite Thin." *Poetry* [Chicago] 58, 1 (April 1941): 14–15.

CRITICISM
- "Archibald Lampman." *The Canadian Forum* 13 (May 1933): 301–3.
- "The Future of Canadian Literature." *Canadian Mercury*, Dec. 1928; reprinted in *The Making of Modern Poetry in Canada: Essential Articles on Contemporary Canadian Poetry in English*. Ed. Louis Dudek and Michael Gnarowski. Toronto: Ryerson 1970: 34–7.
- "*The Shrouding* Revisited." In *The Shrouding*. Ottawa: Golden Dog 1975: [xvii].
- "Raymond Knister." *The Canadian Forum* 12 (Sept. 1932): 459–61.

## Knister, Raymond

POETRY AND PROSE
- *Collected Poems of Raymond Knister*. Ed. Dorothy Livesay. Toronto: Ryerson 1949.
- *The First Day of Spring: Stories and Other Prose by Raymond Knister*. Ed. Peter Stevens. Toronto: University of Toronto Press 1976.
- *My Star Predominant*. Toronto: Ryerson 1934.
- *Windfalls for Cider: The Poems of Raymond Knister*. Ed. Joy Kuropatwa. Windsor, Ont.: Black Moss 1983.

CRITICISM
- "Canadian Letter." In *The First Day of Spring: Stories and Other Prose by Raymond Knister*. Ed. Peter Stevens. Toronto: University of Toronto Press 1976: 377–82.
- Introduction to *Canadian Short Stories*. Ed. Raymond Knister. Toronto: Macmillan 1928: xi-xix.
- "Katherine Mansfield." In *The First Day of Spring: Stories and Other Prose by Raymond Knister*. Ed. Peter Stevens. Toronto: University of Toronto Press 1976: 427–35.
- "The Poetic Muse in Canada." *Saturday Night*, 6 Oct. 1928, 3, 22.
- "The Poetical Works of Francis Thompson." *The New Outlook*, 15 Dec. 1926, 4.
- "The Poetical Works of Wilfred Campbell." *Queen's Quarterly* 31 (1924): 435–49.
- "The Poetry of Archibald Lampman." *Dalhousie Review* 7 (1927): 348–61.
- "A Shropshire Lad." In *The First Day of Spring: Stories and Other Prose by Raymond Knister*. Ed. Peter Stevens. Toronto: University of Toronto Press 1976: 419–27.
- "The Uses of Poetry." *The New Outlook*, 5 Jan. 1927, 15.

ARCHIVAL MATERIAL
- Raymond Knister Papers. Queen's University Archives, Kingston.
- Raymond Knister Papers. Victoria College Library, Toronto.

– Raymond Knister Papers. William Ready Division of Archives and Research Collections, Mills Memorial Library, McMaster University, Hamilton.

## Mackay, Louis
POETRY AND PROSE
– *The Ill-Tempered Lover and Other Poems*. Toronto: Macmillan 1948.
– "Murder Most Foul." *The Canadian Forum* 17 (Dec. 1937): 314.
– [John Smalacombe]. *Viper's Bugloss*. Toronto: Ryerson 1938.

CRITICISM
– "Bliss Carman." *The Canadian Forum* 12 (Feb. 1933): 182–3.
– "James Gay." *The Canadian Forum* 13 (Sept. 1933): 457–8.

## Ross, William Wrightson Eustace
POETRY AND PROSE
– *Experiment 1923–29*. Toronto: Contact 1956.
– *Laconics*. Ottawa: Overbrook 1930.
– *Shapes and Sounds*. Ed. Raymond Souster and John Robert Colombo. Don Mills, Ont.: Longmans 1968.
– *Sonnets*. Toronto: Heaton 1932.

CRITICISM
– "On National Poetry." *The Canadian Forum* 24 (July 1944): 88.

## Scott, Francis Reginald
POETRY AND PROSE
– "Afterthought." In *The White Savannahs*. By W.E. Collin. Toronto: Macmillan 1936: 192.
– "The Canadian Authors Meet." *McGill Fortnightly Review*, 27 April 1927, 73.
– *Collected Poems*. Toronto: McClelland and Stewart 1981.
– [Bernard March]. "Decadence." *McGill Fortnightly Review*, 2 Feb. 1927, 39.
– "Gertrude Stein Has Tea at the Union." *McGill Fortnightly Review*, 25 March 1927, 62.
– [Brian Tuke]. "A Miniature." *McGill Fortnightly Review*, 5 Dec. 1925, 13.
– *New Provinces: Poems of Several Authors*. Ed. F.R. Scott. Toronto: Macmillan 1936: 51–61.
– *Selected Poems*. Toronto: Oxford University Press 1966.
– "Song of May and Virtue." *McGill Daily Literary Supplement*, 11 March 1925, 4.
– [T.T.] "Sonnet (on reading the results of the examinations)." *McGill Fortnightly Review*, 23 Jan. 1926, 43.
– [Brian Tuke]. "Sonnet [One day you asked me to define delight, ...]." *McGill Fortnightly Review*, 9 Jan. 1926, 30.

- [Brian Tuke]. "Sonnet [Would I Were Angelo, and taking stone ...]." *McGill Fortnightly Review*, 6 March 1926, 64.
- "Sonnet (Written on a May Morning)." *McGill Fortnightly Review*, 17 Nov. 1926, 11.
- "Sweeney Comes to McGill." *McGill Fortnightly Review*, 3 Nov. 1926, 4.
- [Brian Tuke]. "To Beauty." *McGill Fortnightly Review*, 19 Dec. 1925, 20.

CRITICISM
- "A.J.M. Smith." In *Leading Canadian Poets*. Ed. W.P. Percival. Toronto: Ryerson 1948: 234–44.
- "A.J.M. Smith: A Personal Memoir." *Canadian Poetry: Studies, Documents, Reviews* 11 (Fall–Winter 1982): 78–85.
- "F.R. Scott: Discussing Oxford Study Group on Christianity and Social Problems." *Canadian Poetry: Studies, Documents, Reviews* 4 (Spring–Summer 1979): 83–93.
- "Modern Poetry." *Canadian Poetry: Studies, Documents, Reviews* 4 (Spring–Summer 1979): 74–83.
- "New Poems for Old – I. The Decline of Poesy." *The Canadian Forum* 11 (May 1931): 296–8.
- Preface. In *New Provinces: Poems of Several Authors*. Ed. F.R. Scott. Toronto: Macmillan 1936: v.
- Preface. In *Poems of French Canada*. Trans. F.R. Scott. Ottawa: Blackfish 1977: i–vi.

ARCHIVAL MATERIAL
- Letter to Raymond Souster. 30 July 1966. Raymond Souster Papers. Thomas Fisher Rare Book Library, University of Toronto, Toronto. Box 6.


*Smith, Arthur James Marshall*
POETRY AND PROSE
- [T.F.] "At a Fireside." *McGill Daily*, 5 Dec. 1923, 3.
- [S.] "Beauty Dead." *McGill Daily*, 13 Dec. 1922, 3.
- [S.] "The Bird." *McGill Fortnightly Review*, 22 March 1926, 75.
- "Chiaroscuro." *McGill Fortnightly Review*, 20 Feb. 1926, 57.
- [Vincent Starr] and R.S. M'Ing [?]. "Chinoiserie." *McGill Daily Literary Supplement*, 4 March 1925, 3.
- [Anon.] "Conditional Mood." *McGill Daily*, 10 Jan. 1923, 3.
- [Vincent Starr]. "The Cry of a Wandering Gull." *McGill Fortnightly Review*, 5 Dec. 1925, 12.
- "Epitaph." *McGill Fortnightly Review*, 9 Jan. 1926, 30.
- [Tom Fool]. "Epithalamium." *McGill Daily*, 25 March 1924, 3.
- "For Ever and Ever, Amen." *McGill Fortnightly Review*, 1 Dec. 1926, 23.
- "Hellenica." *McGill Daily Literary Supplement*, 19 Nov. 1924, 1.

- [Vincent Starr]. "Here Lies an Honest Man." *McGill Fortnightly Review*, 23 Jan. 1926, 42.
- "Homage to E.S." *McGill Fortnightly Review*, 2 Feb. 1927, 34.
- [S.] "Humouresque." *McGill Daily*, 21 March 1923, 3.
- [Tom Fool]. "A Hymn of Hate." *McGill Daily*, 12 Dec. 1923, 3.
- [Vincent Starr]. "Interior." *McGill Daily Literary Supplement*, 21 Jan. 1925, 1.
- [S.] "In the City." *McGill Daily*, 21 March 1923, 3.
- [Damfull]. "Kindness to Animals." *McGill Daily*, 23 Jan. 1924, 3.
- "Leda." *McGill Fortnightly Review*, 3 Nov. 1926, 7.
- [Vincent Starr]. "Legend." *McGill Fortnightly Review*, 6 March 1926, 65.
- "A Little Death to Laugh About." *Centennial Review* 15 (1971): 426–7.
- "The Lonely Land: Group of Seven." *McGill Fortnightly Review*, 9 Jan. 1926, 30.
- "The Moment and the Lamp." *McGill Fortnightly Review*, 17 Nov. 1926, 15.
- *New Provinces: Poems of Several Authors*. Ed. F.R. Scott. Toronto: Macmillan 1936: 65–77.
- [Vincent Starr]. "Nocturne." *McGill Daily Literary Supplement*, 21 Jan. 1925, 1.
- "Not of the Dust." *McGill Fortnightly Review*, 21 Nov. 1925, 3.
- [S.] "Panic." *McGill Fortnightly Review*, 2 Feb. 1927, 36.
- [Vincent Starr]. "Pastorale." *McGill Fortnightly Review*, 22 March 1926, 73.
- "A Poem [Take in your long arms …]." *McGill Fortnightly Review*, 22 March 1926, 78.
- "Poem [Let us invert the world …]." *McGill Fortnightly Review*, 19 Dec. 1925, 23.
- [Michel Gard]. "Poem [When I was arrested …]." *McGill Fortnightly Review*, 18 Feb. 1927, 47.
- *Poems New and Collected*. Toronto: Oxford University Press 1967.
- [Max]. "Poplar Leaves." *McGill Daily Literary Supplement*, 15 Oct. 1924, 1.
- [S.] "Proud Parable." *McGill Fortnightly Review*, 6 March 1926, 65.
- [Michael Gard]. "Punchinello in a Purple Hat." *McGill Fortnightly Review*, 23 Jan. 1926, 42; reprinted ("Varia 1") in *McGill Fortnightly Review*, 25 March 1927, 62.
- [Anon.] "The Quest for Beauty." *McGill Daily Literary Supplement*, 22 Oct. 1924, 2.
- [S.] "Quiet Haven." *McGill Daily*, 21 Feb. 1923, 3.
- [Vincent Starr]. "Save in Frenzy." *McGill Fortnightly Review*, 20 Feb. 1926, 58.
- [S.] "Silver Birch." *McGill Fortnightly Review*, 6 Feb. 1926, 51.
- "Something Apart." *McGill Fortnightly Review*, 1 Dec. 1926, 23.
- "Testament." *McGill Fortnightly Review*, 10 March 1927, 56.
- [S.] "Theolog at the Symphony." *McGill Fortnightly Review*, 3 Nov. 1926, 2.
- [S.] "To An Olde Tune." *McGill Daily*, 6 Dec. 1922, 3.

- [Vincent Starr]. "To Evening." *McGill Fortnightly Review*, 27 April 1927, 73.
- "Twilight." *McGill Fortnightly Review*, 18 Feb. 1927, 45.
- "Two Epitaphs [I. Under this grassy mound ...] [II. Say not of this lady ...]." *McGill Fortnightly Review*, 27 April 1927, 79.
- [S.] "Vain Comfort." *McGill Daily Literary Supplement*, 28 Jan. 1925, 1.
- [Max]. "The Wave." *McGill Daily Literary Supplement*, 8 Oct. 1924, 4.
- [Vincent Starr]. "What Strange Enchantment." *McGill Fortnightly Review*, 21 Nov. 1925, 7.
- [S.] "When Thought of Her." *McGill Daily*, 31 Jan. 1923, 3.
- [Michael Gard]. "The Woman in the Samovar." *McGill Fortnightly Review*, 5 Dec. 1925, 15.
- [Tom Fool]. "Ye Epicure Wisheth for Himself a Merrie Yuletide." *McGill Daily*, 20 Dec. 1923, 6.

CRITICISM
- "Another Belle Dame sans Merci." Rev. of *The Green Hat*, by Michael Arlen. *McGill Daily Literary Supplement*, 28 Jan. 1925, 4.
- , ed. *The Book of Canadian Poetry: A Critical and Historical Anthology*. Chicago: University of Chicago Press 1943.
- "Canadian Poetry: A Minority Report." *University of Toronto Quarterly* 8 (1939): 125–38.
- "Confessions of a Compulsive Anthologist." *Journal of Canadian Studies* 11 (May 1976): 4–14.
- "Contemporary Poetry." *McGill Fortnightly Review*, 15 Dec. 1926, 31–2.
- "Eclectic Detachment: Aspects of Identity in Canadian Poetry." *Canadian Literature* 9 (Summer 1961): 6–14.
- "F.R. Scott and Some of His Poems." *Canadian Literature* 31 (Winter 1967): 25–35.
- "Hamlet in Modern Dress." *McGill Fortnightly Review*, 3 Nov. 1926, 2–4.
- "Leo Kennedy." *Canadian Review of Music and Art* 3, nos. 3–4 (April–May 1944): 37.
- *On Poetry and Poets: Selected Essays of A.J.M. Smith*. Toronto: McClelland and Stewart 1977.
- , ed. *The Oxford Book of Canadian Verse: In English and French*. Toronto: Oxford University Press 1960.
- "A Poet Young and Old: William Butler Yeats." *University of Toronto Quarterly* 8 (1939): 255–63.
- "The Poetry of W.B. Yeats." M.A. Thesis McGill 1926.
- "The Poetry of W.B. Yeats." *McGill Daily*, 21 Nov. 1923, 3.
- "Refining Fire: The Meaning and Use of Poetry." *Queen's Quarterly* 61 (1954): 353–64.
- "A Rejected Preface." *Canadian Literature* 24 (Spring 1965): 6–9.

- "A Self Review." *Canadian Literature* 15 (Winter 1963): 20–26.
- "Symbolism in Poetry." *McGill Fortnightly Review*, 5 Dec. 1925: 11–12, 16.
- "Turning New Leaves." *The Canadian Forum* 27 (May 1947): 42–3.
- "Wanted – Canadian Criticism." *The Canadian Forum* 8 (Apr. 1928) 600–01.

ARCHIVAL MATERIALS
- A.J.M. Smith Papers. Thomas Fisher Rare Book Library, University of Toronto, Toronto.
- A.J.M. Smith Papers. Trent University Archives, Peterborough.

*Tracy, Neil*
POETRY AND PROSE
- *Collected Poems*. Ottawa: Borealis 1975.
- *The Rain It Raineth*. Sherbrooke: Tribune 1938.


SECONDARY SOURCES

Adams, Robert Martin. "What Modernism Was." *Hudson Review* 31 (1979–80): 19–33.
Aldington, Richard, ed. *The Religion of Beauty: Selections from the Aesthetes*. London: Heinemann 1950.
- ed. *Selected Works of Walter Pater*. London: Heinemann 1948.
Balakian, Anna. "Influence and Literary Fortune: The Equivocal Junction of Two Methods." *Yearbook of Comparative and General Literature* 11 (1962): 24–31.
- *The Symbolist Movement: A Critical Appraisal*. New York: New York University Press 1977.
Barzun, Jacques. *Classic, Romantic and Modern*. Toronto: Little, Brown and Co. 1961.
- *The Use and Abuse of Art*. Princeton: Princeton University Press 1974.
Bassett, Sharon. "The Uncanny Critic of Brasenose: Walter Pater and Modernisms." *Victorian Newsletter* 58 (Fall 1980): 10–14.
Bate, Walter Jackson. *The Burden of the Past and the English Poet*. Cambridge, Mass.: Harvard University Press 1970.
Baudelaire, Charles. *Oeuvres*. Paris: Pléiade 1958.
Beckson, Karl, and John M. Munro. "Symons, Browning and the Development of the Modern Aesthetic." *Studies in English Literature 1500–1900* 10 (1970): 687–99.
Beebe, Maurice. "What Modernism Was." *Journal of Modern Literature* 3 (1974): 1065–84.
Bentley, D.M.R., ed. and introd. *Abram's Plains: A Poem*. By Thomas Cary. London, Ont.: Canadian Poetry 1986.

– "Archibald Lampman on Poets and Poetry." *Essays on Canadian Writing* 9 (Winter 1977–78): 12–25.
– "A New Dimension: Notes on the Ecology of Canadian Poetry." *Canadian Poetry: Studies, Documents, Reviews* 7 (Fall–Winter 1980): 1–20.
– "Not of Things Only, But of Thought: Notes on A.J.M. Smith's Imagistic Poems." *Canadian Poetry: Studies, Documents, Reviews* 11 (Fall–Winter 1982): 26–48.
– "Thomas Cary's *Abram's Plains* and its 'Preface.'" *Canadian Poetry: Studies, Documents, Reviews* 5 (Fall–Winter 1979): 1–28.
– "Through Endless Landscapes: Notes on Charles Sangster's *The Saint Lawrence and the Saguenay.*" *Essays on Canadian Writing* 27 (Winter 1983–84): 1–34.
Betjeman, John. *Collected Poems.* Boston: Houghton Mifflin 1971.
– *Summoned by Bells.* London: John Murray 1960.
Beutler, Bernhard. *Der Einfluß des Imagismus auf die Moderne Kanadische Lyrik Englischer Sprache. European University Papers,* ser. 14, Anglo-Saxon Language and Literature, vol. 57. Frankfurt am Main: Peter Lang 1978.
Birney, A. E[arle]. "The Poetry of Robert Finch." *Canadian Poetry Magazine* 10 (March 1947): 6–8.
Bizot, Richard. "Pater and Yeats." *English Literary History* 43 (1976): 389–412.
Blissett, William. "Pater and Eliot." *University of Toronto Quarterly* 22 (1953): 261–8.
Bloom, Harold. *The Anxiety of Influence: A Theory of Poetry.* London: Oxford University Press 1973.
– *A Map of Misreading.* London: Oxford University Press 1975.
Bradbury, Malcolm. *The Social Context of Modern English Literature.* New York: Schocken 1971.
– and James MacFarlane, eds. *Modernism 1890–1930.* Pelican Guides to European Literature, vol. 7. Harmondsworth, Eng.: Penguin 1976.
Brewster, Elizabeth. "I of the Observer: The Poetry of F.R. Scott." *Canadian Literature* 79 (Winter 1978): 23–30.
Brown, Calvin S. "Symposium on Literary Impressionism." *Yearbook of Comparative and General Literature* 17 (1968): 54–59.
Brown, E.K. "A.J.M. Smith and the Poetry of Pride." *Manitoba Arts Review* 4 (Spring 1944): 30–32.
– *On Canadian Poetry.* Toronto: Ryerson 1943.
Buckler, William E. "*Marius the Epicurean*: Beyond Victorianism." In his *The Victorian Imagination: Essays in Aesthetic Exploration.* New York: New York University Press 1980: 260–85.
Burke, Anne. "A.J.M. Smith: An Annotated Bibliography." In *The Annotated Bibliography of Canada's Major Authors.* Ed. Robert Lecker and Jack David. Vol. 3. Downsview, Ont.: ECW, 1983: 267–370.

– , ed. "Some Annotated Letters of A.J.M. Smith and Raymond Knister." *Canadian Poetry: Studies, Documents, Reviews* 11 (Fall–Winter 1982): 98–135.

Burnett, John. "John Glassco: The Canadian Wordsworth." *Canadian Poetry: Studies, Documents, Reviews* 13 (Fall–Winter 1983): 1–11.

Callaghan, Barry. "Memoir [of W.W.E. Ross]." In *Shapes and Sounds*. By W.W.E. Ross. Ed. Raymond Souster and John Robert Colombo. Don Mills, Ont.: Longmans 1968: 1–7.

*Canadian Who's Who 1938–39*. Toronto: Trans-Canada 1939.

Carter, A.E. *The Idea of Decadence in French Literature 1830–1900*. Toronto: University of Toronto Press 1958.

Cary, Thomas. *Abram's Plains; A Poem*. Ed. D.M.R. Bentley. London, Ont.: Canadian Poetry 1986.

Chamberlin, J.E. "From High Decadence to High Modernism." *Queen's Quarterly* 87 (1980): 591–610.

– *Ripe Was the Drowsy Hour: The Age of Oscar Wilde*. New York: Seabury 1977.

Coffman, Stanley. *Imagism: A Chapter for the History of Modern Poetry*. Norman, Okla.: University of Oklahoma Press 1951.

Collin, W.E. *The White Savannahs*. Toronto: Macmillan 1936.

Craig, Terrence, ed. "Frederick Philip Grove's 'The Dirge.'" *Canadian Poetry: Studies, Documents, Reviews* 16 (Spring–Summer 1985): 55–73.

– ed. "Frederick Philip Grove's 'Poems.'" *Canadian Poetry: Studies, Documents, Reviews* 10 (Spring–Summer 1982): 58–90.

Csengeri, K.E. "T.E. Hulme's Borrowings from the French." *Comparative Literature* 34, no. 1 (Winter 1982): 16–27.

Culler, Jonathan. *The Pursuit of Signs: Semiotics, Literature, Deconstruction*. Ithaca, N.Y.: Cornell University Press 1981.

Daniells, Roy. "Earle Birney et Robert Finch." *Gants du Ciel* 11 (1946): 83–96.

Darling, Michael. "A.J.M. Smith's Revisions to His Poems." *Canadian Poetry: Studies, Documents, Reviews* 11 (Fall–Winter 1982): 7–25.

– "An Interview with A.J.M. Smith." *Essays on Canadian Writing* 9 (Winter 1977–78): 55–61.

– "The Myth of Smith." *Essays on Canadian Writing* 20 (Winter 1980–81): 68–76.

– ed. "On Poetry and Poets: The Letters of W.W.E. Ross to A.J.M. Smith." *Essays on Canadian Writing* 16 (Winter 1979–80): 78–125.

DeLaura, David J. "Pater and Eliot: The Origin of the Objective Correlative." *Modern Language Quarterly* 26 (1965): 426–31.

Dellamora, Richard. "Pater's Modernism: The Leonardo Essay." *University of Toronto Quarterly* 47 (1977–78): 135–50.

Djwa, Sandra. "F.R. Scott." In *The Oxford Companion to Canadian Literature*. Ed. William Toye. Toronto: Oxford University Press 1983: 742–5.

- "F.R. Scott." *Canadian Poetry: Studies, Documents, Reviews* 4 (Spring-Summer 1979): 1–16.
- "F.R. Scott: A Canadian in the Twenties." *Papers of the Bibliographical Society of Canada* 19 (1980): 11–21.
- Introduction to *On F.R. Scott*. Ed. Sandra Djwa and R. St-John Macdonald. Kingston/Montreal: McGill-Queen's University Press 1983: ix-xxii.
- "'A New Soil and a Sharp Sun': The Landscape of a Modern Canadian Poetry." *Modernist Studies* 2, no. 2 (1977): 3–17.
- "Of Metaphysics and Dry Bones." *Studies in Canadian Literature* 3 (Winter 1978): 17–34.
- and R. St-John Macdonald, eds. *On F.R. Scott*. Kingston/Montreal: McGill-Queen's University Press 1983.
- *The Politics of the Imagination: A Life of F.R. Scott*. Toronto: McClelland and Stewart 1987.
Douglas, Lord Alfred. *The Collected Poems of Lord Alfred Douglas*. London: Martin Secker 1919.
Dowling, Linda C. *Aestheticism and Decadence: A Selective Annotated Bibliography*. New York: Garland 1977.
Dowson, Ernest. *The Poetical Works of Ernest Dowson*. Ed. Desmond Flower. London: Cassell's 1967.
Dudek, Louis. "Aesthetic Master of Canadian Poetry [A.J.M. Smith]." *The Montreal Star*, 1 Dec. 1962, Sec. Entertainments, 13.
- "A Decadent in Canada in the 1970s? Yes!". Rev. of *Memoirs of Montparnasse*, by John Glassco. *The Gazette* [Montreal], 7 Feb. 1970, 40.
- "The Meaning of Modernism." In *Technology and Culture: Six Lectures*. Ottawa: Golden Dog 1979.
- "Polar Opposites in F.R. Scott's Poetry." In *On F.R. Scott*. Ed. Sandra Djwa and R. St-John Macdonald. Kingston/Montreal: McGill-Queen's University Press 1983: 31–43.
- *The Theory of the Image in Modern Poetry*. St. John's, Nfld.: Memorial University of Newfoundland 1981.
- and Michael Gnarowski, eds. *The Making of Modern Poetry in Canada: Essential Articles on Contemporary Canadian Poetry in English*. Toronto: Ryerson, 1970.
Duffy, Dennis. "John Richardson." In *The Oxford Companion to Canadian Literature*. Ed. William Toye. Toronto: Oxford University Press 1983: 702–4.
Edel, Abraham. "Decadence." *McGill Fortnightly Review*, 22 March 1926, 77–8.
- "What Is Art?". *McGill Fortnightly Review*, 23 Jan. 1926, 39, 43–4.
Edel, Leon. "The 'I' in A.J.M. Smith." *Canadian Poetry: Studies, Documents, Reviews* 11 (Fall–Winter, 1982): 86–92.
- Introduction to *The Shrouding*. By Leo Kennedy. 1933; reprinted Ottawa: Golden Dog 1975: [xi-xvi].

- "John Glassco (1909–1981) and His Erotic Muse." *Canadian Literature* 93 (Summer 1982): 108–17.
- "The *McGill Fortnightly Review*: A Casual Reminiscence." *McGill News*, 21, no. 1 (Autumn 1939): 19–22, 61.
- "A Note on the Cambridge-McGill Debate." *McGill Fortnightly Review*, 1 Dec. 1926, 23.
- "When McGill Modernized Canadian Literature: Literary Revolution – The 'Montreal Group.'" In *The McGill You Knew: An Anthology of Memories 1920–1960*. Ed. Edgar A. Collard. Don Mills, Ont.: Longmans 1975: 112–22.
- "The Worldly Muse of A.J.M. Smith." *University of Toronto Quarterly* 47 (1978): 200–13.
- "The Young Warrior in the Twenties." In *On F.R. Scott*. Ed. Sandra Djwa and R. St-John Macdonald. Kingston/Montreal: McGill-Queen's University Press 1983: 6–16.
Eliot, T.S. *The Complete Poems and Plays 1909–1950*. New York: Harcourt, Brace & World 1958.
- *Selected Essays*. London: Faber and Faber 1969.
Ellman, Richard, and Charles Feidelson, Jr., eds. *The Modern Tradition: Backgrounds of Modern Literature*. New York: Oxford University Press 1965.
Everett, Barbara. "Eliot's 'Four Quartets' and French Symbolism." *English* 29, no. 133 (Spring 1980): 1–37.
Ferns, John. *A.J.M. Smith*. Boston: Twayne 1979.
Fleissner, Robert F. "'Prufrock,' Pater and *Richard II*: Retracing a Denial of Princeship." *American Literature* 38, no. 1 (March 1966): 120–23.
Fletcher, Ian, ed. *Decadence and the 1890s*. London: Edward Arnold 1979.
Flint, F.S. "Imagisme." *Poetry* [Chicago] 1 (March 1913): 199.
Ford, George H. *Keats and the Victorians*. London: Archon 1962.
Friedrich, Werner P. *Comparative Literature*. Proceedings of the Second Congress of the International Comparative Literature Association, vol. 1. Chapel Hill: University of North Carolina Press 1959.
Fulford, Robert. "Just the Usual Whippings, Lashings, Floggings, etc." *Saturday Night*, April 1976, 10.
Gage, John T. *In the Arresting Eye: The Rhetoric of Imagism*. Baton Rouge: Louisiana State University Press 1981.
Gerber, Philip L. "The Surface and the Terror: The Poetry of Eustace Ross." *The Far Point* 5 (Winter 1970): 46–54.
Gingell, Susan. "Poetry in English 1900–1950." In *The Oxford Companion to Canadian Literature*. Ed. William Toye. Toronto: Oxford University Press 1983: 656–60.
Givens, Imogen. Afterword to *Windfalls for Cider: The Poems of Raymond Knister*. Ed. Joy Kuropatwa. Windsor, Ont.: Black Moss 1983: 77–80.

- "Raymond Knister: Man or Myth?". *Essays on Canadian Writing* 16 (Fall–Winter 1979–80): 5–19.
Gnarowski, Michael. "John Glassco: A Note." *Yes* 15 (Sept. 1966): 12–14.
Goldfarb, Russell. "The Dowson Legend Today." *Studies in English Literature 1500–1900* 4 (1964): 653–62.
Gordon, J. King. "The Politics of Poetry." In *On F.R. Scott*. Ed. Sandra Djwa and R. St-John Macdonald. Kingston/Montreal: McGill-Queen's University Press 1983: 17–28.
Green, Martin. *Children of the Sun: A Narrative of "Decadence" in England after 1918*. New York: Basic 1976.
- *Transatlantic Patterns: Cultural Comparisons of England with America*. New York: Basic 1977.
Green, R.J. "Oscar Wilde's *Intentions*: An Early Modernist Manifesto." *British Journal of Aesthetics* 13 (1973): 397–404.
Greene, E.J.H. "Jules Laforgue et T.S. Eliot." *Revue de littérature comparée* 22 (1948): 363–97.
Guillen, Claudio. "The Aesthetics of Literary Influence." In *Comparative Literature*. Ed. Werner P. Friedrich. Proceedings of the Second Congress of the International Comparative Literature Association, vol. 1. Chapel Hill: University of North Carolina Press 1959. Revised in *Influx: Essays on Literary Influence*. Ed. Robert Primeau. Port Washington: Kennikat 1977: 49–73.
Harmer, J.B. *Victory in Limbo: Imagism 1908–1917*. London: Secker and Warburg 1973.
Hartman, Charles O. *Free Verse: An Essay on Prosody*. Princeton, N.J.: Princeton University Press 1980.
Harvey, Roderick Wilson. "'To Hold in a Poem': Tension and Balance in A.J.M. Smith's Verse." *Canadian Poetry: Studies, Documents, Reviews* 11 (Fall–Winter 1982): 49–55.
Hassan, Ihab. "The Problem of Influence in Literary History: Notes Towards a Definition." *Journal of Aesthetics and Art Criticism* 14 (1955): 66–76. Reprinted in *Influx: Essays on Literary Influence*. Ed. Robert Primeau. Port Washington: Kennikat 1977: 34–46.
Heenan, Michael. "Interview with A.J.M. Smith." *Canadian Poetry: Studies, Documents, Reviews* 11 (Fall–Winter 1982): 73–7.
Herkelots, Hugh C.G. "On Having a Shoe Shine." *McGill Fortnightly Review*, 1 Dec. 1926, 21.
Hermeren, Goran. *Influence in Art and Literature*. Princeton, N.J.: Princeton University Press 1975.
Howarth, Herbert. "Symposium on Literary Impressionism." *Yearbook of Comparative and General Literature* 17 (1968): 40–45.
Hueffer, Ford Madox [Ford]. "On Impressionism." *Poetry and Drama* 2, no.

2 (June 1914); reprinted in *Imagism: A Chapter for the History of Modern Poetry*. By Stanley Coffman. Norman, Okla.: University of Oklahoma Press 1951: 114.

Hulme, T.E. *Speculations: Essays on Humanism and the Philosophy of Art*. 1924; reprinted London: Routledge and Kegan Paul 1949.

Jewinski, Ed. "Troubled Joy: Style and Syntax in Glassco's Poetry." *Canadian Poetry: Studies, Documents, Reviews* 13 (Fall–Winter 1983): 12–20.

Johnson, Lionel. *The Collected Poems of Lionel Johnson*. Ed. Ian Fletcher. New York: Garland 1982.

Juvenis [pseud]. "The Quest." *McGill Fortnightly Review*, 23 Jan. 1926, 38, 44.

Keith, W.J. "How New Was *New Provinces*?". *Canadian Poetry: Studies, Documents, Reviews* 4 (Spring-Summer 1979): 120–24.

Kenner, Hugh. *The Pound Era*. Berkeley: University of California Press 1971.

Kermode, Frank. *The Romantic Image*. London: Routledge 1961.

King, E.H. "James Beattie, William Wordsworth and the Evolution of Romanticism." In *A Festschrift for Edgar Ronald Seary: Essays in English Language and Literature*. Ed. A.A. Macdonald, P.A. Flaherty, and G.M. Story. St. John's, Nfld.: Memorial University of Newfoundland 1975: 116–29.

Klinck, Carl F., gen. ed. *The Literary History of Canada: Canadian Literature in English*. 2nd ed. Toronto: University of Toronto Press 1976. 3 vols.

Kokotailo, Philip. *John Glassco's Richer World: Memoirs of Montparnasse*. Toronto: ECW 1988.

Kristeva, Julia. *La Revolution du langage poétique*. Paris: Seuil 1974.

– *Semeiotiké: recherches pour une sémanalyse*. Paris: Seuil 1969.

– *Le Texte du roman*. Paris: Mouton 1970.

Kronegger, Maria Elisabeth. *Literary Impressionism*. New Haven, Conn.: College and University Press 1973.

LaBossière, Camille R. "Compass of the Catoptric Past: John Glassco, Translator." *Canadian Poetry: Studies, Documents, Reviews* 13 (Fall–Winter 1983): 32–42.

Latham, David. "Leo Kennedy." In *The Oxford Companion to Canadian Literature*. Ed. William Toye. Toronto: Oxford University Press 1983: 406.

– "Charles Sangster." In *The Oxford Companion to Canadian Literature*. Ed. William Toye. Toronto: Oxford University Press 1983: 727–8.

Lauber, John. "Liberty and the Pursuit of Pleasure: John Glassco's Quest." *Canadian Literature* 90 (Autumn 1981): 61–72.

Lecker, Robert, and Jack David, eds. *The Annotated Bibliography of Canada's Major Authors*. 7 vols. to date. Downsview, Ont.: ECW 1979–87.

Levenson, Michael H. *A Genealogy of Modernism: A Study of English Literary Doctrine 1908–1922*. Cambridge: Cambridge University Press 1984.

Levin, Harry. "La Littérature comparée: point de vue d'outre Atlantique." *Revue de Littérature Comparée* 27 (1953): 17–26.

Lindberg-Seyersted, Brita. *Pound/Ford: The Story of a Literary Friendship.* New York: New Directions 1982.

Linnér, Sven. "The Structure and Function of Literary Comparisons." *Journal of Aesthetics and Art Criticism* 26 (1967): 169–79.

Livesay, Dorothy. Review of *News of the Phoenix and Other Poems. First Statement* 2, no. 6 (April 1944): 18–19.

Macdonald, Goodridge. "Lately at Evening." *McGill Daily Literary Supplement*, 11 Feb. 1925, 4.

MacLaren, Ian S. "The Yeatsian Presence in A.J.M. Smith's 'Like An Old Proud King in a Parable.'" *Canadian Poetry: Studies, Documents, Reviews* 4 (Spring–Summer 1979): 59–64.

McGrath, F.C. "Heroic Aestheticism: Yeats, Pater and the Marriage of Ireland and England." *Irish University Review* 8 (1978): 183–90.

McMullen, Lorraine. "Leo Kennedy." *Le Chien d'or/The Golden Dog* 1 (Jan. 1972): 46–62.

Mallarmé, Stéphane. *Oeuvres complètes: poésies.* Paris: Flammarion 1983.

Mandel, Eli. "Masks of Criticism: A.J.M. Smith as Anthologist." *Canadian Poetry: Studies, Documents, Reviews* 4 (Spring–Summer 1979): 17–28.

Marvell, Andrew. *The Complete Poems.* Harmondsworth, Eng.: Penguin 1976.

Mathers, K. "Triumvirate of Robert Finch as Poet, Painter and Pianist." *Saturday Night*, 20 Sept. 1947, 16.

Meisel, Perry. *The Absent Father: Virginia Woolf and Walter Pater.* New Haven: Yale University Press 1980.

Moers, Ellen. *The Dandy.* London: Secker and Warburg 1960.

Moore, George. *Flowers of Passion and Pagan Poems.* 1878, 1881; reprinted New York: Garland 1978.

– ed. *Pure Poetry: An Anthology.* London: Nonesuch 1924.

Morley, Patricia. "The Young Turks: A Biographer's Comment." *Canadian Poetry: Studies, Documents, Reviews* 11 (Fall–Winter 1982): 67–72.

Morris, William. *The Collected Works of William Morris.* 24 vols. London: Longmans Green & Co. 1911.

Murdoch, Charles. "Essential Glassco." *Canadian Literature* 65 (Summer 1975): 28–41.

Nelson, James G. "The Nature of Aesthetic Experience in the Poetry of the Nineties: Ernest Dowson, Lionel Johnson and John Gray." *English Literature in Transition 1880–1920* 17 (1974): 223–32.

Norris, Ken. "The Beginnings of Canadian Modernism." *Canadian Poetry: Studies, Documents, Reviews* 11 (Fall–Winter 1982): 56–66.

O'Brien, Kevin. "Oscar Wilde and Canadian Artists." *Antigonish Review* 1, no. 4 (Winter 1971): 11–28.

Ó Broin, Pádraig. "After Strange Gods (A.J. M. Smith and the Concept of Nationalism)." *The Canadian Author + Bookman* 39, no. 4 (Summer 1964): 6–8.

*Old McGill 1925*. Montreal: McGill University, 1925.

Ower, John. "Isabella Valancy Crawford and the 'Fleshly School of Poetry'." *Studies in Scottish Literature* 13 (1978): 275–81.

Pacey, Desmond. *The Letters of Frederick Philip Grove*. Toronto: University of Toronto Press 1976.

Parker, George L. "Bliss Carman." In *The Oxford Companion to Canadian Literature*. Ed. William Toye. Toronto: Oxford University Press 1983: 102–4.

Pater, Walter. *Imaginary Portraits*. 1887; reprinted New York: Johnson Reprint Corp. 1967.

– *Marius the Epicurean: His Sensations and Ideas*. London: Macmillan 1891.

– *The Renaissance: Studies in Art and Poetry (The 1893 Text)*. Ed. Donald L. Hill. Berkeley: University of California Press, 1980.

Peckham, Morse. "Aestheticism to Modernism: Fulfilment or Revolution?". In his *The Triumph of Romanticism*. Columbia, S.C.: University of South Carolina Press 1970: 202–25.

Perkins, David. *A History of Modern Poetry*. 2 vols. Cambridge, Mass.: Harvard University Press 1976, 1987.

Pound, Ezra. *Literary Essays of Ezra Pound*. Ed. T.S. Eliot. New York: New Directions 1968.

– *Selected Poems*. New York: New Directions 1956.

– "Status Rerum – The Second." *Poetry* [Chicago] 8 (April 1916): 38–43.

Precosky, Don. "'Back to the Woods Ye Muse of Canada': Conservative Response to the Beginnings of Modernism." *Canadian Poetry: Studies, Documents, Reviews* 12 (Spring–Summer 1983): 40–45.

– "Ever With Discontent: Some Comments on Raymond Knister and His Poetry." *CV/II* 4, no. 4 (Spring 1980): 3–9.

Primeau, Ronald, ed. *Influx: Essays on Literary Influence*. Port Washington: Kennikat 1977.

Prince, Jeffrey. "The Iconic Poem and the Aesthetic Tradition." *English Literary History* 43 (Winter 1976): 567–83.

Quintus, John Allan. "The Moral Implications of Oscar Wilde's Aestheticism." *Texas Studies in Literature and Language* 22 (1980): 559–74.

Rosenthal, M.L. "Poor Innocent: The Poetry of A.J.M. Smith." *Modern Poetry Studies* 8 (Spring 1977): 1–13.

Ross, Malcolm. "'A Strange Aesthetic Ferment.'" *Canadian Literature* 68–69 (Spring–Summer 1976): 13–25.

Rossetti, Dante Gabriel. *The Works of Dante Gabriel Rossetti*. Ed. W.M. Rossetti. London: Ellis 1911.

Sade, Donatien Alphonse Francois, le Marquis de. *The Marquis de Sade: Selected Letters*. Ed. Margaret J. Crosland. Trans. W.J. Strachan. London: Peter Owen 1965.

Sandburg, Carl. *Complete Poems*. New York: Harcourt, Brace and World 1950.

Saunders, Thomas. "A Novelist as Poet." *The Dalhousie Review* 43 (1963–64): 235–41.

Scobie, Stephen. "The Mirror on the Brothel Wall: John Glassco's *Memoirs of Montparnasse*." *Canadian Poetry: Studies, Documents, Reviews* 13 (Fall–Winter 1983): 43–58.

– "Road Back to Eden: The Poetry of F.R. Scott." *Queen's Quarterly* 79 (1972): 314–23.

Scott, Clive. "Symbolism, Decadence, and Impressionism." In *Modernism 1890–1930*. Ed. Malcolm Bradbury and James Macfarlane. Harmondsworth, Eng.: Penguin 1976: 206–27.

Shaw, J.T. "Literary Indebtedness and Comparative Literary Studies." In *Comparative Literature: Method and Perspective*. Ed. N.P. Stallknecht and H. Franz. Carbondale, Ill.: Southern Illinois University Press 1961: 58–71.

Shore, Marlene. "'Overtures of an Era Being Born': F.R. Scott: Cultural Nationalism and Social Criticism 1925–1939." *Journal of Canadian Studies* 15 (Winter 1980–81): 31–42.

Sitwell, Edith. *Aspects of Modern Poetry*. London: Duckworth 1934.

– *Collected Poems*. London: Macmillan 1961.

Skelton, Robin. "A Poet of the Middle Slopes." *Canadian Literature* 31 (Winter 1967): 40–44.

Spears, Monroe K. *Dionysus and the City: Modernism in Twentieth Century Poetry*. New York: Oxford University Press 1970.

Spender, Stephen. *The Struggle of the Modern*. Berkeley: University of California Press 1963.

Spettigue, D.O. *FPG: The European Years*. Ottawa: Oberon 1973.

– "Frederick Philip Grove." In *The Oxford Companion to Canadian Literature*. Ed. William Toye. Toronto: Oxford University Press 1983: 324–7.

Stanford, Derek. "Arthur Symons and Modern Poetics." *Southern Review* NS 2 (1966): 347–53.

Stephenson, Glennis. "The Bitter Sweet Rose: The Conception of Woman in Roberts' *The Book of the Rose*." *Canadian Poetry: Studies, Documents, Reviews* 14 (Spring–Summer 1984): 53–63.

Stevens, Peter. "The Legacy of A.J.M. Smith." *Canadian Poetry: Studies, Documents, Reviews* 11 (Fall–Winter 1982): 1–6.

– "Leo Kennedy's Poetry." In *The McGill Movement*. Ed. Peter Stevens. Toronto: Ryerson 1969: 35–50.

– ed. *The McGill Movement*. Toronto: Ryerson 1969.

– "The Old Futility of Art: Knister's Poetry." *Canadian Literature* 23 (Winter 1965): 45–52.

– "On W.W.E. Ross." *Canadian Literature* 39 (Winter 1969): 43–61.

Still, Robert. "F.R. Scott: An Annotated Bibliography." In *The Annotated Bibliography of Canada's Major Authors*. Ed. Robert Lecker and Jack David. Vol. 4. Downsview, Ont.: ECW 1983: 205–65.

Sutherland, Fraser. *John Glassco: An Essay and Bibliography*. Downsview, Ont.: ECW 1984.

Sutherland, John. "The Great Equestrians." *Northern Review*, Oct.–Nov. 1953, 21; reprinted in *The Making of Modern Poetry in Canada: Essential Articles on Contemporary Canadian Poetry in English*. Ed. Louis Dudek and Michael Gnarowski. Toronto: Ryerson 1970: 115.

– "Mr Smith and the Tradition." In *Other Canadians: An Anthology of the New Poetry in Canada 1940–1946*. Ed. John Sutherland. Montreal: First Statement 1947: 5–12.

Sutherland, Kathryn. "The Native Poet: The Influence of Percy's Minstrel from Beattie to Wordsworth." *Review of English Studies* 33 (1982): 414–33.

Swinburne, Algernon Charles. *The Complete Works of Algernon Charles Swinburne*. 20 vols. 1925; reprinted New York: Russell and Russell 1968.

Symons, Arthur. *Collected Works of Arthur Symons*. 9 vols. 1924; reprinted New York: AMS 1973.

– "The Decadent Movement in Literature." *Harper's New Monthly Magazine* 87 (Nov. 1893): 866–7.

– *Studies in Prose and Verse*. London: J.M. Dent 1904.

– *The Symbolist Movement in Literature*. 1899; reprinted New York: Dutton 1958.

Tausky, Thomas. "*Memoirs of Montparnasse*: 'A Reflection of Myself.'" *Canadian Poetry: Studies, Documents, Reviews* 13 (Fall–Winter 1983): 59–84.

Temple, Ruth Z. "Truth in Labelling: Pre-Raphaelitism, Aestheticism, Decadence, *Fin-de-Siècle*." *English Literature in Transition 1880–1920* 17 (1974): 201–22.

Thornton, R.K.R. "'Decadence' in Later Nineteenth-Century England." In *Decadence and the 1890s*. Ed. Ian Fletcher. London: Edward Arnold 1979: 15–30.

– *The Decadent Dilemma*. London: Edward Arnold 1983.

Tovell, Vincent. "The World for a Country: An Edited Interview with F.R. Scott." *Canadian Poetry: Studies, Documents, Reviews* 2 (Spring–Summer 1978): 51–73.

Trehearne, Brian. "A.J.M. Smith: The Poetry of Eclectic Detachment." M.A. Thesis McGill 1981.

Vespasiano [Coulborn, A.P.R.]. "Sentimentalism in Education." *McGill Fortnightly Review*, 5 Dec. 1925, 13.

– "To My Counterblasters." *McGill Fortnightly Review*, 9 Jan. 1926, 30.

– "What Is Art?". *McGill Daily Literary Supplement*, 11 March 1925, 2.

Villiers de l'Isle-Adam, Philippe Auguste. *Axel*. Paris: Courrier du Livre 1969.

Waddington, Marcus. "Raymond Knister: A Biographical Note." *Journal of Canadian Fiction* 14 (1975): 175–92.

Ware, Tracy. "George Longmore's *The Charivari*: A Poem 'After the Manner of Beppo.'" *Canadian Poetry: Studies, Documents, Reviews* 10 (Spring–Summer 1982): 1–17.

Warkentin, Germaine. "Criticism and the Whole Man." *Canadian Literature* 64 (Spring 1975): 83–91.

– "Scott's 'Lakeshore' and Its Tradition." *Canadian Literature* 87 (Winter 1980): 42–50.

Wayne, Joyce, and Stuart Mackinnon. "Quill and Quire Interview: F.R. Scott." *Quill and Quire*, July 1982, 12, 16, 18.

Whiteman, Bruce, ed. *A Literary Friendship: The Correspondence of Ralph Gustafson and W.W.E. Ross.* Toronto: ECW 1984.

Whittington-Egan, Richard. "An Eighties View of the Nineties." *Contemporary Review* 237, no. 1375 (Aug. 1980): 93–7.

– "The Nineties: End or Beginning?". *Contemporary Review* 237, no. 1378 (Nov. 1980): 255–60.

– "Sunflower and Green Carnation." *Contemporary Review* 237, no. 1376 (Sept. 1980): 155–60.

*Who's Who in Canada, 1945–46.* Toronto: International 1946.

Wilde, Oscar. *The Artist as Critic: Critical Writings of Oscar Wilde.* Ed. Richard Ellman. London: W.H. Allen 1970.

– "The Critic as Artist." In *The Artist as Critic: Critical Writings of Oscar Wilde.* Ed. Richard Ellman. London: W.H. Allen 1970: 340–408.

– "The Decay of Lying." In *The Artist as Critic: Critical Writings of Oscar Wilde.* Ed. Richard Ellman. London: W.H. Allen 1970: 290–320.

– *The First Collected Edition of the Works of Oscar Wilde.* Ed. Robert H. Ross. 1908; reprinted London: Dawson's of Pall Mall 1969.

– *The Letters of Oscar Wilde.* Ed. Rupert Hart-Davies. London: Rupert Hart-Davies 1962.

– *The Picture of Dorian Gray.* Vol. 5 of *The First Collected Edition of the Works of Oscar Wilde.* Ed. Robert H. Ross. 1908; reprinted London: Dawson's of Pall Mall 1969.

– *Poems.* Vol. 9 of *The First Collected Edition of the Works of Oscar Wilde.* Ed. Robert H. Ross. 1908; reprinted London: Dawson's of Pall Mall 1969.

– "The Soul of Man Under Socialism." In *The Artist as Critic: Critical Writings of Oscar Wilde.* Ed. Richard Ellman. London: W.H. Allen 1970: 255–89.

Williams, William Carlos. *The Collected Earlier Poems.* New York: New Directions 1951.

Wilson, Jean. "The 'Nineties' Movement in Poetry: Myth or Reality?". *Yearbook of English Studies* 1 (1971): 160–74.

Wilson, Milton. "Second and Third Thoughts About Smith." *Canadian Literature* 15 (Winter 1963): 11–17.

Woodcock, George. "John Glassco." In *The Oxford Companion to Canadian Literature*. Ed. William Toye. Toronto: Oxford University Press 1983: 300–1.

– "Two Aspects of A.J.M. Smith." In his *Odysseus Ever Returning: Essays on Canadian Writers and Writing*. Toronto: McClelland and Stewart 1970: 110–18.

Wordsworth, William. *The Poems*. 2 vols. Harmondsworth, Eng.: Penguin 1977.

– *The Prelude: A Parallel Text*. Ed. J.C. Maxwell. Harmondsworth, Eng.: Penguin 1971.

Yeats, William Butler. *Collected Poems*. New York: Macmillan 1967.

# Index